Creation Compromises

2nd Edition

From The Library Of

Reverdy Lewin Orrell, III

Bert Thompson, Ph.D.

APOLOGETICS PRESS

Apologetics Press, Inc.
230 Landmark Drive
Montgomery, Alabama 36117-2752

Second Edition © Copyright 2000
First Edition © Copyright 1995
ISBN: 0-932859-39-9

Library of Congress Cataloging-in-Publication

Thompson, Bert, 1949 -

  Creation Compromises / Bert Thompson—second edition

  Includes bibliographic references and subject, name, and Scripture indices.

  ISBN 0-932859-39-9

  1. Creation. 2. Science and religion. 3. Apologetics and polemics. I. Title

213—dc21   00-135278

Dedication

To Chad and Cody—

- Two sons whose lives have been a continual blessing to their parents, a good example to their peers, a source of encouragement to their friends, and an inspiration to all who know them

- In the hope that you always will love and defend the Truth, regardless of the consequences

TABLE OF CONTENTS

Preface

Without a doubt, Genesis is the single most vilified book in all the Bible. While men of every age have mocked and attacked the Bible as a whole, no single book has taken the brunt of such attacks more often than the book of Genesis. The reason for the vehemence and frequency of such attacks upon the inspired book should be obvious —both biblical faith and man's world view find their own genesis, their *raison d'être*, within its pages. But, with Genesis neatly dismissed, the remainder of Scripture rests upon a mobile foundation, much like a rotting shack teetering upon a fault line—with collapse imminent.

Think of the significance of this first book of the English Bible. Genesis not only provides the only inspired cosmogony available to man, but in doing so introduces for the first time on written record the Bible's primary theme—the redemption of man through reconciliation to the God against Whom he had sinned. Genesis tells man how to interpret the physical world in which he lives. It gives the divine answers to timeless questions concerning the meaning and result of sin. It tells man of the proper relationship between the sexes. And it even instructs him as to the origin of the multiplicity of human languages.

In fewer words than an average sportswriter would use to present his account of a Friday night high school football game, Moses, by inspiration, discussed in Genesis 3 the breaking of the covenant between man and God, the entrance of sin into the world, and the need for a coming Redeemer—the theme that was to occupy the rest of

Scripture. Were it not for the book of Genesis, man forever would be forced to ask—yet never be competent to answer—such questions as "Whence have I come?" or "Why am I here?" or "Where am I going?" Only in Genesis can the information be found to formulate answers to these questions, which linger in the heart of almost every person. What we as humans so often fail to realize is that we are not involved in a search for truth because **it** is lost; rather, we are involved in a search for truth because without it, **we are**!

But we are not merely on a search; we also are engaged in a battle. When the apostle Paul wrote to first-century Christians in the city of Ephesus, he talked about that battle. He wanted to admonish, to warn, and to encourage. Thus, he penned these words:

> Finally, be strong in the Lord, and in the strength of his might. Put on the whole armor of God, that ye may be able to stand against the wiles of the devil. For our wrestling is not against flesh and blood, but against the principalities, against the powers, against the world-rulers of this darkness, against the spiritual hosts of wickedness in the heavenly places. Wherefore take up the whole armor of God, that ye may be able to withstand in the evil day, and, having done all, to stand (Ephesians 6:10-12).

The volume you hold in your hand is a book about a battle—a battle taking place among us over one of the most important and controversial topics in human history: origins. It is absolutely imperative that we win this battle. Our souls, the souls of our children and grandchildren, the souls of many of our friends, and the souls of many even yet unborn are at stake.

But why is this particular battle of such critical importance? There are a number of reasons, but primarily what makes victory so urgent is best summarized in this one thought: give a man a false, warped view of his origin, and he likewise will possess a false, warped view of his destiny. Origin and destiny are inseparably linked.

In every human activity the process of recognizing, believing, and properly utilizing truth is vitally important. Jesus tried to impress this upon His generation when He said: "Ye shall know the truth, and the truth shall make you free" (John 8:32). The same principle operates even today, two thousand years later. Surely, if **knowing** the truth makes us free, then **not knowing** the truth makes us captives of one sort or another. When we refuse to acknowledge and believe the truth, we become susceptible to every ill-conceived plan, deceptive scheme, and false concept that the winds of change may blow our way. We become slaves to error because we have abandoned the one moral compass—truth—that possesses the ability to show us the way, and thereby to set us free.

The simple fact of the matter, however, is that we are responsible for what we choose to believe. Using the personal volition with which God has endowed us, we may choose freely to believe the truth, or we may choose just as freely to believe error. The choice is up to each individual. And once an individual has made up his mind that he prefers error over truth, God will not deter him, as Paul made clear when he wrote his second epistle to the Thessalonians. In that letter, he spoke of those who "received not the love of the truth" (2: 10), and then went on to say that "for this cause God sendeth them a working of error, that they should believe a lie" (2 Thessalonians 2:11). What a horrible thought—to go through life believing a lie!

But what, exactly, was Paul suggesting when he stated in 2 Thessalonians 2:11 that "God sendeth them a working of error, that they should believe a lie"? Was the apostle teaching that God **purposely** causes men to believe error?

No, he most certainly was not. Paul's point in this passage was that because God has granted man personal volition, and because He has provided within the Bible the rules, regulations, and guidelines to govern the use of that personal volition, He therefore will refrain from overriding man's freedom of choice—even when it violates His law. God will not contravene man's decisions, or interfere with the actions based on those decisions. The prophet Isaiah had recorded God's words on this subject many years before when he wrote:

> Yea, they have chosen their own ways, and their soul delight-
> eth in their abominations: I also will choose their delusions,
> and will bring their fears upon them; because when I called,
> none did answer; when I spake, they did not hear: but they did
> that which was evil in mine eyes, and chose that wherein I de-
> lighted not (Isaiah 66:3-4).

The psalmist recorded God's words on this matter when he wrote: "But my people hearkened not to my voice; and Israel would not hear me. So I let them go after the stubbornness of their heart, that they might walk in their own counsels" (Psalm 81:11-12). In Romans 11:8, Paul (quoting from Isaiah 29:10) stated concerning the rebellious Israelites: "God gave them a spirit of stupor, eyes that they should not see, and ears that they should not hear."

Therefore, as Paul penned his second epistle to the young evangelist Timothy, he urged him to "give diligence to present thyself approved unto God, a workman that needeth not to be ashamed, handling aright the word of truth" (2 Timothy 2:15). Surely it behooves us today as well to "handle aright" so precious a commodity as the "word of truth." The salvation of our own souls, and the souls of those with whom we come in contact and attempt to teach (by word or by deed), will depend on the accuracy of the message.

Some, however, have elected to employ their freedom of choice to ignore and/or disobey the truth. Concerning those people who refused to have God in their knowledge, and who actually preferred believing a lie to accepting the truth, Paul repeatedly stated that "God gave them up" (Romans 1:24,26,28). They **could** have come to a knowledge of the truth, but they **would not**.

Strong words, those—"God gave them up!" Why would the apostle use such terms to describe some of the people of his generation? His reason, according to the text that follows, was because "they exchanged the truth of God for a lie, and worshipped and served the creature rather than the Creator" (Romans 1:25).

Is this not an apt description of evolutionists of our day? Have they not "exchanged the truth of God for a lie, and worshipped and served the creature rather than the Creator"? Is this not what evolution does best—exalting the creature over the Creator? And all in the name of "science"? When Paul wrote his first letter to Timothy, he warned: "O Timothy, keep that which is committed to thy trust, avoiding profane and vain babblings, and oppositions of **science falsely so called**" (1 Timothy 6:20, KJV, emp. added). To the Colossians, the apostle to the Gentiles wrote: "Take heed lest there shall be any one that maketh spoil of you through his **philosophy and vain deceit, after the tradition of men**, after the rudiments of the world" (Colossians 2:8, emp. added).

Those of us who accept the Bible as the inspired, inerrant, authoritative Word of God, and who accept the biblical record of origins at face value, now find ourselves engaged in a fierce battle with not **one**, but **two** antagonists. First, we are involved in a battle with out-and-out evolutionists—men and women who retain no belief whatsoever in God or His Word. To them, their origin is strictly a naturalistic phenomenon—nothing more, but certainly nothing less. Richard Dawkins, author of the widely circulated, anti-creationist book, *The Blind Watchmaker*, suggested that "Darwin's theory is now supported by all the available relevant evidence, and its truth is not doubted by any serious modern biologist" (1982, p. 130). A scant seven years later, Dr. Dawkins even went so far as to state: "It is absolutely safe to say that if you meet somebody who claims not to believe in evolution, that person is ignorant, stupid, or insane (or wicked, but I'd rather not consider that)" [1989, p. 34, parenthetical comment in orig.].

Second, there are the opponents who profess a belief in God and His Word, but who have compromised the biblical account of origins so that many aspects of the evolutionary cosmogony may be incorporated into that divine record. Those in the first group rally under such names as atheist, agnostic, infidel, skeptic, freethinker, and the like. Those in the second group rally under the banners of theistic evolution, progressive creationism, threshold evolution, old-Earth creationism, and other similar concepts.

While we disagree strongly with both groups' views on origins, this book is a discussion about only one of those groups—the one composed of people who have compromised the Word of God with naturalistic theories of origins. Much is at stake, for if the theistic evolutionists, progressive creationists, and their cohorts are correct, we who have understood the biblical record to be taken as a literal, historical account of our ultimate origin are wrong. Our adversaries defend a view which suggests that the account is not to be taken in such a fashion, but instead is to be viewed as a mythical, poetical, or allegorical story that is perfectly consistent with most of the tenets of organic evolution.

Furthermore, if our detractors are right, most (if not all!) of what we **thought** was correct turns out not to **be** correct. Progressive creationists, theistic evolutionists, and their kin would have us believe that while the creation account itself is mythical in nature (and thus cannot be accepted as historically true), that should not affect our faith in any significant fashion. For example, Professor Van A. Harvey of Stanford University has suggested that "the Christian faith is not belief in a miracle, it is the confidence that Jesus' witness is a true one" (1966, p. 274). What does he mean by such a statement? Listen carefully as he explains further:

> If we understand properly what is meant by faith, then **this faith has no clear relation to any particular set of historical beliefs at all**.... The conclusion one is driven to is that **the content of faith can as well be mediated through a historically false story of a certain kind as through a true one**, through a myth as well as through history (pp. 280-281, emp. added).

In other words, biblical faith can be grounded as easily in falsehood as in truth! So, it is not whether Genesis actually **tells** us the truth, but whether we **believe** it tells us the truth that matters.

What strikes one immediately about such a concept is the low estimate of the Bible it entails. If God's Word can use falsehoods to teach on what are alleged to be "peripheral" matters (like creation), why can it not also use falsehoods to teach on "essential" matters (like salvation)? And who among us, then, becomes the final arbiter as to what is true and what is false—what is "historical" as opposed to what is "mythical"?

The fact of the matter is, we serve a God Who cannot lie (Titus 1:2; Hebrews 6:18). What Christ taught, and what the Bible teaches, we, as His disciples, should believe and teach—with the full assurance that we shall be both accurate and safe in so doing.

The sad truth, however, is that all too often people simply are not willing to handle the truth aright. On various occasions, this unwillingness manifests itself even among those who profess to be Christians, and who suggest that their intention is to defend the Word of God while at the same time trying to teach and convert the lost. When they are challenged regarding the inappropriate and incorrect content of their message, the justification they offer (even if it is not usually verbalized in these exact words—although sometimes it is!) is that "the end justifies the means." Some apparently feel that employing **just** straightforward, unadulterated, Bible teaching will not impress people sufficiently to convince them to want to obey God's Word. Add to that the fact that it simply is not popular in our day and age to advocate biblical creationism, and it is easy to understand why the message of the Genesis account of creation frequently is altered (or ignored altogether), and why falsehood then so often is the end result.

But surely the question begs to be asked: What good ultimately results from the teaching of such falsehood? Can we legitimately convert the lost through the teaching of error? Can one be **taught wrongly** and **obey correctly**? The teaching of error may comfort where truth offends. Yes, a person who believes that God created the Universe and populated the Earth via the process of organic evolution can be allowed to think that such a view is correct. But in the end, three things have occurred. First, as a result of having believed error, the sinner may not be truly converted. Second, the church has been filled with theistic evolutionists, progressive creationists, and others who hold to false views. Since "a little leaven leaveneth the whole lump" (Galatians 5:9), the church will be weakened, and others may be lured into accepting the same error through association with those who believe it (and teach it) to be true. Third, the person who perpetrated the false teaching has placed his soul, and the souls of those he taught, in jeopardy because of the error he advocated.

Error is error, regardless of the effects produced. Christians are not called to teach error, but truth (John 14:6). Surely, the question should be asked: What faithful Christian would want to teach, or believe, **any** error? God always has measured men by their attitude toward the truth. And the truth can free us only if we know it, accept it, and obey it. Error never frees; it only enslaves. Spiritual benefits cannot result from the teaching of error.

It is the thesis of this book that there can be no compromise with error. Certainly I do not wish to be harsh or strident, but I do wish to defend firmly the Genesis account of origins as being a literal, historical, and accurate account of the Godhead's activity in the realm of creation. Christ, and the Old and New Testament writers, viewed it as such; therefore we not only are correct in following their example, but absolutely must do so.

While it may be true that there are many today who reject the biblical account of creation and accept the basic tenets of organic evolution (in whole or in part), we must not fall prey to mob psychology—the idea which suggests that because "everyone is doing it," that somehow makes it right.

Christ, in His beautiful "Sermon on the Mount," warned: "Narrow is the gate, and straitened the way, that leadeth unto life, and few are they that find it" (Matthew 7:13-14). Those in the majority ultimately will abandon God's wisdom in favor of their own. In Romans 12:2, Paul admonished Christians: "Be not conformed to this world." His command had its basis both in Christ's teachings, and in those of Moses. In Exodus 23:2, Moses commanded the people of Israel: "Thou shalt not follow a multitude to do evil."

It likewise is the contention of this book that Christians may not ignore, be apathetic toward, or casual about those who teach such error. The Scriptures speak plainly on this subject. It is wrong for Christians to allow false teachers and their erroneous doctrines to go unchallenged (2 John 9-11). To the Christians in Rome, Paul wrote:

> Now I beseech you, brethren, mark them that are causing the divisions and occasions of stumbling, contrary to the doctrine which ye learned: and turn away from them. For they that are such serve their own belly, and by their smooth and fair speech they beguile the hearts of the innocent (Romans 16:17-18).

Jude's exhortation was that we "contend earnestly for the faith which was once for all delivered unto the saints" (Jude 3). Paul told the Christians in Thessalonica to "withdraw yourselves from every brother that walketh disorderly and not after the tradition which they received of us" (2 Thessalonians 3:6). The Greek word translated "disorderly" is an adverbial form of the Greek verb, *atakteo*, a word that, according to Thayer's *Greek-English Lexicon*, is used "of soldiers marching out of order, or quitting the ranks."

The material in this volume is about Bible believers, and in some instances even New Testament Christians, who are "marching out of order" because they have—for all practical purposes—"quit the ranks." Peter spoke of some who were known to be "wresting the Scriptures to their own destruction" (2 Peter 3:16). Many of those discussed within these pages are guilty of that very offense. Equally as important, however, is the fact that by advocating—publicly or privately—their off-beat theories about God's creative activity, they have influenced others to believe incorrectly, and in so doing to imperil their souls.

In 2 Timothy 3:1-4, Paul presented his protégé with a litany of sins that characterized what he termed "grievous times." In addition to those who were selfish, boastful, haughty, disobedient, and without self-control, Paul wrote of men "holding a form of godliness, but having denied the power thereof" (2 Timothy 3:5). Paul's point was that Timothy would encounter some who, from all outward appearances, were moral, truthful, dedicated Christians. But the outward appearance was deceptive because they had become hypocrites whose lives and teachings did not conform to the Gospel. In a similar fashion, many Christians today apparently have ignored the impact on their own faith, and on the faith of others, of not accepting what God has said concerning His creative activity—and that of His Son—as recorded in the book of Genesis.

In commenting on the sinful nature of the first-century Pharisees, Christ Himself said: "Ye also outwardly appear righteous unto men, but inwardly ye are full of hypocrisy and iniquity" (Matthew 23:28). The people described by Paul who exhibited "a form of godliness," but who had "denied the power thereof," possessed the same hypocritical, sinful nature as the Pharisees, which is why Paul commanded Timothy, "from these also turn away" (2 Timothy 3:5).

Will historians of the future, as they look back on the twentieth century, say, as O.M. Gilman did of those in the nineteenth century (when he wrote in his book, *The Evolutionary Outlook: 1875-1900*): "After a generation of argument, educated Americans in general came to accept the fact of evolution and went on to make whatever intellectual adjustments they thought necessary" (1971, p. 2)? Will we give up the inspired testimony of God's Word and simply "make whatever intellectual adjustments" are necessary to accommodate our thinking to the pseudo-scientific trappings of organic evolution? The old adage is correct: "All that is necessary for evil to triumph is for good men to do nothing."

In regard to the "intellectual adjustments" (read that as "compromises") that so many Bible believers have made to incorporate various aspect of evolution into their faith-system, I am inclined to say that the philosopher's satirical point was well made when, in days of old, he said: "*Quos Deus vult pedere pruis dementat!*" ("Whom the gods would destroy, they first make mad!"). The inspired apostle Paul put it in another way: "Professing themselves to be wise, they became fools" (Romans 1:22).

If I may kindly say so, those who boldly step forward to compromise the plain teaching of the inspired Word of God need to know that their compromises will not go unchallenged or unanswered. It is the purpose of this book both to challenge, and to answer, many of those compromises. It is my sincere desire that this volume will provide ammunition for the Christian soldier who is in the heat of the battle, so that "ye may be able to withstand in the evil day, and, having done all, to stand."

Bert Thompson
November 1, 2000

Chapter 1

Introduction:
The Importance of Beliefs
Regarding Origins

To the faithful Christian, there is little of more importance than the proclamation and defense of the Old Jerusalem Gospel that is able to save men's souls. Christianity did not come into the world with a whimper, but a bang. It was not in the first century, nor is it intended to be in the twenty-first, something "done in a corner." While it certainly may be true to say regarding some religions that they flourish best in secrecy, such is not the case with Christianity. It is intended to be presented, and to flourish, in the marketplace of ideas. In addition, it may be stated safely that while some religions eschew open investigation and critical evaluation, Christianity welcomes both. It is a historical religion—the only one of the world's major religions based upon an individual rather than a mere ideology—that claims, and can document, an empty tomb for its Founder.

Christians, unlike adherents of many other religions, do not have an option regarding the distribution and/or dissemination of their faith. The efficacy of God's saving grace as made possible through His Son, Jesus Christ, is a message that all accountable men and women need to hear, and one that Christians are commanded to pronounce (John 3:16; Matthew 28:18-20; cf. Ezekiel 33:7-9).

What sets biblical faith apart from the beliefs of certain other religions is that instead of being rooted solely in an appeal to the emotions, it is rooted in an appeal to both the emotions and the intellect. In other words, biblical faith addresses both the heart and the mind; it is not just felt, but learned as well. This always has been the case. From the moment of man's creation, God sought to teach him how to make correct choices that would keep him in, or return him to, a covenant relationship with his Creator. Thus, as soon as man was placed in the lovely Garden of Eden, God gave the instructions necessary for man's temporal and spiritual well-being (Genesis 1:28; 2:16-17). From that moment forward, God actively taught man how to build, and maintain, a proper relationship with his heavenly Father. This is evident within the pages of both the Old and New Testaments.

The Old Testament, for example, is filled with numerous instances of God's providing people with the instructions that would prompt them to serve Him with their hearts as well as with their intellects. During the Patriarchal Age, God spoke directly to the renowned men of old, and conveyed to them the commandments intended to regulate their daily lives, as well as their worship of Him. The apostle Paul, alluding to the Gentiles, spoke of those who had the law "written in their hearts, their conscience bearing witness therewith, and their thoughts accusing or else excusing them" (Romans 2:15).

Later, during the Mosaical Age, God's instructions were given to the Hebrews in written form so that as they grew numerically, they also would possess the ability to grow spiritually. Jewish parents were instructed to teach God's Word to their children on a continuing basis (see Deuteronomy 4:10; 6:7-9; 11:18-25). Eventually, when national and spiritual reform was needed, God provided numerous kings and prophets to perform this important task (see 2 Kings 23:1-3; 2 Chronicles 7:7-9). It is said of the Old Testament prophet Ezra that he purposely "had set his heart to seek the law of Jehovah, and to do it, and to **teach** in Israel statutes and ordinances" (Ezra 7:10, emp. added). Nehemiah 8:7-8 records that Ezra "caused the people to understand the law: and the people stood in their place, and they **read** in the book, in the law of God, distinctly; and they **gave the sense**, so that they **understood** the reading" (emp. added).

It is clear from such passages that during Old Testament times God placed a premium on knowing, understanding, obeying, and teaching His commandments. The golden thread that runs from Genesis through Malachi—the urgent message that the Savior was coming—could not be expressed through emotion alone; the intellect had to be involved as well. It was not enough for God's people merely to "feel" the message; it had to be **taught** so they could understand it, realize its importance to their salvation, and preserve it for generations yet unborn, to whom it also would be taught.

Similarly, the New Testament stresses the critical nature of teaching. In the first century A.D., the message no longer was "the Savior is coming"; rather, the message was "the Savior **has come**." Once Jesus began His public ministry, teaching His disciples (and others whom He encountered on almost a daily basis) became His primary task. While it is true that today we look upon Him as a miracle worker, prophet, and preacher, He was foremost a teacher. Throughout Galilee, Samaria, Judea, and the surrounding areas, Jesus taught in synagogues, boats, temples, streets, marketplaces, and gardens. He taught on plains, trails, and mountainsides—wherever people were to be found. And He taught as One possessing authority. After hearing His discourses, the only thing the people who heard Him could say was, "Never man so spake" (John 7:46).

The teaching did not stop when Christ returned to heaven. He had trained others—apostles and disciples—to continue the task He had begun. They were sent to the uttermost parts of the Earth with the mandate to proclaim the "good news" through preaching and teaching (Matthew 28:18-20). This they did daily (Acts 5: 42). The result was additional disciples, who then were rooted and grounded in the fundamentals of God's Word (Acts 2:42) so that they, too, could teach others. In a single day, in a single city, over 3,000 people became Christians as a result of such teaching (Acts 2:41). In fact, so effective was this kind of instruction that Christianity's bitterest enemies desperately tried to prohibit any further public teaching (Acts 4:18; 5:28)—but to no avail. Christianity's message, and the unwavering dedication of those into whose hands it had been placed, were far too powerful for even its most formidable foes to abate or defeat. Almost twenty centuries later, the central theme of the Cross still is vibrant and forceful.

But will that continue to be the case if those given the sobering task of teaching the Gospel act irresponsibly and alter its content, or use fraudulent means to present it? The simple fact is, Christianity's success today—just as in the first century—is dependent upon the dedication, and honesty, of those to whom the Truth has been entrusted. God has placed the Gospel into the hands of men and women who have been instructed to teach it so that all who hear it might have the opportunity to obey it and be saved. The apostle Paul commented on this when he wrote: "But we have this treasure in earthen vessels, that the exceeding greatness of the power may be of God, and not from ourselves" (2 Corinthians 4:7). The thrust of the apostle's statement in this particular passage was that the responsibility of taking the Gospel to a lost and dying world ultimately has been given to mortal men.

From time to time, however, Christians may be afflicted with either an attitude of indifference, or spiritual myopia (shortsightedness). Both critically impair effectiveness in spreading the Gospel. A Christian's attitude of indifference may result from any number of factors, including such things as a person's own spiritual weakness, a downtrodden spirit, a lack of serious Bible study, etc. Spiritual myopia, on the other hand, often is the end product of either not having an adequate understanding of the Gospel message itself, or not wishing to engage in the controversy that sometimes is necessary to propagate that message.

One such example of spiritual myopia afflicting some Christians today centers on the Bible's teaching regarding the topic of origins. Because no one is particularly fond of either controversy or playing the part of the controversialist, it is not at all uncommon nowadays to hear someone say: "Why bother getting involved in controversial 'peripheral' issues like creation and evolution? Just teach the Gospel." Or, one might hear it said that "since the Bible is not a textbook of science, and since it is the Rock of Ages that is important —not the age of rocks—we should just 'preach Christ.' "

Such statements are clear and compelling evidence of spiritual shortsightedness, and belie a basic misunderstanding of the seriousness of the Bible's teachings on one of its most important topics. First, those who suggest that we not concern ourselves with "peripheral" issues such as creation and evolution, and that we instead "just preach the Gospel," fail to realize that the Gospel **includes creation** and **excludes evolution**. Second, those who advise us simply to "emphasize saving faith, not faith in creation," apparently have forgotten that the most magnificent chapter in all the Bible on the topic of faith (Hebrews 11) begins by stressing the importance of faith in the *ex nihilo* creation of all things by God (verse 3) as preliminary to any kind of meaningful faith in His promises. Third, in order to avoid the offense that may come from preaching the complete Gospel, some simply would regard creation as unimportant. God, however, considered it so important that it was the topic of His first revelation. The first chapter of Genesis is the very foundation of the rest of the biblical record. If the foundation is undermined, it will not be long until the superstructure built upon it collapses as well. Should the first chapters of the Bible prove untrustworthy, upon what basis would one conclude that those which follow merit any confidence? Fourth, many Christians today have overlooked the impact on their own faith of **not teaching** what God has said about creation. G. Richard Culp stated it well.

> One who doubts the Genesis account will not be the same
> man he once was, for his attitude toward Holy Scripture
> has been eroded by false teaching. Genesis is repeatedly re-
> ferred to in the New Testament, and it cannot be separated
> from the total Christian message (1975, pp. 160-161).

Lastly, however, some Christians—afflicted with spiritual myopia —have advised us to "just preach Christ," all the while ignoring, or being uninformed of, the fact that Christ was the Creator before He became (in a physical sense) the Redeemer, and that His finished work of salvation is meaningful only in light of His finished work of creation (Hebrews 4:3-10). Furthermore, Christ and His inspired writers spoke often on the topic of creation and its relevance. The first eleven chapters of Genesis, sometimes referred to as the "creation chapters," are an integral part of the biblical record. They are not unsightly warts or malignant tumors that may be excised, somehow leaving the remainder of that record intact. If these teachings turn out to be either mythical or false, it impeaches not only their testimony, but that of the Lord as well, for He accepted them as both correct and reliable, and used them often as a basis for His instructions and commandments in the New Testament. The teachings of Moses and Christ are inextricably linked. As Jesus said to the unbelieving Jews of His day: "For if ye believed Moses, ye would believe me; for he wrote of me. But if ye believe not his writings, how shall ye believe my words?" (John 5:46-47). John Whitcomb observed:

> It is the privilege of these men to dispense with an historical
> Adam if they so desire. But they do not at the same time
> have the privilege of claiming that Christ spoke the truth.
> Adam and Christ stand or fall together... (1972, p. 111).

Why is this so? And why is a correct understanding of origins so important? Simply put, the answer is this: "If there is no creation, there is nothing else. If there is no Creator, then there is no Saviour either" (Segraves, 1973, p. 24). Ultimately, a proper understanding of creation depends upon a proper understanding of Christ, and vice versa. In Romans 5:14, Paul spoke of Adam as "a **figure** [*tu-*

pos, type] of him who was to come"—which no doubt explains why, in the great "resurrection chapter" of the New Testament (1 Corinthians 15), the apostle wrote by inspiration:

> The first man Adam became a living soul. The last Adam became a life-giving spirit. The first man is of the earth, earthy; the second man is of heaven...and as we have borne the image of the earthy, we shall also bear the image of the heavenly (vss. 45-48).

Adam was thus a "type" of Christ; the two stand or fall together.

THE IMPLICATIONS AND CONSEQUENCES OF BELIEF SYSTEMS

These concepts merit serious attention. Most rational, reasonable people would agree that actions have consequences. If a man commits a crime, is pursued and apprehended by law enforcement officers, tried by a jury of his peers, and sentenced to life in the penitentiary or death in the electric chair, who is responsible? When an individual decides to act, is it not true that ultimately the consequences of those actions fall squarely on his or her shoulders? Indeed, actions **do** have consequences.

But so do beliefs and ideas. Is that not one reason why the spoken word is so powerful. The ability to elucidate an idea via a speech, lecture, or other oral presentation can produce astonishing consequences. Think, for example, of the late president of the United States, John F. Kennedy, who inspired Americans with his "Ask not what your country can do for you, but what you can do for your country" inaugural speech. On the heels of that idea—presented so eloquently by a dashing, young, newly elected, and extremely popular president—volunteerism in America grew at an unprecedented rate. Or, reflect upon another presentation in our nation's capital by the slain civil rights leader, Martin Luther King Jr. The moving oratory contained in his "I have a dream" speech captured the attention of an entire nation, and culminated in legislation aimed at protecting the rights of **all** citizens, regardless of ethnic background, skin color, or religious beliefs.

Beliefs and ideas presented via the written word are no less powerful. Ponder such documents as the hallowed United States *Constitution* that serves as the basis for the freedoms every citizen enjoys. Or contemplate the beloved *Declaration of Independence* that guarantees to every American man, woman, and child certain "unalienable rights." Throughout the history of mankind, the written word has expressed ideas that manifested the ability to free men and women (e.g. the English *Magna Carta*) or to enslave them (e.g., Adolf Hitler's *Mein Kampf*).

Indeed, beliefs and ideas—like actions—have consequences. Prominent humanist Martin Gardner devoted an entire chapter in one of his books to "The Relevance of Belief Systems," in an attempt to explain that **what a person believes** profoundly influences **how a person acts** (1988, pp. 57-64). In his book, *Does It Matter What I Believe?*, Millard Erickson, wrote that there are numerous reasons

> ...why having correct beliefs is important. Our whole lives are inevitably affected by the real world around us, so what we believe about it is of the utmost importance.... What we believe about reality does not change the truth, nor its effect upon us. Correct belief, however, enables us to know the truth as it is, and then to take appropriate action, so that it will have the best possible effect upon our lives. Having correct beliefs is also necessary because of the large amount and variety of incorrect beliefs which are about (1992, pp. 12,13).

Put simply, it **does matter** what we believe. Especially is this true when it comes to the topics of creation and evolution, since in this area we are dealing with complete cosmogonies (i.e., entire world views). Consider the following.

Evolution and Ethics

Although it is rare to see evolutionists actually admit it, the simple fact of the matter is that belief in evolution produces a society that is not a very pleasant one in which to live. Several years ago, British evolutionist Richard Dawkins [who has described himself as "a fairly militant atheist, with a fair degree of hostility toward religion" (see Bass, 1990, 124[4]:86)] authored a book titled *The Self-*

ish Gene, in which he set forth his theory of genetic determinism. In summarizing the basic thesis of the book, Dawkins said: "You are for nothing. You are here to propagate your selfish genes. There is no higher purpose in life" (Bass, 124[4]:60). Dawkins explained:

> I am not advocating a morality based on evolution. I am saying how things have evolved. I am not saying how we humans morally ought to behave.... My own feeling is that **a human society based simply on the gene's law of universal ruthless selfishness would be a very nasty society in which to live**. But unfortunately, however much we may deplore something, it does not stop it being true (1989, pp. 2,3, emp. added).

Dawkins is correct in his assessment that a society based on the truthfulness of evolution would be "a very nasty" place to live. But why? The answer has to do with the implications of belief in evolution.

Ethics generally is viewed as the system or code by which attitudes and actions are determined to be either right or wrong. But the truth of the matter is that if evolution is correct, and there is no God, man exists in an environment where "anything goes." Russian novelist Fyodor Dostoyevsky, in *The Brothers Karamazov* (1880), had one of his characters (Ivan) say that in the absence of God, everything is allowed. French existential philosopher, Jean Paul Sartre, wrote:

> Everything is indeed permitted if God does not exist, and man is in consequence forlorn, for he cannot find anything to depend upon either within or outside himself.... Nor, on the other hand, if God does not exist, are we provided with any values or commands that could legitimize our behavior (1961, p. 485).

Sartre contended that **whatever** one chooses to do is right; value is attached to the choice itself so that "...we can never choose evil" (1966, p. 279). These men are correct about one thing. If evolution is true and there is no God, "anything goes" is the name of the game. Thus, it is impossible to formulate a system of ethics by which one objectively can differentiate "right" from "wrong." Agnostic philosopher Bertrand Russell observed:

We feel that the man who brings widespread happiness at the expense of misery to himself is a better man than the man who brings unhappiness to others and happiness to himself. I do not know of any rational ground for this view, or, perhaps, for the somewhat more rational view that whatever the majority desires (called utilitarian hedonism) is preferable to what the minority desires. These are truly ethical problems but I do not know of any way in which they can be solved except by politics or war. All that I can find to say on this subject is that **an ethical opinion can only be defended by an ethical axiom, but, if the axiom is not accepted, there is no way of reaching a rational conclusion** (1969, 3: 29, emp. added, parenthetical item in orig.).

With no way to reach a rational conclusion on what is ethical, man finds himself adrift in a chaotic sea of despair where "might makes right," where "the strong subjugate the weak," and where each man does what is right in his own eyes. This is not a system of ethics, but rather a society driven by anarchy.

Evolution and Morality

Morality is the character of being in accord with the principles or standards of right conduct. George Gaylord Simpson, Harvard's late, eminent evolutionist, argued that "man is the result of a purposeless and materialistic process that did not have him in mind," yet admitted that "**good and evil, right and wrong, concepts irrelevant in nature except from the human viewpoint, become real and pressing features of the whole cosmos** as viewed by man...because morals arise only in man" (1967, p. 346, emp. added). Simpson therefore concluded: "Discovery that the universe apart from man or before his coming lacks and lacked any purpose or plan has the inevitable corollary that the workings of the universe cannot provide any automatic, universal, eternal, or absolute ethical criteria of right and wrong" (p. 346).

If such concepts as "good and evil, right and wrong" are "real and pressing features," how, then, should morals be determined? Since man is viewed as little more than the last animal among many to be produced by the long, meandering process of evolution, this becomes problematic. In their book, *Origins*, Richard Leakey and Roger Lewin wrote: "There is now a critical need for a deep awareness that, **no matter how special we are as an animal**, we are still part of the greater balance of nature..." (1977, p. 256, emp. added). Charles Darwin declared: "There is no fundamental difference between man and the higher mammals in their mental faculties" (as quoted in Francis Darwin, 1898, 1:64). A lion is not plagued by guilt after killing a gazelle's infant offspring for its noon meal. A dog does not experience remorse after stealing a bone from one of its peers. Since no other animal throughout evolutionary history has been able to locate and live by moral standards, should we somehow trust a "naked ape" (to use zoologist Desmond Morris' colorful expression from his 1967 book by that title) to do any better? Darwin himself complained: "Can the mind of man, which has, as I fully believe, been developed from a mind as low as that possessed by the lowest animals, be trusted when it draws such grand conclusions?" (as quoted in Francis Darwin, 1898, 1:282).

Matter—in and of itself—is impotent to evolve any sense of moral consciousness. If there is no purpose in the Universe, as Simpson and others have asserted, then there is no purpose to morality or ethics. But the concept of a purposeless morality, or a purposeless ethic, is irrational. Unbelief therefore must contend, and does contend, that there is no ultimate standard of moral/ethical truth, and that morality and ethics, at best, are relative and situational. That being the case, who could ever suggest, correctly, that someone else's conduct was "wrong," or that a man "ought" or "ought not" to do thus and so? The simple fact of the matter is that infidelity cannot explain the origin of morality and ethics.

Evolution and Hedonism

Hedonism is the philosophy which argues that the aim of "moral" conduct is the attainment of the greatest possible pleasure with the greatest possible avoidance of pain. One of the tenets of humanism, as expressed in the *Humanist Manifesto* of 1973, suggested, for example:

> ...we believe that intolerant attitudes, often cultivated by or-
> thodox religions and puritanical cultures, unduly repress sex-
> ual conduct. The right to birth control, abortion, and divorce
> should be recognized. While we do not approve of exploit-
> ive, denigrating forms of sexual expression, neither do we wish
> to prohibit, by law or social sanction, sexual behavior between
> consenting adults. The many varieties of sexual exploration
> should not in themselves be considered "evil." Without coun-
> tenancing mindless permissiveness or unbridled promiscuity,
> a civilized society should be a **tolerant** one. Short of harm-
> ing others or compelling them to do likewise, individuals should
> be permitted to express their sexual proclivities and pursue
> their lifestyles as they desire (pp. 18-19, emp. in orig.).

What have been the consequences of this kind of thinking? Sex-
ually transmitted diseases are occurring in epidemic proportions.
Teenage pregnancies are rampant. Babies are born already infected
with deadly diseases (such as AIDS) because their mothers con-
tracted the diseases during their pregnancies and passed them on
to their unborn offspring. In many places divorces are so common
that they equal or outnumber marriages. Jails are filled to overflow-
ing with rapists, stalkers, and child molesters. What else, pray tell,
will have to go wrong before it becomes apparent that attempts
to live without God are futile?

Evolution and the Value of Human Life

Having grown up under a father who was a veterinarian, and personally having served as a professor in the College of Veterinary Medicine at Texas A&M University for a number of years, I have seen
firsthand the fate of animals that have suffered irreparable injuries,
have become riddled with incurable diseases, or have become too
old and decrepit to control their bodily functions. I have had to stand
by helplessly and watch my own father, or one of my colleagues, dis-
charge a firearm to end the life of a horse because of a broken leg
that could not be healed. I have had to draw into a syringe the life-
ending drug to be inserted into the veins of someone's pet dog to
"put it to sleep" because the combination of senility and disease

had taken a toll that not even the ablest practitioner of the healing arts could reverse. It is neither a pleasant task, nor a pretty sight. But while a pet dog or champion 4-H gelding may have held a place of esteem in a child's heart, the simple fact of the matter is that the dog is not someone's father or mother, and the horse is not someone's brother or sister. These are animals—which is why we shoot horses.

In the evolutionary scheme of things, however, man occupies the same status. He may be more knowledgeable, more intellectual, and more scheming than his counterparts in the animal kingdom. But he still is an animal. And so the question is bound to arise: Why should man be treated any differently once his life no longer is deemed worth living? Truth be told, there is no logical reason that he should. From cradle to grave, life—from an evolutionary vantage point—is completely expendable. And so it should be—at least if Charles Darwin's comments are to be taken at face value. In his book, *The Descent of Man,* he wrote:

> With savages, the weak in body or mind are soon eliminated; and those that survive commonly exhibit a vigorous state of health. We civilised men, on the other hand, do our utmost to check the process of elimination; we build asylums for the imbecile, the maimed, and the sick; we institute poor-laws; and our medical men exert their utmost skills to save the life of everyone to the last moment. There is reason to believe that vaccination has preserved thousands, who from a weak constitution would formerly have succumbed to small-pox. Thus the weak members of civilised societies propagate their kind. No one who has attended to the breeding of domestic animals will doubt that this must be highly injurious to the race of man. It is surprising how soon a want of care, or care wrongly directed, leads to the degeneration of a domestic race; but excepting in the case of man himself, hardly any one is so ignorant as to allow his worst animals to breed (1870, p. 501).

In Darwin's day (and even in the early parts of this century), some attempted to apply this view to the human race via the concept of eugenics.

Introduction:
The Importance of Beliefs Regarding Origins

By 1973, the United States Supreme Court, in a 7-to-2 vote on January 22, decided that the embryo growing within the human womb no longer is "human." Rather, it is a "thing" that may be ripped out, slaughtered, and tossed into the nearest dumpster. And the inordinate lengths to which evolutionists will go in order to justify such a position defy description. As an example, consider the case of the late evolutionist, Carl Sagan, and his wife, Ann Druyan. In an article titled "The Question of Abortion: A Search for the Answers" they coauthored for the April 22, 1990 issue of *Parade*, these two humanists argued for the ethical permissibility of human abortion on the grounds that the fetus—growing within a woman's body for several months following conception—is not a human being. Thus, they concluded, the killing of this tiny creature is not murder.*

And what was the basis for this assertion? Sagan and Druyan argued their case by subtly employing the antiquated concept known as "embryonic recapitulation" (sometimes referred to by its catchphrase, "ontogeny recapitulates phylogeny"), which suggests that as the human embryo develops, the growth of the individual (ontogeny) repeats (recapitulates) the evolutionary history of its ancestors (phylogeny)—traveling through such stages as an amoeba-like blob, a fish, an amphibian, a reptile, etc. Therefore, observing the human embryo growing would be like watching a "silent moving picture" of past evolution. They wrote that the embryo first is "a kind of parasite" that eventually looks like a "segmented worm." Further alterations, they suggested, reveal "gill arches" like that of a "fish or amphibian." Supposedly, "reptilian" features emerge, and later give rise to "mammalian...pig-like" traits. By the end of the second month, according to these two authors, the creature resembles a "primate but is still not quite human" (1990, p. 6).

---

* Dr. Sagan died in December 1996. One year later, in 1997, his book, *Billions and Billions*, was published posthumously. Chapter 15 of that book (pp. 163-179), titled "Abortion: Is It Possible to be both 'Pro-Life' and 'Pro-Choice'?," contains the entire text of the *Parade* article, along with Dr. Sagan's comments about the unnerving public response the magazine received following its publication (380,000 people telephoned *Parade's* offices in a matter of days).

The concept of embryonic recapitulation first was set forth in 1866 by the renowned German scientist and artist, Ernst Haeckel. Shortly thereafter, however, it came to light that Dr. Haeckel had used his art talent to falsify some of the drawings that accompanied his research articles on animal and human embryos, in order to make it appear as if embryonic recapitulation were true—when, in fact, it was not. Eventually, he was found guilty of scientific fraud by a jury of his peers at a trial held at the University of Jena where he taught, and he lived much of the rest of his life in disrepute. Scientists have known for well over a century that Haeckel's theory was based on fraudulent data, that it is without any foundation whatsoever in scientific fact, and that both he and it have been thoroughly discredited. As long ago as 1957, George Gaylord Simpson and his coauthors wrote in their widely used biology textbook, *Life: An Introduction to Biology*: "It is now firmly established that **ontogeny does not repeat phylogeny**" (1957, p. 352, emp. added). Notice, however, the authors' comment to their student readers, which appeared as a footnote at the bottom of the same page:

> You may well ask why we bother you with principles that turned out to be wrong. There are two reasons. In the first place, **belief in recapitulation became so widespread that it is still evident in some writings about biology and evolution**. You should know therefore what recapitulation is supposed to be and **you should know that it does not really occur** (emp. added).

Sadly, even though scientists have known for more than a century that embryonic recapitulation is wrong, Simpson and his coauthors were absolutely correct in their assessment that "belief in recapitulation became so widespread that it is still evident in some writings about biology and evolution." For example, in the October 1981 issue of *Science Digest*, evolutionist Isaac Asimov and creationist Duane Gish participated in a written debate (at the invitation of the magazine's editors) under the title of "The Genesis War." During his portion of the debate, Dr. Gish correctly pointed out:

> The idea of embryological recapitulation—that at successive stages of development a fetus resembles a fish, amphibian, reptile and, finally, mammal—is now a thoroughly discredited theory and should be expunged from textbooks (1981, 89 [9]:83).

Surprisingly, Dr. Asimov replied:

> I don't know what aspect of embryological recapitulation is now "thoroughly discredited" in the eyes of a creationist. However, **the human fetus in the course of its development has a tail and has indications of gills** (89[9]:83, emp. added).

An author of Dr. Asimov's stature (he wrote more than 500 volumes during his lifetime!) and preeminence in the evolutionary community should have known better than to make such statements. As the eminent evolutionist of Great Britain, Sir Arthur Keith, had stated quite bluntly almost fifty years earlier:

> It was expected that the embryo would recapitulate the features of its ancestors from the lowest to the highest forms in the animal kingdom. Now that the appearances of the embryo at all stages are known, the general feeling is one of disappointment; the human embryo at no stage is anthropoid in appearance. **The embryo of the mammal never resembles the worm, the fish, or the reptile. Embryology provides no support whatsoever for the evolutionary hypothesis** (1932, p. 94, emp. added).

Unfortunately, statements like Dr. Asimov's are not restricted to the time period of two decades or more ago. In his 1997 book on the origin of the Universe and life in that Universe, *The Whole Shebang*, evolutionist Timothy Ferris wrote:

> Strong evidence of biological conservancy may also be found in embryology, where it gave rise to the saying that "ontogeny recapitulates phylogeny." **A human embryo grows gills like its fish ancestors**, and then tears them down and rebuilds them into lungs (p. 197, emp. added).

Dr. Ferris could not be more wrong than he is. A biology textbook published well over two decades earlier noted: "Actually these 'gills' are alternating ridges and furrows on the right and left sides of the neck. They **never** develop into gills. They remain covered by a thin membrane and **never** have respiratory function" (Moore and Slusher, 1974, p. 434, emp. in orig.).

Twenty-five years later, evolutionist Jeffrey Schwartz concurred when he wrote in his 1999 volume, *Sudden Origins*:

> For Haeckel, the presumed gill-slit stage in human ontogeny was the equivalent of an adult fish. (**In reality, such a stage does not occur**; there are only the folds of the gill arches, which, among other structures, develop into our hyoid bone, inner ear bones, and jaws.) [p. 164, emp. added)].

Why then—if we have known for well over a hundred years that Haeckel's ideas are wrong—have evolutionists continued to use embryonic recapitulation as a "proof" of evolution? John Tyler Bonner, who served for many years as the head of the biology department at Princeton University, succinctly answered that question when he admitted: "We may have known for almost a hundred years that Haeckel's blastaea-gastraea theory of the origin of the metazoa is probably nonsense, **but it is so clear-cut, so simple, so easy to hand full-blown to the student**" (1961, 49:240, emp. added). Apparently, the fact that it is not true matters little.

Thus, when the time came that Carl Sagan and Ann Druyan desperately needed to find something—anything—within science to justify their personal belief that abortion is not murder, they simply resurrected the antiquated, erroneous concept of embryonic recapitulation, dusted it off, and tried to give it some renewed credibility as an appropriate reason why abortion should not be considered as illegal and homicidal. Surely, this shows the lengths to which evolutionists will go in attempts to substantiate their theory, and the inordinate practices that the theory generates when followed to its logical conclusion.

According to Darwin, "weaker" members of society are unfit and, in keeping with the laws of nature, would not survive under normal conditions. Who is weaker than a tiny baby growing in the womb? The baby cannot defend himself, cannot feed himself, cannot even speak for himself. He (or she) is completely and totally dependent upon the mother for life. Since nature "selects against" the weaker animal, and since man is an animal, why should man expect any deferential treatment?

Once those who are helpless, weak, and young become expendable, who will be next? Will it be the helpless, weak, and old? Will it be those whose infirmities make them "unfit" to survive in a society that values the beautiful and the strong? Will it be those who are lame, blind, or maimed? Will it be those whose IQ falls below a certain point, or whose skin is a different color?

More and more there is a clamoring in this country to kill the handicapped, the weak, the old, the terminally ill, and others with a "diminished quality of life." Richard McCormick of the Kennedy Center for the Study of Reproduction and Bioethics at Georgetown University has suggested: "Life is a value to be preserved only insofar as it contains some potentiality for human relationships" (1974). The renowned Nobel laureate, Francis Crick, has urged that "no newborn infant should be declared human until it has passed certain tests regarding its genetic endowment and...if it fails these tests it forfeits the right to live" (as quoted in Howard and Rifkin, 1977, p. 81). It hardly is surprising, then, to hear Joseph Fletcher (of situation ethics fame) suggest that any individual with an IQ of 20 or less is not a person, and that anyone ranging from 20 to 40 is only marginally so (see Lygre, 1979, p. 63).

Twenty-five years ago, Robert Cooke of the University of Wisconsin testified before a U.S. Senate select subcommittee that an estimated "2,000 infants a year are dying in America because treatment has been withheld or stopped" (as quoted in Marx, 1975, p. 9). Almost thirty years ago, an investigation carried out during a three-year period (from 1970 to 1972) at the Yale/New Haven Hospital in Connecticut uncovered the fact that 43 babies died at this one hospital when doctors decided they were "unfit to live" and therefore withdrew food, water, etc. (Lygre, 1979, p. 65). Lest anyone wonders if such things still are occurring decades later, perhaps we should be reminded of the now-famous "Baby Doe" case in an American hospital (see Davis, 1985, pp. 158ff.). Doctors recommended that the newborn baby girl be allowed to die, due to the fact that, in their opinion, she was too badly deformed to live. [Joan Hodgman of the University of California School of Medicine once admitted: "If we have a baby that I know is malformed beyond hope, I make no attempt to preserve life" (as quoted in Lygre, 1979, p. 66).] The parents accepted the doctors' advice, and the hospital staff withdrew food, water, and other reasonable care. The government stepped in to state that a violation of the baby girl's civil rights had occurred (remember "**life**, liberty, and the pursuit of happiness"?). As President of the United States, Ronald Reagan ordered the Secretary of the Department of Health and Human Services to deliver strict rules to hospitals receiving federal funds—rules which made it clear that all necessary steps were to be taken for the continuation of human life. A callous, depraved view of the value of human life had made such extraordinary governmental intervention necessary.

Bentley Glass once suggested that "no parents will in that future time have a right to burden society with a malformed or a mentally incompetent child" (1971, 171:23-29). in his book, *The Sanctity of Life and the Criminal Law*, Glanville Williams, strongly advocated the legalization of both "humanitarian infanticide" and "euthanasia for handicapped children" (1957). Joseph Fletcher even went so far as to state that we are "morally obliged" to end the lives of all those who are terminally ill (1979, p. 152). William Gaylin, a professor of psychiatry and law at Columbia University, declared: "It used to be easy to know what we wanted for our children, and now the best for our children might mean deciding which ones to kill. We have always wanted the best for our grandparents, and now that might mean killing them" (as quoted in Marx, 1975, p. 3). Some in our society already are calling for just such "cleansing" processes to be made legal, using such household euphemisms as "euthanasia" or "mercy killing." After all, we shoot horses, don't we?

CONCLUSION

Richard Dawkins was correct when he suggested that "a human society based simply on the gene's law of universal ruthless selfishness would be a very nasty society in which to live." Indeed, actions do have consequences. And beliefs do have implications.

Acceptance of the biblical doctrine of creation likewise has implications. It implies, for example, that: (a) there is an eternal Creator; (b) religion is God-ordained; (c) supernatural forces have been at work in the past and therefore nature is not "all there is"; (d) man is a special creation produced by God "in His image"; (e) there is an objective standard for truth that provides guidelines for man's ethical and moral conduct; and (f) after this life, there is another life yet to come.

Similarly, any attempt to merge the two systems of origins has implications as well. That is the subject of this book. Some have suggested that there is not necessarily a dichotomy in the matter of origins—that evolution and creation need not be separate, distinct, and opposing world views but instead may be happily combined (see, for example, Sheler, 1999, pp. 49-56). While not impugning the motives of those who have suggested such a compromise, it is my position that such a marriage is both unwarranted and unscriptural, as well as unworthy of any support from those who revere the Word of God as verbally inspired and authoritative in these matters.

One of the most respected evolutionists in America during the past six decades was the late George Gaylord Simpson quoted above —known affectionately among his colleagues as "Mr. Evolution" because of his lifelong, ardent defense of their theory. It is rare indeed that a creationist finds himself in agreement with an evolutionist. But in his book, *This View of Life,* Dr. Simpson addressed the compromise position of theistic evolution, and commented on it in such a way that I find myself agreeing with him. In discussing three well-known men who tried to defend theistic evolution (LeCompte du Nouy, Theilhard de Chardin, and Edmund W. Sinnot), Dr. Simpson remarked:

> ...Three great men and great souls, and all have flatly failed in their quest. It is unlikely that others can succeed where they did not, and surely I know of none who has. The attempt to build an evolutionary theory mingling mysticism [his euphemism for creation—BT] and science has only tended to vitiate the science. I strongly suspect that it has been equally damaging on the religious side... (1964, p. 232).

Those who attempt to defend various compromises of the biblical account of creation have failed, and will continue to fail, because their efforts represent an illegitimate amalgamation of two views—creation and evolution—that are diametrically opposed and that, therefore, logically cannot be conjoined. While the compromisers no doubt have harmed science, as Simpson suggested, the damage they have inflicted on the religious side has been far worse. The loss of respect for the Bible as the inspired Word of God that eventually results from the acceptance of various creation compromises is utterly tragic.

Even more tragic, however, is the ultimate effect of such compromises on a person's faith. Sooner or later, the Bible believer comes to realize that if the first eleven chapters of Genesis are not trustworthy, neither are those that follow. The number of people who have had their faith weakened, or destroyed, as a result of such compromises is inestimable. Surely it is one of the bitterest of ironies that those who were so determined to find a compromise allowing them to believe the biblical record are those who, because of that very compromise, ended up believing the Bible less and less until finally they believed it not at all. Sadly, the lesson learned far too late was that the compromise was unnecessary in the first place, as the following chapters document.

Chapter 2

Origins and
Atheistic Evolution

Origins. The mere mention of the word has the power to evoke deep-seated emotions, because this is one issue on which almost everyone has an opinion. From the very earliest times, men have inquired about their origin, and the question, "Whence have I come?" has not been far from either their minds or their lips. In our day and age it often is the case that **any** discussion of origins stirs quite a controversy, as proponents of competing theories battle each other in public debates, in the news media, in the classroom, in the courtroom, and through the printed word.

Such controversy, however, is not always bad. While it is true that at times more heat than light has been generated, this is not necessarily the case. Not infrequently, people who have had the temerity to question have been rewarded by the fruits of their inquiry. In many instances, people have been caused for the first time to consider seriously (or reconsider) their own privately held positions on these matters. They have sought answers, and have been amazed at the evidence (or lack of evidence) supporting their belief system

—when previously they may have been somewhat complacent about the matter of their own beginnings. Oftentimes, as people have explored the matter of their ultimate origin, they also have discovered, quite inadvertently, certain implications that invariably accompany the suggested scenarios—implications that affect them in their everyday lives as they consider such weighty matters as ethics, morals, truth, and a host of other concepts of real importance to humankind. The controversy over origins (rather, the end results of that controversy) may have proven either a blight or a blessing, but to those who go to the trouble to investigate, one thing is certain: the quest never is dull.

There are two fundamentally different, and diametrically opposed, explanations for the origin of the Universe, the origin of life in that Universe, and the origin of new types of varying life forms. Each of these explanations is a cosmogony—an entire world view, or philosophy, of origins and destinies, of life and its meaning. One of these cosmogonies is known as **evolution** (often referred to as organic evolution, the theory of evolution, the evolution model, atheistic evolution, etc.). The second alternate and opposing view is **creation** (often referred to as special creation, the theory of creation, the creation model, etc.). In this chapter, I would like to define, and examine, the concept of atheistic evolution. In the chapter that follows, I will examine the concept of creation.

ATHEISTIC EVOLUTION DEFINED

The term "evolution" derives from the Latin word, *evolvere*, which means literally to "unroll, unfold, or change." The word "evolution" may be used legitimately to speak of a bud's development into the flower, the metamorphosis of the butterfly, or even the production of new varieties of organisms.* However, this is not what the average person has in mind when he speaks of evolution. In everyday parlance, the word carries quite a different meaning.

---

* For a comprehensive discussion of the varied definitions of evolution, see Bales (1971, 2[3]:1-4).

In 1960, G.A. Kerkut, the renowned British physiologist and evolutionist, authored *The Implications of Evolution*. In that small-but-powerful volume, he defined two theories of evolution that are of importance for the discussion here. He termed one of those the Special Theory of Evolution.* This is the kind of evolution to which practically all people subscribe, and over which there is no controversy. It suggests that limited change, within narrow limits, occurs throughout all living things. I know of no one who would deny this point. Creationists agree to its factuality, as do atheistic evolutionists. Years ago (to list just three examples), Brangus cattle, cockapoo dogs, and 1,000+ varieties of roses did not exist. But today they do. Why? Simply stated, it is because evolution has occurred.

But as everyone recognizes, this "evolution" produced only small changes that did not cross what biologists refer to as "phylogenetic boundaries." That is to say, the Brangus is still a cow, the cockapoo is still a dog, and (to employ an old adage), a rose by any other name is still a rose. While the Special Theory of Evolution allows for change **within** groups, it does not allow for change **between** groups. It is not the Special Theory of Evolution that I will be investigating in the pages that follow; rather, I intend to examine the other theory of evolution mentioned by Kerkut.

In addition to the Special Theory, Dr. Kerkut also identified, defined, and discussed what he termed the General Theory of Evolution.** He stated: "On the other hand, there is the theory that all the living forms in the world have arisen from a single source which itself came from an inorganic form. This theory can be called the 'General Theory of Evolution'..." (1960, p. 157). This is what is referred to commonly as organic evolution, atheistic evolution, or simply "evolution." Through the years, numerous investigators have offered various definitions of evolution. The same year that Dr. Kerkut offered his definitions, Simpson wrote:

---

* The Special Theory of Evolution sometimes is referred to by the term **microevolution**.

** The General Theory of Evolution sometimes is referred to by the term **macroevolution**.

> Evolution is a fully natural process, inherent in the physical
> properties of the universe, by which life arose in the first
> place, and by which all living things, past or present, have
> since developed, divergently and progressively (1960, 131:
> 969).

This definition has been accepted widely because of: (a) Dr. Simpson's reputation in the evolutionary community; and (b) its succinct statement of what evolution is and allegedly does. Previously, Simpson and his coauthors had defined the theory by suggesting:

> First, there is the theory of evolution in the strict sense. This
> states that all living organisms have evolved from common
> ancestors in a gradual historical process of change and diversification. The theory rejects the notion that all organisms
> were designed and created at the beginning of time (Simpson, et al., 1957, pp. 25-26).

Dr. Simpson's Harvard colleague, the famous zoologist P.D. Darlington, reiterated these same points twenty-three years later.

> The outstanding evolutionary mystery now is how matter has
> originated and evolved, why it has taken its present form in
> the universe and on the earth, and why it is capable of forming itself into complex living sets of molecules. This capability
> is inherent in matter as we know it, in its organization and energy.... It is a fundamental evolutionary generalization that no
> external agent imposes life on matter. Matter takes the form
> it does because it has the inherent capacity to do so. This is
> one of the most remarkable and mysterious facts about our
> universe: that matter exists that has the capacity to form itself
> into the most complex patterns of life (1980, pp. 15,234).

While disavowing its factuality, creationists agree with evolutionists about the definition of their theory. One creationist publication defined evolution as:

> ...the hypothesis that millions of years ago lifeless matter,
> acted upon by natural forces, gave origin to one or more minute living organisms which have since evolved into all living and extinct plants and animals, including man. The theory of evolution has to do with the origin of life and the origin
> of species, and should not be confused with the ordinary development or natural history of living plants and animals which
> we see all around us and which is an entirely different phe-

nomenon. In its wider aspects, the theory of evolution embraces the origin and development of the whole universe... (*Evolution*, n.d., p. 7).

Wilbert H. Rusch, a creationist, defined evolution as:

> ...the theory that large groups or kinds of basic organisms change with the passage of time. Then it is held that their descendants will now be as different from them as they were different from their ancestors. It would follow that, given the passage of a sufficient time span, the life forms at any given point in time will be radically different from the life forms present at any time during the past. It really involves what might be termed transspecific change. According to this theory, modern plants and animals are all the modified descendants of plants and animals from the past. All present taxa are then somehow descended from a common ancestry over vast periods of time. This would call for a continuum from the beginning of life to the present, with no distinct groups. This continuum would be made up of all fossil as well as present forms of life... (1991, pp. 13-14).

Notice the common thread running through each definition. First, evolution is a **fully natural** process. Second, no "external agent" (i.e., "Creator") is responsible for inanimate matter becoming animate; evolution "rejects the notion that all organisms were designed and created...." Third, all life descended (evolved) from a common source, which owes its own existence to inorganic matter. Fourth, evolution is a process of "change and diversification" which ultimately produces living organisms that develop "divergently and progressively." In summary then, by definition evolution precludes the supernatural, a Creator, any divine guidance of the natural processes involved, and the creation of organisms as separate and distinct entities not having descended from a common ancestor.

IS ATHEISTIC EVOLUTION POPULAR?

Although atheistic evolution is not nearly as old a viewpoint as creation, it has amassed to itself a rather large following among the peoples of the world. R.L. Wysong, in his book, *The Creation-Evo-*

lution Controversy, commented that "It is downright hard to find anyone who does not believe in evolution in one form or another" (1976, p. 63). Conway Zirkle stated that "practically every educated man believes in evolution. ...evolution is incorporated in the thinking of our time" (1959, p. 19). A university biology textbook used widely for almost two decades began with these words:

> Organic evolution is the greatest principle in biology. Its implications extend far beyond the confines of that science, ramifying into all phases of human life and activity. Accordingly, understanding of evolution should be part of the intellectual equipment of all educated persons (Moody, 1962, p. 1x).

For the past century, evolution has been in the limelight. And for the past quarter of a century or more, it has been taught as **scientific fact** in many elementary, junior high, and senior high schools, as well as in most colleges and universities. As Stephen J. Gould of Harvard put it: "The fact of evolution is as well established as anything in science (as secure as the revolution of the earth around the sun)..." [1987, 8[1]:64, parenthetical comment in orig.]. There can be little doubt that belief in evolution is popular. But **why** is this the case?

WHY DO PEOPLE BELIEVE IN EVOLUTION?

As we make our way through the pilgrimage called "life," on occasion we invariably stop to reflect upon the nature and meaning of our own existence, because such matters variously enthrall, excite, or intrigue us. Nowhere is this more evident than in regard to our ultimate origin. Few there must be who do not pause, at some point in their earthly sojourn, to ponder such topics as the origin of the Universe, the origin of planet Earth, the origin of various life forms on the Earth, the possibility of life on other planets, and even their own origin and destiny.

One of the most mind-numbing mysteries for those who do **not** believe in evolution is trying to understand the people who **do**. [Perhaps evolutionists feel the same exasperation in regard to creationists' beliefs, but on that point I am less qualified to judge.] This observation is not intended to be derogatory, but is offered merely as a statement of fact. As one who writes and lectures often on the topics of creation and evolution, I frequently am asked the question: "Why do people believe in evolution?" Often the question is phrased in what are intended to be complimentary terms: "Why is it that so many **obviously intelligent** people believe in evolution?" Neither question is easy to answer because generally the querist wants a simple, concise response. It is difficult for him to understand why people whom he accepts as "obviously intelligent" believe a concept such as evolution that he, personally, considers so unworthy of acceptance or recommendation by intelligent people. It has been my experience that rarely is there a singular reply that can provide an answer to such a question, because rarely is there just a single reason that can explain adequately why a person believes what he does. Especially is this true in regard to belief in evolution.

At times, the controversy that centers on the topics of creation and evolution has generated more heat than light. This does not necessarily have to be the case, however. In an open society, the topic of origins, and the varying views that people hold on origins, ultimately will be discussed; in fact, they **should** be discussed. But because the subject matter has to do with deeply held convictions, emotions often run high. One good way to avoid emotional entanglement, and the "more heat than light" syndrome that generally accompanies it, is to work diligently to comprehend the other person's position as completely as possible, and therefore to discuss it as accurately and calmly as possible in any given situation. That task is made easier if there exists—at the beginning of the discussion—a basic understanding of **why** the person believes as he does. Again, especially is this true in regard to belief in evolution.

While it may seem somewhat of a truism to suggest that people believe in evolution for a variety of reasons, realization of this fact, and a legitimate exploration of the reasons people offer for believing what they do, can go a long way toward a better understanding of opposing views found within the creation/evolution controversy. With better understanding comes improved communication. And with improved communication comes increased opportunity for dialogue—which can set the stage for the presentation of other viewpoints that perhaps have not been considered previously (e.g., in this particular instance, persuading the evolutionist to consider the evidence for creation).

As I attempt to respond to the question, "Why do so many **obviously intelligent** people believe in evolution?" I hope to be able to provide a better comprehension of the system of organic evolution, and of the people who accept it. Included among the reasons why people believe in evolution are the following.

Reason #1

There can be little doubt that many today believe in evolution simply because it is what they have been taught. As I stated earlier, for the past quarter of a century or more evolution has been taught as scientific fact in most educational settings—from kindergarten through graduate school. Marshall and Sandra Hall noted:

> In the first place, evolution is what is taught in the schools. At least two, and in some cases three and four generations, have used textbooks that presented it as proven fact. The teachers, who for the most part learned it as truth, pass it on as truth. Students are as thoroughly and surely indoctrinated with the concept of evolution as students have ever been indoctrinated with any unproven belief (1974, p. 10).

In their book, *Why Scientists Accept Evolution*, Bales and Clark confirmed such an observation. "Evolution," they wrote, "is taken for granted today and thus it is uncritically accepted by scientists as well as laymen. It is accepted by them today because it was already accepted by others who went before them and under whose direction they obtained their education" (1966, p. 106). People believe in evolution because they have been taught that it is true.

Reason #2

To suggest that many people today accept evolution as true merely because they have been taught to believe it does not tell the whole story, however. Intellectual pride enters into the picture as well. Who among us does not want to present at least the appearance of being smart and well educated? Over the last century, we have been led to believe that if we wish to be considered intelligent, then we should believe in evolution, because intelligent people all over the world believe in evolution. As Henry Morris well stated the issue: "...the main reason most educated people believe in evolution is simply because they have been told that most educated people believe in evolution!" (1963, p. 26).

Consider the hypothetical example of two college students discussing their professors and courses. One of the students, Joe, asks his friend, Mark, the following question: "Hey, Mark, do you believe in evolution? My professor says all smart folks do." Honestly, what is Mark supposed to say? If he says, "No, Joe, I don't believe in evolution," by definition he has admitted to being outside the sphere of all the "smart folks." On the other hand, if he says, "Yes, Joe, I do believe in evolution," he may be admitting to a belief based not on an examination of the evidence, but on the idea that he does not wish to be viewed by his peers as anything but "smart." Undoubtedly, many people today fall into this category. They do not accept evolution because they have seen evidence that establishes it as true. Rather, they believe it because doing so places them in the same category as others whom they consider to be intelligent.

Reason #3

Further exacerbating the problem is the fact that evolution has been given a "stamp of approval" by important spokespersons from practically every field of human endeavor. While there have been those from politics, the humanities, the arts, and other fields who openly have defended evolution as factual, in no other area has this defense been as pronounced as in the sciences. Because science has seen so many successes, and because these successes have been so visible and well publicized, scientists have been granted an aura of respectability that only can be envied by non-scientists. As a result, when scientists champion a cause, people take notice. After all, it is their workings through the scientific method that have eradicated smallpox, put men on the Moon, prevented polio, and lengthened life spans. We have grown used to seeing "experts" from various scientific disciplines ply their trade in an endless stream of amazing feats. Heart surgery has become commonplace; organ transplants have become routine; space shuttles flying to the heavens have become standard fare.

Thus, when evolution is presented as something that "all reputable scientists believe," there are many who accept such a statement at face value, and who fall in line with what they believe is a well-proven dictum that has been enshrouded with the cloak of scientific respectability. As philosopher Paul Ricci has written: "The reliability of evolution not only as a theory but as a principle of understanding is not contested by the vast majority of biologists, geologists, astronomers, and other scientists" (1986, p. 172).

Such statements leave the impression that evolution simply cannot be doubted by well-informed, intelligent people. The message is: "All scientists believe it; so should you." And many do, because, as Marshall and Sandra Hall have inquired: "How, then, are people with little or no special knowledge of the various sciences and related subjects to challenge the authorities? It is natural to accept what 'experts' say, and most people do" (1974, p. 10).

The simple fact is, however, that truth is not determined by popular opinion or majority vote. A thing may be, and often is, true even when accepted only by the minority. Believing something based on the assumption that "everyone else" also believes it often can lead to disastrous results. As the late Guy N. Woods remarked: "It is dangerous to follow the multitude because the majority is almost always on the wrong side in this world" (1982, 124[1]:2).

Reason #4

Without a doubt, there are many who believe in evolution because they have rejected God. For those who refuse to believe in the Creator, evolution becomes their only escape. They generally make no pretense of believing it based on anything other than their disbelief in God. Henry Fairfield Osborn, one of the most famous evolutionists of the early twentieth century, suggested: "In truth, from the earliest stages of Greek thought man has been eager to discover some natural cause of evolution, and to abandon the idea of supernatural intervention in the order of nature" (1918, p. ix). Henry Morris has noted: "Evolution is the natural way to explain the origin of things for those who do not know and acknowledge the true God of creation. In fact, some kind of evolution is absolutely necessary for those who would reject God" (1966, p. 98).

Sir Arthur Keith of Great Britain wrote: "Evolution is unproved and unprovable. We believe it because the only alternative is special creation, and that is unthinkable" (as quoted in Criswell, 1972, p. 73). Professor D.M.S. Watson, who held the position of the Chair of Evolution at the University of London for over twenty years, echoed the same sentiments when he stated that "evolution itself is accepted by zoologists, not because it has been observed to occur or can be proven by logically coherent evidence to be true, but because the only alternative, special creation, is incredible" (1929, 123:233). Almost seventy years later, evolutionist Richard Lewontin wrote:

> Our willingness to accept scientific claims against common sense is the key to an understanding of the real struggle between science and the supernatural. We take the side of science **in spite** of the patent absurdity of some of its constructs, **in spite** of its failure to fulfill many of its extravagant promises of health and life, **in spite** of the tolerance of the scientific community for unsubstantiated just-so stories, because we have a prior commitment, a commitment to naturalism. It is not that the methods and institutions of science somehow compel us to accept a material explanation of the phenomenal world, but, on the contrary, that we are forced by our *a*

priori adherence to material causes to create an apparatus
of investigation and a set of concepts that produce material
explanations, no matter how counter-intuitive, no matter how
mystifying to the uninitiated. Moreover, that materialism is absolute, for we cannot allow a Divine Foot in the door. The eminent Kant scholar Lewis Beck used to say that anyone who
could believe in God could believe in anything. To appeal to
an omnipotent deity is to allow that at any moment the regu-
larities of nature may be ruptured, that miracles may happen (1997, p. 31, emp. in orig.).

These kinds of statements leave little to the imagination, and make
it clear that those who make them believe in evolution not because
of the evidence, but instead because they have made up their minds,
a priori, that they are not going to believe in God.

In his text, *Man's Origin: Man's Destiny*, the late, eminent United
Nations scientist, A.E. Wilder-Smith, observed: "Darwinism and Neo-
Darwinism, rightly or wrongly, have been used everywhere in the
East and West, in the hands of the atheists and agnostics, as the main
weapon against the biblical doctrine of origins" (1975, p. 31). For
the person who stubbornly refuses to believe in God, belief in evolution becomes automatic. Similarly, opposition to God, the Bible,
and the system of origins the Bible describes, becomes just as automatic. Whenever a person rids himself of God, he simultaneously
(even if unwittingly) embraces evolution. By his disbelief, he has eliminated creation as an option regarding his origin.

Reason #5

Another reason people offer for their belief in evolution has to
do with the fact that there is so much evil, pain, and suffering in the
world. No rational, well-informed person can deny the widespread
and unmistakable occurrence of "bad" things that happen, often en-
gulfing those who seem undeserving of such tragic events. To some,
no explanation from religionists—regardless of how elaborately stated or elegantly defended that explanation may be—ever will provide
an adequate answer to the conundrum of how an omnipotent, omniscient, omnibenevolent God can allow atrocities to fill His specially
created world (see Thompson, 2000b, pp. 95-105).

Evolution, on the other hand, provides what appears to be a perfectly logical explanation for such a scenario. According to evolutionary dogma, throughout the history of the world various species (including man) have been engaged in a struggle for survival and advancement. Charles Darwin (borrowing a phrase from his friend, English philosopher Herbert Spencer) referred to it as "survival of the fittest." The evolutionist—because of the nature of his theory—is forced to view the Universe and everything within it as the end result of numerous purposeless accidents. All living things, including man, exist on the Earth not because of any Grand Plan, but because of fortuitous occurrences that resulted from chance happenings in nature. And, to survive—and thrive—in such a world may seem to justify a "might makes right/strong subjugates the weak/to the victor go the spoils" attitude. "It's a jungle out there"—and in the jungle it is the law of tooth and claw that prevails.

Since man is viewed as little more than a naked ape, why should he somehow be exempt from the perils that continually befall other species of animals? These animals live their entire lives with one eye looking over their shoulder, as it were, because they exist in a dog-eat-dog world with no set moral standard. Man, according to evolutionary theory, is no different. His claim to fame lies in the fact that (so far) he occupies the last rung of the evolutionary ladder.

But nature confers on him no special rights, privileges, or protection. In a world where evolution is considered as true, and "survival of the fittest" is touted as nature's way of weeding out the weak, it should be no surprise that evil, pain, and suffering exist. In fact, from the evolutionary vantage point, whenever competition occurs for such things as food supplies, adequate shelter, reproductive advantages, etc., humanity has to learn to cope with evil, pain, and suffering. Granted, at first this may sound harsh, but from the evolutionists' perspective it is consistent, and offers an attempted explanation for the undeniable existence of "bad" things in our world. Unfortunately, all too often the answers offered by religionists for the problem of evil, pain, and suffering have fallen short of the mark, and as a result people have accepted evolution as providing a legitimate explanation for a very real problem in their lives.

Reason #6

As unpleasant as it is to have to admit it, some people believe in evolution because they have heard about, witnessed, or experienced firsthand the mistakes of religionists through the ages. Whether it is the offering of young virgins to an imaginary deity, the burning of alleged witches at the stake, or the adultery of a highly visible televangelist, the truth of the matter is that on occasion believers in God have set a very poor example—one that sensitive, thinking people naturally would have difficulty following.

To some, the very history of religion makes it suspect from the outset. Attempts to force people to accept a certain religion (as in the Crusades), or misguided attempts to squelch open discussion of important issues (as in the Catholic Church's censure of Galileo), have left a bitter taste in the mouths of many. Add to that the hypocrisy of, or word spoken in anger by, a person who wears the name "Christian," and the damage may be such that even in a lifetime it cannot be repaired. The result is that those who have been offended want nothing whatsoever to do with the God of the Bible, and as they reject Him, they also reject His account of the creation of the world in which they live.

Reason #7

While it is undeniable that some reject creation because of inappropriate conduct on the part of those who advocate it, likewise it is true that some reject God, and creation, to excuse or legitimize their own inappropriate personal conduct. In other words, they believe in evolution because it allows them to avoid any objective moral standard of behavior. It keeps them "out of reach" of any deity. It provides a subjective climate of situation ethics where any and all behavior, no matter how absurd or perverse, is acceptable. It nourishes a "do your own thing" attitude that precludes rules and regulations, in a vain attempt to circumvent the guilt that inevitably comes from doing wrong.

In the evolutionary scenario, humans are merely the last in a long line of amoebas, crocodiles, and orangutans resulting from fortuitous cosmic accidents. In such an arrangement, it is futile to speak of "personal responsibility." There exists, in the grand scheme of things, no reason why one "ought" or "ought not" to act a certain way, or to do/not do a certain thing. Aldous Huxley stated the matter succinctly in his article, "Confessions of a Professed Atheist":

> I had motives for not wanting the world to have meaning; consequently, assumed it had none, and was able without any difficulty to find reasons for this assumption.... The philosopher who finds no meaning in the world is not concerned exclusively with a problem in pure metaphysics; he is also concerned to prove there is no valid reason why he personally should not do as he wants to do.... For myself, as no doubt for most of my contemporaries, the philosophy of meaninglessness was essentially an instrument of liberation. The liberation we desired was simultaneously liberation from a certain political and economic system and liberation from a certain system of morality. **We objected to the morality because it interfered with our sexual freedom** (1966, 3:19, emp. added).

If Huxley and his cohorts had abandoned belief in evolution and accepted the existence of God, it would have "interfered with their sexual freedom." Realizing that, they chose instead to abandon belief in God. That left them with only one option—belief in evolution. It was not something they did because of the weight of the evidence. Rather, it was something they did because they desired to avoid personal accountability to the Creator. Their actions belied their motives. As Woods remarked: "Convince a man that he came from a monkey, and he'll act like one!" (1976a, 118[33]:514).

Reason #8

Lastly, we may state that some people accept evolution because they are convinced that it is the correct answer to the question of origins. They have examined the evidence and, on the basis of their examination, have concluded that evolution is the only plausible explanation for the Universe and all that it contains. These people generally are both sincere and open-minded. They are not attempting to rid themselves of the idea of God. They do not feel the need to be "intellectually correct." They are not reacting to unkind treatment at the hand of religionists. They are not searching for a way to justify worldly behavior. They simply believe the evidence favors evolution, and thus have accepted it as the correct view of origins.

IS EVOLUTION A "FACT" OF SCIENCE?

When we talk about the origin of the Universe and those things in it, we cannot speak as eyewitnesses or firsthand observers. None of us was present when the origin of the Universe occurred. Therefore, any scientific discussion must be based on assumptions, hypotheses, and theories put in place after the fact.

An **assumption** is something taken for granted, and represents a legitimate starting point for an investigation. A **hypothesis** is an educated guess or tentative assumption. A **theory** is a plausible or scientifically acceptable general principle or body of principles to explain phenomena.

It generally is alleged by the more spirited evolutionists that evolution has been proven, and therefore must be spoken of not as theory, but fact. As far back as 1944, evolutionist W.W. Howells wrote in *Mankind So Far* that "there is also the mystery of how and why evolution takes place at all.... Evolution is a fact, like digestion..." (p. 5). On May 2, 1966, Nobel laureate Hermann J. Muller circulated a manifesto that affirmed:

> It has for many years been well established scientifically that all known forms of life, including man, have come into being by a lengthy process of evolution. There are no hypotheses, alternative to the principle of evolution with its "tree of life," that any competent biologist of today takes seriously. Moreover, the principle is so important for an understanding of the world we live in and of ourselves that the public in general,

including students taking biology in high school, should be
made aware of it, and of the fact that it is firmly established
even as the rotundity of the earth is firmly established (1966,
p. 2).*

Affixing their names to Dr. Muller's manifesto to signify their agreement were 177 of the world's most eminent evolutionary scientists.

In this day and age, most evolutionists no longer speak of the
"theory" of evolution, but refer instead to the "fact" of evolution.
The widely accepted Biological Sciences Curriculum Study, finan-
ced by the National Science Foundation, organized the entire treatment of biological science around the "fact" of the evolutionary
framework of life history. Almost all books on biology published by
secular publishers for at least the past two generations have been
written as though evolutionary presuppositions were fact instead
of theory. In introducing the papers in the three-volume work on
evolution stemming from the 1959 Darwinian Centennial Convocation in Chicago, Sir Julian Huxley eulogized Darwin as follows:

> Charles Darwin has rightly been described as the "Newton
> of biology"; he did more than any single individual before or
> since to change man's attitude to the phenomena of life and
> to provide a coherent scientific framework of ideas for biol-
> ogy, in place of an approach in large part compounded of hear-
> say, myth, and superstition. He rendered evolution inescap-
> able as a fact, comprehensible as a process, all-embracing
> as a concept (1960b, pp. 1-2).

Huxley maintained that "after Darwin it was no longer necessary
to deduce the existence of divine purpose for the facts of biological
adaptation" (1946, p. 87). Compare also Huxley's categorical statement at the Chicago convocation: "In the evolutionary pattern of
thought there is no longer need or room for the supernatural. The
earth was not created; it evolved. So did all the animals and plants

---

* Muller's manifesto was published originally in the February 1967 issue of *Bulletin
of the Atomic Scientists*. In his book, *Forty-Two Years on the Firing Line*, James
D. Bales gives the entire text of the manifesto (n.d., pp. 71-72) and a listing of the
177 scientists who signed it (pp. 73-77).

that inhabit it, including our human selves, mind, and soul as well as brain and body. So did religion" (1960c, pp. 252-253). Jacques Barzun, in his book, *Darwin, Marx, Wagner*, raised this question:

Why was evolution more precious than scientific suspense of judgment? Why do scientists to this day speak with considerable warmth of "the fact of evolution," as if it were in the same category as the fact of combustion, which "may be observed by anyone who will take the necessary trouble"? (1958, p. 65).

Barzun went on to point out why evolution is accepted as a fact, by stating that it gave scientists complete freedom over "everything in heaven and earth without restriction." He also observed that it put everything under one cause (1958, p. 65).

The codiscoverer of the DNA molecule, James Watson, is on record as stating: "Today the theory of evolution is an accepted fact for everyone but a fundamentalist minority" (1987, p. 2). Joining Dr. Watson in that assessment is Harvard paleontologist, Stephen J. Gould, one of the evolutionary establishment's fieriest apologists, and an indefatigable crusader on behalf of organic evolution. He is a cogent writer, a gifted speaker, and a tireless worker for "the cause." He also is one of science's most prolific and best-read authors (along with such late colleagues as Carl Sagan and Isaac Asimov), and is highly regarded in many scientific circles (the January 1983 issue of *Discover* magazine voted him "Scientist of the Year"). Through the years, Dr. Gould's articles have appeared not only in refereed scientific journals (e.g., *Nature, New Scientist, Science*, et al.), but in popular science magazines as well (*Discover, Omni, Science Digest*, et al.). Therefore, when Dr. Gould speaks, many people listen. To quote him directly: "When we come to popular writing about evolution, I suppose that my own essays are as well read as any" (1987, 8[1]:65). And therein lies the problem.

In the January 1987 issue of *Discover*, Dr. Gould authored a lengthy article titled, "Darwinism Defined: The Difference Between Fact and Theory." In this particular article, Gould expressed his extreme agitation at the inability of certain people (who should know better, he said) to properly address evolution by its rightful designation—as a **fact**, not a theory. The specific cause (this time) for his discomfiture was an article in the September 30, 1986 issue of the *New York Times* by Irving Kristol ("Room for Darwinism and the Bible"). Dr. Gould acknowledged both his dismay and dissatisfaction at the apparent inability of people like Mr. Kristol to distinguish (to use his own words) "the central distinction between secure fact and healthy debate about theory" (p. 64). Dr. Gould then explained himself when he noted:

> Facts are the world's data; theories are explanations proposed to interpret and coordinate facts. The fact of evolution is as well established as anything in science (as secure as the revolution of the earth about the sun), though absolute certainty has no place in our lexicon. Theories, or statements about the causes of documented evolutionary change, are now in a period of intense debate—a good mark of science in its healthiest state. Facts don't disappear while scientists debate theories (p. 64, parenthetical comment in orig.).

Later, Gould commented that "...evolution is also a fact of nature, and so do we teach it as well, just as our geological colleagues describe the structure of silicate minerals, and astronomers the elliptical orbits of the planets" (p. 65).

What could be clearer? Dr. Gould wants everyone to know that evolution is a fact. **How** evolution occurred may be considered by some to be merely a "theory," but **that** evolution has occurred is a fact not open for further discussion. Gould even commented, "I don't want to sound like a shrill dogmatist shouting 'rally 'round the flag boys,' but biologists have reached a consensus...about the fact of evolution" (p. 69). [In a guest editorial in the August 23, 1999 issue of *Time* magazine, Dr. Gould boasted that "evolution is as well documented as any phenomenon in science, as strongly as the earth's revolution around the sun rather than vice versa. In this sense, we can call evolution a 'fact'" (1999, 154[8]:59).] Dr. Gould is upset because there are those who refuse to acknowledge evolution as a fact.

According to him, "Evolution is a fact, like apples falling out of trees" (as quoted in Adler, 1980, p. 95). Gould's colleagues could not agree more. In the March 1987 issue of *Natural History*, Douglas J. Futuyma wrote in his review of Richard Dawkins' book, *The Blind Watchmaker:*

> In the last ten years or so, evolution has been under severe attack, especially in the United States. It is important here to recognize the distinction between the proposition that evolution has occurred and the theory that describes the causes of evolutionary change. That evolution has occurred—that diverse organisms have descended from common ancestors by a history of modification and divergence—is accepted as fact by virtually all biologists. "Fact" here means a proposition, like the proposition that the earth revolves about the sun, supported by so much evidence that to disbelieve it would require disbelieving a large, successful edifice of scientific achievement. The historical reality of evolution is doubted chiefly by creationists, mostly on doctrinaire religious grounds (96[3]:34).

Of course, such renowned scientists as Gould and Futuyma are not even willing to concern themselves with creationists. In fact, Dr. Gould commented:

> I don't speak of the militant fundamentalists who label themselves with the oxymoron "scientific creationists," and try to sneak their Genesis literalism into high school classrooms under the guise of scientific dissent. I'm used to their rhetoric, their dishonest mis- and half-quotations, their constant repetition of "useful" arguments that even they must recognize as nonsense.... Our struggle with these ideologues is political, not intellectual. I speak instead of our allies among people committed to reason and honorable argument (1987, 8[1]: 64).

This point should not be overlooked. Gould suggests that his concern is about people who are "committed to reason and honorable argument." That, by his definition, would eliminate any and all "creationists."

The purpose of the writings of Gould and Futuyma (and other evolutionists) is to convince people to stop speaking of the "theory" of evolution, and to speak instead of the "fact" of evolution. But, in order to accomplish this, they have to redefine the word "fact" as it is used in science. I might note here that they are by no means the first to attempt such a redefinition. Simpson and Beck tried the exact same thing in their biology text, *Life: An Introduction to Biology*, and ended their "redefining" section by claiming that theories ultimately

> ...may be just as certain—merit just as much confidence—as what are popularly called "facts." Belief that the sun will rise tomorrow is the confident application of a generalization. The theory that life has evolved is founded on much more evidence than supports the generalization that the sun rises every day. In the vernacular, we are justified in calling both "facts" (1965, p. 16).

A fact usually is defined as an actual occurrence or something that has actual existence. With that standard-usage definition in mind, consider the following.

Charles Darwin, in his *Origin of Species*, stated: "Long before the reader has arrived at this part of my work, a crowd of difficulties will have occurred to him. Some of them are so serious that to this day I can hardly reflect on them without being in some degree staggered" (1859, p. 158). Theodosius Dobzhansky, the late, eminent geneticist of the Rockefeller University, stated in his book, *The Biological Basis of Human Freedom*: "Evolution as a historical fact was proved beyond reasonable doubt not later than in the closing decades of the nineteenth century." Yet two pages later he stated: "There is no doubt that both the historical and the causal aspects of the evolutionary process are **far from completely known**. ...The causes which have brought about the development of the human species **can be only dimly discerned**" (1956, pp. 6,8,9, emp. added). Notice Dobzhansky's admission that both the historical (what Gould refers to as the "fact" of evolution) and the causal (what Gould refers to as the "theory" of evolution) are "far from completely known."

In other words, on the one hand evolution is declared to be a fact, yet on the other hand it is acknowledged that the process is "far from completely known," with its causes "only dimly discerned," and the difficulties "staggering." Evolutionist W. LeGros Clark wrote: "What was the ultimate origin of man? ...Unfortunately, any answers which can at present be given to these questions are based on indirect evidence and thus **are largely conjectural**" (1955, p. 174, emp. added). Kerkut, as an evolutionist, stated:

> ...I believe that the theory of Evolution as presented by orthodox evolutionists is in many ways a satisfying explanation of some of the evidence. At the same time I think that the attempt to explain all living forms in terms of evolution from a unique source...is premature and **not satisfactorily supported by present-day evidence**. ...the supporting evidence remains to be discovered.... We can, if we like, believe that such an evolutionary system has taken place, but I for one do not think that "it has been proven beyond all reasonable doubt." ...It is very depressing to find that many subjects are being encased in scientific dogmatism (1960, pp. vii, viii, emp. added).

After listing and discussing the seven **non-provable assumptions** upon which evolution is based, Dr. Kerkut then observed: "The first point that I should like to make is that these seven assumptions by their nature **are not capable of experimental verification**" (p. 7, emp. added).

This stinging rebuke of the alleged factuality of evolution is not an isolated instance. W.R. Thompson, while Director of the Commonwealth Institute of Biological Control in Canada, penned the "Introduction" to the 1956 edition of Darwin's *Origin of Species, in which he wrote:*

> Darwin did not show in the *Origin* that species had originated by natural selection; he merely showed, on the basis of certain facts and assumptions, how this **might** have happened, and as he had convinced himself he was able to convince others.... On the other hand, it does appear to me that Darwin in the *Origin* was not able to produce palaeontolog-

ical evidence sufficient to prove his views but that **the evidence he did produce was adverse to them**; and I may note that the position is not notably different today. The modern Darwinian palaeontologists are obliged, just like their predecessors and like Darwin, to **water down the facts** with subsidiary hypotheses which, however plausible, are in the nature of things unverifiable (pp. xii, xix, emp. added).

Lest someone think that Dr. Thompson was speaking from ignorance, I would like to introduce this quotation from Charles Darwin when he wrote in a November 23, 1859 letter to his brother Erasmus, one day before the *Origin of Species* was published: "Concerning species, in fact the *a priori* reasoning is so entirely satisfactory to me that if the facts won't fit, why so much the worse for the facts, in my feeling" (see Francis Darwin, 1888, 2:29).

Evolutionists dogmatically assert that evolution is a fact, yet admit that it: (a) is based upon **non-provable assumptions** that are "not capable of experimental verification"; (b) bases its conclusions upon answers that are "largely conjectural"; (c) is faced with evidence "adverse" to the available facts; (d) must continually be found guilty of "watering down the facts"; and (e) has both historical and causal aspects that "are far from completely known." Little wonder Dr. Kerkut stated concerning the theory of evolution: "The evidence that supports it is not sufficiently strong to allow us to consider it anything more than a working hypothesis" (1960, p. 157). Robert Millikan, Nobel laureate in physics, opined: "The pathetic thing is that we have scientists who are trying to prove evolution, which no scientist can ever prove" (1925). What a far cry from the assessments of Gould and his colleagues in the modern evolutionary camp.

Someone might object, however, that the quotations I have employed (from evolutionists such as Dobzhansky, Clark, and others) to document the nonverifiability of evolution were written during the 1950s and 1960s. Much scientific research on evolution has occurred in the decades that followed, and thus it might be considered unfair to rely on such "dated" critiques of a concept like evolution that changes so rapidly and that has been studied so intently.

My response to such an objection would be to point out that I used the quotations from the 1950s and 1960s intentionally, in order to document that the situation over the past four decades has not improved. By the 1970s, for example, little had changed. At the height of his professional career, Pierre-Paul Grassé was considered by many to be France's greatest living zoologist. In fact, Dobzahansky wrote of him: "Now one can disagree with Grassé, but not ignore him. He is the most distinguished of French zoologists, the editor of the 28 volumes of *Traité de Zoologie*, author of numerous original investigations, and ex-president of the Academie des Sciences. His knowledge of the living world is encyclopedic" (1975, 29:376). In 1977, Grassé wrote in *The Evolution of Living Organisms:*

> Today our duty is to destroy the myth of evolution, considered as a simple, understood, and explained phenomenon which keeps rapidly unfolding before us. Biologists must be encouraged to think about the weaknesses and extrapolations that theoreticians put forward or lay down as established truths. The deceit is sometimes unconscious, but not always, since some people, owing to their sectarianism, purposely overlook reality and refuse to acknowledge the inadequacies and falsity of their beliefs.

> Their success among certain biologists, philosophers, and sociologists notwithstanding, **the explanatory doctrines of biological evolution do not stand up to an objective, in-depth criticism**. They prove to be either in conflict with reality or else incapable of solving the major problems involved (pp. 8,202, emp. added).

Three years later, in 1980, British physicist H.S. Lipson produced a thought-provoking piece in the May issue of *Physics Bulletin*, a refereed science journal. In his article, "A Physicist Looks at Evolution," Dr. Lipson commented first on his interest in life's origin and, second, on his non-association with creationists. He then noted: "In fact, evolution became in a sense a scientific religion; almost all scientists have accepted it and many are prepared to 'bend' their observations to fit with it." Dr. Lipson went on to ask how well evolution has withstood the years of scientific testing, and suggested that "to my mind, the theory does not stand up at all."

After reviewing many of the problems (especially from thermodynamics) involved in producing something living from something nonliving, he asked: "If living matter is not, then, caused by the interplay of atoms, natural forces, and radiation, how has it come into being?" After dismissing any sort of "directed evolution," Lipson concluded: "I think, however, that we must go further than this and admit that the only acceptable explanation is **creation**." Like other evolutionists who have voiced similar views, Dr. Lipson hardly is ecstatic about his conclusion—a fact he made clear when he wrote: "I know that this is anathema to physicists, as indeed it is to me, but we must not reject a theory that we do not like if the experimental evidence supports it" (31:138, emp. in orig.).

Just a little over a year later, on November 5, 1981, the late Colin Patterson (who at the time was the senior paleontologist of the British Museum of Natural History in London, the editor of the professional journal published by the museum, and one of the world's foremost fossil experts) delivered a public address to his evolutionist colleagues at the American Museum of Natural History in New York City. In his speech, Dr. Patterson astonished those colleagues when he stated that he had been "kicking around" non-evolutionary, or "anti-evolutionary," ideas for about eighteen months. As he went on to describe it:

> One morning I woke up and something had happened in the night, and it struck me that I had been working on this stuff for twenty years and there was not one thing I knew about it. That's quite a shock to learn that one can be misled so long. Either there was something wrong with me, or there was something wrong with evolution theory (1981).

Dr. Patterson said he knew there was nothing wrong with him, so he started asking various individuals and groups a simple question: "Can you tell me anything you know about evolution, any one thing that is true? I tried that question on the geology staff at the Field Museum of Natural History, and the only answer I got was silence." He tried it on the Evolutionary Morphology Seminar at the University of Chicago, a very prestigious body of evolutionists, and all he got there "was silence for a long time and eventually one person said, 'I do know one thing—it ought not to be taught in high school.' " He then remarked, "It does seem that the level of knowledge about evolution is remarkably shallow. We know it ought not to be taught in high school, and that's all we know about it."

Dr. Patterson went on to say: "Then I woke up and realized that all my life I had been duped into taking evolution as revealed truth in some way." But more important, he termed evolution an "anti-theory" that produced "anti-knowledge." He also suggested that "the explanatory value of the hypothesis is nil," and that evolution theory is "a void that has the function of knowledge but conveys none." To use Patterson's wording, "I feel that the effects of hypotheses of common ancestry in systematics has not been merely boring, not just a lack of knowledge, I think it has been positively anti-knowledge" (1981; cf. Bethell, 1985, 270:49-52,56-58,60-61).

Dr. Patterson made it clear, as I wish to do here, that he had no fondness for the creationist position. Yet he did refer to his stance as "anti-evolutionary," which was quite a change for a man who had authored several books (one of which was titled simply, *Evolution*) in the field that he later acknowledged was capable of producing only "anti-knowledge."

Colin Patterson was not the only one expressing such views, however. Over the past two decades, distinguished British astronomer Sir Fred Hoyle has stressed the serious problems—once again, especially from the fields of thermodynamics—with various theories about the naturalistic origin of life on the Earth. The same year that Dr. Patterson traveled to America to speak, Dr. Hoyle wrote:

> I don't know how long it is going to be before astronomers generally recognize that the combinatorial arrangement of not even one among the many thousands of biopolymers on which life depends could have been arrived at by natural processes here on the Earth. Astronomers will have a little difficulty in understanding this because they will be assured by bi-

ologists that it is not so, the biologists having been assured in their turn by others that it is not so. The "others" are a group of persons who believe, quite openly, in mathematical miracles. They advocate the belief that tucked away in nature, outside of normal physics, there is a law which performs miracles (provided the miracles are in the aid of biology). This curious situation sits oddly on a profession that for long has been dedicated to coming up with logical explanations of biblical miracles.... It is quite otherwise, however, with the modern miracle workers, who are always to be found living in the twilight fringes of thermodynamics (1981a, 92:526, parenthetical comment in orig.).

In fact, Dr. Hoyle has described the evolutionary concept that disorder gives rise to order in a rather picturesque manner.

The chance that higher forms have emerged in this way is comparable with the chance that a tornado sweeping through a junk-yard might assemble a Boeing 747 from the materials therein (1981b, 294:105).

And, in order to make his position perfectly clear, he provided his readers with the following analogy:

At all events, anyone with even a nodding acquaintance with the Rubik cube will concede the near-impossibility of a solution being obtained by a blind person moving the cubic faces at random. Now imagine 10^{50} blind persons each with a scrambled Rubik cube, and try to conceive of the chance of them all **simultaneously** arriving at the solved form. You then have the chance of arriving by random shuffling at just one of the many biopolymers on which life depends. The notion that not only biopolymers but the operating programme of a living cell could be arrived at by chance in a primordial organic soup here on the Earth is evidently nonsense of a high order (1981a, 92:527, emp. in orig.).

Hoyle and Chandra Wickramasinghe (who is a professor of astronomy and applied mathematics at the University College, Cardiff, Wales) went even further. Using probability figures applied to cosmic time (not just geologic time here on the Earth), their conclusion was:

Once we see, however, that the probability of life originating at random is so utterly minuscule as to make the random concept absurd, it becomes sensible to think that the favourable properties of physics on which life depends, are in every respect deliberate.... It is therefore almost inevitable that our own measure of intelligence must reflect in a valid way the higher intelligences...even to the extreme idealized limit of **God** (1981, pp. 141,144, emp. in orig.).

Hoyle and Wickramasinghe suggested, however, that this "higher intelligence" did not necessarily have to be, as far as they were concerned, what most people would call "God," but simply a being with an intelligence "to the limit of God." They, personally, opted for "directed panspermia," a view which suggests that life was "planted" on the Earth via genetic material that originated from a "higher intelligence" somewhere in the Universe. But just one year later, in 1982, Dr. Hoyle wrote:

A common sense interpretation of the facts suggests that **a superintellect** has monkeyed with physics, as well as with chemistry and biology, and that there are no blind forces worth speaking about in nature. The numbers one calculates from the facts seem to me so overwhelming as to put this conclusion almost beyond question (20:16, emp. added).

Three years after that, in 1985, molecular biologist Michael Denton authored *Evolution: A Theory in Crisis*, in which he stated:

In this book, I have adopted the radical approach. By presenting a systematic critique of the current Darwinian model, ranging from paleontology to molecular biology, I have tried to show why I believe that the problems are too severe and too intractable to offer any hope of resolution in terms of the orthodox Darwinian framework, and that consequently the conservative view is no longer tenable.

The intuitive feeling that pure chance could never have achieved the degree of complexity and ingenuity so ubiquitous in nature has been a continuing source of scepticism ever since the publication of the *Origin*; and throughout the past century there has always existed a significant minority of first-rate biologists who have never been able to bring themselves to accept the validity of Darwinian claims. In fact, the number of biologists who have expressed some degree of disillusionment is practically endless.

> The anti-evolutionary thesis argued in this book, the idea that
> life might be fundamentally a discontinuous phenomenon,
> runs counter to the whole thrust of modern biological thought.
> ...Put simply, no one has ever observed the interconnecting
> continuum of functional forms linking all known past and pres-
> ent species of life. The concept of the continuity of nature has
> existed in the mind of man, **never** in the facts of nature (pp.
> 16,327,353, emp. in orig.).

In 1987, two years after Denton's book was published, Swedish biologist Søren Løvtrup wrote in an even stronger vein:

> After this step-wise elimination, only one possibility remains:
> **the Darwinian theory of natural selection**, whether or
> not coupled with Mendelism, **is false**. I have already shown
> that the arguments advanced by the early champions were
> not very compelling, and that there are now considerable
> numbers of empirical facts which do not fit with the theory.
> Hence, **to all intents and purposes the theory has been
> falsified**, so why has it not been abandoned? I think the an-
> swer is that current evolutionists follow Darwin's example
> —they refuse to accept falsifying evidence (p. 352, emp. added).

In his 1988 book, *The Cosmic Blueprint: New Discoveries in
Nature's Creative Ability to Order the Universe*, Australian physicist Paul Davies wrote: "There is for me powerful evidence that there
is something going on behind it all. It seems as though somebody
has fine-tuned nature's numbers to make the Universe. **The impression of design is overwhelming**" (p. 203, emp. added). That
same year, George Greenstein wrote:

> As we survey all the evidence, the thought insistently arises
> that some supernatural agency—or, rather, Agency—must be
> involved. Is it possible that suddenly, without intending to, we
> have stumbled upon scientific proof of the existence of a Su-
> preme Being? Was it God who stepped in and so providen-
> tially crafted the cosmos for our benefit? (1988, p. 27).

In 1992, Arno Penzias (who fourteen years earlier had shared the
1978 Nobel Prize in physics with Robert W. Wilson for their discovery of the so-called "background radiation" left over from the Big
Bang) declared:

Astronomy leads us to a unique event, a universe which was created out of nothing, one with the very delicate balance needed to provide exactly the conditions required to permit life, and one which has an underlying (one might say "supernatural") plan [p. 83, parenthetical comment in orig.].

In his 1994 book, *The Physics of Immortality*, Frank Tipler (who coauthored with John D. Barrow the massive 1986 volume, *The Anthropic Cosmological Principle*) wrote:

When I began my career as a cosmologist some twenty years ago, I was a convinced atheist. I never in my wildest dreams imagined that one day I would be writing a book purporting to show that the central claims of Judeo-Christian theology are in fact true, that these claims are straightforward deductions of the laws of physics as we now understand them. I have been forced into these conclusions by the inexorable logic of my own special branch of physics (Preface).

One year later, NASA astronomer John O'Keefe admitted:

We are, by astronomical standards, a pampered, cosseted, cherished group of creatures.... If the Universe had not been made with the most exacting precision we could never have come into existence. It is my view that these circumstances indicate the universe was created for man to live in (1995, p. 200).

Then, in 1998, evolutionist Michael Denton shocked everyone with his new book, *Nature's Destiny*, when he admitted:

Because this book presents a teleological interpretation of the cosmos which has obvious theological implications, it is important to emphasize at the outset that the argument presented here is entirely consistent with the basic naturalistic assumption of modern science—that the cosmos is a **seamless unity which can be comprehended ultimately in its entirety by human reason and in which all phenomena, including life and evolution and the origin of man, are ultimately explicable in terms of natural processes**....

Although this is obviously a book with many theological implications, my initial intention was not specifically to develop an argument for design; however, as I researched more deeply into the topic and as the manuscript went through successive drafts, it became increasingly clear that the laws of nature were fine-tuned on earth to a remarkable degree and that the emerging picture provided powerful and self-evident support for the traditional anthropocentric teleological view of the cosmos. Thus, by the time the final draft was finished, the book had become in effect an essay in natural theology in the spirit and tradition of William Paley's *Natural Theology* (pp. xvii-xviii,xi-xii, emp. in orig.).

Such quotations could be multiplied almost endlessly. Even a cursory examination documents that there is much more that is "unknown" than "known" in the evolutionary scenario.

First, evolution cannot be proven true unless nonliving can give rise to living—that is to say, spontaneous generation must have occurred. Evolution, in its entirety, is based on this principle. But what evidence is there that the concept of spontaneous generation is, in fact, correct? What evidence is there that life arose from nonlife? In their 1965 biology textbook, *Life: An Introduction to Biology*, evolutionists Simpson and Beck begrudgingly admitted that the spontaneous generation of life "does not occur in any known case" (p. 261). Twelve years later, in his book, *Until the Sun Dies*, Robert Jastrow, the founder and former director of the Goddard Institute for Space Studies at NASA, summarized the situation as follows:

> According to this story, every tree, every blade of grass, and every creature in the sea and on the land evolved out of one parent strand of molecular matter drifting lazily in a warm pool. What concrete evidence supports that remarkable theory of the origin of life? There is none (1977, p. 60).

Four years after that, in 1981, renowned British astrophysicist Sir Fred Hoyle complained in *Nature* magazine:

> The likelihood of the spontaneous formation of life from inanimate matter is one to a number with 40,000 noughts after it.... It is big enough to bury Darwin and the whole theory of evolution. There was no primeval soup, neither on this planet nor on any other, and **if the beginnings of life were not random, they must therefore have been the product of purposeful intelligence** (1981b, 294:148, emp. added).

A decade later, in 1991, Hoyle and Wickramasinghe published in *New Scientist* an article with a catchy title ("Where Microbes Boldly Went") but a dismal message—dismal, that is, for evolutionists who are forced by their theory to believe in the concept of biochemical evolution, which allegedly produced the first life on Earth by chance processes.

> Precious little in the way of biochemical evolution could have happened on the Earth. It is easy to show that the two thousand or so enzymes that span the whole of life could not have evolved on the Earth. If one counts the number of trial assemblies of amino acids that are needed to give rise to the enzymes, the probability of their discovery by random shufflings turns out to be less than 1 in $10^{40,000}$ (91:415).

Those "40,000 noughts" with which Dr. Hoyle was struggling in 1981 still were a thorn in his side ten years later. And the situation has not improved in the years since. One of the "scientific heavyweights" in origin-of-life studies from an evolutionary viewpoint is Leslie Orgel, who has spent most of his professional career attempting to uncover the secrets of how life began on this planet. In the October 1994 issue of *Scientific American*, Dr. Orgel authored an article titled "The Origin of Life on Earth" in which he admitted:

> It is extremely improbable that proteins and nucleic acids, both of which are structurally complex, arose spontaneously in the same place at the same time. Yet it also seems impossible to have one without the other. **And so, at first glance, one might have to conclude that life could never, in fact, have originated by chemical means**....

> We proposed that RNA might well have come first and established what is now called the RNA world.... This scenario could have occurred, we noted, **if prebiotic RNA had two properties not evident today**: a capacity to replicate without the help of proteins and an ability to catalyze every step of protein synthesis....

> The precise events giving rise to the RNA world remain unclear. As we have seen, investigators have proposed many hypotheses, but evidence in favor of each of them is fragmen-

tary at best. **The full details of how the RNA world, and
life, emerged may not be revealed in the near future**
(271:78,83, emp. added).

It is not enough, of course, "just" to establish the possibility of
spontaneous generation/biochemical evolution. Evolutionists also
must explain the origin of the dazzlingly complex DNA/RNA genetic
code that is the basis of every living organism. But, just as their fan-
ciful-but-failed scenarios for the explanation of the naturalistic origin of life have left them lacking any substantive answers, so their theories regarding the origin of the genetic code have failed just as
miserably. One evolutionist, John Maddox, confessed as much in
a curiously titled but revealing article, "The Genesis Code by Numbers," in *Nature*.

> It was already clear that the genetic code is not merely an ab-
> straction but the embodiment of life's mechanisms; the con-
> secutive triplets of nucleotides in DNA (called codons) are in-
> herited but they also guide the construction of proteins.
>
> **So it is disappointing that the origin of the genetic code
> is still as obscure as the origin of life itself** (1994, 367:
> 111, emp. added).

Second, not only is the inability of **how** to get life started a serious stumbling block for evolutionists, but now the **where** of this supposed happening has been called into question as well. Hoyle and
Wickramasinghe have argued that life fell to Earth from space after having evolved from the warm, wet nucleus of a comet (see Gribbin, 1981, 89[3]:14; Hoyle and Wickramasinghe, 1981). Sir Francis
Crick, codiscoverer of the DNA molecule, has suggested that life actually was sent here from other planets (1981). Meanwhile, back on
Earth, Sidney Fox and colleagues have proposed that life began on
the side of a primitive volcano on our primeval planet when a number of dry amino acids "somehow" formed there at exactly the right
temperature, for exactly the right length of time, to form exactly the
right molecules necessary for living systems (1977). Evolutionists are
fond of saying (remember Gould?) that there is no controversy over
the **fact** of evolution; it is only the "how" about which they disagree. Not true. They cannot even agree on the "where."

Of course, some evolutionists will attempt to argue that such matters are not properly discussed as a part of the evolutionary process, and that evolution *per se* only applies to biological change. Dobzhansky, however, settled that issue when he stated:

> Evolution comprises all the stages of development of the universe: the cosmic, biological, and human or cultural developments. Attempts to restrict the concept of evolution to biology are gratuitous. Life is a product of the evolution of inorganic matter, and man is a product of the evolution of life (1967, 55:409).

Third, in his January 1987 *Discover* article, Dr. Gould, discussed some of the "data" that establish evolution as a "fact" (his statement was that "facts are the world's data"). An examination of these data **disproves** the very thing that Gould was attempting to prove —the "factuality" of evolution. He commented:

> We have direct evidence of small-scale changes in controlled laboratory experiments of the past hundred years (on bacteria, on almost every measurable property of the fruit fly *Drosophila*), or observed in nature (color changes in moth wings, development of metal tolerance in plants growing near industrial waste heaps) or produced during a few thousand years of human breeding and agriculture (8[1]:65, parenthetical items in orig.).

Dr. Gould thus wants us to believe that such changes **prove** evolution to be a fact. Yet notice what the professor conspicuously omitted. He failed to tell the reader what he stated publicly during a speech at Hobart College, February 14, 1980, when he said:

> A mutation doesn't produce major new raw material. You don't make new species by mutating the species.... That's a common idea people have; that evolution is due to random mutations. A mutation is **not** the cause of evolutionary change (as quoted in Sunderland, 1984, p. 106, emp. in orig.).

On the one hand, Gould wants us to believe that bacteria and fruit flies have experienced "small-scale changes" via genetic mutations and thus serve as excellent examples of the "fact" of evolution. But on the other hand, he tells us that mutations ("small-scale changes") don't cause evolution. Which is it?

On March 4, 1982, Colin Patterson participated in a radio interview for the British Broadcasting Corporation. In that interview, he admitted: "No one has ever produced a species by mechanisms of natural selection. No one has ever gotten near it and most of the current argument in neo-Darwinism is about this question: how a species originates" (1982). If evolution does not occur by mutation, and it does not occur by natural selection, how, then, could evolution be considered a "fact"? The only two known mechanisms have been admitted—even by evolutionists—to be completely impotent in this regard. Keith Thompson, professor of biology and dean of the graduate school at Yale University, admitted as much when he wrote in the *American Scientist*:

> Twenty years ago Mayr, in his *Animal Species and Evolution* seemed to have shown that if evolution is a jigsaw puzzle, then at least all the edge pieces were in place. But today we are less confident and the whole subject is in the most exciting ferment. Evolution is both troubled from without by the nagging insistence of antiscientists [his term for creationists —BT] and nagged from within by the troubling complexities of genetic and developmental mechanisms and new questions about the central mystery—speciation itself (1982, p. 529).

Further, notice that in his article Gould made the same mistake that Darwin made 128 years earlier—extrapolating far beyond the available evidence. Darwin looked at finches' beaks, and from small changes he extrapolated to state that evolution from one group to another had occurred. Gould looked at changes in fruit flies or bacteria and did exactly the same thing, all the while failing to tell the reader that the bacteria never changed into anything else, and the fruit flies always remained fruit flies. If the "data" are the "facts," and if the "data" actually **disprove** evolution, how is it then that evolution can be called, in any sense of the word, a "fact"?

The standard-usage dictionary definition of a fact is something that is "an actual occurrence," something that has "actual existence." Can any process be called "an actual occurrence" when the knowledge of how, when, where, what, and why is missing? Were some-one to suggest that a certain skyscraper had merely "happened," but that the how, when, where, what, and why were complete un-knowns, would you be likely to call it a fact, or an "unproven asser-tion"? To ask is to answer. Gould, Futuyma, Simpson, and other evolutionists may ask us to believe that their unproven hypothesis somehow has garnered to itself the status of a "fact," but if they do, they will have to come up with something based on evidence to sub-stantiate their wishful thinking. Merely trying to alter, for their own purposes, the definition of fact will not suffice. Pardon us for our in-credulity, but when the best they can offer is a completely insuffi-cient explanation for life's origin in the first place, an equally insuffi-cient mechanism for the evolution of that life once it "somehow" got started via naturalistic processes, and a fossil record full of "miss-ing links" to document its supposed course through time, we will con-tinue to relegate their "fact" to the status of a theory (or better yet, a hypothesis). Adulterating the definition of the word fact is a poor attempt by Gould (and others) to lend credence to a theory that lacks any factual merit whatsoever.

Theodore N. Tahmisian, a nuclear physicist with the Atomic Energy Commission, once stated:

> Scientists who go about teaching that evolution is a fact of life are great con men, and the story they are telling may be the greatest hoax ever. In explaining evolution we do not have one iota of fact.... It is a tangled mishmash of guessing games and figure jaggling (as quoted in Jackson, 1974, p. 37).

James E. Lloyd, editor of the *Florida Entomologist*, condemned evolution with faint praise (while simultaneously attempting to prop up its alleged factuality) when he wrote:

> Evolution is, for all practical purposes, fact. Natural selection, though it may be tautological and philosophically a poor the-ory in the various ways it is usually stated (e.g., "survival of the fittest"), and perhaps not even capable of being falsified, is nevertheless profound and axiomatic. It provides the most useful insight for problem solving that biological science has, and is the heart and soul of behavioral ecology (1982, 65:1).

Natural selection, says Lloyd, is a tautology (i.e., it reasons in circles). Yet its major flaws notwithstanding, evolution is to be accepted as a "fact" all the same. If this is the best evolutionists have to offer as support for their claim of evolution's factuality, it should be obvious to even the most casual observer that such a claim is completely vacuous. Little wonder, then, that evolutionist Michael Denton wrote concerning Darwin:

> His general theory that all life on earth had originated and evolved by a gradual successive accumulation of fortuitous mutations, is still, as it was in Darwin's time, a highly speculative hypothesis entirely without direct factual support and very far from that self-evident axiom some of its more aggressive advocates would have us believe (1985, p. 77).

Chapter 3

Origins and Creation

The alternate and opposing theory to atheistic evolution is creation (also known as special creation, the theory of creation, or the creation model). Whereas evolution is based solely on the concept of **naturalistic** processes, creation is based on the concept of **supernatural** processes. That there is indeed a dichotomy here (and that these two models are, in fact, diametrically opposed to each other) is granted by many on both sides of the issue. Some years ago, Nobel laureate George Wald of Harvard University authored a lengthy, award-winning article for *Scientific American* on the origin of life. In his article, Dr. Wald commented that, as an evolutionist, he felt "the reasonable view was to believe in spontaneous generation; the only alternative, to believe in a single, primary act of supernatural creation. **There is no third position**" (1979, p. 287, emp. added).

While creationists strongly disagree with Dr. Wald's suggestion regarding the feasibility of spontaneous generation, they just as strongly agree with his assessment that "there is no third alternative." We are here either as the result of natural forces (evolution), or supernatural forces (creation). Morris and Parker observed:

The fact is, however, there are **only two** possible models of origins, evolution or creation.... Either the space/mass/time universe is eternal, or it is not. If it is, then evolution is the true explanation of its various components. If it is not, then it must have been created by a Creator. These are the only two possibilities—simply stated, either it happened by accident (chance)...**or it didn't** (design).... There are only these two possibilities. There may be many evolution submodels...and various creation submodels..., but there can be only two basic models—evolution or creation (1987, p. 190, emp. and parenthetical items in orig.).

One or the other of these two models must be correct. That is to say, all things either can, or cannot, be explained in terms of ongoing, natural processes within a self-contained Universe. If they can, then evolution is true. If they cannot, then they must be explained, at least in part, by extranatural processes that can account for a Universe which itself was created. That is where creation becomes an option.

CREATION DEFINED

The creation model that I am discussing in this book derives its legitimacy from the Bible as the inspired Word of God. As a God-breathed revelation (2 Timothy 3:16-17; 2 Peter 1:20-21; 1 Corinthians 2:12-13), the Bible speaks correctly and with authority on each matter with which it deals. The creation model maintains that the Universe is **not self-contained**. Rather, everything in the Universe, and in fact, the Universe itself, came into being through the design, purpose, and deliberate acts of a supernatural Creator Who, using processes that are not continuing as natural processes in the present, created the Universe, the Earth, and all life on the Earth, including all basic types of plants and animals, as well as humans. Creation maintains, in keeping with the account found in Genesis 1 (and referenced in other portions of the Bible), that God, as the Creator, is omnipotent, omniscient, and omnipresent, having created the Universe and all that is in it through divine fiat "by the word of His power" (Hebrews 1:3).

Irenaeus (A.D. 130-200), one of the early church writers, expressed it like this: "He Himself called into being the substance of His own creation, when previously it had no existence" (n.d., 2.X.iv). Generally, this is referred to as creation *ex nihilo*, indicating that God created the Universe and its inhabitants from substance(s) not previously in existence. Wilbert H. Rusch summarized the creation model (as it applies to life) by stating that:

> ...we could then hold that God made the plants and the animals according to His own plan. This would seem to have involved the creation of certain basic **kinds** of plants and animals, each with the ability to vary within a circle of the **kind** to a greater or lesser degree. However, it would imply that there are definite limits, beyond which plants and animals may not vary (1991, p. 15, emp. in orig.).

Quite obviously, the creation model differs drastically in a number of ways from the evolution model. The evolution model posits a Universe that is able to explain its own existence (viz., it is self-contained); the creation model posits a Universe that is not able to explain its own existence (viz., it is not self-contained). The evolution model posits no Creator; the creation model posits an omnipotent Creator. The evolution model posits a Universe that is the end product of purely naturalistic forces; the creation model posits a Universe that is the end product of the Creator's intelligent and purposeful design. The evolution model advocates the view that life originated by accident; the creation model advocates the view that life was specially created. Other important disparities between the two models could be listed, but these will become evident throughout the remainder of this book.

IS CREATION POPULAR?

A thousand times over the death knell of creation has been sounded, the funeral procession formed, the inscription cut on the tombstone, and the committal read. But somehow the corpse never stays put. Concerning the premature funeral of creation, Morris has penned these words:

The bells had tolled for any scientific belief in special creation. The Scopes trial (1925) had ended in a nominal victory for the fundamentalists, with the teacher Scopes convicted of teaching evolution in the high school, contrary to Tennessee law. In the press, however, Clarence Darrow and his evolutionist colleagues had resoundingly defeated William Jennings Bryan and the creationists. Evolution henceforth was almost universally accepted as an established fact of modern science, and special creation relegated to the limbo of curious beliefs of a former age....

But if creationism once was dead, it has recently risen from the dead! Today there are hundreds of outspoken scientists advocating a return to creation and abandonment of evolution, and their numbers are increasing. The evolutionary "establishment" is becoming alarmed, as multitudes of disillusioned youth are recoiling from the precipice of animalistic amoralism and survival-of-the-fittest philosophy to which two generations of evolutionary indoctrination had led them (1974b, pp. 9,13).

Since the publication in 1961 of *The Genesis Flood* by John C. Whitcomb and Henry M. Morris, belief in creation has increased in popularity in a drastic fashion. The formation in 1963 of the Creation Research Society did much to heighten that popularity, as did the establishment in 1970 of the California-based Institute for Creation Research. No longer are creationists considered to be on the "peripheral fringe" and thus not much of a threat to the evolutionary establishment. Creation is enjoying a groundswell of support in both the popular and the scientific communities. There are scores of creationist organizations—local, regional, national, and even international. And the interest is growing daily.

In the past, evolutionists often swayed audiences with bombast, accusations, and insinuations. But no longer. Basil Overton, author of the book, *Evolution Or Creation?*, offered this assessment:

Evolutionists are dogmatic in what they offer as an alternative to believing the Bible account of creation. They ask us not to believe the Bible and then dogmatically ask us to believe their theories instead. Dr. H.H. Newman says that the doctrine of evolution has no rival except what he calls "the outworn and completely refuted" story of creation. He says the story of creation is no longer believed by any except the ignorant, the dogmatic, and the prejudiced. (See: *Outlines of General Zoology*, by H.H. Newman, page 407.)

It is unfortunate that such men as Dr. H.H. Newman make such rash statements, because such a view as he has expressed classifies many of the world's greatest minds as being ignorant, dogmatic, and prejudiced. Dr. Newman so classifies such great scientists and thinkers as: Dr. A. Cressy Morrison; Dr. Heribert Nilsson of the Swedish Botanical Institute; Dr. John Klotz, an American Man of Science, and author of a classic entitled: *Genes, Genesis, and Evolution*; Dr. Henry Morris, and Dr. John Whitcomb, authors of the celebrated book, *The Genesis Flood*; Dr. Frank Lewis Marsh of Andrews University, and a host of others (1973, p. 15, parenthetical comment in orig.).

There has been an interesting turn of events over the past years.

In spite of the overwhelming monopoly that evolutionists have developed over educational and communications media, however, there does exist a tremendous reservoir of intelligent anti-evolutionary Christian conviction in this and other countries. And if well-written scholarly literature of this nature could somehow be channeled to the great body of educated "men of good will," who are inclined to believe in evolution simply because of a brainwashing to which they have been subjected ever since entering the public schools but whose minds are not closed to new considerations, then there is no doubt that a much greater body of anti-evolutionary sentiment could be quickly developed (Morris, 1963, p. 28).

Actually, the very thing that Dr. Morris predicted in 1963 has happened. There is, in fact, a "body of anti-evolutionary sentiment" that has developed, and correspondingly a body of "pro-creation sentiment." In 1975, James Coppedge made the following statement in his book, *Evolution: Possible or Impossible?*:

The growing evidence against evolution will eventually force American evolutionists to face the fact that the position is untenable. Some will then openmindedly explore the idea of creation, while others will doubtless persist in materialism at any cost (p. 180).

As it turns out, the predictions made by both Morris and Coppedge contained a kernel of truth. Certainly, it is not the case that evolutionists are abandoning their theory in droves. However, two observations may be made about recent happenings. First, it is from among the evolutionists themselves that have come some of the most stinging rebukes of their theory. Second, among the general populace there is a marked increase in support for creation. As evidence—in addition to the quotations from evolutionists like Grassé, Denton, and Løvtrup introduced in the previous chapter—I offer the following.

In 1971, Harvard-trained lawyer, Norman Macbeth, wrote a biting rebuttal of evolution titled *Darwin Retried*. Somewhat later, in a published interview about the book and its contents, he observed that evolutionists still were "not revealing all the dirt under the rug in their approach to the public. There is a feeling that they ought to keep back the worst so that their public reputation would not suffer and the Creationists wouldn't get any ammunition" (1982, 2:22). It is too late, however, because the evolutionists' public reputation **has** suffered, and the creationists **have** garnered to themselves additional ammunition, as is evident from the following.

In a center-column, front-page article in the June 15, 1979 issue of the *Wall Street Journal*, there appeared an article by one of the *Journal's* staff writers commenting on how creationists, when engaging in debates with evolutionists, "tend to win" the debates, and that creationism was "making progress." In 1979, Gallup pollsters conducted a random survey, inquiring about belief in creation versus evolution. The poll had been commissioned by *Christianity Today* magazine, and was reported in its December 21, 1979 issue. This poll found that 51% of Americans believe in the special creation of a literal Adam and Eve as the starting place of human life. In the March 1980 issue of the *American School Board Journal* (p. 52), it was reported that 67% of its readers (most of whom were school board members and school administrators) favored the teaching of the scientific evidence for creation in public schools. *Glamour* magazine conducted a poll of its own and reported the results in its August 1982 issue (p. 28). The magazine found that 74% of its readers favored teaching the scientific evidence for creation in public schools. One of the most authoritative polls was conducted in October 1981 by the Associated Press/NBC News polling organization. The results were as follows:

> "Only evolution should be taught" 8%
> "Only creation should be taught" 10%
> "Both creation and evolution should be taught" . . . 76%
> "Not sure which should be taught" 6%

Thus, nationwide no less than 86% of the people in the United States believe that creation should be taught in public schools. In August 1982, another Gallup poll was conducted, and found that 44% of those interviewed believed not only in creation, but in a recent creation of less than 10,000 years ago. Only 9% of the people polled believed in atheistic evolution.

On November 28, 1991 results were released from yet another Gallup poll regarding the biblical account of origins. The results may be summarized as follows. On origins: 47% believed God created man within the last 10,000 years (up 3% from the 1982 poll mentioned above); 40% believed man evolved over millions of years, but that God guided the process; 9% believed man evolved over millions of years without God; 4% were "other/don't know." On the Bible: 32% believed the Bible to be the inspired Word of God, and that it should be taken literally; 49% believed the Bible to be the inspired Word of God, but that it should not always be taken literally; 16% believed the Bible to be entirely the product of men; 3% were "other/don't know" (see Major, 1991, 11:48; John Morris, 1992, p. d). Two years later, a Gallup poll carried out in 1993 produced almost the same results. Of those responding, 47% stated that they believed in a recent creation of man; 11% expressed their belief in a strictly naturalistic form of evolution (see Newport, 1993, p. A-22). Four years after that poll, a 1997 Gallup survey found that 44% of Americans (including 31% who were college graduates) subscribed to a fairly literal reading of the Genesis account of creation, while another 39% (53% of whom were college graduates) believed God played at least some part in creating the Universe. Only 10% (17% college graduates) embraced a purely naturalistic, evolutionary view (see Bishop, 1998, pp. 39-48; Sheler, 1999, pp. 48-49). The results of a Gallup poll released in August 1999 were practically identical: 47% stated that they believed in a recent creation of man; 9% expressed belief in strictly naturalistic evolution (see Moore, 1999).

In its March 11, 2000 issue, the *New York Times* ran a story titled "Survey Finds Support is Strong for Teaching 2 Origin Theories," which reported on a poll commissioned by the liberal civil rights group, People for the American Way, and conducted by the prestigious polling/public research firm, DYG, of Danbury, Connecticut. According to the report, 79% of the people polled felt that the scientific evidence for creation should be included in the curriculum of public schools (see Glanz, 2000, p. A-1).

The amazing thing about all of this, of course, is that these results are being achieved after more than a century of evolutionary indoctrination. As a result, anti-creationist hysteria is in full swing. Resolutions against creation are being passed, pro-evolution pamphlets are being distributed, "committees of correspondence" are being formed, debates with creationists are being avoided (so that the creationists no longer "tend to win"), and anti-creationist books are streaming from the presses at an unprecedented rate. For example, in 1977 the American Humanist Association fired a major salvo by publishing a *Manifesto* affirming evolution as "firmly established in the view of the modern scientific community" (see *The Humanist*, 1977, 37:4-5). Following that, Dorothy Nelkin, a professor of sociology at Cornell University, published the first of what became a series of anti-creationist books when she wrote *Science Textbook Controversies and the Politics of Equal Time* (1977).

Since then, a lengthy list of such books can be documented. As samples, I might list such volumes as: (1) *The Darwinian Revolution* by Michael Ruse (1979); (2) *Abusing Science: The Case Against*

Creationism by Philip Kitcher (1982); (3) *The Monkey Business* by Niles Eldredge (1982); (4) *Scientists Confront Creationism*, edited by Laurie Godfrey (1983); (5) *Science on Trial: The Case for Evolution* by Douglas J. Futuyma (1983); (6) *Science and Creationism*, edited by Ashley Montagu (1984); (7) *Creation and Evolution: Myth or Reality?* by Norman D. Newell (1985) (8) *The Blind Watchmaker* by Richard Dawkins (1986); (9) *Science and Creation* by Robert W. Hanson (1986); (10) *Cult Archaeology and Creationism* by Francis B. Harrold and Raymond A. Eve (1987); (11) *Anti-Evolution Bibliography* by Tom McIver (1988a); (12) *Evolution—The Great Debate* by Vernon Blackmore and Andrew Page (1989); (13) *Evolution and the Myth of Creationism* by Tim Berra (1990); (14) *The Creationist Movement in Modern America* by Francis B. Harrold and Raymond A. Eve (1991); (15) *The Creationists: The Evolution of Scientific Creationism* by Ronald L. Numbers (1992); (16) *The Myth-Maker's Magic—Behind the Illusion of "Creation Science"* by Delos B. McKown; (17) *Creationism's Upside-Down Pyramid: How Science Refutes Fundamentalism* by Lee Tiffin (1994); (18) *Science and Earth History: The Evolution/Creation Controversy* by Arthur N. Strahler (1999); and (19) T*he Triumph of Evolution and the Failure of Creationism* [the sequel to his 1982 volume, *The Monkey Business*] by Niles Eldredge (2000).

This list could be lengthened considerably, but I think the point is clear. Creation no longer is being taken lightly. A "call to arms" has been made by the evolutionary establishment, and is being answered by many in the evolutionary community. Creationism is enjoying renewed popularity. Were that not the case, evolutionists would not be so busily engaged in meeting what they perceive as a very real threat to the status quo that they have enjoyed for so long.

WHY DO PEOPLE BELIEVE IN CREATION?

Those who believe in creation do so for a number of reasons. First, they believe in creation because they have seen the evidence that proves God's existence. Creationists understand that where there is a painting, there must by necessity be a painter. Where there is a poem, there must by necessity be a poet. Where there is a law, there must by necessity be a lawgiver. Where there is design, there must by necessity be a designer. Because the Universe is intricately designed, creationists find it impossible to believe that it "just happened." To them, the only logical conclusion is that the Universe had a designer—the God of the Bible.

Second, it is true that Christians believe in creation because of faith. But this is not "blind faith," for that phrase is not descriptive of biblical faith (see Thompson, 1994, 14:25-27,29-31). The Christian's faith is based on evidence (Hebrews 11:1), not mere guesswork. Christianity is no "pie-in-the-sky-by-and-by" religion. While Christians readily admit that, at times, they walk by faith and not by sight (2 Corinthians 5:7), they also are quick to point out that God has not left Himself without witness of Himself in nature (Romans 1:18-20; Acts 14:17), which makes faith evidence-based and evidence-established. Since faith comes by hearing, and hearing by the Word of God (Romans 10:17), wherever there is no evidence from God, there will be no faith.

Third, those who believe in creation do so because they have examined both the empirical and the *prima facie* evidence that is available. And such evidence points to a Creator—not to a Universe that is self-created or self-explained. Upon critical examination, creationists have found the "proofs" of evolution not to be "proofs" at all. Nonliving matter does not give rise to life. The "missing links" are still missing. Evolution has no adequate mechanism. Such solely human traits as morals, values, and ethics remain unexplained by any evolutionary process. And so on. On the other hand, each of these issues is answered quite adequately by creation.

IS CREATION A "FACT" OF SCIENCE?

The concepts of creation and evolution both share one fundamental similarity—the idea that the Universe and life are the products of one or more **unique** events. Evolutionists speak of such things as the Big Bang and the origin of living from nonliving. Neither of these events, however, is occurring today. In a similar fashion, creationists speak of the Universe and life as the products of divine creative acts, and of a worldwide Flood that helped shape the present Earth. These events also are unique.

Science (in the sense that most people understand the word) normally deals with empirical events and processes—things that can be observed with the five senses. Furthermore, science usually concerns itself with those things that are universal, dependable, timeless, and repeatable. That is to say, a scientist in China can use the same methodology as a scientist in America and obtain the same results today, tomorrow, next year, or at any time in the future.

It should be obvious to all concerned that neither evolution nor creation falls into such a category. Certain of the basic concepts involved (the Big Bang, the creation of man, etc.) cannot be tested using these criteria. Yet there are certain things about both creation and evolution that **can** be tested. In order to distinguish the things within each model that can be tested from those that cannot, some authors have suggested that science itself be divided into two distinct categories. For example, in their 1984 book, *The Mystery of Life's Origin*, Charles Thaxton, Walter Bradley, and Roger Olsen recommended separating **operation science** from **origin science**. Others (e.g., Geisler and Anderson, 1987) have followed suit.

Operation science deals with regular, recurring events in nature that require natural causes (eclipses, volcanoes, reproduction, etc.), while origin science deals with singularities that may or may not require a natural cause (the Big Bang, creation, etc.). The term "origin science" may be new but, in fact, it works by the time-honored, standard principles of causality and uniformity. The **principle of causality** says that every material effect must have a prior, necessary, and adequate cause. The **principle of uniformity** (or analogy) says that similar effects have similar causes. In other words, the kinds of causes that we observe producing effects today can be counted on to have produced similar effects in the past. What we see as an adequate cause in the present, we assume to have been an adequate cause in the past; what we see as an inadequate cause in the present, we assume to have been an inadequate cause in the past.

None of us denies that creation occurred in the distant past as the results of events that now are unable to be studied experimentally in the laboratory. In this sense, creation is no more a "fact" of science than evolution. But the same limitations are inherent in evolutionary scenarios. Anyone familiar with the works of evolutionists like Robert Jastrow and Fred Hoyle is aware of the fact that these scientists, and others, have pointed out that the origin of the Universe, and of life itself, occurred in the distant past under conditions not necessarily experimentally reproducible and therefore not able to be studied in a strictly scientific manner. Paul Ehrlich and L.C. Birch, both evolutionists, also have addressed these issues.

> Our theory of evolution has become...one which cannot be refuted by any possible observations. Every conceivable observation can be fitted into it. It is thus "outside empirical science" but not necessarily false. No one can think of ways in which to test it. Ideas, either without basis or based on a few laboratory experiments carried out in extremely simplified systems have attained currency far beyond their validity. They have become part of an evolutionary dogma accepted by most of us as part of our training (1967, 214:349).

That would seem, to the unbiased observer, to put creation and evolution on equal footing. Evolutionists likely will disagree, as Trevor Major has observed:

> Still, evolutionists may argue that creationists have done themselves no service by making a separate science out of singularities. Defining a nonempirical science is one thing; proposing supernatural causes is quite another. For this reason, they will always view creationism as unscientific. But the idea that history consists of an unbroken stream of natural causes and effects is merely a **presumption** on their part. Perhaps they fear a new generation of doctoral students invoking God when they cannot explain something in their research projects. Yet this fear is unfounded. As stated earlier, most scientists of the past had no problem with divine intervention. In-

deed, one of the driving forces of early Western science was
the idea that the Universe, as God's creation, was open to rational investigation. In doing good operation science, these
scientists would seek natural causes for regularly occurring
events. Many of them recognized, however, that unique events
may require a cause beyond nature. Only analogy with the
present can determine whether the cause is miraculous or naturalistic (1994a, 14:21, emp. in orig.).

It is not a justifiable criticism to say simply that "creation is based
on supernatural processes in the distant past" and therefore is not
scientific. The "supernatural" beginnings of creation are no less available for scientific examination than are the "unique" (though allegedly
natural) beginnings of evolution.

Furthermore, whoever defined science as "naturalism"? The word
"science" derives from the Latin *scientia*, meaning "knowledge."
Scientists are supposed to be men and women who are on a lifelong search for truth and knowledge, regardless of where that search
may lead. Science is based on an observation of the facts and is directed at finding patterns of order in the observed data. **There is
nothing about true science that excludes the study of created objects and order!**

To assume that knowledge can be acquired solely on the basis
of naturalism, and that **only** those items that might have come about
"naturally" may be studied, is to beg the question entirely. It is at
least possible that creation could be the true explanation of origins,
and thus it is premature and bigoted for certain scientists to exclude
it from the domain of science by definition, all the while leaving the
theory of evolution within that domain.

Chapter 4

Voices of Compromise

Where would we be without revelation from God? Such a revelation is both possible and necessary. It is possible because God, being all-powerful, is able to do anything He wishes that is not contrary to His divine nature (Job 42:2; Matthew 19: 26). It is necessary due to the fact that otherwise man would have no way to know fully and adequately the things it is imperative for him to know. For example, it is essential to have a divine revelation in order for man to know: (a) **The character of God**. While something of God's essence and power can be gleaned vaguely from nature itself (as I shall show shortly), it takes the fullness of actual communication from God to reveal His holiness, justice, mercy, grace, love, and other attributes. (b) **The origin of man**. Were it not for divine revelation, man would have no way to know of his lofty origin. The confusion of modern-day evolutionary theories is evidence aplenty of this. (c) **The origin of evil**. Man needed to be educated concerning the source of his sinful predicament. Else, how could he know about the sinful state in which he finds himself? (d) **Man's purpose**. Divine revelation was necessary if man was to comprehend his purpose while here on Earth, and especially the provisions for his redemption. With no defined purpose, man surely would wander endlessly through the centuries, with neither goals nor objectives at hand. (e) **Man's destiny**. In the absence of God's revelation, none of us would know anything of the heaven to be gained, or the hell to be shunned. The urgency of this knowledge is made all the more real by the general despair of those who reject the concept of supernatural revelation.

Revelation designates the unveiling of facts and truths by God —things that man, on his own, could not have known previously. Revelation has reference to the communication of knowledge. **Revelation** discovers new truth to men (1 Corinthians 2:10); **inspiration** guides and controls the giving of truth (1 Corinthians 2:13), ensuring that God gets written correctly what He wants written. Inspiration extends to the whole of truth, although the subject matter is of two kinds: revelation and known facts (or as we would call it, history). The Bible speaks forthrightly about its inspiration (2 Timothy 3:16-17; 2 Peter 1:20-21; 1 Corinthians 2:13; et al.). Basically, this claim amounts to the declaration that the Bible is God's will and way in the world, a record and interpretation of God's activity, and a guide for man in service to the Lord. The Bible thus is regarded (based on evidence) as a repository of absolute Truth that may be studied faithfully, the result being that one knows God's will.

In discussing God's revelation, students of Scripture have spoken of that revelation as being two-fold: (1) natural (or general) revelation; and (2) special (or supernatural) revelation. **Natural revelation** comes to man through nature. The first six verses of Psalm 19 declare that God has given a revelation of Himself in nature that constantly is testifying to the existence of the Creator. The apostle Paul, speaking through inspiration in Romans 1:20, clearly stated that God's "invisible nature, namely, his eternal power and deity, has been clearly perceived in the things that have been made. So they are without excuse." Natural revelation is rooted in creation and in the ordinary relationship of God to man. The Scriptures teach that natural revelation is universal. At no time in all of history has God left Himself without a witness of Himself in nature (Acts 14:17).

The Scriptures likewise make it clear, however, that God has given a second revelation—**special revelation**. This revelation is found only in the Bible. It has become inscripturated; it is of word and of fact, and is historical in nature. God, in using this kind of revelation, disclosed Himself in at least three different ways: (a) **Theophanies** (i.e., veiled appearances of Himself). He appeared in fire, clouds, and smoke (Genesis 15:17; Exodus 3:2; 19:9,16ff.; 33:9). He appeared in stormy winds (Job 38:1; 40:6; Psalm 18:10-16). Theophany reached its highest point in the incarnation in which Jesus Christ became flesh and dwelt among us (Colossians 1:19; 2:9). (b) **Direct communications**. God spoke through an audible voice on occasion (Genesis 2:16; 3:8-19; 4:6-15; Exodus 19:9; 1 Samuel 3:4). He communicated through visions (Isaiah 6:1ff.; 21:6ff.; Ezekiel 1-3; Daniel 1:17). He also communicated through the Holy Spirit (Mark 13:11; Luke 12:12; John 14:17; 15:26; Acts 6:10). (c) **Miracles**. God, through miracles, chose to reveal His power and presence. Such miracles emphasized great truths, and were intended as confirmation of His word, His prophecy, and His power.

The careful student of Scripture has long been aware of the two types of revelation, and similarly has been aware that as great as natural revelation is, in and of itself it is deficient. At this point in time, nature has ceased to be a perspicuous revelation of God (at least to some). It may have been so before sin occurred, but even if it were, man now has been so blinded by sin that he cannot read the divine script in nature. Natural revelation simply is not enough; it never was intended to be. It does not afford man the reliable knowledge of God, and the spiritual things man needs for his ultimate salvation. Therefore, it is inadequate as a total foundation for man's faith. From nature, man never can infer the need for a personal Savior. Thus, God gave special revelation. The two combined represent God's message adequately communicated to man. When viewed in their proper perspectives, God's two revelations form important testimony to His power and His saving grace.

THE DOUBLE REVELATION THEORY

Unfortunately, some today have abandoned any confidence in what God's special revelation has to say regarding man's origin, in deference to evolutionary speculations. Numerous others, not willing to forsake the totality of their faith, have sought an illegitimate amalgamation between biblical and evolutionary views.

For example, advocates of what has come to be known as the Double Revelation Theory maintain that natural revelation and special revelation are fully authoritative in their respective realms. Since these two revelations are given by the same self-consistent God of Truth, they cannot, and will not, contradict each other. The **theologian**, therefore, is viewed as the God-appointed interpreter of Scripture, while the **scientist** is seen as the God-appointed interpreter of nature, each reading (through "special lenses") his own "book of revelation."

According to proponents of this idea, whenever there is an apparent conflict between the conclusions of the scientist and the conclusions of the theologian—especially with regard to such questions as the origin of the Universe, the solar system, plant life, animal life, and man—it is the theologian who must rethink his interpretation of Scripture in such a way as to bring the Bible into harmony with the scientists' consensus. Since "the Bible is not a textbook on science," and since these problems overlap the territory in which science alone must give us detailed and authoritative answers, the theologian is the one who should "correct" his views. It is held that this is necessarily the case because if a grammatical/historical interpretation of any biblical account should lead the Bible student to adopt conclusions that are contrary to the prevailing views of trained scientists concerning the origin and nature of the material Universe, then that Bible student would be guilty of making God a deceiver of mankind in these vitally important matters. But a God of Truth cannot lie (Titus 1:2; Hebrews 6:18). Therefore, so the argument goes, the Bible account must be "interpreted" in such a manner as to bring it into full agreement with the generally accepted views of contemporary scientists.

There is a variety of ways by which advocates of the Double Revelation Theory hope to accomplish this highly unusual dichotomy. If one is speaking of Genesis 1-11, for example, these chapters are not to be viewed as literal or historical. Instead, they must be viewed as "mythical" or "allegorical." The Bible, so we are told, is intended to provide answers to important "spiritual questions" such as "Who?" or "Why?" Scientists, on the other hand, must provide the answers to important questions such as "When?" and "How?"

It is not difficult to document examples revealing the popularity of the Double Revelation Theory. In fact, John Whitcomb devoted an entire appendix in one of his books to listing proponents of the Double Revelation Theory (1978, pp. 163-165), and currently there are many more names that could be added to his list. For example, on June 13, 1986, Henry Morris (creationist and then-president of the Institute for Creation Research) and Lewis Mammel (theist, but anti-creationist and researcher at AT&T Bell Research Laboratories) debated the subject of the age of the Earth. During the closing moments of the debate, in response to a question from the audience, Dr. Mammel stated, in speaking about Christians and creationists, "I think they would be able to adjust their interpretation to agree with what we see in the natural world. **I think it's a mistake to elevate doctrine above our reason and the evidence of our senses**" (see Mammel and Morris, 1986, emp. added).

There are others, of course, who agree with Dr. Mammel in this approach. Davis A. Young, as a professor of geology at Calvin College, advocated similar views. In his book, *Creation and the Flood*, he acknowledged that the literal-day interpretation of the Genesis account of creation is "the obvious view," and that the Bible teaches a universal Flood. Nevertheless, he felt compelled to reject (and did reject!) these teachings of Scripture because "geology" (i.e., geology as interpreted through an evolutionary framework) has "disproved" them (1977, pp. 44,172). In his book, *Christianity and the Age of the Earth*, Dr. Young stated:

> The Bible is indeed the infallible, inerrant Word of God. It is absolutely true in matters of science and history as much as in matters of salvation and religion. But nature is also from God, and nature would lead us to believe that the Earth is extremely old. Scientific investigation of the world God gave us is an exciting enterprise that God would have us engage in. We do not need the flight-from-reality science of creationism (1982, p. 163).

Young has made it clear that while he verbally professes a belief in God's Word as infallible and inerrant, that Word will not be allowed to dictate to him the truth in certain areas.

Another religionist who has accepted the Double Revelation Theory is Pattle P.T. Pun, professor of biology at Wheaton College, who has written:

> It is apparent that the most straightforward understanding of the Genesis record, without regard to all the hermeneutical considerations suggested by science, is that God created heaven and earth in six solar days, that man was created in the sixth day, that death and chaos entered the world after the Fall of Adam and Eve, that all of the fossils were the result of the catastrophic universal deluge which spared only Noah's family and the animals therewith....

> However, the Recent Creationist position has two serious flaws. First, it has denied and belittled the vast amount of scientific evidence amassed to support the theory of natural selection and the antiquity of the earth. Secondly, much Creationist writing has "deistic" implications...the stipulation that the varieties we see today in the biological world were present in the initial Creation implies that the Creator is no longer involved in creation in a dynamic way (1987, 39:14).

Dr. Pun's accusation that creationists' teachings have "deistic" implications is both unwarranted and unfair. Creationists do not teach or imply that all the varieties of plants and animals were present in the initial creation, but only the basic "kinds"—which is exactly what Genesis says no less than ten times in its first chapter. Furthermore, the fact that God **no longer is creating** (Genesis 2:1) does not mean that He somehow is inactive in the present world. Jesus Himself stated, in fact, that His Father "worketh even until now" (John 5:17). While God's work of **creation** is complete, His work of **redemption** continues. Creationists cannot be accused justifiably of advocating deism in any form. [NOTE: For an up-to-date discussion and refutation of deism from a creationist point of view, see Thompson, 2000b, pp. 33-42.] The real reason that Dr. Pun rejects what he admits is the "most straightforward understanding of the Genesis record" is that it conflicts with the "vast amount of scientific evidence amassed to support the theory of natural selection and the antiquity of the earth." He therefore suggests that the biblical record be interpreted via "hermeneutical considerations suggested by science." Here is a perfect example of the Double Revelation Theory at work. Scientific theory has become the controlling factor in biblical exegesis.

One last example bears mentioning, because it shows the end results of the Double Revelation Theory. In 1991, Hugh Ross authored *The Fingerprint of God* as an apologetic for progressive creationism. In that volume, he made the following comments:

> More than speaking merely of God's existence, the creation, according to Romans 1, also reveals essential truths about God's character, which would include His desire and means to form a relationship with man. As an illustration of the accessibility of that information, the Bible includes an account of an ancient character, Job (Job 7-19) who, **without** the aid of scriptures, and in opposition to the religion of his peers, discerned all the elements of "the gospel," the good news of how man can find eternal life in God. The creation, thus, reveals all the necessary steps to develop a right relationship with God. These steps are uniquely corroborated by the Bible (pp. 181-182, emp. in orig.).

This is a perfect example of where the Double Revelation Theory will lead. It begins with natural and special revelation being equal. Eventually, however, natural revelation takes a position of preeminence—because, after all, it is based on **empirical** evidence. Finally, Ross' position triumphs. Man no longer needs God's special revelation to instruct him on the plan of salvation; rather, that is evident through nature, and the Bible merely "corroborates" it. Harold Lindsell, while serving as editor of *Christianity Today* magazine, addressed this idea when he wrote:

> ...to accept the story of Eve's beginnings as given in Genesis in any historical sense is to knock the theory of evolution into a cocked hat. It brings to bear upon the creative process divine intervention that drives the uniformitarian hypothesis and the endless eons of evolutionary development into the ground. If, in the face of the biblical data, the theistic evolutionist chooses to accept the hypothesis of some scientists, he at least should be conscious of what he is doing to the Bible in the process. He no longer makes it the source book for his knowledge of origins. In place thereof he chooses the verdict of science and allows it to sit in judgment on the Bible rather than letting the Bible sit in judgment on science (1977, pp. 15-17).

When Dr. Lindsell spoke of the fact that science ultimately will be allowed to "sit in judgment" on the Bible by the person who accepts the Double Revelation Theory, he was absolutely correct. On May 5-7, 2000, I had the opportunity to speak at a large gathering of young people in Elizabethtown, Kentucky. During one of the lectures, I discussed the literal nature of the account found in Genesis 1-11, and how that account clearly was in opposition to the General Theory of Evolution. During the question and answer session that followed one of my lectures, a young girl who appeared to be roughly of high school age (I learned later that she was, in fact, a junior in high school) raised her hand. When I called on her, she expressed strong disagreement with such a view, and went on to say that she believed firmly in evolution and viewed Genesis 1-11 as nothing more than a convenient mythology fabricated by Hebrews who did not have the vast scientific data that we possess today.

In my response, I very kindly disagreed with her conclusion, and went to great lengths to explain that both the Lord and His inspired writers not only viewed Genesis 1-11 as literal and historical, but frequently used the content of those chapters to construct fundamental Bible doctrine (e.g., Matthew 19, where the Lord quoted

Genesis 2:24 to discuss marriage, divorce, and remarriage with the Pharisees; Matthew 24, where Christ used the global, Noahic Flood to draw a comparison to the destruction of the Earth at His Second Coming; 1 Corinthians 15:47, where Paul discussed Adam, "the first man, of the earth, earthy" and compared him to Christ as the "last Adam," etc.). When I demonstrated to the young lady the damage that ultimately is inflicted upon the biblical record by a full-fledged acceptance of theistic evolution (the position she was attempting to defend), she retorted: "But **science** supports my view!" In response, I said very simply: "No ma'am, **true** science does **not** support your view. And more important, the Bible as the Word of God indicates that Genesis 1-11 is literal and historical." She then raised her voice to be heard and exclaimed: "Well, **science is my God!**"

That is exactly where belief in the Double Revelation Theory leads—which is why it **must be rejected** by Bible-believing Christians. As noted Old Testament scholar Edward J. Young remarked:

> What strikes one immediately upon reading such a statement is the low estimate of the Bible which it entails. Whenever "science" and the Bible are in conflict, it is always the Bible that, in one manner or another, must give way. We are not told that "science" should correct its answers in the light of Scripture. Always it is the other way around. Yet this is really surprising, for the answers which scientists have provided have frequently changed with the passing of time. The "authoritative" answers of pre-Copernican scientists are no longer acceptable; nor, for that matter, are many of the views of twenty-five years ago (1964, p. 53).

Indeed, why is it that God's **unchanging** revelation in the Bible should be "reinterpreted" to fit the **ever-changing** theories of modern scientists?

The writers of the Bible deal abundantly with matters of fact in science and history (unlike the writings of Buddhism, Confucianism, Hinduism, etc., which deal almost exclusively with faith/conduct matters). To take the position that the Bible is unreliable when it

95

deals with verifiable data of science and history inevitably will cause thinking inquirers to reject its teachings on theological beliefs. Jesus said, "If I have told you earthly things, and ye believe not, how shall ye believe if I tell you of heavenly things?" (John 3:12). If Jesus and His writers have told us about "earthly" things and we are not pre-disposed to believe such, how can we be expected to believe statements from these same men with regard to spiritual matters such as redemption, sanctification, justification, etc.?

The Bible must be accepted as inerrant and authoritative on all matters with which it deals. Otherwise, it is not really the Word of God. If any man, or group of men, is empowered to tell us **author-itatively** what God's Word means, then we may as well entrust him (or them) with a commission to rewrite the Bible altogether. Man seeks to become God (whether he is a theologian or scientist) if he insists that **his** word must be accepted over and above what **God's** Word says. While the Double Revelation Theory may be popular in certain circles, it fails to address certain realities—not the least of which are the tremendous limitations that inhabit the scientific method. As Michael Poole has suggested:

> Public opinion about science ranges between making it into a god, and despising it. Some people have regarded science as the sole means to peace and prosperity on earth. But, when the god failed to deliver the goods, they despised it. To treat science as a secular substitute for God is not only naive, it is idolatry. To abuse it because it fails to provide the solution to the world's ills is childish. It compares with the infant who kicks its toy because it will not do something for which it was never designed. Between these two extremes lies the rosy-spectacled view that, although science and technology have caused a lot of problems, they will also be the means of solving them.
>
> Science and technology are the activities of imperfect people. The tendencies to misuse and exploit for personal gain operate here as in every other department of life. But the answer to abuse is not disuse, but responsible use (1990, p. 126).

Furthermore, science cannot deal with once-for-all, utterly unique events. Science is impotent when it comes to dealing with moral and/or spiritual (thus, empirically elusive) realities that give significance to human endeavor. Science fails most conspicuously, however, whenever it is forced into the position of trying to analyze the supernatural and miraculous acts of God. These events undeniably form the foundation of the Judeo-Christian world view. The scientist or theologian who accepts the Double Revelation Theory would have us believe that even in matters such as these, science always takes precedence. How so?

Acceptance of the Double Revelation Theory also fails to consider the effects of sin. While it is true that the heavens declare the glory of God (Psalm 19:1), it also is true that the eyes of man's understanding, blinded by sin, do not always read the heavens aright. The noetic effects of sin often lead to anti-theistic presuppositions. Much is presented as "scientific fact" that is hostile to the conclusions presented in the Bible. Whitcomb has commented:

> Those who exclusively employ the scientific method in historical sciences (e.g., paleontology) uncritically apply this method in a uniformitarian manner by extrapolating present natural processes forever into the past. Furthermore, they ignore the possible anti-theistic bias of the scientist himself as he handles the facts of nature in arriving at a **cosmology** (i.e., a theory concerning the basic structure and character of the universe) and a **cosmogony** (i.e., a theory concerning the origin of the universe and its parts). To the extent that such theorists fail to give careful and honest recognition to these essential limitations of the scientific method and of the investigator himself, they fail to give a true and undistorted picture of reality as a whole, and they fail also to point men to the only true source for understanding its mysteries (1978, p. 56, emp. and parenthetical items in orig.).

It certainly is true that God cannot deny Himself (2 Timothy 2:13). God's Word always will agree with God's world, for the Author of the one is the Creator of the other. God's revelation in nature often can amplify and illustrate His Word, but His written revelation

97

always must inform and constrain our interpretation of nature. Yes, God has spoken to us through nature. Numerous passages attest to that fact (Job 12:7-8; 26:13-14; Psalm 19:1-2; 97:6; Acts 14:17; 17:24-28; Romans 1:20-21). The proper use of science and technology not only helps man to implement the Edenic commission to "subdue and have dominion over the earth" (Genesis 1:28), but also teaches men more and more about the person and work of their Creator-God. God's revelation in nature, therefore, always must **supplement** and **confirm** His revelation in Scripture. It cannot be used to correct or interpret it. **If there is an apparent conflict —one that cannot be resolved by a more careful study of the relevant data of both science and Scripture—then the written Word always must take priority!**

THEISTIC EVOLUTION

In 1 Kings 18:21, Elijah chastised the people of God for not taking a stand for their God. He asked, "How long halt ye between two opinions? If the Lord be God, follow Him: but if Baal, then follow Him." Henry Morris, in commenting on this passage, stated:

> The spirit of compromise that prevailed among the people of God in Elijah's time also manifested itself in the mid-nineteenth century, as Christians labored to accept both God and evolution, both the Bible and the ages of geology. This was not surprising, for in every age there has been conflict between God and the Devil and a corresponding tension between the world-system and the community of the saints, and always there have been those among the latter who seek to ease the tension by yielding up some of the distinctives of the Bible-founded separatism to which they were called. Neither is it surprising then that the same spirit of compromise is moving strongly today among erstwhile Bible-centered Christians (1966, p. 97).

Some today prefer a "middle-of-the-road" approach to the matter of origins—a concept generally known as "theistic evolution" (sometimes referred to as "religious evolution," "mitigated evolution," or "spiritual evolution"). What, exactly, is theistic evolution?

The word "theistic" derives from the Greek word, *theos*, meaning God. Therefore, when one claims to be a "theistic" evolutionist, he is claiming to believe in both God and evolution at the same time. It is not always easy to provide a simple, comprehensive definition for theistic evolution because the concept is altered by its adherents to suit their own personal situations. Some, for example, would suggest that God created the initial building blocks of matter and then allowed the evolutionary process to take over—including the spontaneous generation of life. Others contend that God created not only the primary building blocks of matter, but also life itself, and then placed into operation natural laws through which evolution operated over eons of time. Still others would argue that God not only created the building blocks and gave life a "push," but actually intervened from time to time, even though evolution was the mode of operation. Generally speaking, those in this last group prefer to be called "progressive creationists" rather than out-and-out theistic evolutionists. Their views will be discussed later in chapter 12. The following definitions from the literature offer a summary of the concept known as theistic evolution.

> Many Christians, including men of science as well as theologians, accommodate the discoveries of science in their religion by suggesting that God did not create the world (in its present form) supernaturally. Rather, He used natural processes as His "method of creation," and guided evolution to the final realization of man. In this view, Adam's body was produced as a result of the process of evolution, and God then completed His "creation" of man by giving him an eternal soul. The creation of life as described in Genesis is thus recognized to be essentially poetic, or at least to be flexible enough to permit God a wide latitude in His **method** of creation. This interpretation is generally referred to as "theistic evolution" (Young, 1985, p. 46, emp. and parenthetical item in orig.).

> The theistic evolutionist holds a position somewhat between that of the absolute evolutionist and the creationist. He believes that God created the materials of our universe and then guided and superintended the process by which all life has

evolved from the very simplest one-celled form on up to the sophisticated forms which we know today. Evolution was God's method of bringing about the present development, though originally the materials were created by God (Baxter, 1971, p. 159).

What is theistic evolution? Believers in God generally take the position that God made the universe, including the laws of nature, so that the universe moves along in response to these laws. If one drops an object to earth, it is expected to behave in accordance with the law of gravitation as formulated by scientists as a result of their observation. Both theists (believers in God) and atheists (disbelievers in God) believe that there are natural laws by which the universe operates. The atheist believes that there was no FIRST CAUSE but that this system has gone on for eternity, so that prior to each effect there has existed a totally adequate natural cause. When a natural effect occurs for which there was not a totally adequate natural cause, then supernatural INTERVENTION has occurred. Theistic evolution postulates that such intervention accounts for some actions in evolution (Camp, 1972, p. 192, emp. and parenthetical items in orig.).*

IS THEISTIC EVOLUTION POPULAR?

Is theistic evolution popular? Indeed it is. Many today have accepted it as a "way out" of having to make a decision in favor of either creation or evolution. Thus, it has become the "middle of the road" position that so many Christians already have taken on a myriad of other issues (e.g.: verbal inspiration, the virgin birth, the resurrection, miracles, etc.). As Wysong has observed:

---

* On occasion, there is some confusion about the definition of theistic evolution in regard to natural laws. Camp has addressed this matter: "The expression 'theistic evolution' is sometimes used to refer to the concept that God created natural laws which would cause evolution to take place and thus in this guiding principle, God can be said to be the author of life. This notion cannot be said to be 'theistic evolution' in any meaningful sense. One might as well refer to theistic rain, theistic thunder, theistic earthquakes, etc. These natural phenomena can be observed, yet we believe that they have totally adequate natural causes though a theist will no doubt believe God created those natural forces while an atheist will not believe in God. The phenomena are not regarded to be a result of divine intervention into the laws of nature" (1972, p. 63).

Theistic evolution has been advocated in the past by men like Augustine and Aquinas. Today it is vogue. It is downright hard to find anyone who does not believe in evolution in one form or another, and it is also difficult to find anyone who does not believe in a creator in one form or another. This hybrid belief has given reprieve to those not wishing to make a total commitment to either side (1976, p. 63).

Henry Morris assessed the current trend in this manner:

The sad fact is that evolutionism has also deeply affected evangelical schools and churches. After all, even modern ultra-liberal theological schools (e.g., Harvard, Yale) and denominations (e.g., Methodist, Episcopalian) were once orthodox and zealous for the Scriptures. These institutions have traveled down the road of compromise with evolutionary humanism farther than most, but many evangelicals today seem to have embarked on the same icy road, unaware of the dangers ahead and impatient with those who would warn them. Evangelicals (meaning those who accept the inerrant authority of the Bible and believe in the deity of Christ and his substitutionary death and bodily resurrection) generally "dare not call it compromise" and perhaps are not even aware of it. But compromise they have, in many, many instances. Some have accepted full-blown theistic evolution, but many more believe in either "progressive creation" or "reconstructive creation" (i.e., the so-called Gap Theory). ...the sad truth is that many evangelical leaders, who **profess** to believe in biblical inerrancy and authority, have also compromised with evolution (1989, pp. 101,104, emp. and parenthetical items in orig.).

Sadly, the proof substantiating Dr. Morris' statements is not hard to come by. For example, Stanley Beck, of the American Lutheran Church, once remarked:

To call himself reasonably well-educated and informed, a Christian can hardly afford not to believe in evolution. Evolution, including human evolution, is no longer in contention. Evolution has been demonstrated so thoroughly...even produced experimentally, that it has ceased to be a matter of opinion. And to announce that you do not believe in evolution is as irrational as to announce that you do not believe in electricity (1963, pp. 316-317).

J.D. Thomas offered this summary:

> This view is also commonly accepted by many others who accept biological evolution. Major religious groups today which hold for some form of theistic evolution include the Roman Catholics who count it to be their official doctrine of the origin of man. Some Jews, particularly the extremely liberal ones, hold to this view, and the Protestant theologians which are normally counted as Liberals are very strong in favor of theistic evolution (where they accept God); and the Neo-Orthodox or Existentialist theologians follow in this same pattern since they also accept much of the "Scientific Naturalism" that Liberalism has held to over the years. There are also several who wear the label of conservative theologians, some of them quite outstanding, who have accepted theistic evolution in some manner, believing that the arguments favoring evolution are strong enough that they must be accepted; and they have felt that this is the best way to find agreement between the Bible and science.... Some call their view "progressive creationism," some "threshold evolution...." Each of these terms implies that there is something about the general doctrine of evolution which must be accepted (1965, pp. 177-178, parenthetical item in orig.).

The evidence suggests that belief in theistic evolution has been popular in the past, and remains popular today.

WHY DO PEOPLE BELIEVE IN THEISTIC EVOLUTION?

Why do people choose to believe in theistic evolution? First, no doubt many believe in theistic evolution because they feel that the evidence for organic evolution actually having occurred is just too strong to ignore. Nobel laureate George W. Beadle put it this way:

> One must accept all of evolution or none. And the evidence for organic evolution is overwhelmingly convincing. ...belief in evolution, including the spontaneous origin of life from non-living antecedents, need in no way conflict with religion (as quoted in Buffaloe, 1969, pp. 17,20,21).

Jan Lever of the Free University of Amsterdam remarked:

> ...when we thus place side by side the knowledge which we possess of the higher life of the Primates of the Pleistocene Epoch and the revelation that man has been brought forth within that which has been created, then we may not reject in advance the **possibility** that the genesis of man occurred by way of a being that, at least with respect to the characteristics of its skeleton, was an animal, according to our norms and criteria. ...we may not reject in advance the possibility that there has existed a genetic relation between man and animal (1958, pp. 197,221, emp. in orig.).

In a symposium on "Origins and Christian Thought Today" held at Wheaton College on February 17, 1961, Walter Hearn stated:

> ...surely we know that processes have been involved in bringing **us** into existence. Why shudder, then, at the idea that processes were involved in bringing Adam into existence? Granted that we do not yet know details of the processes, why may we not assume that God **did** use processes? (1961, p. 42, emp. in orig.).

Edward L. Kessel presented the theistic evolution point of view by suggesting:

> Once He had established the material of Nature, and the laws of Nature to govern its activities, He used this mechanism to continue creation—creation by evolution (evolvement, development).... Just as an open-minded scientist must heed the evidence and recognize that there must be a God, the nonscientist must likewise heed the evidence and recognize that creational evolution was God's method of creation, once He had produced the material of the universe and established its laws (as quoted in Baxter, 1971, pp. 159-160, parenthetical item in orig.).

In speaking of James Orr, the conservative theologian of the latter part of the nineteenth century and the early part of the twentieth, Davidheiser suggested that he "...entertained views of theistic evolution. Dr. Orr had the theory of evolution thrust upon him and he had to deal with it. He seems to have been convinced that the scientists had proved evolution to be true and that he had to do the best he could with it" (1969, p. 38).

This appears to be the attitude of many today. They have had the theory of evolution "thrust upon them," and the only way they know of "doing the best they can with it" is to attempt to incorporate it into the biblical record. They therefore make a conscious decision to become theistic evolutionists.

Second, some people believe in theistic evolution because they are convinced in their own minds that it not only is not contradictory to the Bible, but is, in fact, quite compatible with the Divine Record. Albertus Pieters, in his *Notes on Genesis*, wrote:

> If a Christian believer is inclined to yield as far as possible to the theory of organic evolution, he can hold that man's body was prepared by God through such a natural process, and that, when this process had reached a certain stage, God took one of the man-like brutes so produced, and made him the first human being, by endowing him with a human soul and a morally responsible nature.... In such a conception there is nothing contrary to the Bible (1947, p. 201).

James Hefley, writing in *Eternity* magazine, stated: "A distinguished university professor and respected Christian told me, I believe that science has proved certain forms of evolution.... I believe this does not conflict with the Biblical account of creation" (1965, p. 21).

Neal Buffaloe, writing in *Mission* magazine, said that he believed "the concept of evolution is neither degrading to man, detrimental to human dignity, nor in conflict with the Bible" (1969, pp. 17,20, 21). John N. Clayton, a lecturer on Christian evidences and editor of a bi-monthly journal titled *Does God Exist?*, is on record as stating: "If we look carefully at the issues about which we are talking, however, we can find that evolution and the Bible show amazing agreement on almost all issues and that one is not mutually exclusive of the other" (1976b, p. 130).

In the September/October 1984 issue of his *Does God Exist?* magazine, John Clayton published, approvingly, an article titled "Monism, Belief, and Scientific Explanations" by Pepperdine University biology professor Norman Hughes. In his article, Dr. Hughes wrote:

It is unfortunate that so many believers seem to have accepted an idea that has grown out of philosophical monism: the idea that there is either a naturalistic explanation (discovered by man and therefore understandable by man, i.e., "scientific") for a natural event, or there is a supernatural explanation (not known or understood by man, except to whatever degree divine revelation may have enlightened him for the same event). This brief essay is an attempt to set forth the thesis that such a choice is neither necessary nor beneficial. In fact, the essence of the dualism of Scripture is that **the believer can accept both natural and supernatural explanations at the same time**.... The idea that to whatever extent one accepts **evolutionary explanations**, to that degree one has eliminated God's role in the creation of life is an idea based on a fallacy (1984a, 11[5]:16, emp. added, parenthetical items in orig.).

Was Dr. Hughes advocating theistic evolution? Indeed he was. And one does not have to "read between the lines" to reach such a conclusion because Hughes himself settled the matter once and for all in a letter he wrote to the editor of the *Journal of the American Scientific Affiliation* in which he stated: "I am a theist—I believe in God and in Jesus Christ as His revelation to humankind. I am an evolutionist—I find many biological phenomena which are not explainable except by the theory of evolution. But please, don't call me a theistic evolutionist!" (1986, 384[4]:282). [One wonders exactly what Dr. Hughes would expect to be called, if not a theistic evolutionist. Perhaps he would prefer "evolutionary theist."]

After reading Dr. Hughes' article in John Clayton's journal, Wayne Jackson of Stockton, California, wrote to inquire if he was, in fact, a theistic evolutionist. [In the December 1984 issue of the monthly paper he edits, *The Christian Courier*, Jackson authored an article titled "A Pepperdine Professor and Evolution" that documents all of these facts (1984, 20:29-31).] On November 23, 1984, Dr. Hughes graciously responded by letter as follows:

I do insist again that the basic thesis of the article is valid, i.e., that one can hold both a naturalistic and a supernatural explanation for the origin and the continuation of natural phenomena at the same time.... As a scientific theory, organic evolution has a number of weaknesses, but at the same time, it provides explanations for certain natural phenomena which I could not otherwise explain. To the extent that I find evolutionary theory useful, I have no hesitancy in using it (1984b, p. 1).

Apparently people like Buffaloe, Clayton, Hughes, and others who think like them, believe that there is no conflict whatsoever between the Genesis account of creation and evolution; therefore, anyone who wishes to espouse theistic evolution is free to do so, without worrying about any contradiction (real or alleged) that it might present in regard to the biblical material on origins.

Third, there are those who believe that the concept of theistic evolution somehow heightens God's glory by having allowed Him to create the Universe via an evolutionary process. They feel this makes God "more believable," and simultaneously bestows more honor on Him. Paul Amos Moody, in his book, *Introduction to Evolution*, addressed the issue in this fashion.

> It is just as possible to worship a God who works through natural laws, slowly evolving life on this planet, as it is to worship a God who creates by sudden command. In fact, is not our concept of the Creator immeasurably heightened when we understand more and more of the intricate workings of this marvelous universe? Such a Creator is of far greater stature than would be a miracle worker who created things once and for all back in 4004 B.C. (1970, p. 496).

In commenting on this idea, Davidheiser remarked:

> Theistic evolution is as old as the acceptance of evolution by the nominal Christian church. Those who hold this position consider evolution to be a fact, but they believe that it has been divinely directed instead of coming about through natural processes. It is frequently said by those who advocate theistic evolution that it is a grander concept to think of God working in this way than to think of Him producing living creatures by fiat creation. However, what is important is what the Bible says, and not what men may think is grander (1969, p. 168).

106

Fourth, no doubt there are some theistic evolutionists who believe it "just doesn't matter" one way or the other. J.D. Thomas reviewed this position in his book, *Facts and Faith*.

> In connection with a study of evolution it is important that we consider the question of theistic evolution or "religious" evolution, which question is a real problem to some people. The reasoning is, that inasmuch as so many people do believe in evolution, what is the use of "making a big fuss about it"? They feel that we might accept some basic principles about evolution and yet hold for the existence of God and for creation in some way—that perhaps God simply used evolution as the means of getting man here (1965, p. 15).

In commenting on theistic evolution, John Clayton suggested that "While there is no evidence biblically or scientifically to support such a position, these people do have one very excellent point, and that is that this whole subject is totally irrelevant to the question of the existence of God" (1976b, p. 131). Edward John Carnell, in his book, *The Case for Orthodox Theology*, assessed the matter rather bluntly when he wrote: "If God was pleased to breathe His image into a creature that had previously come from the dust, so be it" (1959, p. 95). Buffaloe—with what might best be described as a "shrug of the shoulders" attitude—said: "What do we care that man the animal is a product of evolution as long as man the spirit is begotten of God?" (1969, pp. 17,20,21).

Fifth, theistic evolution is popular among some people because they feel Genesis has not told us **how** God created. Russell Mixter, former president of the American Scientific Affiliation, was a proponent of this view. He felt that "Genesis 1 is designed to tell **Who is the creator, and not necessarily how** the full process of creation was accomplished" (1961, p. 25, emp. in orig.).

There are other reasons, of course, that could be listed to document why so many Bible-believing people choose to accept evolution. Many, no doubt, are influenced by the steady stream of evolutionist propaganda appearing in such widely read publication as *National Geographic, Reader's Digest, Weekly Reader, Discover,*

Scientific American, and a host of others. Fear of being viewed as "anti-intellectual" likely causes some to opt for theistic evolution. The influence of co-workers, friends, or peers also cannot be ruled out. Pressure to conform to the status quo is quite severe, especially in the scientific community. The love of "all things worldly" likely is responsible for many falling prey to theistic evolution. And, the desire to avoid controversy at all cost probably is responsible for the acceptance of theistic evolution among certain groups of people.

THEISTIC EVOLUTION AND THE VOICES OF COMPROMISE

In attempting to help people see the effects of the compromise of theistic evolution, Paul Zimmerman asked:

> Is it possible for us, as faithful interpreters of Scripture and believers in God's Word, to accept theistic evolution? If we do so, what are the consequences, if any? Have we perhaps, out of a stubborn conservative spirit, been dragging our feet when we should have gone along with evolution? There are many who feel that our insistence on creation as opposed to evolution imposes an intellectual obstacle to the faith of young people in today's scientific age (1972, p. 97).

Many in the religious community believe Christians simply should "go along with evolution." Bernard Ramm is just one example. In *The Christian View of Science and Scripture,* he wrote:

> We have noted that already orthodox thinkers (Protestant and Catholic) have affirmed that evolution, properly defined, can be assimilated into Christianity. **This is strong evidence that evolution is not metaphysically incompatible with Christianity**. The final answer, however, must come from one with responsible leadership. It must come from the best of evangelical scholarship which is **fair, competent, and learned**. It must come from our better thinkers in biology, geology, and theology, and not from more vocal or less able men. It must not come by the cheap anti-evolutionary tract nor from pulpiteering, but from that evangelical scholarship which is loyal to the best academic scholarship and to the sound teachings of Holy Scripture (1954, pp. 292-293, emp. and parenthetical item in orig.).

Thus, Ramm asks us to "check our brains at the church house door" so to speak, and let "competent scholarship" do our thinking for us. In light of such a suggestion, a good question might be: "What position will 'competent scholarship' urge upon us?" In his book, *The Long War Against God,* Henry Morris provided the answer.

> In 1973 an unofficial survey was conducted among the science teachers in the Christian College Consortium, an association of a dozen or so prestigious evangelical colleges (Wheaton, Gordon, Westmont, etc.). The report of the survey included the following summary: "Efforts to characterize and identify with the departmental positions results in all respondents calling themselves 'theistic evolutionists,' 'progressive creationists,' or infrequently 'fiat creationists'." The great majority of these teachers thus teach either theistic evolution or progressive creation—that is, when they do not bypass the subject altogether... (1989, p. 104, parenthetical item in orig.).

Dr. Morris went on to discuss the results of a second survey taken in 1980. Of 69 schools to whom questionnaires were sent, 52 responded. Of those, 48 replied that they did not consider the topic of origins important, and 31 stated categorically that they did not teach the Genesis account of creation to be literally true (1989, p. 105).

In some cases, it appears that Dr. Ramm has gotten his wish. "Competent scholarship" has spoken—and what has it said? James Jauncey, in *Science Returns to God,* commented that:

> There are a great number of biologists who at least tentatively believe in evolution, but who nevertheless are active members of Christian churches and find no problem at all. The general attitude is that even if evolution were proved to be true, instead of making God unnecessary, it would merely show that this was the method God used (1961, p. 20).

Dr. Jauncey stated further:

> This kind of thinking would consider the evolutionary process as the means that God is using. The point that the author wishes to make here is that even if the origin of man from the evolutionary hypothesis were proved to be correct, there still would be no insoluble difficulty for the Christian interpreter (p. 49).

In 1954, Ramm said:

> To this point we have shown that evolution with all neces-
> sary qualifications has been adopted into both Catholic and
> Protestant evangelical theology and has not meant the dis-
> ruption of either. **To charge that evolution is anti-Chris-
> tian, and that theistic evolution is not a respectable
> position, is very difficult to make good** in view of the
> evidence we have given (pp. 289-290, emp. added).

Fifteen years later, when Bolton Davidheiser wrote his classic volume, *Evolution and Christian Faith*, he observed:

> In recent years a new thing has happened, and this is more
> dangerous to Christian faith than the attacks and ridicule of
> the evolutionists. Men of science who profess to be Bible-
> believing Christians are telling conservative Christian audi-
> ences that it is not only all right to believe at least a certain
> amount of evolution, but that it actually is necessary to do
> so (1969, p. 39).

The evidence suggests that many Bible believers, especially young
people, are falling prey to the idea that they can believe in evolution
in one form or another. Hugo McCord, while professor of Bible and
biblical languages at what was then Oklahoma Christian College
(now Oklahoma Christian University of Science and Arts), wrote of
his experiences with the freshmen in his Bible classes.

> It is my privilege of teaching all Oklahoma Christian College
> Freshmen in their first Bible course on this campus. Since we
> start with Genesis it is not long till the subject of evolution
> arises. It is distressing that some from Christian homes are
> quite firm believers in evolution. Each year, after students
> listened to a taped lecture on "The Bible and Evolution," ques-
> tions are written out and handed to me. One of the ques-
> tions shows that there is the belief in theistic evolution: "What
> is so wrong about believing that such things really occurred
> gradually, with the help of God? I have no problems corre-
> lating evolution and my religion" (1968, pp. 771,777).

It is not surprising that youngsters are so willing to accept theistic
evolution, considering what "competent scholarship" urges upon
them. In 1986, for example, students in the biology classes of two
professors at Abilene Christian University (ACU)—Kenneth Williams

and Archie Manis—were taught that "the fact of evolution is beyond dispute." Dr. Manis urged his students to study the Genesis account (he had given them a photocopy of Genesis 1 from his personal Bible, with the words "myth, hymn" scribbled in the margin beside Genesis 1:1), and then to synthesize a "personal statement of belief about origins" (see Thompson, 1986, pp. 10-16). A serious and sustained controversy erupted when alumni of the University (including a number of alumni from the biology department itself) discovered that Genesis was being labeled a myth and evolution was being taught as fact. Those alumni, and others who opposed the teaching of evolution as the correct view of origins, rose up in arms against ACU. Financial support to the school decreased. Parents who had planned to send their children to ACU decided against doing so. And so on.

Tragically, rather than admit the obvious and correct the problem, the University Administration and Board of Directors publicly denied that there was any problem with the professors' teachings —in spite of firm, eye-witness testimony from former and current students. Friends of the University counseled then-president, William J. Teague, that one way to convince the institution's many financial supporters and alumni that the charges against its biology professors were false was to publish a book on the very topic of the controversy—creation and evolution.

Two years later, in 1988, University officials did just that, and released for distribution the volume titled *Evolution and Faith*. Ironically (or perhaps not), the University chose as editor of the book J.D. Thomas, former chairman of ACU's Bible department and a well-known advocate of the Gap Theory (1961, p. 54). At first, it seemed odd that the University would choose a man who for so long has been recognized for compromising the creation account. However, after reading the volume that he edited for ACU, it was apparent that he was chosen **because** of this reputation, **not in spite of it**. Assisting Thomas were other ACU faculty members, and one Board member (J.T. Ator). The book addressed such topics as biology (J.R. Nichols), chemistry (P.C. Reeves, dean of the College of Science), physics (M.E. Sadler), astronomy (J.T. Ator), origins and the Bible (I.A. Fair, Bible department chairman), and the week of creation (N.R. Lightfoot). Interestingly, there was an appendix by John N. Clayton of South Bend, Indiana—who is known widely for his many compromises of the creation record (for documentation, see Jackson and Thompson, 1992). President Teague penned the foreword.

The thrust of the book was crystal clear. For example, an entire chapter (by Sadler) was devoted to the proposition that "experimental evidence indicates that we live in a universe that was created over 10 billion years ago, after which the heavier elements were formed. The age of our solar system is about 4-5 billion years." Where does this line of reasoning lead? Dr. Sadler continued:

> The Bible does not say how old the earth is, much less the solar system or the universe. **To judge as heretics all those who believe that the present universe has evolved from a big bang is unfair and creates controversy over something that is certainly not a central part of Christianity** (1988, p. 93, emp. added).

Do certain teachers at ACU present the evolutionary Big Bang scenario as the method of the origin of the Universe? Yes indeed, as is evinced from the fact that one of the authors of the book, Arlie J. Hoover, subsequently published an article on "God and the Big Bang" in which he suggested that "it is entirely possible" that "God used a big bang as His method of creation." Dr. Hoover went on to suggest: "Because the Bible does not specify how God did it, we are left to choose the hypothesis that seems to have the best supporting material." He concluded his article by stating: "The big bang theory is far from being established, but we should not reject it as if it necessarily contradicted the biblical account of Creation" (1992, 134[9]:34-35).

Dr. Sadler suggested that these things are not "a central part of Christianity," and Dr. Hoover stated that "the Bible does not specify how God did it." Yet a comparison between the evolutionary Big

Bang scenario and the Genesis record of origins establishes numerous contradictions between the two. [NOTE: For an in-depth discussion of those contradictions, see Jackson, 1993, 28:41-43.]

In the chapter following Dr. Sadler's, ACU Board member Ator instructed the reader not to place "unnecessarily restrictive" limitations on Genesis 1. He then stated that the days of Genesis were not really "days" at all, but long periods of time (1988, pp. 96-97), from which he concluded: "The data just reviewed has [sic] driven scientists to the conclusion that the universe must have an age of between fifteen and twenty billion years" (p. 105). His entire chapter was devoted to the idea that "one should not 'force fit' his or her own ideas into the brief, beautiful, pristine creation account in Genesis" (p. 115), and then he proceeded to do just that. Oddly, one chapter later Bible Department chairman Ian Fair wrote:

> While it is possible to consider the term "day" in the Hebrew language to mean "time" or "age," this does seem to strain the simplest interpretation of Genesis 1:3ff. We will notice below that the Biblical theologian should have no difficulty with the "24-hour day" interpretation **if the text is permitted to speak in its own literary context and within its own purpose**... (1988, pp. 146-147, emp. in orig.).

However, in the following chapter Neil Lightfoot wrote regarding the word "day" as used in Genesis 1: "Obviously this is not a simple question with a clear-cut answer. ...here dogmatism is not only unwise but **unscriptural**" (1988, pp. 172,173, emp. in orig.).

Here is a book—whose alleged purpose is to build faith in the creation account among college-age youngsters—which suggests that the Gap Theory (espoused by Thomas and Clayton) is correct. No, ignore that. The Day-Age Theory (espoused by Sadler and Ator) is correct. No, ignore that. The days of Genesis are to be accepted as 24-hour periods (according to Fair). No, ignore that. There is no way to come to any clear-cut answer regarding the length of the days of Genesis (says Lightfoot). No, ignore that. The Big Bang scenario is the correct view of the origin of the Universe (Hoover and Sadler think). Pity the poor ACU student reading this volume. What is he or she to believe? From beginning to end, the book is filled with contradictions and false teachings on the creation account and related passages.

Neal Buffaloe, professor of biology at the University of Central Arkansas in Conway, and a member of the Christian Church (Disciples of Christ), teaches his students that:

> It is simply a fact that it [evolution—BT] produced that wonder which we know as the human species.... We have sought to show that evolution is not **in itself** the enemy of Theism, as the Creationists mistakenly assume, but rather can reasonably be interpreted as providing support for the doctrine of divine creation (Buffaloe and Murray, 1981, p. 20, emp. in orig.).

In 1999—eighteen years after Dr. Buffaloe wrote his college textbook, and thirteen years after the fiasco at Abilene Christian University—Mike Gipson, a science professor at Oklahoma Christian University of Science and Arts in Oklahoma City, Oklahoma (which is supported by individual members and congregations of the churches of Christ), penned a letter to the editor of Oklahoma City's largest and most prominent newspaper, the *Daily Oklahoman*. His letter (which appeared in the "Your Views" section of the November 24, 1999 issue of the paper under a general heading titled "Textbook Disclaimer Advocacy") was written in response to a November 14, 1999 editorial discussing a State-proposed "disclaimer" being considered for inclusion in all books used in Oklahoma that discussed evolution. The editor of the *Daily Oklahoman* had suggested that the disclaimer (which pointed out to students that evolution is not a fact, and is only one possible explanation of how the Universe and its contents came to be) was "elegant and non-offensive." Dr. Gipson wrote in strong disagreement.

First, he complained because the disclaimer "implies no gradualism at all in the fossil record." Second, he complained because the disclaimer "suggests that the hundreds of transitional forms claimed by paleontologists automatically have no merit. In my judgment, this is not...intellectually honest." Gipson then concluded: "Evolutionary theory, like all science, is tentative. Within the realm of faith, many of us hold religious explanations for the source of the diversity of life around us. Within the realm of science, **evolution**—though theoretical—currently **appears to be the best explanation**" (Gipson, 1999, A-8, emp. added).

Little wonder so many young people today are confused on what to believe regarding the biblical account of creation, considering the exposure they receive to this kind of material (much of it from professors who claim to be Christians!). Can evolution "reasonably be interpreted" to fit the Genesis account? Is evolution really "the best explanation" for the origin of the Universe and its inhabitants? Can we believe (and still be true to the Scriptures) that "such things occurred gradually, with the help of God"—and not affect adversely either our faith or our salvation? I suggest the answer to these kinds of questions is an apodictic "No!" And I agree wholeheartedly with Coppedge when he observed: "Some believers in God are not clearly aware that the Bible and evolution are not compatible. They suppose that theistic evolution is a philosophy acceptable to the Christian faith, not having thought through the contradiction involved" (1975, p. 177).

The remainder of this book examines that contradiction, and attempts to help people see that theistic evolution and its counterparts undermine the authority of both God and His Word. Were it possible somehow to take a comprehensive poll of church members, that poll likely would show that many today quite willingly espouse theistic evolution as "God's method of creation." While this is unfortunate indeed, it should not be all that surprising—in light of the minuscule amount of teaching we have offered in the past on this topic. While teaching on sin, heaven, hell, the resurrection, grace, faith, and love (all important topics), many times we have failed to teach Genesis 1 in its proper perspective. The result is a membership that believes in theistic evolution without really knowing its ramifications or end results. As Hosea said long ago, "My people are destroyed for lack of knowledge" (Hosea 4:6).

Were Christians to be made aware of the logical implications of their belief in evolution, some would retreat from the ranks of theistic evolutionists post-haste. The problem appears to be that many Christians are not aware that it is an "either...or" situation when it comes to belief in creation and evolution—not a "both...and." That dichotomy is the topic of the next chapter.

Chapter 5

"Either...or," Not "Both...and"

During the late 1940s, Woolsey Teller, second president of the American Association for the Advancement of Atheism, debated James D. Bales of Harding College (now University). During one of his speeches, Mr. Teller exclaimed: "If evolution is accepted, Adam and Eve go out! That story, the Bible fable, is interesting mythology but it doesn't present the true picture of the origin of man" (1976, p. 54).

The point is well taken. If one accepts evolution, the Bible does not present the "true picture" of the origin of man or, for that matter, anything else in the Universe. The thrust of Mr. Teller's argument was this: It is an "either...or" proposition, not a "both...and." **Either** one accepts evolution, **or** one accepts creation. But it is not possible, logically, to accept both evolution and creation.

The key word here is "logically." Theism, by definition, entails supernaturalism; evolution, by definition, entails solely naturalistic processes. This is why, in chapter 2, I presented in such detail the evolutionists' definitions of their theory. As Dr. Simpson emphatically stated, evolution is a **fully natural process**. Zimmerman couched the problem in these terms:

> In other words, once the premise of evolution is granted that matter interacts with itself under the guidance of the process of natural selection, there is no need of God. Theistic evolutionists of course deny this. In effect they would attempt to baptize the theory and to make it Christian. After two decades of reading evolutionary literature, both philosophical and scientific, I am of the opinion that this baptizing cannot be effected. The theory is based on the interaction of matter with matter. It is based on the changes which are produced by chance and which are then developed by natural selection. **If one places God's guidance into the process, he violates one of the basic tenets of the theory** (1972, p. 121, emp. added).

Evolution is based, in its entirety, on naturalism; creation requires supernaturalism. One cannot, with consistency, inject the supernatural into evolutionary theory and have it remain evolutionary theory. There is no such thing as "supernatural naturalism."

Of course, there are those who assert that belief in both creation and evolution **is** possible because, they say, they are the living proof of exactly that—people who **do** believe in both. "Can't we be Christian evolutionists?" they ask. In his book, *King of Creation*, Henry Morris dealt with this very issue:

> Yes, no doubt it is possible to be a Christian and an evolutionist. Likewise, one can be a Christian thief, or a Christian adulterer, or a Christian liar! Christians can be inconsistent and illogical about many things, but that doesn't make them right! (1980, pp. 83-84).

The question for a person who accepts the Bible as the inspired Word of God is not whether he can hold to a belief in theistic evolution. Rather, the question is whether he can believe in theistic evolution and remain **logically consistent**, without impugning the Bible or its Author. To put it another way: "Is it **right**?" A second, equally important question is: "Where will such a belief eventually lead?" Darrel Kautz, in *The Origin of Living Things*, concluded:

The theistic-evolution approach to biblical interpretation is highly rationalistic; that is, greater weight is given to human logic than to the reality of divine inspiration. When such a methodology is employed, it is just a matter of time until the Bible, in all its parts, is viewed merely as an ordinary book, and no longer as a fully trustworthy, divinely inspired document. Man's word supplants God's Word, and biblical truth becomes clouded—even lost. It is not difficult for a perceptive individual to see that theistic evolution leads to double talk. The Scripture is and is not God's word; it is and is not trustworthy; it is and is not history; it is and is not the ultimate source of Christian theology (1988, p. 30).

Wysong observed what occurs once a person begins this journey toward belief in theistic evolution.

Many hold to evolution while at the same time espousing belief in a creator. The result is a sort of hybrid, a baptized evolution called theistic evolution.... The creator is used here as a vindicator of evolutionary difficulties. With time, as evolutionists explained more and more by naturalism, the creator was crowded further and further back in time and given less and less responsibility. For many, theistic evolution is only believed transitorily. The position is often only a filler, an easily passed bridge from theism to atheism (1976, p. 63).

The long-range results of belief in theistic evolution can be tragic indeed. The sad part is that so few Christians realize it until it is too late. Over a century ago, during the time of Darwin, James M. Wilson held the position of the Canon of Worcester as a minister, and simultaneously taught science. In his discussion of the transformation that belief in evolution brought upon his life, he stated clearly the reasons that caused him to all but abandon his faith.

The evolution of man from lower forms of life was in itself a new and startling fact, and one that broke up the old theology. I and my contemporaries, however, accepted it as a fact. The first and obvious result of this experience was that we were compelled to regard the Biblical story of the Fall as not historic, as it had long been believed to be.... But now, in the light of the fact of evolution, the Fall, as a historic event ...was excluded and denied by science.... If there is no historic Fall, what becomes of the redemption, the Salvation through Christ? How does Jesus save His people from their sins? (1925).

Julian Huxley boasted: "Darwin pointed out that no supernatural designer was needed; since natural selection could account for any known form of life, there was no room for a supernatural agency in its evolution" (1960d, p. 46). The cost of opting for evolution is much higher than many at first realize.

"LOGICAL ILLITERATES, SCIENTIFIC SIMPLETONS, FOOLS, AND MENACES"

On Thursday evening, May 23, 1985 I participated in a televised debate with renowned evolutionist and humanist, Delos McKown. The setting was the Tracey Larkin show on Alabama Public Television. The audience was composed of the people of Alabama. The show aired at 6:30 p.m.

The day before, I had received a telephone call from Mr. Larkin, asking if I might be willing to meet Dr. McKown in order to discuss the creation/evolution controversy. I gladly accepted the invitation. Dr. McKown was no stranger to me. He is well known in evolutionist/humanist circles. At the time of our debate, he was the chairman of the philosophy department at Auburn University (he since has retired), and wrote often for anti-creation publications such as the humanist journal *Creation/Evolution*. In fact, he had just authored a fictional novel, *With Faith & Fury* (1985), which depicted a fundamentalist preacher who tangled with an evolutionist and (of course) lost. The novel was published by the humanist publishing firm, Prometheus Press, of Buffalo, New York. Eight years later, in 1993, Dr. McKown authored (and Prometheus published) *The Myth-Maker's Magic—Behind the Illusion of "Creation Science,"* which was a frontal attack on biblical creationism.

As the debate opened, Dr. McKown fired a salvo intended to leave the audience with the impression that **all** legitimate scientists of repute are evolutionists. He quoted from a booklet that had just been published by the National Academy of Sciences (the 1984 volume, *Science and Creationism: A View from the National Academy* *of Sciences*) that sought to present evolution as a scientific fact. He suggested that evolution is accepted by "all scientists" as representative of the truth regarding human origins. Dr. McKown then opined that the only view that should be presented in public schools was the evolutionary scenario. I quickly reminded him, however, that by taking such a position he had put himself at odds with his famous mentor, Charles Darwin, as well as the great public defender of evolutionary theory, Clarence Darrow. Darwin, for example, stated in the "Introduction" to his 1859 publication, *The Origin of Species*:

> I am well aware that there is scarcely a single point discussed in this volume on which facts cannot be adduced, often apparently leading to conclusions directly opposite to those at which I have arrived. **A fair result could be obtained only by fully stating and balancing the facts on both sides of each question** (emp. added).

During the famous 1925 "Scopes Monkey Trial," Clarence Darrow stated that it was "sheer bigotry" to teach only one theory of origins. [Of course, at the time Darrow had reference to the teaching of only creation, in the absence of evolution, but his statement is true nonetheless.] I asked Dr. McKown what would be wrong with allowing students to have access to **all** the evidence, so they could examine it at their leisure and then make up their minds without fear of undue coercion. The Auburn philosophy professor recoiled in utter shock at such a suggestion, and stated that exposing students to such concepts would be tantamount to putting astrology back into astronomy, or the stork back into obstetrics. He stated that if we put the "so-called evidences" (to use his exact terminology) for creation into the public schools, students quickly would see that they had been "sold a bill of goods."

I hastened to point out to Dr. McKown that students in public schools **already** had been "sold a bill of goods," in that they were being allowed to see only one small segment of the evidence regarding origins—**the side the evolutionists wanted them to see**. The fact of the matter is that creationists have an impressive arsenal of evidence at their disposal which helps to establish the conclusion that the creation model fits the available scientific facts far better than the evolution model. [See my book, *The Scientific Case for Creation* (1999e), for a presentation and discussion of much of that evidence.] The one-sided indoctrination of students in this materialistic philosophy in the tax-supported schools of our pluralistic, democratic society is a violation of both academic and religious freedoms. Furthermore, it is **poor education** and **poor science**. To remedy this intolerable situation, creation scientists insist that only after students have had an opportunity to weigh **all** the data, consider each alternative, and examine the implications and consequences of both positions, are they then able to determine correctly which is more credible and rational. **That is good education, and good science!** But, as Harvard-trained lawyer Norman Macbeth accurately pointed out in his book, *Darwin Retried* (1971), evolutionists (and this certainly would include Dr. McKown) are almost irrationally fearful of creationists, and are determined to prevent them—at all costs—from presenting any scientific evidence that supports creationism.

In the last 60 seconds of the debate, the television host, Mr. Larkin, was wrapping up the evening's discussion when he remarked to Dr. McKown that the creationists seemed to be making a good bit of progress in their efforts to set forth the scientific evidence for creation. Upon hearing this, Dr. McKown exploded in a burst of incensed rhetoric, and stated in no uncertain terms that, indeed, creationists **were** making a good deal of headway—but due only to the fact that our nation is filled with (and this is a direct quote from Dr. McKown) "logical illiterates and scientific simpletons."

While such a statement may have been as shocking to the people of Alabama as it was insulting, Dr. McKown hardly is the only evolutionist making such public, inflammatory statements. Just a brief four years after Delos McKown's tirade, the eminent British evolutionist, Richard Dawkins, offered the following blunt assessment of those who choose to believe in creation as opposed to evolution: "It is absolutely safe to say that **if you meet somebody who claims not to believe in evolution, that person is ignorant, stupid, or insane (or wicked**, but I'd rather not consider that)" [1989, p. 34, emp. added, parenthetical comment in orig.].

In 1991, Phillip Johnson, a lawyer with impeccable credentials from both Harvard and the University of Chicago, and a professor at the University of California at Berkeley, authored a volume titled *Darwin on Trial*. His book—which became practically an overnight best seller—presented a withering critique of Darwinian evolution, and included this assessment:

> The official scientific organizations, however, are at war with creationism, and their policy is to demand unconditional surrender.... To the zealots, people who say they believe in God are either harmless sentimentalists who add some vague God-talk to a basically naturalistic worldview, or they are creationists. **In either case they are fools, but in the latter case they are also a menace** (p. 128, emp. added).

"Oh, to see ourselves as others see us," as the old adage goes. To those who have helped develop, and who ardently defend, the concept known as the General Theory of Evolution, those people who believe in God are fools, and creationists are worse by far because they are logical illiterates, scientific simpletons, and fools who are ignorant, stupid, insane, wicked menaces!

Why is it that theistic evolutionists, progressive creationists, and old-Earth creationists cannot see what atheists, evolutionists, and secularists see so clearly? In an article titled "What do Evolutionists Think about Theistic Evolution?" Trevor Major wrote:

> It is precisely this compromise that worries many defenders of evolution:...theistic evolution is as unacceptable as special creation. Darwin's victory was hollow, they complain, if it can be shown that something outside nature is necessary to explain the Universe or life.... Evolution renders God superfluous, if not nonexistent (1994b, 14:55).

While the theistic evolutionist is trying to find more ways to weave evolutionary theory into the biblical text, the secularists are telling him not to bother because the attempt is futile. Some evolutionists even have gone so far as to applaud strict creationists publicly for their consistency, if not for their beliefs. One evolutionist's applause went like this:

> Cheer Number One goes to the creationists for serving rational religion by demonstrating beautifully that we must take the creation stories of Genesis at face value.... Many Christians have taken the dishonest way of lengthening the days into millions of years, but the creationists make it clear that such an approach is nothing but a makeshift that is unacceptable Biblically and scientifically.... Creationists deserve Cheer Number Two for serving rational religion by effectively eliminating "theistic evolution".... Creationists rightly insist that evolution is inconsistent with a God of love.... Three cheers, then, for the creationists, for they have cleared the air of all dodges, escapes and evasions made by Christians who adopt non-literal interpretations of Genesis and who hold that evolution is God's method of Creation (Mattell, 1982, pp. 17-18).

Michael Denton, certainly no friend of either the Bible or its doctrine of creation, addressed the damage to Christianity resulting from a consistent belief in evolution when he wrote:

> As far as Christianity was concerned, the advent of the theory of evolution and the elimination of traditional teleological thinking was catastrophic. The suggestion that life and man are the result of chance is incompatible with the biblical assertion of their being the direct result of intelligent creative activity. Despite the attempt by liberal theology to disguise the point, **the fact is that no biblically derived religion can really be compromised with the fundamental assertion of Darwinian theory**. Chance and design are antithetical concepts, and **the decline in religious belief can probably be attributed more to the propagation and advocacy by the intellectual community of the Darwinian version of evolution than to any other single factor** (1985, p. 66, emp. added).

In one of His parables, recorded in Luke 16:8, Jesus made this observation: "The sons of this world are for their own generation wiser than the sons of light." Oh, how true—and what a tragic state of affairs! We have God's inspired Word at our fingertips in our own mother tongue. We have the wisdom of the ages contained within that single volume. We have the word of the Creator on what He did, and how He did it. We even have it laid out before us in chronological, day-by-day detail. And we then ignore it, in favor of the man-made doctrine of evolution—a concept invented in the first place for the very purpose of ridding man of his Creator.

Little wonder that Julian Huxley stated concerning theistic evolution: "God is unnecessary" (1960a, p. 45). George Gaylord Simpson referred to Christianity as a higher form of superstition that in many ways actually is inferior to the superstitions of native tribes, and referred to church services as "higher superstitions celebrated weekly in every hamlet of the United States" (1964, p. 4). Erasmus Darwin, Charles Darwin's grandfather, had absolutely no use for Christianity and its concept of origins—a point he made abundantly clear when he said: "As for the being of a God, the existence of a soul, or a world to come, who can know anything about them? Depend upon it...these are only the bugbears by which men of sense govern fools" (as quoted in Camp, 1972, p. 176). Thomas H. Huxley regarded Genesis 1 as "the cosmogony of the semi-barbarous Hebrews" and hated ministers so much that he stated he wanted to get the heel of his shoe "into their mouths and sc-r-r-unch it around" (as quoted in Himmelfarb, 1959, p. 216).

More often than not, the theistic evolutionist has not followed his belief to its logical end. Evolutionists like Kirtley F. Mather of Harvard University have, however. Dr. Mather wrote:

> When a theologian accepts evolution as the process used by the creator, he must be willing to go all the way with it. Not only is it an orderly process, it is a continuing one. Nothing was finished on any seventh day; the process of creation is still going on. The golden age for man—if any—is in the fu-

ture, not in the past.... Moreover the creative process of evolution is not to be interrupted by any supernatural intervention. ...the spiritual aspects of the life of man are just as surely
a product of the processes called evolution as are his brain
and nervous system (1960, pp. 37-38).

During the 1959 Darwin Centennial Convocation at the University of Chicago to celebrate the one-hundredth anniversary of the
publication of *The Origin of Species*, Sir Julian Huxley stated:

Darwinism removed the whole idea of God as the creator of
organisms from the sphere of rational discussion.... There was
no sudden moment during evolutionary history when "spirit"
was instilled into life, any more than there was a single moment when it was instilled into you.... I think we can dismiss
entirely all idea of a supernatural overriding mind being responsible for the evolutionary process (1960d, pp. 45,46).

Simpson later remarked: "Purpose and plan are not characteristic of organic evolution and are not a key to any of its operations"
(1967, p. 293). British agnostic Bertrand Russell wrote:

Religion, in our day, has accommodated itself to the doctrine
of evolution.... We are told that...evolution is the unfolding
of an idea which has been in the mind of God throughout. It
appears that during those ages...when animals were tortur-
ing each other with ferocious horns and agonizing stings, Omnipotence was quietly waiting for the ultimate emergence of
man, with his still more widely diffused cruelty. Why the Creator should have preferred to reach His goal by a process,
instead of going straight to it, these modern theologians do
not tell us (1961, p. 73).

Donald G. Barnhouse was at one time the editor of *Eternity* magazine. He believed in God, but he also believed in evolution—except
for the evolution of man, whom, he felt, had been specially created
by God. He said: "May we not hold that...God intervened in the past,
even in the midst of a long evolutionary process, and created man
as an entirely new factor?" (1960, p. 8). He desperately wanted—
to use Julian Huxley's phrase—"a sudden moment during evolutionary history when 'spirit' was instilled into life." Bolton Davidheiser
correctly concluded that such is wishful thinking.

> Biologists in general, of course, would not consider this for a
> moment. This is an unstable position. It is unreasonable to
> think that evolution would go just so far and no further. Some
> think they can maintain this position, but students cannot be
> expected to stop believing in evolution at the human level if
> they are taught that everything else evolved. The trend today
> is to indoctrinate students with the concept that man is an
> animal, so why should they stop short of man in accepting
> evolution if they are told they may accept the rest? (1969,
> pp. 173-174).

Biologist Lorraine L. Larison—who has seen what Dr. Barnhouse and others like him have not—issued this warning:

> Evolution is a hard, inescapable mistress. There is just no room
> for compassion or good sportsmanship. Too many organisms
> are born, so, quite simply, a lot of them are going to have to
> die, because there isn't enough food and space to go around.
> You can be beautiful, fat, strong, but it might not matter. The
> only thing that does matter is whether you leave more chil-
> dren carrying your genes than the next person leaves. It's true
> whether you're a prince, a frog, or an American elm. Evolu-
> tion is a future phenomenon. Are your genes going to be in
> the next generation? That is all that counts (1977, 82:46).

The essence of Darwinism is captured quite accurately in the phrase
"survival of the fittest" because it is a life-or-death struggle for existence that results in extermination of the weak and unfit. British
poet Lord Tennyson described nature as "red in tooth and claw."
The renowned philosopher of science, David Hull, observed:

> [The] evolutionary process is rife with happenstance, contin-
> gency, incredible waste, death, pain and horror.... Whatever
> the God implied by evolutionary theory and the data of nat-
> ural history may be like, He is not the Protestant God of waste
> not, want not. He is also not a loving God who cares about
> His productions. He is not even the awful God portrayed in
> the book of Job. [He] is careless, wasteful, indifferent, almost
> diabolical. He is certainly not the sort of god to whom any-
> one would be inclined to pray (1991, 352:486).

As Henry Morris noted: "Many theologians wrote about evolution
as 'God's method of creation,' forgetting conveniently that it was all
supposed to be accomplished by a brutal struggle for existence, with

the weak perishing and only the fittest surviving" (1984, p. 112). In addition, it would behoove us to remember:

> Evolution has no place for a man starting in a good world, a man starting with a knowledge of righteousness and true holiness (Eph. 4:24; Col. 3:10). Man does not fall from a lofty position. Rather he is climbing upward under his own power from a lower position and achieving a higher one. This is the basic rationale of evolution and cannot be separated from it (Zimmerman, 1972, pp. 121-122).

That is exactly what Dr. Simpson meant when he said:

> Man stands alone in the universe, a unique product of a long, unconscious, impersonal, material process with unique understanding and potentialities. These he owes to no one but himself, and it is to himself alone that he is responsible. He is not the creature of uncontrollable and undeterminable forces, but is his own master. He can and must decide and manage his own destiny (1953, p. 155).

It is true, of course, that some evolutionists **appear** to be open-minded about the co-existence of religion and science. But that is generally all it is—appearance. As a lawyer, Johnson has observed from personal experience: "Mixing religion with science is obnoxious to Darwinists only when it is the wrong religion that is being mixed" (1991, p. 128). In other words, the evolutionists will go so far, and no farther, in their willingness to accommodate religious concepts. Here is a perfect example.

Evolutionists recognize that most Americans are religious. They also know that certain organizations that dispense research funds do not take kindly to science publicly attacking religion. So, it often is stated for public consumption that "religion and science may co-exist peacefully because they operate in different spheres." That is exactly what happened in 1984 when the National Academy of Sciences mailed to every American school district its publication, *Science and Creationism: A View from the National Academy of Sciences.* In the Preface to that document (which was a vicious attack against creationism), Frank Press, the Academy's President, said that it is

false...to think that the theory of evolution represents an irreconcilable conflict between religion and science. A great
many religious leaders accept evolution on scientific grounds
without relinquishing their belief in religious principles. As
stated in a resolution by the Council of the National Academy of Sciences in 1981, however, "Religion and science are
separate and mutually exclusive realms of human thought
whose presentation in the same context leads to misunderstanding of both scientific theory and religious belief" (1984).

From a simple, straightforward reading of Dr. Press' statements,
one would get the impression that there is no "irreconcilable conflict" between evolution and religion. But this, too, is wishful thinking, suggests William Provine, a historian of science at Cornell University. Dr. Provine, in speaking specifically about Dr. Press' comments, said that "these rationalizations are politic, but intellectually
dishonest." Strong words indeed, but as Provine went on to explain:

Modern science directly implies that the world is organized
strictly in accordance with mechanistic principles. There are
no purposive principles whatsoever in nature. There are no
gods and no designing forces that are rationally detectable.
...Second, modern science directly implies that there are no
inherent moral or ethical laws, no absolute guiding principles
for human society. Third, human beings are marvelously complex machines. The individual human becomes an ethical person by means of two primary mechanisms: heredity and en-
vironmental influences. That is all there is. Fourth, we must
conclude that when we die, we die and that is the end of us.
...Finally, free will as it is traditionally conceived—the freedom to make uncoerced and unpredictable choices among alternative possible courses of action—simply does not exist.
...There is no way that the evolutionary process as currently
conceived can produce a being that is truly free to make choices
(n.d., pp. 25-29).

The idea that evolutionists are willing to allow a peaceful coex-
istence between creation and evolution is a pipe dream. Evolutionist Douglas Futuyma, to cite just one example, made that point clear:

Anyone who believes in Genesis as a literal description of
history must hold a world view that is entirely incompatible
with the idea of evolution, not to speak of science itself....

Where science insists on material, mechanistic causes that can be understood by physics and chemistry, the literal believer in Genesis invokes unknowable supernatural forces.

Perhaps more important, if the world and its creatures developed purely by material, physical forces, it could not have been designed and has no purpose or goal. The fundamentalist, in contrast, believes that everything in the world, every species and every characteristic of every species, was designed by an intelligent, purposeful artificer, and that it was made for a purpose. Nowhere does this contrast apply with more force than to the human species. Some shrink from the conclusion that the human species was not designed, has no purpose, and is the product of mere mechanical mechanisms—but this seems to be the message of evolution (1983, pp. 12-13).

Furthermore, there is compelling evidence that the evolutionary community will not sit by idly while creationists (or theistic evolutionists) attempt to provide an alternative to students. The American Scientific Affiliation (ASA) is composed of scientists who believe in God and yet who, for the most part, openly advocate theistic evolution and/or progressive creation in matters of origins. In what was a calculated and direct response to the National Academy of Sciences' 1984 pamphlet on *Science and Creationism,* in 1987 the ASA produced and distributed a 48-page booklet, *Teaching Science in a Climate of Controversy: A View from the American Scientific Affiliation.* The general tenor of the booklet was to encourage "open-mindedness," especially in light of what the ASA called "open questions" having to do with origins. But, as Johnson noted: "Persons who claim to be scientists, but who try to convince school teachers that there are 'open questions' about the naturalistic understanding of the world, are traitors..." (1991, p. 128).

No doubt the naive members of the ASA were shocked at the events that transpired subsequent to the publication of their booklet. Their evolutionary colleagues were not willing to be nearly as tolerant as they at first had indicated in their political diatribes. In fact, retribution against the ASA booklet was swift and merciless. Evolutionary biologist William Bennetta organized a group of his evolutionist colleagues to respond to the ASA publication, labeling it "an attempt to replace science with a system of pseudoscience devoted to confirming Biblical narratives" (1987, pp. 36-43). In *The Science Teacher* of May 1987, there appeared a collection of essays edited by Bennetta, and written by nine scientific heavyweights such as Stephen Jay Gould, Niles Eldredge, Douglas Futuyma, Vincent Sarich, and others.

The authors of the ASA booklet were shocked and bewildered at the response of their evolutionary colleagues. Dr. Press had assured them that there was no "irreconcilable conflict between religion and science." But when a group of theistic evolutionists from the ASA attempted to take him at his word and make their views known as publicly as the National Academy of Sciences' had been, suddenly they had a war on their hands. What had happened, they wondered, to the "open-mindedness" of their scientific colleagues? Although he wrote twenty-three years before this controversy, the late James D. Bales nevertheless offered an explanation as to why people such as the members of the National Academy of Sciences would not be likely to tolerate—much less accept—the position of theistic evolution as advocated by those in the American Scientific Affiliation.

> Evolution is based on the assumption that one must explain all things naturally. It is inconsistent to bring in God at the very beginning of the process, or anywhere along the line. If one calls on God to perform a miracle to put the spirit—the image of God—in an evolved body, this is just as much a miracle as if the body had been created directly by God.... The theistic evolutionist who believes that God miraculously put the image of God in an animal body, and made man, will be looked down upon as being as ignorant and prejudiced as the man who says that the body of man was also miraculously created. In fact, some of them will have greater scorn for the theistic evolutionist because he is supposed to know that evolution did take place, but he refuses to accept the logical consequences of the hypothesis.... If one brings God, and the miraculous, in at any place why not in all the places which

are indicated in the Bible? **The introduction at any place of God and the miraculous destroys scientific explanations**, because by the very definition of terms a scientific explanation is a natural explanation which can be proven experimentally. Consistent evolutionism cannot accept the natural evolution of plants and animals, and the supernatural creation of man (1974, 116:52-53, emp. added).

There is no compromise that will please the leaders of evolutionary thought, short of people completely abandoning belief in any form of creation whatsoever. Yet many Christians remain convinced that the road of compromise is the path to travel. Once they have begun their journey, however, they rarely return to their starting place. In the first chapter of this book, I provided a quote from G. Richard Culp that spoke to this very point. Dr. Culp correctly observed: "One who doubts the Genesis account will not be the same man he once was, for his attitude toward Holy Scripture has been eroded by false teaching" (1975, pp. 160-161).

Compromise is a one-way street that ends at a dangerous precipice. In the case of the compromise of theistic evolution, its logical outcome is apostasy from the Christian faith. Eventually, the theistic evolutionist finds himself (or herself) having compromised so much, and so often, that nothing of Christianity remains but a hollow shell. Eventually the theistic evolutionist becomes just like the young high school girl I discussed in chapter 4 who boasted unashamedly: "**Science is my God!**"

The tragic part about all of this is that it is so very unnecessary. God's revelation is complete, self-consistent, and wonderfully satisfying. No compromise ever will improve on it, as the information presented in the following chapters documents.

Chapter 6

Genesis 1-11:
Mythical or Historical?

On November 24, 1859, J.M. Dent & Sons of London released for distribution Charles Darwin's book, *The Origin of Species*—a volume that would change forever the perceptions held by many people regarding their ultimate origin. However, long before Darwin wrote his book, he had seen his own perceptions of origins change as well. When he was but a young man, his parents sent him to Cambridge University to become a minister. In fact, somewhat ironically, the only earned degree that Charles Darwin ever held was in theology. But while studying theology, he also was studying geology and biology. After his graduation, and a subsequent five-year voyage at sea aboard the *H.M.S. Beagle*, Darwin's attitudes and views had changed drastically.

In 1959, Nora Barlow edited Darwin's autobiography, and included additional material that previously had been unavailable. In that volume, this amazing statement can be found:

> I had gradually come, by this time, to see that the Old Testament from its manifestly false history of the world and from

its attributing to God the feelings of a revengeful tyrant, was
no more to be trusted than the sacred books of the Hindoos,
or the beliefs of any barbarian (pp. 85-86).

Before Darwin could give himself over wholly to the doctrine of evolution, he first had to abandon all confidence in the historicity of the
Old Testament and any belief in its teachings on origins. That accomplished, he then was able to imbibe evolutionary scenarios without obvious discomfort.

There is an important moral to this real-life, historical account.
The Genesis account—taken at face value—stands in stark contra-
distinction to evolutionary theory. Thus, for people who claim to
view the Bible as the Word of God (as Darwin himself once did),
and yet who are determined to retain a belief in evolution (in whole
or in part), there is a very real conflict that must be resolved.

In an attempt to resolve this conflict, some have gone so far as
to suggest that Genesis contains **no world view at all**. Donald
England, a distinguished professor of chemistry at Harding University in Searcy, Arkansas, took just such a position in his book, *A
Christian View of Origins:**

> I recognize certain irreconcilable differences between the pro-
> nouncements of science concerning origins and the general
> impressions a person gets from reading Genesis 1. However,
> I feel that this dissonance need not necessarily be disturbing
> to a Christian's faith.... **[T]here is no world view presented
> in Genesis 1**. I believe the intent of Genesis 1 is far too sub-
> lime and spiritual for one to presume that it teaches anything
> at all about a cosmological world view. **We do this pro-
> found text a great injustice by insisting that there is in-
> herent within the text an argument for any particular
> world view** (1972, pp. 102,124, emp. added).

Dr. England has acknowledged the "irreconcilable differences" between Genesis and what he terms "the pronouncements of science,"
but he feels no discomfiture over this "dissonance" because he dis-
avows **any** world view whatsoever in Genesis, thereby leaving himself completely free to accept whatever happens to be in vogue scientifically at the time.

---

* Donald England's "Non-World View" will be treated more fully in chapter 12.

For those who wish to retain some semblance of a world view in Genesis, however, what kind of amalgamation of the "irreconcilable differences" between Genesis and evolution can be effected? John Rendle-Short discussed the solution suggested by many today.

> Theistic evolutionists generally believe that God has revealed all that can be known of the world and man in two books, the book of Nature and the book of Scripture. Since both originate from God they must be compatible; there can be no final disagreement. Evolution, they believe, is a scientifically accepted fact (granted the proviso that God, not chance, was in control)....
>
> Theistic evolutionists are well aware that in Genesis 1 and 2 the creation of man is recorded as having taken place in six days after the "beginning." They also know that according to evolution man was created millions of years after the origin of life. Here is the discrepancy. How to resolve it? Since there can be no discordance between the book of Nature and the book of Scripture, and since both appear true, the error, they feel, must lie in our interpretation and understanding of the Genesis account (1984, p. 13, parenthetical comment in orig.).

Once evolution has been accepted as factual, then it is the "interpretation and understanding of the Genesis account" that must be addressed. Therefore, theistic evolutionists (and their counterparts—progressive and old-Earth creationists) must find a way to reinterpret the biblical account of origins in order to accommodate it to various evolutionary scenarios. The first step in achieving this goal is to "reevaluate" the literary style of Genesis. As Zimmerman observed:

> In asking whether or not theistic evolution may be found in the text, we must come to grips with the question as to what kind of literature we have in Genesis 1. Unless we decide the kind of literature we are dealing with, we cannot perform good exegesis. If it is historical prose, that is one thing. If it is poetry or myth or saga or symphony, that is quite another (1972, p. 102).

The question then becomes: "What kind of literature **is** the Genesis account of creation? May we accept it at face value as literal history —i.e., representing events that took place exactly as described? Or, should we view the creation account simply as poetic mythology—i.e., a beautiful story (on the level of a pagan myth, for example), but certainly not literal history?

IS GENESIS 1-11 MYTHICAL OR HISTORICAL?

Is Genesis 1-11 Mythical?

If one accepts that Genesis contains at least **some** world view, then the creation account must be either literal or non-literal. For the theistic evolutionist, of course, that question already has been answered. There is no possibility whatsoever that a theistic evolutionist will accept the Genesis account as literal history, since to do so would align it squarely against evolution. Eventually, then, the events recorded in the first eleven chapters of Genesis somehow must be relegated to the status of a myth or an allegory; they **cannot** be viewed as literal, historical events that actually transpired. This simply is not an option for the theistic evolutionist.

The literature produced by those supporting theistic evolution proves this to be the case. In fact, it did not take long after the publication of *The Origin of Species* for compromise to occur. As early as 1923, William W. Keen wrote the following in his book, *I Believe in God and in Evolution:*

> In this age of general education, I can hardly believe that the most sincere literalist can insist that while Adam was made unconscious, an actual rib was taken from his body and out of it was fashioned a woman; and that Eve and a serpent actually conversed together in intelligible speech. To those who are familiar even in a general way with Oriental literature, all this is clearly to be understood figuratively and not literally (p. 8).

John L. McKenzie, writing on "Myth and the Old Testament" in *The Catholic Biblical Quarterly,* stated: "It is not a tenable view that

God in revealing Himself also revealed directly and in detail the truth about such things as creation and the fall of man; the very presence of so many mythical elements in their traditions is enough to eliminate such a view " (1959, 21:281).

In referring to the creation account in Genesis, A.M. Ramsey, one-time Archbishop of Canterbury and a former president of the World Council of Churches, concluded: "It is the story of disobedience of Adam and Eve. There is no necessity for a Christian to believe it to be history; indeed, there are reasons **why it cannot be literal history**" (as quoted in Hedegard, 1964, pp. 190-191, emp. added). The authors of the popular *Westminster Dictionary of the Bible* asserted: "The recital of the facts of creation is obviously not a literal, historical record" (n.d., p. 119).

Bernard Ramm, in his influential book, *The Christian View of Science and Scripture*, suggested that Genesis "is a purified ancient world myth. But through it shines the truth that God as Lord is God as Creator" (1954, p. 222). Well-known, neo-orthodox theologian Rudolf Bultmann spoke of the Israelites as a nation that, "like other nations, had its creation myths. God was depicted as the workman, forming the earth and all that is therein out of pre-existent matter. Such myths lie behind the creation stories of Genesis 1 and 2" (1969, p. 16).

Albert Wells, in *The Christian Message in a Scientific Age*, attacked the literal nature of the Genesis record when he wrote: "It is hardly necessary to regard the Genesis account of creation as literal truth in order to obtain its true meaning and relevance" (n.d., p. 113). In fact, Wells even went so far as to question the inspiration of the account by suggesting: "The fact of creation is thus not to be considered a direct revelation from God, unconditional by historical contingencies. It was, rather, an essential component of both the prophetic and the priestly mind" (n.d., p. 121). In his text, *Adam and the Ape: A Christian Approach to the Theory of Evolution*, R.J. Berry stated:

The creation of woman from Adam's side need not be interpreted literally; the teaching of Genesis 2:21-22 is obviously about the complementarity of the sexes and the meaning of marriage rather than the evolution of sex or mechanisms of sexual differentiation (1975).

J. Frank Cassel, a member of the American Scientific Affiliation,
wrote in that society's professional journal:

> The Adam-Eve sequence can be explained as spiritual. Wheth-
> er this is true or a dodge is of course an academic question,
> for is it not the spiritual message which God seeks to impart
> to us? Then why worry about what passages are to be inter-
> preted literally and which figuratively? Look, rather, to God
> to reveal himself more fully and more directly to you from
> each passage according to your need (1960, 12:2).

M.H. Hartshorne believed: "The Biblical account of creation is a
myth, which means that it expresses the fundamental assumptions
concerning the nature and meaning of human existence that the
men of the Bible held" (1958, p. 85).

In 1981, Neal Buffaloe and N. Patrick Murray coauthored a booklet, *Creationism and Evolution*, in which they addressed the type
of literature they perceived Genesis 1-11 to be.

> In other words, the Genesis poems are significant not be-
> cause they tell us how things **were**, or the way things hap-
> pened long ago. Rather, they are talking about man's situa-
> tion **now**—the eternal importance of man's relationship to
> God, and the primordial disruption of that fellowship that
> lies at the root of human nature and history. When we read
> the ancient Hebrew accounts of the creation—Adam and
> Eve, the Garden of Eden, man's "fall" by listening to the se-
> ductive words of a serpent, and God's Sabbath rest—we must
> understand...that "these things never were, but always are.
> ...The stories are told and retold, recorded and read and re-
> read not for their **wasness** but for their **isness**" (p. 8, emp.
> in orig.).

In speaking of Exodus 20:11, which records God's creation of
"the heavens, the earth, the seas, and all that in them is" in six days,
John Clayton remarked that the acceptance of this verse by Christians as literal history is "a very shallow conclusion" that is "incon-

sistent with the Genesis record as well as other parts of the Bible" (1976a, 3[10]:5). This is the case, he explained, because "Exodus 20:11 is a quote of Genesis 2 and **Genesis 2 is not a historical account**" (1979a, 7[4]:3, emp. added).

Two years before making that statement, in speaking of Genesis 2 Clayton had written: "This is, incidentally, why the order of life in Chapter II is different than in Chapter I—**it has a different non-historical purpose**" (1977, 49[6]:7, emp. added). When both the radical nature and the accuracy of that statement were challenged (see Jackson and Thompson, 1979), Clayton then went on the defensive in an attempt to "explain" what he "really" meant.

> First of all, I believe Genesis 1 is a literal, historical account. Its purpose is to tell us the history of the earth. But I do not believe that Genesis 2 is that kind of historical document.... Now **it is historical, and it is historically correct. But it is not primarily a historical document** the way Genesis 1 is, in my view (1980b).

So Genesis 2 is historical. And it is historically correct. But it is not primarily a historical document? Some "explanation"!

This extremely unorthodox (and completely illogical) assessment by Mr. Clayton then led him to offer a discussion on the difference, as he saw it, between Genesis 1 and Genesis 2.* In speaking of Moses, he said: "**Only an idiot would write a history and then rewrite it—and especially rewrite it backwards**" (1980b, emp. added).

The implication of such a statement is crystal clear: If both Genesis 1 and Genesis 2 are the same kind of literal, historical narrative, then an idiot's mentality is reflected! Here, in summary form, is Clayton's argument.

---

* One of John Clayton's errors is his inability to recognize that an account may be presented **out of chronological sequence** and yet still be **literal and historical**. Acts 10, regarding the outpouring of the Holy Spirit upon Cornelius, is not totally chronological in arrangement (cf. Acts 11, especially vs. 4), but what Christian would go so far as to deny that it is **literal history**? Similarly, the fact that Genesis 2 is not arranged from a strictly chronological viewpoint **has nothing to do with the fact that it is literal history**.

(1) If Genesis 1 and Genesis 2 are the same kind of literal, historical documents, then they are contradictory and reflect an idiot's mentality.

(2) But they are not really contradictory (hence, not idiotic) since they are not the same kind of writing; Genesis 1 is literal history, Genesis 2 is not.

(3) Since Genesis 2 is not a literal, historical account, if Exodus 20:11 is taken from Genesis 2 (as Clayton wrongly suggests it is), then it is not literal history either.

(4) But Exodus 20:11 **is** based on Genesis 2 (his wrong assumption).

(5) Therefore, Exodus 20:11 is **not literal history** and we are not obliged to believe that the creation occurred in six, literal, historical days.

From the biblical perspective, however, the Mosaic affirmation —that in six days Jehovah made the heavens, the earth, the seas, and everything in them (Exodus 20:11)—is a clear reference to Genesis 1, **not Genesis 2**. And so, if Exodus 20:11 is based on Genesis 1 (which it is), and if Genesis 1 is literal history (which Clayton admits), then Exodus 20:11 **is a literal, historical account**. If Genesis 2 is not historical, these questions are appropriate.

(1) Did God literally form Adam from the dust of the ground?

(2) Was the Garden of Eden a real, historical place?

(3) Was there an actual tree of knowledge of good and evil?

(4) Did Adam really name all the animals?

(5) Was Eve really made from Adam's side?

If Genesis 2 is not historical, none of these questions can be answered with certainty. Clayton's position is nothing short of rank modernism.

Approximately a decade after John Clayton began calling into question the historicity of the Genesis account, another progressive creationist, Davis A. Young, joined in the fray when he wrote: "I suggest that we will be on the right track if we stop treating Genesis 1 and the flood story as scientific and **historic** reports" (1987, 49:303, emp. added). Three years later, in 1990, he added:

> The most acceptable view of Genesis 1 does not regard it as
> a chronicle of successive events during the first seven days
> (however long) of cosmic history. Rather, Genesis 1 should be
> regarded as a highly structured theological cosmology that
> extensively employs a royal-political metaphor because of
> the great importance of kingship in the world of ancient Is-
> rael. In contrast to the pagan, polytheistic myths of the cultures
> that surrounded the infant nation of Israel, Genesis 1 portrays
> God as the sovereign King who calls into existence by his royal
> decrees those creatures that the nations sinfully worshiped
> and the myths deified. The days are part of the literary por-
> trayal of the royal council of divine creation and may be em-
> ployed analogously to a temporal succession of decrees by an
> earthly kind. The days are days in the sphere of divine action,
> a sphere that transcends time, not the first seven days of cos-
> mic history. Genesis 1 is therefore a theological statement and
> should not be used to answer scientific questions about the
> age and historical unfolding of the cosmos that would have
> been alien to the Israelites. Genesis 1 tells us that God is the
> Creator, but it does not tell us when or how he created (pp.
> 58-59, parenthetical item in orig.).

Six years later, in 1996, two important books were produced by
leading authors and subsequently published by highly respected com-
panies. The first was by Karen Armstrong, the *New York Times* best-
selling author of *A History of God*. In her book, *In the Beginning:
A New Interpretation of Genesis* (published by Ballantine), she defended the standard Graf-Wellhausen Documentary Hypothesis,
which suggests that the Pentateuch was not written by Moses, but
instead was produced by a multiplicity of authors and/or redac-
tors, including those known as J,E,D, and P. When writing about
those authors' attempts to produce the book of Genesis, she stated:

> The authors of Genesis do not give us historical information
> about life in Palestine during the second millennium BCE. In
> fact, as scholars have shown, they knew nothing about the
> period. **Frequently, they made mistakes.... Our authors
> are not interested in historical accuracy**.... The tales of
> Genesis have a timeless quality because they address those
> regions of the spirit that remain opaque to us and yet exert
> an irresistible fascination.... Yet precisely because the authors

of Genesis are dealing with such fundamental and difficult matters, they give us few precise teachings. The are no glib or facile messages in Genesis. **It is impossible to find a clear theology in its pages.**

...[T]he editors of Genesis seem to have introduced their readers to P's version of a serene and omnipotent deity only to dismantle it in later chapters. The God who dominates the first chapter of the Bible has disappeared from the human scene by the end of Genesis. Story after story reveals a much more disturbing God: as we shall see, the omnipotent God of the first chapter soon loses control of his creation; the immutable deity is seen to change his mind and even to feel threatened by humanity. The benevolent Creator becomes a fearful Destroyer. The impartial God who saw all his creatures as "good" now has favorites and teaches his protégés to behave in an equally unfair manner to their dependents. **It is impossible to come away from the Book of Genesis with a coherent notion of God** (1996, p. 13, emp. added).

The second significant volume published that year, *The Bible as Literature*, was authored by John B. Gabel, Charles B. Wheeler, and Anthony York, and was published by Oxford University Press. Gabel and his coauthors likewise accepted the Graf-Wellhausen documentary hypothesis, and therefore wrote:

This hypothesis explains certain obvious repetitions and contradictions.... We are not citing these problems to undermine the authority of scripture, as used to be the fashion when professional skeptics would lecture to audiences on "the mistakes of Moses" [a reference to the famous, nineteenth-century infidel Robert Ingersoll—BT]. We are merely supplying some of the data on which the documentary theory rests. Efforts to reconcile contradictions or explain away problems have been made and will be made by persons who feel that the integrity of the text (which for them means its divine authority) must be preserved at all costs. The costs, however, tend to be rather high. Whenever there are contradictions or other problems, the documentary theory usually presents a more reasonable alternative, and it is accepted by a great many scholars who do not feel their faith threatened by the possibility that the Bible text, being a product of human history, experienced some adventures in reaching the point where it is now... (1996, pp. 112-113, parenthetical comment in orig.).

They then asserted that there are two completely different (and contradictory) "creation accounts" in Genesis 1 and 2, and that the Genesis "stories" drew from a "shared tradition" with earlier works (such as the so-called Gilgamesh epic and the Babylonian *Enuma Elish*).* The authors continued:

> Until archaeology and the recovery of ancient languages made it possible to go behind biblical narratives, there was no way for a reader of, say, Genesis 8:6-12 to know that the author was drawing upon an older narrative tradition for details in his story....

> Since the detail about sending out birds from the ark is found in none of the earlier narratives except the Gilgamesh epic, **we know that this is the version adapted for the Hebrew Bible**, where all the key elements of the tradition are found.... **The use of a shared tradition, and especially its adaptation to the new use, is perhaps best shown in the creation story of Genesis 1. This is a reworking of the Babylonian creation story "Enuma Elish,"** sometimes called the "Babylonian Genesis" (pp. 49,50, emp. added).

Then, late in 1999, Jeffery L. Sheler, a religion writer for *U.S. News & World Report*, authored a significant—and highly publicized—volume, *Is the Bible True?* He, too, defended the Graf-Wellhausen position, and suggested:

> Nowhere has the question of literary genre been more central than in the wrangling over the Bible's veracity than in regard to what many scholars refer to as the "primordial history" in the opening chapters of Genesis. What are we to make of the stories of creation and of Noah's ark and the worldwide flood? Should they be taken as literal history, as religious myth, or perhaps as some kind of literary hybrid that combines features of both?...

---

* For an examination and refutation of the idea that pagan mythology such as the Gilgamesh epic influenced biblical writers, see Brantley, 1993b, 7:49-53. For an examination and refutation of the idea that the Genesis account of creation was influenced by, and contains elements of, ancient pagan myths such as the Babylonian *Enuma Elish*, see Brantley, 1995, pp. 75-92.

While most biblical scholars consider the story of the flood a myth or a folktale or assign it to some other category of literature that allows for an allegorical interpretation, many conservatives have little difficulty imagining that an omnipotent God could pull off precisely what the Genesis story describes. **As with the creation narrative, however, the evidence and arguments from science stack up overwhelmingly against a literal interpretation of the flood story.... [T]here is little doubt that a lack of compelling evidence makes a purely literal reading of the Bible's primordial history a most difficult position to sustain**. ...Today, a growing number of conservative scholars, harking back to Augustine, are convinced that more **nuanced views of the biblical creation account are required to accommodate the knowledge revealed in science** (pp. 48,54,55,52, emp. added).

The positions of the theistic evolutionist, and those sympathetic with him, are quite clear. Genesis 1-11 cannot be accepted as literal history, but must be "reinterpreted" as: (a) mythical; (b) spiritual; (c) a royal-political metaphor; (d) a discussion of "things that never were"; (e) a commentary on man's condition **now**; (f) a "priestly discussion" for the Israelite people **then**; (g) etc.

Is Genesis 1-11 Literal?

Contradictory claims of theistic evolutionists aside, the question remains: "Is the material contained in the first eleven chapters of the Bible mythical or literal?" Zimmerman has commented:

We cannot make any progress in answering the question until we decide whether or not Genesis is patently unscientific. By this I do not mean to deal with the question of whether or not it is a scientific textbook. This red herring ought to be buried permanently. The question rather is, "Does it contain information which is correct in substance?" (1968, 1:55).

It is my contention that **the material in Genesis 1-11 is historically true**, and that it represents believable, literal history that is "correct in substance." I share the view of the eminent Old Testament scholar, Edward J. Young, when he wrote:

> The position adopted in this article is that the events record-
> ed in the first chapter of the Bible actually took place. They
> were historical events, and Genesis one, therefore, is to be
> regarded as historical. In employing the word "historical,"
> we are rejecting the definition which would limit the word to
> that which man can know through scientific investigation
> alone. We are using the word rather as including all which
> has transpired. Our knowledge of the events of creation we
> receive through the inscripturated revelation of God (1964,
> pp. 50-51).

Before I present the evidence documenting Genesis 1-11 as literal history, I would like to comment on the statement that the Bible should be accepted as "literally" true. Oftentimes, creationists
are asked: "Do you believe that **everything** in the Bible is **literally**
true?" The answer to such a question depends on the definition of
the word "literally." In his book, *Christ and the Cosmos*, E.H. Andrews presented an excellent discussion of this issue. Although it
is somewhat lengthy, I wish to present it here because of its clarity.

> First of all, creationism does not insist on a completely literal
> interpretation of the Bible. It calls rather for a **literary** inter-
> pretation. Let me explain. The word "literal" creates all kinds
> of difficulties in people's minds. Usually, those who oppose
> the creationist viewpoint attach the label "literalist" to the cre-
> ationist and then use this assignation to ridicule him. But this
> is wholly unfair, for the creationist makes no such claim. In-
> deed, if we try to interpret the Bible literally at all points we
> find ourselves in all kinds of trouble, for a literal statement is
> a statement of precise fact, or as close to that as human lan-
> guage will allow....

> We see, therefore, that there are different literary forms em-
> ployed in Genesis 1 and 2. We recognize that the Bible uses
> literary devices such as metaphor, simile, anthropomorph-
> ism and dramatic forms to convey its message....

> Having established, then, that we do not necessarily interpret
> Scripture in a slavishly literal manner, but rather according to
> its literary genre and therefore according to the intention of
> the author, we nevertheless insist that those passages where
> the form and content are historical must be interpreted as
> genuine history....

When we turn to such passages as Genesis 1 to 3, and to the flood narrative, for example, we find that their contents are presented plainly as historical fact. Those facts may be expressed using a variety of dramatic and literary devices, but the author nevertheless claims to be relating events that actually took place. The narratives are accounts, not of myth, but of reality. So then, creationism adopts a historical approach to these historical portions of Scripture (1986, pp. 80-83, emp. in orig.).

For generations biblical creationism has adopted a historical approach to the first eleven chapters of Genesis, and for good reason —**these chapters discuss real, literal, historical events**. There is nothing in the biblical record that suggests Genesis 1-11 should be viewed as containing mythical or allegorical material. And such a claim is supported quite adequately by the available evidence. Here is a portion of that evidence.

1. The style of these early chapters of Genesis does not suggest a mythical or allegorical approach. Thomas H. Horne, in his classic, multi-volume set, *An Introduction to the Critical Study and Knowledge of the Holy Scriptures*, wrote: "The style of these chapters, as indeed, of the whole book of Genesis, is strictly historical, and betrays no vestige whatever of allegorical or figurative description; this is so evident to anyone that reads with attention as to need no proof" (1970, 5:6). In his work, *Genesis: Historical or Mythological?*, Edward C. Wharton commented in the same vein.

From the outset, the Bible is written in the context and appearance of sane and sober history. There is not the slightest intimation that these Scriptures contain myth. The historical and literal nature of the Record is easily determined in contrast to the parables, allegories, and symbolisms which are usually defined within the context. We know, for an illustration, that Luke 8:4-15 is a parable for it is so stated at the beginning. We know that Galatians 4:21-31 is an allegory for the same reason. Where the Bible teaches by allegory or parable or symbolism it is distinctly so labeled or otherwise easily understood in the context. To read the Bible's parables, allegories, *etc.*, and then to read Genesis is to know that Genesis bears no faint resemblance to any of these, but that it appears to be what it asks us to believe it is—historical fact (n.d., p. 2).

Edward J. Young declared:

> Genesis one is not poetry or saga or myth, but straightforward, trustworthy history, and, inasmuch as it is a divine revelation, accurately records those matters of which it speaks. That Genesis one is historical may be seen from these considerations: (1) It sustains an intimate relationship with the remainder of the book. The remainder of the book (i.e., The Generations) presupposes the Creation Account, and the Creation Account prepares for what follows. The two portions of Genesis are integral parts of the book and complement one another. (2) The characteristics of Hebrew poetry are lacking. There are poetic accounts of the creation and these form a striking contrast to Genesis one (1964, p. 105).

Concerning Dr. Young's final point, Raymond Surburg wrote:

> To discern the difference between the historical narrative of Genesis 1:1-2:3 as a prosaic account and a truly poetic version of the creation miracle, the reader needs only to compare Genesis 1 with Psalm 104:5-9; Psalm 12; Job 38-39; Proverbs 8:23-31. These are extremely poetic in character. In Psalms 8 and 19 poetic statements describe the heavenly bodies but there is a real difference between these statements and Genesis 1-2 (1969, p. 2).

In his book, *The Biblical Basis for Modern Science*, Henry Morris commented:

> Genesis 1-11 is certainly recorded as serious and sober history, and it leads directly and naturally into Genesis 12 and the rest of Genesis. Genesis in turn is the necessary foundation for all the rest of Scripture. If these first eleven chapters are not historical, then our entire Biblical foundation has been removed (1984, p. 116).

2. The Genesis narrative is to be accepted as literal history because this is the view adopted by Jesus Christ. As Whitcomb has said:

> ...It is the privilege of these men to dispense with an historical Adam if they so desire. But they do not at the same time have the privilege of claiming that Jesus Christ spoke the truth.

Adam and Jesus Christ stand or fall together, for Jesus said: "If ye believed Moses, ye would believe me. But if ye believe not his writings, how shall ye believe my words?" (John 5:46-47). Our Lord also insisted that "till heaven and earth pass away, one jot or one tittle shall in no wise pass from the law **(and this includes Genesis)** till all things be accomplished" (Matthew 5:18) [1972, pp. 110-111, emp. and parenthetical comment in orig.].

In Matthew 19, a discussion between Christ and the Pharisees is recorded, the topic of which was marriage, divorce, and remarriage. The passage makes it clear that the Pharisees' intent was to trick the Lord into contradicting the Law of Moses and thereby turn the people against Him, because most of the Israelites viewed Moses with great respect—and rightly so. On that occasion, however, the Lord did not fall prey to the Jewish leaders' trap because He understood their strategy. Instead, He pointedly asked those hypocrites: "Have ye not read [citing Genesis 1:27 —BT] that He who made them from the beginning made them male and female?" (Matthew 19:4). Concerning this discourse, Wayne Jackson observed:

Here Jesus plainly affirms that: (1) There was a **beginning**, (2) The first couple was **made**, (3) They were **male and female**. When Christ spoke of Adam and Eve being "made," He used the aorist Greek verb epoisesen, stressing the fact that this pair was made by **single acts** of creation. Had the Lord subscribed to the notion that the first humans evolved over vast ages of time, he would have employed the Greek imperfect tense, which is designed to emphasize **progressive** action at some time in the past. Thus, Christ actually verbally refuted the concept of evolutionary development. And certainly the Lord was in a position **to know** what took place in the beginning, for He was there (John 1:1), and was the active agent of creation (Colossians 1:16) [1974, pp. 26-27, emp. in orig.].

In the words of Henry Morris: "Denying the historical validity of the Creation account also undermines the authority of the New Testament and of Christ Himself!" (1966, p. 92). Whitcomb concluded: "If Genesis is not historically dependable, then Jesus is not a dependable guide to all truth, and we are without a Savior" (1972, p. 111).*

3. The Genesis narrative is to be accepted as literal and historical because inspired writers of the New Testament not only referred often to the narrative, but also made doctrinal arguments that depended upon the historical validity of the Genesis account.** Paul contended that woman was "of" (*ek*—a Greek preposition meaning "out of") man (1 Corinthians 11:8,12). He called Adam and Eve by name in 1 Timothy 2:13, and based his instructions to Christians for woman's work in the church on the actual **order** of creation. The apostle considered Adam as historical as Moses (Romans 5:14), and he clearly said that "the serpent deceived Eve by his craftiness" (2 Corinthians 11:3).

The creation itself is attributed to the word of God (Hebrews 11:3), and Peter referred to the emerging of the Earth as an event that actually occurred (2 Peter 3:5b). There was no question in Paul's mind about God's fiat creation (2 Corinthians 4:6). Likewise, in 1 Corinthians 11:7 the apostle stated that man had been made in the image of God, and he spoke specifically about man's

---

* Some writers, influenced by German rationalism, contend that in reality Jesus did not accept the historicity of Genesis; rather, He merely accommodated Himself to the ignorance of first-century Judaism. Such a charge not only is without foundation, but impugns the deity of Christ. H.S. Miller emphasized that Christ "was completely and eloquently silent concerning any error, contradiction, inaccuracy, myth, legend, or forgery in the Old Testament; strangely and criminally silent, if such existed. These either did or did not exist. If they did exist, He was either (1) ignorant of them, in which case He was not omniscient, hence not the unique Son of God, hence an impostor, hence a sinner, hence no Savior; or, He (2) did know of them and deliberately chose to be silent, to deceive the people, in which case He was a dishonest man, a deceiver, an impostor, a sinner, and no Savior" (as quoted in Jackson, 1974, p. 26).

** In his book, *The Genesis Record*, Henry Morris provides several appendices, one of which is titled "Quotations from or Allusions to Genesis in the New Testament" (1976, pp. 677-682). In Appendix #4, Dr. Morris lists some 200 specific references to Genesis from the New Testament—powerful testimony to the literal, historical nature of the Genesis narrative.

creation in Matthew 19:4 and Mark 10:6. Christ was called by Paul "the last Adam" (1 Corinthians 15:45). If the **first** Adam was a myth, then is the **last** (Jesus Christ) also a myth? Will theistic evolutionists actually be willing to go this far? Alan Hayward wrote:

> Worse still, if we treat the Fall of Adam as a piece of religious fiction we strike at the very heart of the Christian gospel. The liberal is forced to reinterpret Paul's teaching about salvation through Christ's Cross in this fashion:
>
> For as in [the fictitious] Adam all die, so also in the [real] Christ shall all be made alive.... Just as we have borne the image of the [fictitious] man of dust, we shall also bear the image of the [real] man of heaven (I Corinthians 15:22,49).
>
> If, because of one [fictitious] man's trespass, death reigned through that one [fictitious] man, much more will those who receive the abundance of grace and the [real] free gift of righteousness [truly] reign in life through the one [real] Jesus Christ (Romans 5:17).
>
> Such a blend of fact and fiction is a flimsy foundation on which to build a doctrine of eternal life. Observe how Paul weaves Adam's sin and Christ's righteous death together into the very fabric of salvation. Paul evidently regarded Adam and Christ as the two key characters in human history, each playing a vital role in the destiny of mankind. But if Paul was mistaken, and Adam's fall is actually little more than a touching tale for tiny tots, then why should we believe Paul when he tells us that Christ rose miraculously from the dead? And "if Christ has not been raised, your faith is futile," Paul warns us (I Corinthians 15:17) [1985, p. 191, bracketed items in orig.].

4. The Genesis narrative is to be accepted as literal and historical because any attempt to "mythologize" it represents an overt attack upon God's nature. Wayne Jackson has explored this point.

> The Bible teaches that the creation of the heavens, the earth, and the inhabitants thereof, was for the glorification of Almighty God. Any attempt, therefore, to nullify the doctrine of **creation** is in reality an assault upon **God Himself**. "The heavens declare the glory of God and the firmament show-

eth His handiwork" (Psalms 19:1). "Even everyone is called by My name, for I have created him for My glory. I have formed him, yea, I have made him" (Isaiah 43:7). "For in Him, and through Him, and to Him, are all things; to whom be glory forever!" (Romans 11:36) [n.d., p. 10, emp. in orig.].

5. The Genesis narrative is to be accepted as literal and historical because genuine science has not discredited, and from the very nature of the scientific method cannot discredit, the Genesis account of origins. George Howe has discussed this point.

> The topic of origins is usually treated as if it lay exclusively in the domain of science. Such classification is unfortunate and erroneous when the limitations of the scientific method are evaluated. Science is properly equipped to cope with problems of "how" here and now. For example, such matters as: "how chromosomes migrate in dividing cells," "how water ascends in the trunks of trees," and "how sugars move in phloem tissue" fall clearly in the sphere of science. Yet none of these sample problems has been thoroughly and absolutely settled. If scientific methods as yet cannot completely solve contemporary problems, how can these same methods be expected to yield absolute answers about origins? This does not belittle the amazing achievements of experimental science, but throws the limitations of the method into full focus (1964, p. 24).

Many theistic evolutionists have concluded that "science" has proven evolution true, and in turn has disproven the biblical account of creation. But their beginning premise is incorrect; science has not proven evolution true. Nor will it ever do so, for such a task falls far beyond the scope of the scientific method.

6. The Genesis narrative is to be accepted as literal and historical because:

> Denying the historical accuracy of the Bible in the account of creation leads to a doctrinal position known as **modernism**. If men evolved from the beast, the sin nature is an inherited animal characteristic and cannot be due to the fall of man through disobedience. This denies the need of a Redeemer, and thus the atonement of Christ is neglected or denied (Davidheiser, 1969, pp. 168-169, emp. in orig.).

Or, as Culp stated:

> One who doubts the Genesis account will not be the same
> man he once was, for his attitude toward Holy Scripture
> has been eroded by false teaching. Genesis is repeatedly re-
> ferred to in the New Testament, and it cannot be separated
> from the total Christian message (1975, pp. 160-161).

ARE THERE TWO (CONTRADICTORY) CREATION ACCOUNTS IN GENESIS?*

It is common for liberal critics of the Bible to assert that the book of Genesis contains two accounts of the creation of the Earth and mankind (the first in Genesis 1:1-2:3, and the second in Genesis 2:4-25). Allegedly, these two accounts reflect different authors, different time periods, etc. Further, critics charge that the narratives contradict each other in several particulars. As one author lamented: "It is evident that the Pentateuch cannot be the continuous work of a single author. This is shown by the existence of **two differing** accounts (doublets) of the same event: thus e.g. the story of the creation in Gen. 1 and 2:4ff." (Weiser, 1961, pp. 72-73, emp. and parenthetical item in orig.).

This peculiar, unorthodox view of Scripture is not the exclusive property of radically liberal theologians; it has made its presence felt in conservative circles as well. Some, for example, speak of the "two different creation accounts" (e.g., Buffaloe and Murray, 1981, p. 7) or the "two 'creation hymns'" (see Manis as quoted in Thompson, 1986, p. 16).

One of the foundational assumptions of this viewpoint (often referred to as "higher criticism") is that the Pentateuch (a grouping of the first five books of the Bible) was not authored by Moses. Supposedly, several ancient writers contributed to this collection. These

---

* I would like to thank my friend and colleague, Wayne Jackson, for permission to edit and reproduce portions of this material from *Reason & Revelation*, the monthly journal on Christian evidences that he and I formerly co-edited (and for which I currently serve as editor).

authors are referred to as J, E, P, and D. Some scholars subdivide them even further, e.g., J^1, J^2, etc. "J" stands for "Jehovah," since that name for God is prominent in certain sections. "E" signifies *Elohim*, another divine name allegedly identifying certain portions. "P" purports to be a "Priestly Code," and "D" identifies what is known as the "Deuteronomic" writer. The critics claim that all of these writings eventually were collected and combined by a "redactor" (editor). This theory, known as the Documentary Hypothesis, became popular in the nineteenth century when Jean Astruc, a French physician, claimed that he had isolated certain "source" authors in the Pentateuch. His views were expanded and popularized by others so that by the end of the century numerous biblical commentators had gravitated to this liberal concept. Though this approach is widely circulated today, it will not bear the weight of scholarly investigation.*

In the case of the "two creation accounts," Genesis 1 is said to be a "P" document (dating from the Babylonian or post-Babylonian captivity period), while Genesis 2 is a "J" narrative from the ninth century B.C. Basically, the arguments in support of this viewpoint are twofold. (1) It is claimed that the two creation stories show evidence of **different styles** of writing. (2) It is argued that the **accounts conflict** in that they reflect strangely divergent concepts of deity and a mismatched order of creation. I would like to examine these assertions.

Stylistic Variation

Professor Kenneth Kitchen of the University of Liverpool has suggested that "stylistic differences are meaningless" (1966, p. 118). Such differences may as much indicate a variance in the subject addressed as the suggestion of multiple authors. On the basis of archaeological evidence, Kitchen has shown that the "stylistic" the-

---

* For further discussion and refutation of the Documentary Hypothesis, see: Jackson, 1990a; McDowell, 1999.

ory simply is not credible. For example, a biographical inscription of Uni, an important Egyptian official who lived about 2400 B.C., reflects at least four different styles, yet no one denies the singularity of its authorship (1966, p. 125).

The plural authorship of the "creation accounts" is supposed to be indicated by the use of two names for deity in these sections. "God" (*Elohim*) is employed in Genesis 1, whereas "Jehovah" (Yahweh) is found in 2:4ff. In response it may be observed, first, that solid biblical research has shown the use of different appellations for deity to reflect possibly a **purposeful theological emphasis**. For example, *Elohim*, which suggests "strength," exalts God as the mighty Creator. Yahweh is the name that expresses the essential moral and spiritual nature of deity, particularly in terms of His relationship to the nation of Israel (see Stone, 1944, p. 17).

Second, the multiple employment of titles was common in the literature of antiquity as a device of literary variety. Archaeological discoveries have illustrated this point quite amply. Consider, as an example, Genesis 28:13 where the Lord spoke to Jacob and remarked: "I am Jehovah (Yahweh), the God (*Elohim*) of Abraham, the God (*Elohim*) of Isaac...." Would anyone argue for the multiple authorship of this single sentence upon the basis of the use of two Hebrew names for the Creator? Hardly. One scholar pointedly observed:

> To conclude that differences in style or vocabulary unmistakably indicate different authors is invalid for any body of literature. It is well known that a single author may vary his style and select vocabulary to fit the themes he is developing and the people he is addressing. It goes without saying that a young graduate student's love letter will vary significantly in vocabulary and style from his research paper (Davis, 1975, p. 23).

It must be concluded that arguments for "two creation accounts" in Genesis, based upon a subjective view of "style," are both speculative and unconvincing.

154

So-Called Contradictions

As I mentioned earlier, the alleged discrepancies between chapters 1 and 2 involve an imagined difference in the perception of God on the part of the hypothetical "authors," and the alleged contradictory order of events mentioned in the respective records.

First, it is supposed that in Genesis 1 the Creator is a transcendent Being, majestically and distantly bringing the creation into existence. In Genesis 2, however, He is characterized by naive anthropomorphisms (human terminology applied to deity) that imply an inferior status. For example, in Genesis 2 the writer says that Jehovah "formed," "breathed," "planted," etc. (vss. 7-8).

While it is true that such expressions are found in chapter 2, what many critics have failed to observe and acknowledge is that anthropomorphic terminology also is employed in Genesis 1:1-2:4 where God "called," "saw," "rested," etc. (1:8,12; 2:1). There is no validity whatsoever to this argument, and thus one should not be surprised that various scholars have labeled it "illusory" in nature (e.g., Kitchen, 1966, p. 118).

Second, as indicated above, some reversed language order, as seen in the two chapters, also is supposed to demonstrate conflicting creation accounts. The well-known theological liberal, E.A. Speiser, observed for example: "The first account starts out with the creation of 'heaven and earth' (1:1). The present narrative begins with the making of 'earth and heaven' (2:4b)." Speiser then went to great lengths to emphasize that in the first record heavenly activity was in focus, while in the latter account man became the center of interest. He then concluded: "This far-reaching divergence in basic philosophy would alone be sufficient to warn the reader that two separate sources appear to be involved, one heaven-centered and the other earth-centered" (1964, pp. 18-19).

This particular argument for a dual authorship of Genesis 1 and 2 is similarly unconvincing. Note Genesis 2:4. "These are the generations of the **heavens and the earth** when they were created, in the day that Jehovah God made **earth and heaven**." In this one verse there is contained the heaven/earth and earth/heaven motif. Does this mean that two people must have written this one sentence? Even the Bible's most liberal and outspoken critics do not so contend!

Third, the claim is made that in chapter 1 man is represented as having been made "in the image of God" (27), yet in chapter 2, he merely is "formed...of the dust of the ground" (7), thus suggesting a distinct contrast. The point of comparison, however, is too limited, hence unfair. As Professor John Sailhamer remarked:

> ...we should not overlook the fact that the topic of the "creation of man" in chapter 2 is not limited merely to v. 7. In fact, the topic of the creation of the man and the woman is the focus of the whole of chapter 2. What the author had stated as a simple fact in chapter 1 (man, male and female, was created in God's likeness) is explained and developed throughout the narrative of chapter 2. We cannot contrast the depiction of the creation of man in chapter 1 with only one verse in chapter 2; we must compare the whole of the chapter (1990, 2:40-41, parenthetical item in orig.).

Fourth, Genesis 1 and 2 are said to contradict each other in the relative creation-order of plants and man. In chapter 1, critics argue, plants were created on the third day of the initial week (vss. 11-12) and man was made on the sixth day (vss. 26ff.), whereas in chapter 2 the plants and herbs seem not to appear until after the formation of man (vss. 5ff.). But the problem exists only in the mind of the critic. There are possible ways by which to resolve the alleged difficulty.

Some have suggested that in Genesis 1 the original **creation** of the botanical world is in view, while in Genesis 2 the emphasis is upon the fact that plant **reproduction** had not commenced, since as yet there was neither sufficient moisture nor a cultivator of the ground—factors that later were remedied in verses 6-7 (see Jacobus, 1864, 1:96).

Others agree that entirely different matters are in view in these respective accounts. In Genesis 1:11-12 vegetation in general is under consideration, but in Genesis 2:5ff. the writer is discussing the specific sort of vegetation that requires human cultivation. Browne observed:

> The words rendered **plant, field**, and **grew**, never occur in the first chapter; they are terms expressive of the produce of labour and cultivation; so that the historian evidently means that no cultivated land and no vegetables fit for the use of man were yet in existence on the earth (1981, 1:39, emp. in orig.).

Another view is that Genesis 2:5 does not refer to the condition of the Earth at large; rather, the writer simply is discussing the preparation of the beautiful garden in which man was to live (Young, 1964, p. 61). In any event, the point needs to be stressed that whenever there is the **possibility of legitimate reconciliation** between passages that **superficially appear to conflict**, no contradiction can be charged.*

Fifth, it is argued that Genesis 1 represents animals as existing before man (24-26), yet Genesis 2 has Adam created before the animals are formed (19). The text of Genesis 2:19 merely suggests that the animals were formed before being brought to man; it says nothing about the relative origins of man and beast in terms of specific chronology. Critics are reading something into the text that simply is not there. William Green pointed out that when noted scholar Franz Delitzsch (1813-1890), an early advocate of the Documentary Hypothesis, first authored his famous commentary on the book of Genesis, he employed this argument as proof of a discrepancy between Genesis 1 and 2. However, in the last edition of his work, after he had matured and his knowledge had increased, he repudiated this quibble and argued for the harmony of 2:19 with chapter 1 (Green, 1979, p. 26).

---

* For two excellent discussions of principles to be used when dealing with both biblical difficulties and alleged contradictions, see: Jackson (1983, 3:25-28); Jackson and Bromling (n.d.).

The Real Explanation

Are there differences in the narratives of Genesis 1 and 2? Yes, there are. But mere differences do not necessarily imply contradictions, much less multiple authorship. The real question is this: Is there a **purpose** to these variations? Yes, there is. Furthermore, numerous factors militate against the notion that Genesis 1 and 2 are independent, contradictory accounts of the creation.

First, careful analysis reveals that there is deliberate purpose in the individuality of these two sections of Scripture. In Genesis 1, there is a broad outline of the events of the creation week, which reaches its climax with the origin of mankind in the very image of God. In Genesis 2, there is the special emphasis upon man, the divine preparation of his home, the formation of a suitable mate, etc. Edward J. Young has provided a good statement of this matter.

> There are different emphases in the two chapters...but the reason for these is obvious. Chapter 1 continues the narrative of creation until the climax, namely, man made in the image and likeness of God. To prepare the way for the account of the fall, chapter 2 gives certain added details about man's original condition, which would have been incongruous and out of place in the grand, declarative march of chapter 1 (1960, p. 53).

This type of procedure was common in the literary methodology of antiquity. Gleason Archer has observed that the

> technique of recapitulation was widely practiced in ancient Semitic literature. The author would first introduce his account with a short statement summarizing the whole transaction, and then he would follow it up with a more detailed and circumstantial account when dealing with matters of special importance (1964, p. 118).

These respective sections have a different literary motif. Genesis 1 is **chronological**, revealing the sequential events of the creation week, whereas Genesis 2 is **topical**, with special concern for man and his environment. [This procedure is not unknown elsewhere in biblical literature. Matthew's account of the ministry of Christ is more topical, while Mark's record is more chronological.]

Second, there is clear evidence that Genesis 2 never was an independent creation account. There are simply too many crucial elements missing for that to have been the case. For instance, there is no mention in Genesis 2 of the creation of the Earth, Sun, Moon, stars, etc. Nor is there any reference to the oceans or fish. Archer has noted that there is not an origins record in the entire literature collection of the ancient Near East that omits discussing the creation of the Sun, Moon, seas, etc. (1982, p. 69). Obviously, Genesis 2 is a sequel to chapter 1. The latter presupposes the former, and is built upon it.

Even Howard Johnston, while sympathetic to the Documentary Hypothesis, was forced to concede:

> The initial chapter [Genesis 1] gives a general account of the creation. The second chapter is generally declared by critics to be a second account of the creation, but, considered in the light of the general plan, that is not an accurate statement. Evidently the purpose of this chapter is to show that out of all the creation we have especially to do with man. Therefore only so much of the general account is repeated as is involved in a more detailed statement concerning the creation of man. There is a marked difference of style in the two accounts, but the record is consistent with the plan to narrow down the story to man (1902, p. 90).

The following summary statement by Kitchen is worthy of notice.

> It is often claimed that Genesis 1 and 2 contain two different creation-narratives. In point of fact, however, the strictly **complementary** nature of the "two" accounts is plain enough: Genesis 1 mentions the creation of man as the last of a series, and without any details, whereas in Genesis 2 man is the centre of interest and more specific details are given about him and his setting. There is no incompatible duplication here at all. Failure to recognize the complementary nature of the subject-distinction between a skeleton outline of **all** creation on the one hand, and the concentration in detail on man and his immediate environment on the other, borders on obscurantism (1966, pp. 116-117, emp. in orig.).

One final, yet forceful, point needs to be made. In Matthew 19: 4-5, Jesus combined quotations from Genesis 1 and Genesis 2. He declared: "He who made them from the beginning made them male and female [Genesis 1:26], and said, 'For this cause shall a man leave his father and mother, and shall cleave to his wife; and the two shall become one flesh' [2:24]." If the liberal viewpoint is true, how very strange that Christ gave not the slightest hint that the two accounts involved a multiple authorship and contradictory material! Obviously, the Son of God did not endorse "higher criticism" with its esteemed Documentary Hypothesis.

When the texts of Genesis 1 and 2 considered carefully, one thing is clear: An objective evaluation reveals neither discrepancies nor dual authorship. Students of the Bible should not be disturbed by the fanciful, plentiful, and ever-changing theories of liberal critics. The Word of God was not written merely for the benefit of "scholars," but for the common person as well. The Scriptures assume that the average man or woman is able to understand the message and to know that the source is divine.

For many Bible believers today, the rebuke offered by the Lord to the two on the road to Emmaus is applicable: "O fools and slow of heart to believe all that the prophets have spoken" (Luke 24:25). Jesus accused some of His day of erring because "ye know not the Scriptures, nor the power of God" (Mark 12:24). Thomas Whitelaw summarized the issue well.

> If we are to listen to many expositors of no mean authority, we must believe that what seems so clearly defined in Genesis—as if very great pains had been taken that there should be no possibility of mistake—is not the meaning of the text at all.... A person who is not a Hebrew scholar can only stand aside and admire the marvelous flexibility of a language which admits of such diverse interpretations (n.d., 1:4).

If we are unwilling to accept Genesis 1-11 as historical, how, then, will we be able to accept: (a) **any** biblical concept of man's origin; (b) the unifying concept of both Old and New Testaments (i.e., the need for a coming Redeemer, which is based on information found in Genesis 3); (c) God's personally designed plan of salvation; (d) the Sonship of Christ (since Jesus so often testified to the accuracy of the Genesis account); (e) the truthfulness of the Old and New Testament writers; and (f) the overall authority of the Scriptures as the inspired Word of God?

Chapter 7

The Bible and the Age of the Earth—Time, Evolution, and Biblical Chronology

In the controversy over creation and evolution, it is a rare event indeed to find something on which those in both camps agree wholeheartedly. Generally speaking, the two world views are light-years apart from start to finish. There is one thing, however on which both creationists and evolutionists **do** agree: Evolution is impossible if the Earth is young (with an age measured in thousands, not billions, of years). R.L. Wysong addressed this point in his book, *The Creation-Evolution Controversy.*

> Both evolutionists and creationists believe evolution is an impossibility if the universe is only a few thousand years old. There probably is no statement that could be made on the topic of origins which would meet with so much agreement from both sides. Setting aside the question of whether vast time is competent to propel evolution, we must query if vast time is indeed available (1976, p. 144).

It may be somewhat ironic that so much discussion has resulted from something on which both sides seemingly agree, but it should not be at all surprising. Apart from the most basic issue of the controversy itself—i.e., whether creation or evolution is the correct view of origins—the single most serious area of conflict between those who accept the biblical account of creation and those who accept the theory of organic evolution (in whole or in part) is the chronological framework of history—viz., the age of the Earth. And, of course, this subject is of immense interest not only to those who promulgate atheistic evolution, but to those who are sympathetic with certain portions of that theory as well. While a young Earth/Universe presents no problem at all for creationists who accept the biblical account of origins at face value, it is the death knell to every variety of the evolutionary scenario.

A simple, straightforward reading of the biblical record indicates that the Cosmos was created in six days only a few thousand years ago. Standing in stern opposition to that view is the suggestion of atheistic evolutionists, theistic evolutionists, progressive creationists, and so-called "old-Earth creationists" that the current age of the Universe can be set at roughly 8-12 billion years, and that the Earth itself is almost 5 billion years old. Further complicating matters is the fact that the biblical record plainly indicates that living things were placed on the newly created Earth even before the end of the six-day creative process (e.g., plant life came on day three). The evolutionary scenario, however, postulates that primitive life evolved from nonliving chemicals roughly 3.5-4.0 billion years ago, and that all other life forms gradually developed during the alleged "geologic ages" (with man arriving on the scene, in one form or another, approximately 1-2 million years ago).

Even to a casual observer, it is apparent that the time difference involved in the two models of origins is significant. Much of the controversy today between creationists, atheistic evolutionists, theistic evolutionists, progressive creationists, and old-Earth creationists centers on the age of the Earth. The magnitude of the controversy is multiplied by three factors. First, atheistic evolution itself is apodictically impossible to defend if the Earth is young. Second, the concepts mentioned above that are its "theistic cousins" likewise are utterly impossible to defend if the Bible is correct in its straightforward teachings and obvious implications about the age of the Earth. Third, there is no possible compromise that will permit the old-Earth/young-Earth scenarios to coexist; the gulf separating the biblical and evolutionary views in this particular area simply is too large. As Henry Morris correctly observed:

> Thus the Biblical chronology is about a million times shorter than the evolutionary chronology. A million-fold mistake is no small matter, and Biblical scholars surely need to give primary attention to resolving this tremendous discrepancy right at the very foundation of our entire Biblical cosmology. This is not a peripheral issue that can be dismissed with some exegetical twist, but is central to the very integrity of scriptural theology (1984, p. 115).

In the earlier quote from Dr. Wysong, it was suggested that we must "query if vast time is indeed available." That is my intention here. Indeed, a million-fold mistake is no small matter. Exactly how old is the Earth according to God's Word?

THE IMPORTANCE OF TIME TO EVOLUTIONISTS AND THOSE SYMPATHETIC TO THEM

There is no doubt about the critical nature of time in the evolutionary scenario. Quotations to this effect from the available literature could be multiplied many times over. For example, in his award-winning (and oft'-reproduced) article in *Scientific American* a number of years ago, Nobel laureate George Wald of Harvard University minced no words when he wrote:

> To make an organism demands the right substance in the right proportions and in the right arrangement. We do not think that anything more is needed—but that is problem enough.... One has only to contemplate the magnitude of this task to concede that the spontaneous generation of living organisms is impossible. Yet here we are—as a result, I believe, of spontaneous generation....

In such a problem as the spontaneous generation of life, we have no way of assessing probabilities beforehand, or even of deciding what we mean by trial. The origin of a living organism is undoubtedly a step-wise phenomenon, each step with its own probability and its own conditions of trial. Of one thing we can be sure, however: whatever constitutes a trial, more such trials occur the longer the interval of time.

The important point is that since the origin of life belongs in the category of "at-least-once" phenomena, time is on its side. However improbable we regard this event, or any of the steps it involves, **given enough time**, it will almost certainly happen at least once. And for life as we know it, with its capability for growth and reproduction, once may be enough. **Time is in fact the hero of the plot**. The time with which we have to deal here is of the order of two billion years. What we regard as impossible on the basis of human experience is meaningless here. Given so much time, the "impossible" becomes possible, the possible becomes probable, and the probable virtually certain. One has only to wait; **time itself performs the miracles** (1979, pp. 290,291,293-294, emp. added).

Other well-known evolutionary scientists have echoed the same sentiments. Harold Blum, writing in *Time's Arrow and Evolution*, remarked: "The origin of life can be viewed properly only in the perspective of an almost inconceivable extent of time" (1968, p. 151). Leo Koch, in an article he authored for *Scientific Monthly*, commented that, given enough time, "...the highly improbable occurs regularly, and indeed is inevitable" (1957, p. 250). Keosian went on to observe: "The mechanists were not discouraged by the enormous span of time required for this chance event. They point out that, given enough time, the most improbable event becomes a statistical certainty" (1968, p. 10).

DOES TIME ITSELF "PERFORM MIRACLES"?

It is ironic that time—which evolution needs as its friend—has become its worst enemy. Why is this the case? There are two reasons. First, time itself—contrary to Dr. Wald's wishful thinking—does not "perform miracles" and, in fact, is quite impotent. Second, time works **against** ordered systems, in keeping with the Second Law of Thermodynamics. These two points need to be examined.

A.I. Oparin, the Russian evolutionist credited with inventing the phrase, "origin of life," and one of the first researchers in this area, once stated that while there is much speculation on the origin of life as a result of vast amounts of time, the actual documentation (what he called "quantitative arguments") is conspicuously missing.

> It is sometimes argued in speculative papers on the origin of life that highly improbable events (such as the spontaneous formation of a molecule of DNA and a molecule of DNA-polymerase in the same region of space and at the same time) become virtually inevitable over the vast stretches of geological time. No serious quantitative arguments, however, are given in support of such conclusions (1961, p. 31, parenthetical comment in orig.).

While Oparin's comments were made as long ago as 1961, the same assessment prevails today. The origin of life, viewed from a purely mechanistic standpoint, remains as much a mystery as it was in Dr. Oparin's time—and for good reason. The simple fact is that, in nature, **time works against the spontaneous generation of living organisms**. Dr. Wald addressed this point, and, in fact, called it "the most stubborn problem that confronts us," when he wrote:

> In the vast majority of processes in which we are interested the point of equilibrium lies far over toward the side of dissolution. That is to say, spontaneous **dissolution** is much more probable, and hence proceeds much more rapidly, than spontaneous **synthesis**.... The situation we must face is that of patient Penelope waiting for Odysseus, yet much worse; each night she undid the weaving of the preceding day, but here a night could readily undo the work of a year or a century (1955, p. 17, emp. added).

In nature, things don't "automatically" go toward self-organization. In fact, Wald admitted, left to themselves, in nature they go toward **spontaneous dissolution**, which is the process not of assembling, but of degrading. Wald even went so far as to complain that what "nature" could have taken a year, or a century, to accomplish (if ever) could be undone in an instant. For every step forward, there are a dozen (or a hundred, or a thousand) backwards. And the addition of more time merely makes the problem worse.

There are other factors to be considered as well, however. Whitcomb has elucidated one of them.

> Time is the deadliest enemy of the theory of evolution. Why? Because according to the second law of thermodynamics and the entropy principle, any ordered system through the passing of time will disintegrate and become more and more disordered. High level energy will dissipate into low level energy, so that its force and power for useful work can never be regained. Take, for example, the plight of a young man trying to lift himself up into the air by his shoestrings. How desperately wrong would be the challenge that an evolutionary scientist would give to this young man—that is, to keep on trying and not give up, because given enough time he could make it! Of course, this illustration is silly, but the principle remains; any effort to contradict basic laws of the universe can only be frustrated by the addition of time. The young man after a period of time would lose what energy he had and collapse to the floor; given a hundred and fifty years, all of his efforts would cease by the inexorable experience of death, and nothing would remain as an evidence of his experiment but dry bones and dust. This is the inevitable effect of time upon any ordered system in the universe as understood in this world today (1973a, 2:61-62).

Wysong has written in agreement.

> Similarly, it is conceivable that wind might blow a pile of toothpicks dumped from a picnic table into an arrangement resembling a model airplane. Given enough time, it could happen. But if that freak event does happen, would it remain if still subject to time and gale winds? Would it ever complexify? Isn't time not only the creator, but more efficiently the enemy of the freak event? Will time not surely destroy the order fortuitously created? The creationist asks: "How then can time be actually cited as the very cause of the almost infinite complexity of life?..."

> The creationist argues that time is only a measure of natural decay. Time does not complexify, it does not originate or build up anything without a predesigned "motor," rather, it dissipates, degenerates, melts, dissolves and removes available energy (1976, pp. 139,141,142).

Thus, time—which the evolutionist took to be his best friend—has become his worst enemy.

> A billion years with no creative power equals less than nothing. That is the formula for the failure of the god of evolution. But the formula for creationism is this: infinite power with almost no duration of time equals a fantastic creation. In other words, the magnitude and glory and complexity of creation is not a function of time, but of the power of God, who spoke it into existence by His Word. God's Word tells us that in six days He created the heavens, the Earth, the seas, and all that in them is (Whitcomb, 1973a, 2:65).

This expresses the creationist's viewpoint perfectly. Time cannot, and does not, "perform miracles." That is a process best left to the Creator.

THE AGE OF THE EARTH—"WAIT AND SEE"

As I begin this investigation into the age of the Earth, I first would like to define the scope of the present inquiry. It is not my intention here to examine and refute the scientific evidences that allegedly establish an ancient Earth. There already are a number of books available that provide such information (see for example: Henry Morris, 1974a,1989; Wysong; 1976, Ackerman, 1986; Morris and Parker, 1987; Kautz, 1988; Jackson, 1989; John Morris, 1994; Woodmorappe, 1999). The reader interested in a discussion of the scientific aspects of this controversy is referred to these works, or others like them.

Obviously, then, I am not writing with the atheistic evolutionist in mind. I am well aware that my arguments would carry no weight whatsoever with the person who falls into that category. Rather, this discussion is intended for those who: (a) believe in the God of the Bible; (b) claim to accept the Bible as His inspired, authoritative Word; and (c) are convinced that what God has said can be understood. For such a person, the Bible is the final authority on any subject that it addresses. Edward J. Young expressed this point when he wrote:

> It is of course true that the Bible is not a textbook of science, but all too often, it would seem, this fact is made a pretext for treating lightly the content of Genesis one. Inasmuch as the Bible is the Word of God, whenever it speaks on any subject, whatever that subject may be, it is accurate in what it says (1964, p. 43).

The question then becomes: "**Does** the Bible speak on the subject of the age of the Earth?" Yes, it does. But before we delve into what it says, there are two popular, prevailing attitudes that need to be discussed.

First, I acknowledge that some religionists regard this as a question that simply cannot be answered at present. We are urged to "withhold judgment," "wait and see," or "reserve judgment."

Jack Wood Sears, former chairman of the biology department at Harding University, wrote for example:

> When conflicts do occur, the part of wisdom is to withhold judgment until the facts are all in. For example, there is difficulty with the age of life on the earth. Science, as I indicated earlier, has seemed to indicate that the life has been here much longer than we have generally interpreted the Bible to indicate. However, scientific determination of the ages of geological strata is not absolute and is subject to much difficulty and uncertainty. The Bible, as we have shown, does not date creation, and **the intimations it seems to present** may not be properly understood. Since I hold science to be a valid approach to reality, and since I have concluded upon much and sufficient evidence, that the Bible is inspired and therefore true, the only rational recourse, it seems to me, is to withhold judgment about a seeming contradiction. **Wait and see** (1969, p. 97, emp. added).

Four years later, J. Frank Cassel wrote in a similar vein:

> The thoughtful person respects present knowledge in both
> areas (science and Biblical research) and keeps searching
> for new information and insight. In the meantime he must **re-
> serve judgment**, saying simply "I don't know where the
> proper synthesis lies." The tension remains as the search con-
> tinues (1973, pp. 251-252, emp. added, parenthetical item
> in orig.).

While at first glance such suggestions may appear to be praise-
worthy and laudable, I would like to suggest that they are nothing
but a carefully planned ruse. Authors of such sentiments no doubt
want **others** to adhere to their advice, but they themselves have
absolutely no intention of doing so.

Cassel, for example, has written often about the accuracy of the
so-called geologic timetable, and is a well-known apologist for the
old-Earth scenario. Further, in November of 1983 I personally debated Dr. Sears on the topic of the age of the Earth.* I confidently
affirmed the proposition that the Bible does **not** allow for an ancient Earth; Dr. Sears affirmed the proposition that it **does**. The debate occurred some 14 years **after** Dr. Sears penned his "wait and
see" statement. Had he discovered additional information during
those years that no longer made it necessary to wait and see? Apparently not, since during the debate he told the audience that he was
"still waiting" (an exact quote from the transcript) for information
that would allow him to make a decision regarding the age of the
Earth. If he were still waiting, why, then, would he be willing to engage in a public debate to defend the idea that the Bible allows for an
ancient Earth? Where is the consistency in such a position?

In reality, what these writers mean when they claim that "we"
should "wait and see," or that "we" should "reserve judgment," is that
those who believe in a young Earth should wait and see or reserve judgment. In the meantime, they will continue to advocate publicly their position that an ancient Earth is wholly consistent with
the biblical record.   •

---

* The debate is available in printed, audio, and video formats. The printed manuscripts
of the debate are in McClish (1983), pp. 405-434. Audio and video tapes are available from the offices of Apologetics Press.

Second, there are some in the religious community who suggest that the Bible is conspicuously silent on the age of the Earth. It is not uncommon to hear statements suggesting that since the Bible does not address this matter, a person is free to believe whatever he or she wishes in this regard. Typical of such a mind-set are the following statements by Donald England and John Clayton.

> However, nowhere does a Biblical writer give us an age for earth or an age for life on earth.... Inasmuch as Scripture does not state how old the earth is or how long life has existed on earth, one is free to accept, if he wishes, the conclusions of science (England, 1983, pp. 155-156).

> Genesis 1:1 is an undated verse. No time element is given and no details of what the Earth looked like are included. It could have taken place in no time at all, or God may have used eons of time to accomplish his objectives (Clayton, 1976b, pp. 147-148).

This, of course, is but another ruse. Beware when a writer or speaker suggests that the Bible is "silent" on the topic of the age of the Earth, or that a person is free to accept the varied "conclusions of science." What those who make such statements **really** mean is that **they** are free to accept the conclusions, not of science, but of uniformitarian geology, and in so doing to defend the same old-Earth position as their evolutionist colleagues. Both England and Clayton, for example, are on record as defending an ancient Earth (see: England, 1972, pp. 103-106; Clayton as documented in Jackson and Thompson, 1992, pp. 99-110).

CHRONOLOGY AND THE BIBLE

The truth of the matter is that the Bible, as a book grounded in history, is filled with chronological data that may be used to establish a relative age for the Earth. It is not "silent" on this topic, and thus there is no need to "wait and see" or to "reserve judgment." Professor Edwin Thiele, the man who unlocked much of the mystery of Old Testament chronology, declared:

> We know that God regards chronology as important, for
> He has put so much of it into His Word. We find chronology
> not only in the historical books of the Bible, but also in the
> prophetic books, in the Gospels, and in the writings of Paul
> (1977, p. 7).

The Bible, for example, provides impressive chronological data from Adam to Solomon. Combining information from the Assyrian Eponym Lists and the Black Obelisk, the death of Ahab has been determined to be 853-852 B.C. (Packer, et al., 1980, p. 48), and therefore the reign of Solomon (some forty years, 1 Kings 11:42) can be dated at 971-931 B.C. (Merrill, 1978, p. 97; Packer, et al., 1980, p. 50; Brantley, 1993a, 13:83). According to 1 Kings 6:1, 480 years before Solomon's fourth year of reign (967-966 B.C.), Moses brought the Israelites out of Egypt. The date of the Exodus is 1446/1445 B.C. (Unger, 1973, pp. 140-152; Archer, 1970, pp. 212-222; Packer, et al., 1980, p. 51; Jackson, 1981, 1:38; 1990b, 10:17).

To this date is added the years of sojourn in Egypt (430 years, Exodus 12:40),* thereby producing the date of 1876 B.C. as the year Jacob went to Egypt (Packer, et al., 1980, p. 50). Interestingly, the Bible records Pharaoh's query of Jacob's age (and Jacob's answer —130 years) in Genesis 47:9. This would make the year of Jacob's birth 2006 B.C. (Genesis 25:26). Abraham was 100 years old when

---

* The length of the Israelites' sojourn in Egypt is a matter of some controversy. There are two major views. The first view suggests that the Israelites **actually lived in Egypt** for 430 years [see, for example: Archer (1994), pp. 205-212; Keil and Delitzsch (1974), 2:29; Kitchen, (1966), pp. 53-56; and Unger 1954), pp. 106,150]. The second view suggests that the time period of "the sojourning of the children of Israel, who dwelt in Egypt 430 years" (Exodus 12:40-41; cf. Galatians 3:17) **begins with the call of Abraham** and God's promise to him (Genesis 12:1-3) **and ends with the Exodus** [see, for example: Barnes (n.d., p. 121; Clarke (n.d.), 1:358; Henry (n.d.), 1:322; Mauro (n.d.), pp. 31-32; Rohl (1995), pp. 329- 332; and Thiele (1963), pp. 166-167]. Placing the time that the Israelites **actually lived in Egypt** as 215 years rather than 430 years has no impact on the point I am making in this section regarding biblical chronology, since it actually would **decrease** the number of years in the chronology rather than **increase** it, which is why I intentionally chose to employ the larger of the two figures (430 years) in the above discussion. Such a usage on my part avoids the critics' potential charge of "artificially reducing" the chronology via use of the 215-year figure.

he begat Isaac, giving the date of 2166 B.C. for Abraham's birth
(Genesis 21:5; Packer, et al., 1980, p. 54). The chronology from
Abraham to Adam is recorded very carefully in two separate genealogical tables—Genesis 5 and 11. According to Genesis 12:4,
Abraham was 75 when he left Haran, presumably after Terah died
at 205 years; thus, Abraham was born when Terah was 130 years
old, albeit he is mentioned first by importance when Terah started
having sons at the age of 70 (Genesis 11:27; 12:4; Acts 7:4; see Beechick, 1997, p. 100, note #1).

Having established the birth date of Abraham at 2166 B.C. (Archer, 1970, pp. 203-204), it is possible to work from the time of
Adam's creation to Abraham in order to discern the chronology of
"the beginning." The time from the creation of Adam to Seth was
130 years (Genesis 5:3), the time from Adam to Noah was 1056
years (Packer, et al., 1980, pp. 56-57), and the time from Noah's
birth to the Flood was 600 years (Genesis 7:6), or 1656 A.A. (After Adam). It appears that Shem was about 100 years old at the
time of the Flood (Genesis 5:32; 11:10), and begat Arphaxad two
years after the Flood (the Earth was not dry for more than a year;
cf. Genesis 7:11 with 8:14; see also Genesis 11:10 and Beechick,
1997, p. 100, note #2) in approximately 1659 A.A.

Arphaxad begat Salah in his 35th year; however, Luke 3:36 com-
plements the chronological table of Genesis 11 with the insertion of
Cainan between Arphaxad and Salah, which indicates that likely
Arphaxad was the father of Cainan. Proceeding forward, one ob-
serves that Terah was born in 1879 A.A. and bore Abraham 130
years later (in 2009 A.A.). Simple arithmetic then—2166 B.C. added to 2009 A.A.—would place the date of the Creation at approximately 4175 B.C. Thus, the Flood would have occurred around
2519 B.C.

Numerous objections have been leveled at the literal and consecutive chronological interpretation of Scripture. For example,
some have suggested that the tables of Genesis 5 and 11 are neither literal nor consecutive. Yet five of the patriarchs clearly were

the **literal** fathers of their respective sons: Adam named Seth (Genesis 4:25), Seth named Enos (4:26), Lamech named Noah (5:29), Noah's literal, consecutive sons were Shem, Ham, and Japheth (cf. 5:32 with 9:18), and Terah fathered Abraham directly (11:27, 31).

Jude's record in the New Testament counts Enoch as "the seventh from Adam" (1:14), thereby acknowledging the genealogical tables as both literal and consecutive. Moreover, how better could Moses have expressed a literal and consecutive genealogy than by using the terms "lived...and begat...begat...after he begat...all the days...and he died"? Without question, Moses noted that the first three individuals (Adam, Seth, and Enos) were consecutive, and Jude stated by inspiration that the first seven (to Enoch) were consecutive. Enoch's son, Methuselah, died the year of the Flood, and so by three simple steps the chronology of Adam to Noah can be proven to be both literal and consecutive, producing a trustworthy biblical chronology/genealogy.

There also have been those who have objected to the suggestion that God actually would be concerned with providing accurate, trustworthy information on the age of the Earth and humanity in the first place. Their point is that the Bible was intended to provide spiritual, not chronological, insight. But the numerous chronological tables permeating the Bible prove that theirs is a baseless objection. God, it seems, **was very concerned** about giving man exact chronological data and, in fact, was so concerned that He provided a precise knowledge of the period back to Abraham, plus two tables—with ages—from Abraham to Adam. The ancient Jewish historians (e.g., 1 Chronicles 1:1-27) and the New Testament writers (e.g., Luke 3:34-48) understood the tables of Genesis 5 and 11 to be literal and consecutive. The Bible explains quite explicitly that God created the Sun and Moon as timekeepers (Genesis 1:16) for Adam and his descendants (notice how Noah logged the beginning and the ending of the Flood using these timekeepers, Genesis 7:11; 8:14).

Still others have suggested that the two tables somehow are symbolic. But the use (or even repetitive use) of a "unique" number does not necessitate a symbolical interpretation. Special numbers (such as 7,10,12,40, etc.) employed in Scripture may be understood as literal despite the frequency of their use. Are there not three **literal** members of the Godhead? Did not Sceva have seven **literal** sons? Were there not ten **literal** commandments? Were there not twelve **literal** apostles? Was Christ's fast in the wilderness not forty **literal** days? Moreover, those who study history routinely recognize that it abounds with numerical "coincidences." To say that the tables of Genesis 5 and 11 are "symbolic" of long periods of time flies in the face of the remainder of the biblical record.

Those who believe that the Bible is **unconcerned** with chronology would do well to spend time studying the lineages of the Hebrew kings in the Old Testament. James Jordan explained why.

> Chronology **is** of concern to the writers of the Bible. From this perspective we should be **surprised** if the Bible did not include chronological data regarding the period from Creation to Abraham, especially since such data can now be obtained from no other source. That chronology is of concern to the Bible (and to its Author) can also be seen from the often difficult and confusing chronology of the Kings of Israel. Thus, we find that it is the intention of the Bible to provide us with chronology from Abraham to the Exile. Some of that chronology is given in summary statements...but some is also given interspersed in the histories of the Kings. Is it therefore surprising or unreasonable that some should be given along with genealogies as well? (1979/1980, 2:21, emp. and parenthetical item in orig.).

While it is true that genealogies (and chronologies) serve various functions in Scripture, one of their main purposes is to show the historical connection of great men to the unfolding of Jehovah's redemptive plan. These lists, therefore, are a link from the earliest days of humanity to the completion of God's salvation system. **In order to have any evidential value, they must be substantially complete.**

For example, the inspired writer of Hebrews, in contending for the heavenly nature of Christ's priesthood, argued that the Savior could not have functioned as a priest while living upon the Earth since God had in place a **levitical** priesthood to accomplish that need (Hebrews 8:4). Jesus did not qualify for the levitical priesthood because "it is **evident** that our Lord hath sprung out of **Judah**" (Hebrews 7:14, emp. added). How could it have been "evident" that Jesus Christ was from the tribe of Judah—**unless there were accurate genealogical records by which such a statement could be verified**? The writer of Hebrews based his argument on the fact that the various readers of his epistle would not be able to dispute the ancestry of Christ due to the reliable nature of the Jewish documentation available—i.e., the genealogies.

It has been argued that secular history is considerably older than 4000 B.C. But ponder this. When the studies of various Egyptologists are examined, no two provide the same dates for the Old Kingdom (III-VI Dynasties). Breasted (1912) gave the date as 2980-2475 B.C., Baikie (1929) dated the period as being 3190-2631 B.C., White (1970) suggested 2778-2300 B.C., Aling (1981) dated it at 2800-2200 B.C., and Rohl (1995) offered 2650-2152 B.C. With such variability in the last "sure" period of Egypt's history, how can dogmatism prevail for the **pre**dynastic period? Scientists and historians influence Christendom with their "established limits" of history. And theologians influence Christianity with evolution-based bias as well. For instance, Gleason Archer has stated:

> The problems attending this method of computation are compounded by the quite conclusive archaeological evidence that Egyptian Dynasty I went back to 3100 B.C., with a long period of divided kingdoms in the Nile valley before that. These could hardly have arisen until long after the Flood had occurred and the human race had multiplied considerably (cf. Genesis 10). It therefore seems necessary to interpret the figures of Genesis 5 and 11 differently, especially in view of the gaps in other biblical genealogical tables (1979, 1:361).

Obviously Archer is completely willing to override Scripture with the "scientific" message of archaeology. This mind-set—which requires the Bible to submit to science (geology, paleontology, archaeology, anthropology, etc.)—undermines the authority of the Word of God. In one prominent example from a few years back, the then-editor of *Christianity Today* stated:

> But one fact is clear: the genealogies of Genesis will not permit us to set any exact limit on the age of man. Of that we must remain ignorant **unless the sciences of geology and historical anthropology give us data from which we may draw tentative scientific conclusions** (Kantzer, 1982, p. 25, emp. added).

The fact of the matter is that **both** scientists **and** theologians should be concerned with fitting the scientific data to the truth—God's Word—not with molding God's Word to fit current scientific theories (which, in a few short years may change—e.g., in Charles Darwin's day, the Earth had been "proven" scientifically to be 20 million years old, while today it has been "proven" scientifically to be 4.6 billion years old).

Furthermore, archaeologists often use speculative (and inaccurate) techniques such as radiocarbon dating, dendrochronology (tree-ring analysis), and pottery dating schemes. Yet each of these methods is beset with serious flaws, not the least of which are the basic assumptions upon which they are constructed. In two timely, well-researched articles ("Dating in Archaeology: Radiocarbon & Tree-Ring Dating," and "Dating in Archaeology: Challenges to Biblical Credibility"), Trevor Major (1993, 13:74-77) and Garry Brantley (1993a, 13:81-85) explained the workings of these various methods and exposed the faulty assumptions upon which each is based. After listing and discussing five important problem areas associated with carbon-14 dating, and after discussing the problems associated with obtaining accurate tree-ring growth rates, Major wrote:

> Radiocarbon dating assumes that the carbon-12/carbon-14 ratio has stayed the same for at least the last hundred thousand years or so. However, the difference between production and decay rates, and the systematic discrepancy between radiocarbon and tree-ring dates, refute this assumption.... Simi-

larly, we should not accept the claims for dendrochronology at face value. Bristlecones may add more than one growth ring per year, and the "art" of cross dating living and dead trees may be a considerable source of error. Both radiocarbon dating and dendrochronology face technical problems, and are loaded with old Earth ideas. They assume that nature works today the same as it has worked for millions of years, yet the facts do not support this contention. **Neither method should give us cause to abandon the facts of biblical history** (1993, 13:77, emp. added).

In his article, Brantley addressed the problems associated with subjectivism in archaeological chronology in general, and pottery dating in particular. He then drew the following conclusions:

...we must recognize that archaeological evidence is fragmentary and, therefore, greatly limited. Despite the amount of potsherds, bones, ornaments, or tools collected from a given site, the evidence reflects only a paltry fraction of what existed in antiquity (Brandfon, 1988, 14[1]:54). Unearthed data often are insufficient, inconclusive, and subject to biased interpretation....

...the paucity of archaeological evidence provides fertile soil for imaginative—and often contradictory—conclusions. We must not overlook the matter of subjectivity in interpretations. ...Finally, **archaeology is an imprecise science, and should not serve as the judge of biblical historicity**. The pottery dating scheme, for example, has proved to be most helpful in determining relative dates in a tell. But, at best, pottery can place one only within the "chronological ball park." John Laughlin, a seasoned archaeologist, recognized the importance of potsherds in dating strata, but offered two warnings: (1) a standard pottery type might have had many variants; and (2) similar ceramic types might not date to the same era—some types may have survived longer than others, and different manufacturing techniques and styles might have been introduced at different times in different locales. Further, he mentioned the fact of subjectivity in determining pottery: "...in addition to its observable traits, pottery has a 'feel' to it" (1992, 18[5]:72). **Therefore, we must recognize archaeology for what it is—an inexact science with the innate capacity for mistakes** (1993a, 13:84-85, emp. added).

Wayne Jackson accurately summarized the importance of biblical chronology when he wrote:

> The purpose of biblical chronology is to determine the correct dates of events and persons recorded in the Bible as accurately as possible, in order that we may better understand their role in the great plan of Jehovah.... The Bible is the inspired Word of God (II Tim. 3:16). Its testimony is, therefore, always reliable. Whenever it speaks with reference to chronological matters, one may be sure that it is **right**! No chronology is thus to be trusted which contradicts plain historical/chronological data in the sacred text, or which requires a manipulation of factual Bible information (such as is frequently done by compromisers who have been romanced by the chronological absurdities of the theory of evolution) [1981, 1:37, emp. and parenthetical comment in orig.].

Was chronology of importance to the biblical writers? Indeed it was. Does the Bible speak, then, in any sense, concerning the age of the Earth or the age of humanity on the Earth? Indeed it does. I am not suggesting, of course, that one can settle on an **exact** date for the age of the Earth (as did John Lightfoot [1602-1675], the famed Hebraist and vice-chancellor of Cambridge University who taught that creation occurred the week of October 18 to 24, 4004 B.C., and that Adam and Eve were created on October 23 at 9:00 A.M., forty-fifth meridian time [see Ramm, 1954, p. 121]).

I **do** contend, however, that the Bible gives a chronological framework that establishes a **relative** age for the Earth—an age confined to a span of only a few thousand years. The chapters that follow present the evidence to support such a conclusion.

Chapter 8

The Bible and the Age of the Earth— The Day-Age Theory

D.D. Riegle, in his book, *Creation or Evolution?*, observed: "It is amazing that men will accept long, complicated, imaginative theories and reject the truth given to Moses by the Creator Himself" (1962, p. 24). Some of the theories being discussed in this book are indeed "long, complicated, and imaginative." Why is this the case? Even proponents of the old-Earth view admit that a simple, straightforward reading of the biblical text "seems to present" a young Earth. Jack Wood Sears, quoted earlier, has admitted concerning the biblical record that "the intimations **it seems to present** may not be properly understood" (1969, p. 97, emp. added).

These "intimations" of a young Earth have not escaped those who opt for an old Earth. In 1972, Donald England wrote in *A Christian View of Origins*:

> But why do some people insist that the earth is relatively re-
> cent in origin? First, I feel that it is because **one gets the gen-
> eral impression from the Bible that the earth is young**.
> ...It is true that Biblical chronology leaves one with the gen-
> eral impression of a relatively recent origin for man... (p. 109,
> emp. added).

Eleven years later, when Dr. England authored his book, *A Scientist Examines Faith and Evidence*, apparently his views had not
changed.

> A reading of the first few chapters of Genesis **leaves one
> with the very definite general impression that life has
> existed on earth for, at the most, a few thousand years**
> (1983, p. 155, emp. added).

Both Sears and England admit that the Bible "intimates" a young
Earth, and that a reading of the first chapters of Genesis "leaves
one with the general impression" of a youthful planet. Do these two
men then accept a young Earth? They do not. The question is: Why?
If a simple, plain, straightforward reading of the biblical text indicates a young Earth, what reason(s) do they give for not accepting
what the Bible says? Here is Dr. England's 1983 quotation again,
but this time reproduced with his introductory and concluding remarks:

> Third, it is not recommended that one should allow a general
> impression gained from the reading of Scripture to crystallize
> in his mind as absolute revealed truth. A reading of the first
> few chapters of Genesis leaves one with the very definite im-
> pression that life has existed on earth for, at the most, a few
> thousand years. **That conclusion is in conflict with the
> conclusions of modern science that the earth is ancient**
> (1983, p. 155, emp. added).

In his 1972 volume, he had stated: "**From the many scientific dating methods** one gets the very strong general impression that the
earth is quite ancient" (p. 103, emp. added). Dr. Sears added: "**Science**, as I indicated earlier, **has seemed to indicate** that life has
been here much longer than we have generally interpreted the Bible to indicate" (1969, p. 97, emp. added).

The professors' point, explained in detail in their writings, is this: **Uniformitarian dating methods take precedence over the Bible!** Once again, scientific theory has become the father of biblical exegesis. The question being asked is not "What does the Bible say?," but rather "What do evolutionary dating methods indicate?" In order to force the biblical record to accommodate geologic time, defenders of these dating methods do indeed find it necessary to invent "long, complicated, and imaginative" theories.

One of the most important questions, then, in the controversy over the age of the Earth is this: If the Earth is ancient, **where** in the biblical record will the time be placed to guarantee that antiquity? There are but three options. The time needed to ensure an old Earth might be placed: (a) **during** the creation week; (b) **before** the creation week; or (c) **after** the creation week. If the time needed to account for an old Earth cannot be inserted successfully into one of these three places, then it quickly becomes obvious that an old-Earth view is unscriptural. Therefore, I would like to examine each of these.

WHY THE NEED FOR THE DAY-AGE THEORY?

The attempt to place the eons of time necessary for an ancient Earth **during** the creation week generally is known as the Day-Age Theory—a view which suggests that the days of Genesis 1 were not literal, 24-hour days, but instead were lengthy, indefinite periods or eons of time. Arthur F. Williams observed:

> There are certain areas of biblical interpretation in which Christians find themselves in serious disagreement. One of these is the Genesis account of creation. Some interpret the record **literally**, believing each of the six days to have been cycles of 24 hours, on the sixth of which God created man in His own image by divine fiat from the dust of the earth. They believe that God breathed into man's nostrils the breath of life and he became a living soul. They, likewise, believe that this occurred at a time not longer than a few thousand years ago. Others interpret the entire record of creation "parabolically,"

and insist that the six days represent a vast period of time, extending into millions or billions of years (1970, p. 24, emp. in orig.).

Surburg noted:

> Another group of interpreters has adopted what is known as the "concordistic theory." They say that the "days" of Genesis possibly are periods of time extending over millions of years. They believe that this interpretation can be made to correspond to the various geological periods or ages. This is sometimes referred to as the "day-age" theory (1959, p. 57).

John Klotz addressed this point in *Genes, Genesis, and Evolution*: "It is hardly conceivable that anyone would question the interpretation of these as ordinary days were it not for the fact that people are attempting to reconcile Genesis and evolution" (1955, p. 87). Guy N. Woods concluded: "The day-age theory is a consequence of the evolutionary theory. But for that speculative view such a hypothesis would never have been advanced" (1976b, p. 17).

IS THE DAY-AGE THEORY POPULAR?

Is the Day-Age Theory popular? Yes, and it has been advocated by a number of influential people in the religious community.

> Many sincere and competent Biblical scholars have felt it so mandatory to accept the geological age system that they have prematurely settled on the so-called day-age theory as the recommended interpretation of Genesis 1. By this device, they seek more or less to equate the days of creation with the ages of evolutionary geology (Morris, 1976, p. 53).

Among those "competent Biblical scholars" to whom Dr. Morris referred are the following. Wilbur M. Smith, former dean of Moody Bible Institute, went on record as stating: "First of all, we must dismiss from our mind any conception of a definite period of time, either for creation itself, or for the length of the so-called six creative days" (1945, p. 312). Bernard Ramm called the belief that the days of creation were 24-hour days the "naive, literal view" (1954, pp. 120-121).

Merrill Unger, in his *Bible Handbook*, wrote that the view which understands the days of Genesis 1 to be literal 24-hour days is "generally recognized as untenable in an age of science" (1966, p. 38). Kenneth Taylor, producer of the *Living Bible Paraphrased*, added footnotes to the text of Genesis 1 in that volume in an attempt to explain to the reader that the Hebrew phrase "evening and morning" (used repeatedly throughout the chapter) actually means a long period of time. In his book, *Evolution and the High School Student*, Taylor wrote:

> To me it appears that God's special creative acts occurred many times during 6 long geological periods capped by the creation of Adam and Eve perhaps more than 1 million years ago. This idea seems to do justice both to the Bible and to what geologists and anthropologists currently believe. If they change their dates up or down, it will make no difference to this belief, unless to move Adam's age forward or backward (1974, p. 62).

Edward John Carnell of Fuller Theological Seminary advised: "And since orthodoxy has given up the literal-day theory out of respect for geology, it would certainly forfeit no principle if it gave up the immediate-creation theory out of respect for paleontology. The two seem to be quite parallel" (1959, p. 95).

In more recent times, the Day-Age Theory has been championed by such writers as Davis A. Young (*Creation and the Flood*, 1977, p. 132), Alan Hayward (*Creation and Evolution: The Facts and the Fallacies*, 1985, p. 164), Howard J. Van Till (*The Fourth Day*, 1986, pp. 75-93; *Portraits of Creation*, 1990, pp. 236-242), and Hugh Ross (*Creation and Time*, 1994, pp. 45-90). Others have lent it their support as well. For example, in his audio-taped lecture, *Questions and Answers: Number One*, John Clayton remarked:

> I believe it is totally inconsequential as to whether or not the days of Genesis were 24-hour days or not. It isn't until the fourth day until the Sun and Moon were established as chronometers. There were no days, seasons, etc.—at least as we know them—before the fourth day! (n.d.[c]).

Jack Wood Sears,* mentioned earlier, also is on record as advocating this particular viewpoint.

There are some who go through the motions of appearing to be "neutral," when in fact they clearly are not. For example, in the April 4, 1986 edition of *Gospel Minutes* (a weekly publication produced by and distributed among members of the churches of Christ), then-coeditor Clem Thurman spent a page-and-a-half answering a reader's question on whether or not the days mentioned in Genesis 1 should be considered as literal 24-hour periods (1986, 35[14]: 2-3). He offered three extremely (and conspicuously!) brief points—using only two column inches of space—discussing why the days "might" be considered as literal, and almost **two full columns** suggesting reasons why they could not be. Then, of course, he urged each reader to "decide for himself" what the "correct" answer was. Why not just be honest and openly advocate the Day-Age Theory without going through all the unnecessary machinations?**

---

* In December 1977, Dr. Sears and I shared the platform at a week-long series of lectures in Salisbury, the capital of Rhodesia (now Zimbabwe). During the lectureship, in response to a question from a young man in the audience, I stated that the days of creation in Genesis 1 were literal, 24-hour periods. As I returned to my chair, Dr. Sears leaned over to me and said: "There's not a Hebrew scholar in the world who would agree with you on that point. You are very much mistaken in believing the days of creation to be 24-hour days." In his lecture the following day, he politely took issue with my comment that the days were of a 24-hour duration. In my debate with him in Denton, Texas in November 1983, he once again made clear his position that the days of Genesis likely were long epochs. Audio and video tapes of that debate are available from the offices of Apologetics Press.

** One of the strangest concepts set forth regarding the days of Genesis 1 has been suggested by Gerald L. Schroeder in his book, *Genesis and the Big Bang*. "God might have plunked man down in a world that was ready-made from the instant of creation. But that was not on the Creator's agenda. There was a sequence of events, a development in the world, which led to conditions suitable for man. This is evident from the literal text of Genesis 1:1-31. **By God's time frame, the sequence took six days. By our time frame, it took billions of years**" (1990, p. 85, emp. added; see also Schroeder, 1997). Most readers no doubt will wonder how, by "God's time," it took six days, yet in "our time" it took billions of years? Why is it that writers cannot be forthright and simply admit that they have no intention whatsoever of believing the "literal text" (to use Schroeder's own words) of the Genesis account as it is written?

There are still others, however, who are quite cautious not to reveal their predisposition toward the Day-Age Theory, and who go to great lengths to suggest that this is best left an "open matter" because there are "good arguments on both sides of the issue." Burton Coffman took such a position in his *Commentary on Genesis* (1985).

DO ALL THOSE WHO ADVOCATE THE DAY-AGE THEORY BELIEVE IN EVOLUTION?

Is it the case that all those who advocate the Day-Age Theory are either evolutionists or theistic evolutionists? No, not necessarily. There are some who prefer to be called simply "old-Earth creationists" because they claim to accept neither evolution nor theistic evolution. As Surburg observed:

> Many Christians who today hold this view are not necessarily evolutionists. They do not believe that God employed the evolutionary method to produce man, and they endeavor to reconcile the process indicated by paleontology with the creative days of Genesis (1959, p. 57).

Williams agreed, but cautioned:

> ...we do not mean to imply that all who hold to the day-age theory are evolutionists. We do insist, however, that such a view can be maintained only by an acceptance of the mental construct known as the geologic column, which is based upon the assumption of evolution (1970, p. 25).

Indeed, if evolutionary dogma (with its accompanying uniformitarian-based dating methods) had not been allowed to sit in judgment on the biblical record in the first place, there would have been no need for the Day-Age Theory. As Williams went on to point out, there also is an inherent danger in accepting such a theory.

> The day-age theory, though espoused by some men who are sincere Christians, is fraught with dangerous consequences to the Christian faith. This question is not merely academic, as some assert, but it directly affects biblical theology.... The first chapters of Genesis must be regarded as the seed plot

of the entire Bible, and if we err here, there is reason to believe that those who come under false interpretations of the Genesis account of creation will sooner or later become involved in error in other areas of divine revelation. It is our conviction that **once the interpretation of the six days of creation which makes them extended periods of perhaps millions of years in duration is accepted, the door is opened for the entire evolutionary philosophy** (1970, pp. 24-25, emp. added).

Henry Morris was correct when he said: "The day-age theory is normally accompanied by either the theory of theistic evolution or the theory of progressive creation. ...neither theistic evolution nor progressive creation is tenable Biblically or theologically. Thus the day-age theory must likewise be rejected" (1974a, p. 222). Weston W. Fields said that he has noticed:

> ...the underlying presupposition of the day-age theory is that geologic evolutionists are correct in their allegations about the immense eons of time necessary to account for the geological features of the earth, and the biological evolutionists are at least partially correct when they say that in some sense higher forms came from lower forms. Thus, many (though not all) day-age theorists are also theistic evolutionists and progressive creationists (1976, p. 166, parenthetical item in orig.).

IS THERE LEXICAL AND EXEGETICAL EVIDENCE TO SUPPORT THE DAY-AGE THEORY?

In examining whether or not there is lexical and exegetical support for the Day-Age Theory, the question should be asked: "If the author of Genesis wanted to instruct his readers on the fact that all things had been created in six literal days, what words might he have used to convey such a thought?" Henry Morris has suggested:

> ...the writer would have used the actual words in Genesis 1. If he wished to convey the idea of long geological ages, however, he could surely have done it far more clearly and effectively in other words than in those which he selected. It was clearly his intent to teach creation in six literal days.

Therefore, the only proper way to interpret Genesis 1 is not
to "interpret" it at all. That is, we accept the fact that it was
meant to say exactly what it says. The "days" are literal days
and the events described happened in just the way described
(1976, p. 54).

A second question that must be asked is this: "Is there adequate
(or, for that matter, any) lexical and exegetical evidence to suggest
that the days of creation should be interpreted as ages of time?" In
my estimation, the most thorough rebuttal of the Day-Age Theory
(and, coincidentally, of the Gap Theory) ever put into print is *Unformed and Unfilled* by Weston W. Fields. In that volume, Dr.
Fields addressed the complete **lack** of evidence—from the biblical
text itself—for the Day-Age Theory.

> With the Gap Theory the Day-Age Theory shares the advan-
> tage of allowing unlimited amounts of time. But it also has an
> advantage which the Gap Theory does not: it allows the ge-
> ologist the **sequence** he wants (assuming he ignores the bibli-
> cal sequences), and it allows the biologists to have partial or
> complete evolution. However, it also shares one disadvantage
> with the Gap Theory—indeed, it outdoes the Gap Theory in
> this particular: it rests on very scanty exegetical evidence. The
> lexical exility on which it is based is almost unbelievable; con-
> sequently, we must conclude that it springs from presuppo-
> sitions—a fact transparent even to the casual reader (1976,
> pp. 156-166, emp. in orig.).

Fields then proceeded to present the lexical evidence.

> ...As in the case of other problems involving meanings of
> words, our study must begin with Hebrew lexicography. Nearly
> all the defenders of the theory fail, however, to give any lexi-
> cal backing to the theory. The reader is left completely unin-
> formed concerning the use of *yom* (day) in the Old Testament.
> Therefore, we have listed a complete summary of both Brown,
> Driver, and Briggs's as well as Koehler and Baumgartner's
> listings. Nothing less than a **complete** examination of the
> evidence will suffice. In the lexicon of Brown, Driver, and
> Briggs, there are seven primary meanings for *yom* (day), with
> numerous subheadings:

1. Day, opposite of night. Listed under this heading are Genesis 1:5,15,16,18.
2. Day, as a division of time.
   a. working day.
   b. a day's journey.
   c. to denote various acts or states such as seven days, Genesis 7:4.
   d. day as defined by evening and morning. Listed here are Genesis 1:5,8,13,19,23,31.
   e. day of the month.
   f. day defined by substantive, infinitive, etc., such as the "snowy day."
   g. particular days defined by proper name of place, such as the Sabbath Day.
   h. your, his, or their day, as in the sense of the day of disaster or death: "your day has come."
3. The day of Yahweh, as the time of his coming in judgment.
4. The days of someone, equaling his life, or his age: "advanced in days."
5. Days.
   a indefinite: some days, a few days.
   b. of a long time: "many days."
   c. days of old: former or ancient times.
6. Time.
   a. vividly in general sense as in the "time of harvest."
   b. used in apposition to other expressions of time, such as a "month of days" equals a "month of time."
7. Used in phrases with and without the prepositions.
   a. such as with the definite article, meaning "today."
   b. in the expression "and the day came that," meaning "when."
   c. in an expression such as "lo, days are coming."
   d. in construct before verbs, both literally, **the day of**, and (often) in general sense—**the time of** (forcible and pregnant representing the act vividly as that of a single day). Under this definition is listed Genesis 2:4.
   e. day by day (*yom yom*).
   f. in expressions such as "all the days" meaning always, continually.

g. in an additional phrase with *bet* meaning **on** a particular day.

h. with *kap*, meaning as, like the day.

i. with *lamed*, meaning on or at the day.

j. with *min*, meaning since the day or from the day.

k. with *lemin*, meaning since the day.

l. with *'ad*, meaning until the day.

m. with *'al*, meaning upon the day.

Koehler and Baumgartner list the usages of *yom* under ten different headings:

1. Day, bright daylight, as opposite of night.

2. Day, of 24 hours. Listed under this heading is Genesis 1:5.

3. Special days, such as the "day of prosperity," or the "day of adversity."

4. Yahweh's day.

5. Plural or day, such as "seven days."

6. Plural of day, such as "the days of the years of your life."

7. Plural of day in a usage to refer to a month or year.

8. Dual, such as in the expression, "a day or two."

9. With the article, "that day."

10. With a preposition such as *bet*, "on the day," or "when."

Now **these** are the meanings the lexicons give. For the reader interested in **all** the evidence, here it is. We must immediately raise the question: where is the lexical support for identifying the days of Genesis as **long periods of time**? Far from supporting the notion that the creative days of Genesis 1 are vast ages, extending, perhaps, over millions of years, the lexicons suggest that "day," as used to refer to creation is of the normal 24 hours duration. This is the **natural** interpretation (1976, pp. 169-172, emp. in orig.).

The evidence supporting the days of creation being 24-hour periods is overwhelming, as Fields has amply documented. In addition to that evidence, I would like to offer the following for consideration.

EVIDENCE SUBSTANTIATING THE DAYS OF GENESIS 1 AS LITERAL, 24-HOUR PERIODS

1. The days of creation should be accepted as literal, 24-hour periods because the context demands such a rendering.

> The language of the text is simple and clear. Honest exegetes cannot read anything else out of these verses than a day of 24 hours and a week of 7 days. There is not the slightest indication that this is to be regarded as poetry or as an allegory or that it is not to be taken as a historical fact. The language is that of normal human speech to be taken at face value, and the unbiased reader will understand it as it reads. There is no indication that anything but a literal sense is meant (Rehwinkle, 1974, p. 70).

It is true that the word in the Hebrew for day (*yom*), as in other languages, can be employed with a variety of meanings. But, as in all other languages, the context in which the word is used is critical in determining what the word means in any given instance. Henry Morris noted:

> There is no doubt that *yom* can be used to express time in a general sense. In fact, it is actually translated as "time" in the King James translation 65 times. On the other hand, it is translated as "day" almost 1200 times.... Whenever the writer really intended to convey the idea of a very long duration of time, he normally used some such word as *'olam* (meaning "age" or "long time") or else attached to *yom* an adjective such as *rab* (meaning "long"), so that the two words together *yom rab*, then meant "long time." But *yom* by itself can apparently never be proved, in one single case, to **require** the meaning of a long period of time, and certainly no usage which would suggest a geologic age (1974a, p. 223, emp. in orig.).

The following quotation from Arthur Williams documents several important points in this controversy, especially in light of the Day-Age theorists' inconsistency. We are told that *yom* in Genesis 1 is an "age." Yet Day-Age proponents are unwilling to translate the word in this fashion elsewhere, for it makes no sense to do so, and destroys the meaning of the passages.

What did the word *yom* (day) mean to Moses and to Israel in the day in which the books of Moses were written?...

In the Genesis account of creation the word "day" occurs 14 times, always a translation of the Hebrew word *yom*. Those who hold to the day-age theory ask us to give the word "day" a meaning which it has nowhere else in the five books of Moses....

As if the consistent significance of the word *yom* throughout the writings of Moses were not enough to establish the meaning of the English word "day," God added statements which are difficult to interpret otherwise. "...God divided the **light** from the **darkness**. And God called the light **Day** and the darkness he called **Night**. And the **evening** and the **morning** were the first day." In the light of cultural considerations of hermeneutics, can anyone honestly believe that these terms as used in the Genesis account of creation had a meaning almost infinitely removed from the meaning which they had elsewhere in the writings of Moses? The word "day" would have had no meaning to Moses or to his contemporaries other than that which was limited by reference to the sun. It would be impossible to prove from Scripture that the Israelites in the days of Moses had any concept of a "day" in terms of millions or billions of years. The evidence arising from serious consideration of the cultural meaning of the word *yom* as used by Moses and understood by the Israelites is wholly on the side of the 24-hour day in the Genesis account of creation. Such a view is consistent with its meaning as used by Moses throughout his writings (1970, pp. 26-28, emp. in orig.).

As an example of the point Dr. Williams is making, consider the use of *yom* in Numbers 7:12,18. In this context, the discussion is the offering of sacrifices by the princes of Israel. Verse 12 records: "And he that offered his oblation the first day was Nahshon, the son of Amminadab, of the tribe of Judah." Verse 18 records, "On the second day Nethanel the son of Zuar, prince of Issachar, did offer." Notice the sequential nature involved via the use of "first day" and "second day." Do Day-Age theorists suggest that Moses meant to say "in the first eon," or "in the second age" the events recorded transpired? Of course not. Why, then, should the treatment of the word *yom* in Genesis 1 be any different? Indeed, it would not be, were it not for the desire to incorporate evolutionary theory into the biblical text.

2. The days of creation should be accepted as literal, 24-hour periods because God both **used and defined** the word *yom* in the context of Genesis 1. It is nothing short of amazing to discover the evidence built into the text for "interpreting" what kind of days these were. In Genesis 1:5, Moses wrote: "And God called the light Day, and the darkness He called Night. And the evening and the morning were the first day." Thus, the "first day" is defined as a period of both day and night—i.e., a normal day.

Further, Genesis 1:14 is instructive in this matter: "And God said, 'Let there be lights in the firmament of heaven to divide the day from the night; and let them be for signs and for seasons, and for days and for years.'" If the "days" are "ages," then **what are the years**? If a day is an age, then what is a night? The entire meaning of the passage is lost when one "reinterprets" the word "day." Marcus Dods, writing in the *Expositor's Bible*, said simply: "If the word 'day' in this chapter [Genesis 1—BT] does not mean a period of 24 hours, the interpretation of Scripture is hopeless" (1948, 1:4-5). Klotz correctly observed:

> It is a general principle of Biblical interpretation that a word is to be taken in its everyday meaning unless there is compelling evidence that it must be taken in a different sense.... But there is nothing in the text or context of Genesis 1 which indicates that these were long periods of time. Sound principles of Biblical interpretation require that we accept this "day" as being an ordinary day (1955, pp. 84-85).

Fields summarized the argument by stating: "The farther we read in the creation account, the more obvious it is that Moses intended his readers to understand that God created the universe in six 24-hour days. Nothing could be **more** obvious!" (1976, p. 174, emp. in orig.).

3. The days of creation should be accepted as literal, 24-hour periods because whenever *yom* is preceded by a numeral in Old Testament non-prophetical literature (viz., the same kind of literature found in Genesis 1), it **always** carries the meaning of a normal day. Arthur Williams spoke to this point in the *Creation Research Annual* when he wrote: "We have failed to find a single example of the use of the word 'day' in the entire Scripture where it means other than a period of twenty-four hours when modified by the use of the numerical adjective" (1965, p. 10). Henry Morris concurred:

> It might still be contended that, even though *yom* never **requires** the meaning of a long age, it might possibly **permit** it. However, the writer of the first chapter of Genesis has very carefully guarded against such a notion, both by modifying the noun by a numerical adjective ("first day," "second day," etc.), and also by indicating the boundaries of the time period in each case as "evening and morning." Either one of these devices would suffice to limit the meaning of *yom* to that of a solar day, and when both are used, there could be no better or surer way possible for the writer to convey the intended meaning of a literal solar day.
>
> To prove this, it is noted that whenever a limiting numeral or ordinal is attached to "day" in the Old Testament (and there are over 200 such instances), the meaning is always that of a literal day (1974a, pp. 223-224, emp. and parenthetical items in orig.).

Raymond Surburg was invited to contribute to the book, *Darwin, Evolution, and Creation*, edited by Paul Zimmerman. In his chapter, Dr. Surburg quoted from a letter written by renowned Canadian anthropologist, Arthur C. Custance, and sent to nine contemporary Hebrew scholars, members of the faculties of nine leading universities—three in Canada, three in the United States, and three in England. In the letter, Dr. Custance inquired about the meaning of *yom* as used in Genesis. For example, he asked: "Do you understand the Hebrew *yom*, as used in Genesis 1, accompanied by a numeral, to be properly translated as: (a) a day as commonly understood, or (b) an age, or (c) an age or a day without preference for either?" Seven of the nine replied, and all stated that the word *yom* means "a day as commonly understood" (as quoted in Surburg, 1959, p. 61). Thus, when the writer stated in Exodus 20:11 that God created the Earth and everything in it in six days, he meant what he said—six literal, 24-hour days.

4. The days of creation should be accepted as literal, 24-hour periods because whenever *yom* occurs in the plural (*yamim*) in Old Testament non-prophetical literature (viz., the same kind of literature found in Genesis 1), it always carries the meaning of a normal day. *Yamim*, the Hebrew word for "days," appears over 700 times in the Old Testament. In each of these instances where the language is non-prophetical in nature, it **always** refers to literal days. Thus, in Exodus 20:11, when the Scriptures say that "in six days the Lord made heaven and earth, the sea, and all that in them is," there can be no doubt that six literal days are meant. Even the most liberal Bible scholars do not attempt to negate the force of this argument by suggesting that Genesis 1 and Exodus 20:11 are prophetical.

5. The days of creation should be accepted as literal, 24-hour periods because whenever *yom* is modified by the phrase "evening and morning" in Old Testament non-prophetical literature (viz., the same kind of literature found in Genesis 1), it always carries the meaning of a normal day.

> Having separated the day and night, God had completed His first day's work. "The evening and the morning were the first day." This same formula is used at the conclusion of each of the six days; so it is obvious that the duration of each of the days, including the first, was the same.... It is clear that, beginning with the first day and continuing thereafter, there was established a cyclical succession of days and nights—periods of light and periods of darkness.

> The writer not only defined the term "day," but emphasized that it was terminated by a literal evening and morning and that it was like every other day in the normal sequence of days. In no way can the term be legitimately applied here to anything corresponding to a geological period or any other such concept (Morris, 1976, pp. 55-56).

Addressing the text from the perspective of one who had studied the original languages of the Bible for over fifty years, the late Guy N. Woods wrote:

> The "days" of Genesis 1 are divided into light and darkness exactly as is characteristic of the day known to us. "And God saw the light, that it was good; and God divided the light from the darkness. And God called the light Day, and the darkness He called Night. **And the evening and the morning were the first day**" (Genesis 1:4,5). This simple and sublime statement is decisive of the matter. Of what was the first day composed? Evening and morning. Into what was it divided? Light and darkness. The Hebrew text is even more emphatic. The translation, "And the evening and the morning were the first day" is literally, "And evening was, and day was, day one." The two periods—evening and morning—made one day. The Jewish mode of reckoning the day was from sunset to sunset; i.e., evening and morning, the two periods combining to make **one** day (1976b, p. 17, emp. in orig.).

This phrase "evening and morning" is important as a modifier, especially in light of the fact that Day-Age theorists insist that these days were long epochs of time. The question must be asked: "Has anyone ever seen an 'eon' with an evening and morning?"

Some have suggested, of course, that literal, 24-hour days would not have been possible until at least the fourth day, because the Sun had not been created yet. Notice, however, that the same "evening and morning" is employed **before** Genesis 1:14 (i.e., the creation of the Sun) as after it. Why should there be three long eras of time before the appearance of the Sun, and only 24-hour days after its creation? Both Klotz and Woods have addressed this objection.

> Insofar as the view is concerned that these could not be ordinary days because the sun had not been created, we should like to point to the fact that we still measure time in terms of days even though the sun does not appear or is not visible. For instance, north of the Arctic Circle and south of the Antarctic Circle the sun does not appear for periods of time up to six months at the poles themselves. We would not think

of measuring time in terms of the appearance or lack of appearance of the sun in these areas. No one would contend that at the North or South Pole a day is the equivalent of six months elsewhere (Klotz, 1955, p. 85).

...If to this the objection is offered that the sun did not shine on the earth until the fourth day, it should be remembered that it is the function of the heavenly bodies to **mark** the days, not **make** them! It is night when no moon appears; and the day is the same whether the sun is seen or not (Woods, 1976b, p. 17, emp. in orig.).

By way of summary, it may be said that:

(a) The phrase "evening and morning" was the Hebrew way of describing a literal, 24-hour day.

(b) There are no instances in the non-prophetical Old Testament passages where the phrase "evening and morning" represents anything more than a literal, 24-hour day.

(c) The presence of the Sun and Moon do not regulate the day and the night. The Earth's rotation on its axis does that. Since the phrase "evening and morning" is used both before and after the Sun's creation, the days are obviously literal, 24-hour days.

6. The days of creation should be accepted as literal, 24-hour periods because Moses had at his disposal the means by which to express long periods of time, but purposely did not use wording in the original Hebrew that would have portrayed such an idea. Fields commented:

Perhaps the most telling argument against the Day-Age Theory is, "what else could God say to convey the idea that the days of creation were **literal** days?" He used the **only** terms available to him to communicate that idea. There was a word, on the other hand, which Moses could have used had he wanted to signify **ages** or vast **periods of time**. He could have used the word *dor* which has that very meaning. But instead he used the word "day," and we think the reason he did is very obvious to the unbiased reader: He wanted to tell his readers that all of creation took place in six literal 24-hour days! (1976, pp. 177-178, emp. in orig.).

7. The days of creation should be accepted as literal, 24-hour periods because of the problems in the field of botany if the days are pressed into becoming long periods of time. Woods wrote:

> Botany, the field of plant-life, came into existence on the third day. Those who allege that the days of Genesis 1 may have been long geological ages, must accept the absurd hypothesis that plant-life survived in periods of total darkness through half of each geologic age, running into millions of years (1976b, p. 17).

Henry Morris also has addressed this issue:

> The objection is sometimes raised that the first three days were not days as they are today since the sun was not created until day four. One could of course turn this objection against those who raise it. The longer the first three days, the more catastrophic it would be for the sun not to be on hand during those days, if indeed the sun is the only possible source of light for the earth. The vegetation created on the third day might endure for a few hours without sunlight, but hardly for a geologic age! (1974a, p. 224).

In addition, there is a serious problem regarding reproduction of plants. The Genesis text indicates that plants were created on day three. Yet other living things were not created until days five and six. How could plants have survived that are pollinated solely by insects? Clover is pollinated by bees, and the yucca plant has the pronuba moth as its only means of pollination. How did plants multiply if they were growing millions of years before the insects came into existence?

8. The days of creation should be accepted as literal, 24-hour periods because of plain statements about them within the Scriptures.

   (a) "for in six days Jehovah made heaven and earth, the sea, and all that in them is" (Exodus 20:11).

   (b) "For He spake, and it was done; He commanded, and it stood fast" (Psalm 33:9).

(c) "Let them praise the name of Jehovah; for he commanded and they were created" (Psalm 148:5).

(d) "for in six days Jehovah made heaven and earth, and on the seventh day he rested, and was refreshed" (Exodus 31:17).

Does a simple, straightforward reading of these verses imply a long period of evolutionary progress, or six literal, 24-hour days and instantaneous creation? Riegle answered:

> The Hebrew text implies that the Creative acts were accomplished instantly. In Genesis 1:11 God's literal command was, "Earth, sprout sprouts!" In the very next verse we find the response to the command—"The earth caused plants to go out." There is no hint that great ages of time were required to accomplish this phase of the Creation. It could have been done in only minutes, or even seconds, as far as God's creative power is concerned (1962, pp. 27-28).

In its appropriate context, each of these passages can be understood correctly to be speaking only of literal days and instantaneous creation.

9. The days of creation should be accepted as literal, 24-hour periods because of God's explicit command to the Israelites to work six days and rest on the seventh, just as He had done. He told them not only **what** to do, but **why** to do it.

> Remember the sabbath day, to keep it holy. Six days shalt thou labor, and do all thy work; but the seventh day is a sabbath unto Jehovah thy God: in it thou shalt not do any work, thou, nor thy son, nor thy daughter, thy manservant, nor thy maidservant, nor thy cattle, nor thy stranger that is within thy gates: for in six days Jehovah made heaven and earth, the sea, and all that in them is, and rested the seventh day: wherefore Jehovah blessed the sabbath day, and hallowed it (Exodus 20:8-11).

The Sabbath command can be understood properly only when the days of the week are recognized as being 24-hour days. A.E. Wilder-Smith aptly summarized the problem that results (in regard to the Sabbath) if the days are not accepted as literal, 24-hour days.

Another difficulty arises if one tries to apply the age-equals-day interpretation. The whole important biblical doctrine of the Sabbath is weakened by this view. For God is reported as having rested on the seventh day after working the six days. The implication is that man should also rest on the seventh day as God did. But did God rest for an age, maybe of millions of years? The whole biblical concept of the Sabbath is coupled with six working days and one day of rest in seven. God certainly did not need to rest, but presumably set us a pattern with the Sabbath rest (1975, p. 44).

OBJECTIONS CONSIDERED

Three specific objections to 24-hour creation days often are mentioned by those who advocate an old Earth.

"One Day Is With The Lord As A Thousand Years"

The first objection has to do with the passage found in 2 Peter 3:8.

> [I]n the last days, mockers shall come with mocking, walking after their own lusts, and saying, "Where is the promise of his coming? for, from the day that the fathers fell asleep, all things continue as they were from the beginning of the creation." For this they willfully forget, that there were heavens from of old, and an earth compacted out of water and amidst water, by the word of God; by which means the world that then was, being overflowed with water, perished: but the heavens that now are, and the earth, by the same word have been stored up for fire, being reserved against the day of judgment and destruction of ungodly men. But forget not this one thing, beloved, that one day is with the Lord as a thousand years, and a thousand years as one day. The Lord is not slack concerning his promise, as some count slackness; but is longsuffering to you-ward, not wishing that any should perish, but that all should come to repentance. But the day of the Lord will come as a thief... (emp. added).

Some have suggested that this passage indicates that the "days" of Genesis could have been thousands of years in duration, rather than 24-hour periods. The passage, however, is not discussing the length of the days in Genesis 1. Nor is it speaking of the length of "God's days" in general. Those who suggest that support can be found in Peter's statements for increasing the length of the creation days have failed to take into account the context of Peter's comments —a context that is critical to an understanding of the apostle's message. John C. Whitcomb observed:

> Note carefully that the verse does **not** say that God's days last thousands of years, but that "one day is with the Lord **as** a thousand years." In other words, God is completely above the limitations of time in the sense that he can accomplish in one literal day what nature or man could not accomplish in thousands of years, if ever. Note that one day is **as** a thousand years, not **is** a thousand years, with God. If "one day" in this verse means a long period of time, then we would end up with the following absurdity: "a long period of time is with the Lord as a thousand years." Instead of this, the verse reveals how much God can accomplish in a 24-hour day, and thus sheds much light upon the events of Creation Week (1975, 36:68, emp. in orig.).

Peter is discussing specific things that will take place "in the last days" when mockers shall ask, "Where is the promise of his coming?" The apostle is not referring to, nor does his discussion center on, "the first days" (i.e., the days of Genesis 1). Rather, he is warning against those living in the Christian dispensation who, after Christ's resurrection and ascension, doubted that He would return as He had promised. Guy N. Woods elucidated the thrust of Peter's comments when he wrote:

> The passage should be considered in the light of its context. The material heavens and earth are to suffer destruction by fire, despite the mockers who scoff at such predictions and who allege, in the face of the earth's earlier destruction by water, that all things must continue as they are from the beginning (2 Peter 3:1-7). All such are "willingly ignorant," and refuse to accept the clear and obvious lessons of history. Faithful followers of the Lord are not to be influenced by these skeptics, but to remember "that one day is with the Lord as a thousand years, and a thousand years as one day."

By this the apostle meant that the passing of time does not, in any way, affect the performance of God's promises or threats. He is not influenced by the passing of the centuries; and the lapse of time between the promise or threat, and the performance, is no factor, at all. With man, it definitely is. That which we promise to do tomorrow, we are much more likely to do, than that which we promise next year, or in the next century, since we may not be here then to fulfill the promise. But, this limitation, so characteristic of man, does not influence Deity. The passing of a thousand years, to God, does not alter his plans and purposes any more than a day, and he will carry them out as he has planned, regardless of the amount of time which is involved (1976b, p. 146).

In his commentary on Peter's epistles, R.C.H. Lenski brilliantly explained both the purpose of the apostle's comments and the impact those comments were intended to have on his readers.

Entirely too much escapes the mockers, hence their ignorant mocking (v. 5-7). This is a point that may escape even Peter's readers, which he, therefore, wants them to note well: "that one day with the Lord is as a thousand years, and a thousand years as one day." This is Peter's own statement which is based on Ps. 90:4: "A thousand years in thy sight are as yesterday when it is passed and as a watch in the night." God created time....

With the Lord time is evidently not what it is to us who live in time. He is above time. Peter does not say that the Lord is timeless, which he, of course, is, but that **his** relation to time must never be confused with **our** relation to time. A day seems short to us, a thousand years a very long period. With the Lord a single day is "as a thousand years," and vice versa. Let us not overlook the two ὡς, "as." Peter does not say: "A single day **is** a thousand years, and a thousand years **are** a day...." Whether it be a day or a thousand years as we count time, both are really the same with the Lord; neither hampers nor helps him. Those who apply this dictum to the word "day" in Genesis 1 and make "day" in Genesis 1 equal to a period that consists of millions of years find no support in this passage (1966b, pp. 344-345, emp. in orig.).

Henry Morris noted:

> Similarly, the familiar verse in 2 Peter 3:8 has been badly mis-
> applied when used to teach the day-age theory. In the con-
> text, it teaches the opposite, and one should remember that
> a "text without a context is a pretext." Peter…is saying that,
> despite man's naturalistic scoffings, God can do in one day
> what, on uniformitarian premises, might seem to require a
> thousand years. God does not require aeons of time to ac-
> complish His work of creating and redeeming things. It is even
> interesting that on the above equation—one day for a thou-
> sand years or 365,000 days—the actual duration of God's
> work with the earth and man—say about 7,000 years becomes
> about two-and-a-half-billion years, which is at least of the or-
> der of magnitude of the "apparent age" of the world as cal-
> culated by uniformitarianism! (1974a, pp. 226-227).

Biblical language scholar Weston W. Fields commented on the
passage in this manner.

> This verse is often used to support the Day-Age Theory. Yet
> far from supporting the theory, it actually disproves it! What
> the verse indicates is that things which are so complex that
> from the human standpoint they would seem to have taken
> God a thousand years to accomplish, are things God can do
> in one day. This verse shows us how God can do such a fan-
> tastic amount of work in such a short period of time (1976,
> p. 177).

This particular passage in 2 Peter 3:8 serves to illustrate that
time is of little essence with God. Peter's obvious intent was to stress
that in a short period time—namely, a 24-hour day—God can do
the work that would take man or nature a thousand years (if ever)
to accomplish. Similarly, God does not tire, although thousands of
years may pass, because with Him a thousand years are as a day.
This passage may be (and, in fact, is!) a wonderfully moving commentary on the eternal nature of God, but there is nothing whatsoever in it to intimate that the days of Genesis were eons of time.
Those days should not to be reinterpreted via a gross misapplication of 2 Peter 3:8.

Too Much Activity On Day Six

The second objection to the days of Genesis being literal, 24-hour periods is that the sixth day could not have been a normal day because **too much activity** occurred on that day. Alan Hayward, who accepts this criticism as legitimate because he holds to the Day-Age Theory, has explained why he believes this to be a valid argument against the 24-hour days.

> Finally, there is strong evidence that the sixth day of creation must have lasted more than 24 hours. Look how much took place in that sixth day! To begin with, God created the higher animals, and then created Adam. After that:
>
> "And the Lord God planted a garden in Eden.... And out of the ground the Lord God made to grow every tree..." (Genesis 2:8,9). Then **every** living animal and **every** bird was brought to Adam for naming.
>
> In all that long procession of living things, Adam saw that "there was not found a helper fit for him" Genesis 2:20). So God put Adam to sleep, created Eve, and presented her to Adam, who joyfully declared:
>
> This **at last** is bone of my bones and flesh of my flesh; she shall be called Woman, because she was taken out of Man (Verse 23).
>
> All commentators are agreed that the expression translated "at last" in the RSV means just that. They usually express the literal meaning of the Hebrew as "now, at length," and some of them quote numerous other passages in the Old Testament where this Hebrew word carried the same sort of meaning. Thus, the Hebrew indicates that Adam had been kept waiting a long time for his wife to appear—and all on the sixth day (1985, pp. 164-165, emp. in orig.).

This is one of the few attempts to prove that the days of creation were long periods of time by actually appealing to the Bible itself. Generally no such attempts are made by those holding to the Day-Age Theory. Instead, they routinely base their case on scientific arguments that appeal to the apparent antiquity of the Earth, to geological phenomena, etc. Here, however, their position is as follows:

(1) there is textual evidence in Genesis 2 that the sixth day of creation could not have been a literal day (as suggested by Hayward, above); (2) but obviously it was the same type of "day" as each of the previous five; (3) thus, none of the "days" of the creation week is to be viewed as literal.

The argument (from Hayward's statement of it) is two-pronged. First, it is said that after God created Adam on the sixth day, He commissioned him to name the animals **before Eve was fashioned** later on that same day—a task that would have taken a much longer period than a mere 24-hour day. Second, it is alleged that when Adam first saw Eve, he exclaimed: "This is **now** [Hayward's "at last"] bone of my bones...," and his statement thus reflects that he had been without a mate for quite some time—certainly longer than a few hours. This compromise is advocated not only by Hayward, but by Gleason Archer in his *Encyclopedia of Biblical Difficulties* (1982, pp. 58ff.) and by Hugh Ross in *Creation and Time* (1994, pp. 50-51).

Significantly, Professor Archer reveals that he has been influenced by the assertions of evolutionary geochronology. His discussion of this matter is in response to the question: "How can Genesis 1 be reconciled with the immense periods of time indicated by the fossil strata?" He has claimed that there is conflict between Genesis and the beliefs of evolutionary geologists only if one understands "Genesis 1 in a completely literal fashion," which, he asserts, is unnecessary. Dr. Archer has suggested that "God gave Adam a major assignment in natural history. He was to classify **every species of animal and bird** found in the preserve" (1982, p. 59). He further stated that it

> ...must have taken a good deal of study for Adam to examine each specimen and decide on an appropriate name for it, especially in view of the fact that he had absolutely no human tradition behind him, so far as nomenclature was concerned. It must have required some years, or, at the very least, a considerable number of months for him to complete this comprehensive inventory of all the birds, beasts, and insects that populated the Garden of Eden (p. 60).

One would be hard pressed to find a better example of "the theory becoming father to the exegesis" than this.* Archer simply has "read into" the divine narrative the assumptions of his baseless view. Let us take a careful look at the Bible **facts**.

First, apparently only those animals that God "brought" unto Adam were involved, and this seems to be limited (as Archer concedes) to Eden. Second, certain creatures were excluded. There is no mention, for example, of fish or creeping things. Third, the text does not suggest how broad the categories were that Adam was to name. It is sheer assertion to claim that he was to name "**every species**." God created living organisms according to "kinds"—a word that, as it is used in the Bible, appears to be a rather elastic term. It translates the Hebrew word *min*, which sometimes seems to indicate species, sometimes genus, and sometimes family or order. [But, as Walter C. Kaiser, chairman of the department of Old Testament and Semitic languages, Trinity Divinity School, has observed: "This gives no support to the classical evolutionist view which requires developments across kingdom, phyla, and classes" (see Harris, et al., 1980, 1:504).] Fourth, why should it be assumed that Adam had to "give a good deal of study" to this particular situation? He never had to "study" such things as walking, talking, or tilling the ground; clearly Adam had been endowed miraculously with a mature knowledge that enabled him to make his way in that antique environment. He needed no "human tradition" behind him; he was "of God" (see Luke 3:38). Let us examine what some other scholars have said about this. C.F. Keil observed that although Adam and Eve were created on the same day, "there is no difficulty in this, since it would not have required much time to bring the animals to Adam to see what he would call them, as the animals of paradise are all we have to think of" (1971, 1:87). H.C. Leupold concurred:

---

* I would like to thank my friend and colleague, Wayne Jackson, for permission to edit and reproduce portions of this material from *Reason & Revelation*, the monthly journal on Christian evidences that he and I formerly co-edited (and for which I currently serve as editor).

> [T]hat there is a limitation of the number of creatures brought before man is made apparent by two things. In the first place, the beasts are described as beasts **of the field** (*haseh*), not beasts **of the earth**, as in 1:24. Though there is difficulty in determining the exact limits of the term "field" in this instance, there is great likelihood (cf. also v. 5) that it may refer to the garden only. In the second place, the fish of the sea are left out, also in v. 20, as being less near to man. To this we are inclined to add a third consideration, the fact, namely, that the garden could hardly have been a garden at all if all creatures could have overrun it unimpeded. Since then, very likely, only a limited number of creatures are named, the other difficulty falls away, namely, that man could hardly have named all creatures in the course of a day (1942, 1:130-131, emp. in orig.).

As Henry Morris has pointed out,

> ...the created kinds undoubtedly represented broader categories than our modern species or genera, quite possibly approximating in most cases the taxonomic family. Just how many kinds were actually there to be named is unknown, of course, but it could hardly have been as many as a thousand. Although even this number would seem formidable to us today, it should be remembered that Adam was newly created, with mental activity and physical vigor corresponding to an unfallen state. He certainly could have done the job in a day and, at the very most, it would have taken a few days even for a modern-day person, so there is nothing anywhere in the account to suggest that the sixth day was anything like a geological age (1984, p. 129, emp. in orig.).

As it turns out, Dr. Archer's argument about the animals is much ado about nothing.

Archer further contended that this extended period of naming the animals left Adam with a "long and unsatisfying experience as a lonely bachelor" and so he was "emotionally prepared" when Eve finally arrived on the scene. One writer declared concerning Adam: "It seems that he had been searching diligently for a long time for a suitable mate, and when he found her, he burst out, **This at last** [literally, 'this time'] **is bone of my bones**, etc." (Willis, 1979, p. 113, emp. and bracketed item in orig.).

Again, one can only express amazement at how some scholars so adroitly "read between the lines." There is nothing in the statement, "This is now bone of my bones" that hints at—much less demands—a long, lonely bachelorhood for Adam. The Hebrew word translated "now" is *pa'am*. The term does not require a protracted span of time, as asserted by Willis. It can denote simply a contrast with that which has been recorded previously, as it does in this context. Professor M.W. Jacobus observed that the term denoted "**this time—in this instance**, referring to the other **pairs**," and so simply expressed Adam's satisfaction with his mate in contrast to the animals he had been naming (1864, p. 110, emp. in orig.). Robert Jamieson wrote:

> ...**this time**, is emphatic (cf. 30:30; 46:30). It signifies "now indeed," "now at last," as if his memory had been rapidly recalling the successive disappointments he had met with in not finding, amidst all the living creatures presented to him, any one capable of being a suitable companion to him (1945, 1:46, emp. in orig.).

There is, therefore, nothing in Genesis 2 that is in conflict with the plain, historical statements of Genesis 1:27ff.: "And God created man in his own image, in the image of God created he him; male and female created he them.... And there was evening and there was morning, the sixth day." As I have pointed out repeatedly, the Scriptures indicate that the creation week of six days was composed of the same kind of "days" that the Hebrews employed in their observance of the Sabbath (Exodus 20:8-11), and though this argument has been ridiculed, **it never has been answered**.

There is another point, from the New Testament, that is worthy of consideration. In 1 Timothy 2:13, Paul wrote: "For Adam was first formed, **then** Eve." Of special interest here is the word "then" [Greek, *eita*]. This term is an adverb of time meaning "then; next; after that" (Thayer, 1962, p. 188). It is found 16 times in the New Testament in this sense. [Once it is employed in argumentation to add a new reason and so is rendered "furthermore" (Hebrews 12:9).] The word, therefore, generally is used to suggest a logical sequence between two occurrences and **there never is an indication that a long lapse of time separates the two**. Note the following:

(a) Jesus "girded himself. Then [*eita*] he poureth water into the basin" (John 13:5).

(b) From the cross, Jesus said to Mary, "Woman, behold thy son! Then [*eita*] saith he to the disciple..." (John 19:26-27). Compare also John 20:27—"Then [*eita*] saith he to Thomas..." and Mark 8:25.

(c) In Luke 8:12, some seed fell by the wayside, "then [*eita*] cometh the devil and taketh away the word from their heart." And, note Mark's parallel: "Straightway cometh Satan, and taketh away the word" (4:15). These examples reveal no long lapses of time.

(d) James said a man "is tempted when he is drawn away by his own lust, and enticed. Then [*eita*] the lust, when it hath conceived, beareth sin" (1:14-15). How long does that take?

(e) Christ appeared to Cephas; "then [*eita*] to the twelve" (1 Corinthians 15:5) and this was on the same day (Luke 24:34-36). See also 1 Corinthians 15:7.

(f) In speaking of Christ's coming, Paul declared: "Then [*eita*] cometh the end" (1 Corinthians 15:23-24). Will there be a long span of time (1,000 years), as the millennialists allege, between Christ's coming and the end? Indeed not.

(g) For the other uses of *eita*, see Mark 4:17, Mark 4:28, 1 Corinthians 12:28, and 1 Timothy 3:10.

So, "Adam was first formed, then [*eita*] Eve" (1 Timothy 2:13). Paul's use of this adverb, as compared with similar New Testament usages elsewhere, is perfectly consistent with Moses' affirmation that Adam and Eve were made on the same literal day of history.

God's Sabbath Rest Still Is Continuing

Day-Age theorists sometimes suggest that the seventh "day" still is continuing. Their argument is that since "evening and morning" is not mentioned in regard to the seventh day, it must not have been a 24-hour day. Therefore, we are living in the seventh day—a position they must defend to remain consistent. There are, however, a number of serious problems with this approach. The first has been explained by Woods.

> Jehovah finished his labors at the end of the sixth day, and on the seventh rested. The narrative provides no basis for the assumption that the day he rested differed in any fashion from those which preceded it. It evidently was marked out and its length determined in the same manner as the others. If it was not a day of twenty-four hours, it sustains no resemblance to the sabbath which was given to the Israelites (1976b, pp. 17-18).

Moses' obvious intent was for the reader to understand that God: (1) rested (past tense); and (2) gave the seventh day (the Sabbath) as a day of rest because He had rested on that day.

There is a second problem with the view that the seventh day still is continuing. James Pilgrim has addressed that problem.

> ...if the "day-age" theorists accept day seven as an "age" also, we ask, "What about day eight, or day nine, or day ten...?" On the **assumption** that the earth is 7,000 years old (a most distinct possibility), let the "day-age" proclaimers put 2,555,000 days (7,000 years at 365 days per year) on a page. Now let them circle the day which began the normal 24-hour day. Let them also give just one scripture reference to substantiate the validity of that circle. Can they do it? No! Will they do it? No! (1976, 118[33]:522, emp. in orig.).

The third problem with the idea that the seventh day is continuing has to do with Adam, as Woods has noted:

> Adam, the first man, was created in the **sixth** day, lived through the **seventh** day, and into at least a portion of the **eighth** day. If these days were long geologic periods of **millions** of years in length, we have the interesting situation of Adam hav-

ing lived in a portion of **one** age, through the whole of **another** age, and into at least a portion of a third age, in which case he was many millions of years old when he finally died! Such a view of course is absurd; and so are the premises which would necessitate it (1976b, p 18, emp. in orig.).

Whitcomb has explained **why** these things are true:

...Genesis 2:2 adds that He rested on the seventh day. That day also must have been literal, because otherwise the seventh day which God blessed and sanctified would have been cursed when God cursed the world and cast Adam and Eve out of the Garden. You see, the seventh day must have ended and the next week commenced before that Adamic curse could have come. Adam and Eve lived through the entire seventh day and into the following week, which is simply a confirmation of the fact that each of the days, including the seventh, was literal (1973a, 2:64-65).

It also has been suggested that Hebrews 4:4-11, where the writer speaks of the **continuation** of God's Sabbath rest, provides support for the Day-Age Theory. First, I would like to present the passage in question along with the argument made from it. Then I would like to offer an explanation of why the passage does not lend credence to the Day-Age Theory and why the argument based on it is faulty. Here is the passage.

For he hath said somewhere of the seventh day on this wise, "And God rested on the seventh day from all his works"; and in this place again, "They shall not enter into my rest." Seeing therefore it remaineth that some should enter thereinto, and they to whom the good tidings were before preached failed to enter because of disobedience, he again defineth a certain day, "Today," saying in David so long a time afterward (even as hath been said before), "Today if ye shall hear his voice, Harden not your hearts." For if Joshua had given them rest, he would not have spoken afterward of another day. There remaineth therefore a sabbath rest for the people of God. For he that is entered into his rest hath himself also rested from his works, as God did from his. Let us therefore give diligence to enter into that rest, that no man fall after the same example of disobedience.

Here is the argument. Proponents of the Day-Age Theory suggest that since God's Sabbath Day (the seventh day of the creation week) continues to this very day, then it follows logically that the other days of the creation week were long periods of time as well (see Ross, 1994, pp. 48-49,59-60; Geisler and Brooks, 1990, p. 230). In support of this position, Hugh Ross wrote: "Further information about the seventh day is given in Hebrews 4. ...we learn that God's day of rest continues" (1994, p. 49).

Wrong! Here is the correct meaning of the passage. While the text speaks clearly of the cessation—beginning on the seventh day—of God's creative activity, that text nowhere suggests that God's seventh day has continued from the past into the present. Nor does the passage speak of the duration of the seventh day. Van Bebber and Taylor have addressed this point.

> Like David in the Psalms, the writer of Hebrews is warning the elect not to be disobedient and hard-hearted. Thus, he alludes to Israel in the wilderness who because of their hard hearts could not receive God's promise of rest in Canaan. "Rest," as used in these verses by both David and the writer of Hebrews, had a specific historic reference to the promised land of Canaan. The Hebrew word used by David for "rest" was *menuwchah*, which is a general term for rest which has a special **locational** emphasis (e.g., "**the resting place or abode of resting**") [see Brown, et al., 1979, p. 629b]. This concept is echoed by the author of Hebrews who uses the Greek word *katapausis*, which also may refer to an abode or location of resting (Hebrews 4:1,3-5,8).

> At the climax of this passage, the author promises a future day of rest (Hebrews 4:9, Greek: *Sabbatismos*). This is the only time in the New Testament that this word for "rest" is employed. It seems to be a deliberate reference to Day Seven of Creation. The author does not say, however, that the seventh day continues on into the future. He uses *Sabbatismos* without an article (like saying **a** Sabbath, rather than **the** Sabbath). In Greek, this grammatical structure would generally represent the character or nature of Day Seven, **without really being Day Seven**. That is, the context makes it clear that the future day of rest will be similar to the original sev-

> enth day. The task will be complete; we will live with Christ eternally—our work on earth will be done (1996, pp. 72-73, emp., parenthetical, and bracketed items in orig.).

The passage in Hebrews is using the **essence** of the seventh day of creation to refer to the coming **essence** of heaven—i.e., a place of rest. It is not speaking about the actual **length** of that seventh day. Furthermore, the fact that God has not been involved in creative activity since the close of day six says absolutely nothing about the duration of the individual days of creation. When God completed the creation, He "rested"—but **only from His work of creation**. He is very much at work now—but **in His work of redemption**, not creation. Jesus Himself said: "My Father worketh even until now" (John 5:17). While it **is correct** to say that God's rest from creative activity continues to this very hour, it **is not correct** to say that His Sabbath Day continues. That was not the point the Hebrew writer was trying to make, and to suggest that it was represents either a misunderstanding or misuse (or both) of the passage.

God was not saying, via the Hebrew writer, that He wanted to share a **literal** Sabbath Day's rest with His creation. Rather, He was saying that He intended to enjoy a rest that was **typified** by the Sabbath Day's rest. The Israelites who rebelled against God in the wilderness were not able to share either a "rest" by entering into the physical presence of the promised land or a "rest" by entering into the eternal presence of God. Lenski commented on the text as follows:

> **The point lies in taking all these passages together**. The rest from which the Jews of the Exodus were excluded, into which we are entering, is God's rest, the great Sabbath since the seventh day, of course not of the earthly days and years that have rolled by since then and are still continuing but the timeless, heavenly state that has been established and intended for men in their glorious union with God.
>
> These are not different kinds of rest: the rest of God since creation and a future rest for his people; or a rest into which men have already entered and one that has been established

since the redemptive work of Jesus, into which they are yet to enter; or a rest "at the conclusion of the history of mankind." **The seventh day after the six days of creation was a day of twenty-four hours**. On this day God did not create. Thus God made the first seven-day week (Exod. 20:8-11; 31:12-17), and the Sabbath of rest was "a sign" (v. 17) so that at every recurrence of this seventh day Israel might note the significance of this sign, this seventh day of rest being a **type** and a **promise** of the rest instituted for man since the days of creation. Like Canaan, the Sabbath was a type and a promise of this rest (1966a, pp. 132-133, emp. added).

Additionally, even if it could be proven somehow that the seventh day of creation were longer than the others (which it cannot), that still would establish only one thing—that the **seventh day** was longer. It would say absolutely nothing about the length of the other six days. And concerning those days, the Bible could not be any clearer than it is in explaining their duration of approximately twenty-four hours. Genesis 1 defines them as periods of "evening and morning" (1:5, 8,13,19,23,31). While God's **activity** within each literal day may have been miraculous, there is nothing miraculous about the **length** of the days themselves. They were, quite simply, the same kinds of "days" that we today enjoy. Attempts to reinterpret the message of Hebrews 4 do not alter that fact.

I would like to offer those who are enamored with the Day-Age Theory the following challenge (as set forth by Fields) for serious and thoughtful consideration:

It is our conclusion, therefore, that the Day-Age Theory is impossible. It is grammatically and exegetically preposterous. Its only reason for existence is its allowance for the **time** needed by the evolutionary geology and biology. We would like to suggest two courses of action for those who so willingly wed themselves to such extravagant misinterpretations of the Scripture: either (1) admit that the Bible and contemporary uniformitarian geology are at odds, reject biblical creation, and defend geological and biological evolution over billions of years; or (2) admit that the Bible and contemporary uniformitarian geology are at odds, study all the geological indications of the **recent creation** of the earth, accept the implications of Noah's flood, and believe the recent creationism of the Bible. One must choose either the chronological scheme of uniformitarianism or the chronological scheme of the Bible, **but the inconsistencies of this sort of interpretation of the Hebrew text for the purpose of harmonizing mutually exclusive and hopelessly contradictory positions can no longer be tolerated** (1976, pp. 178-179, emp. in orig. except for last sentence).

Chapter 9

The Bible and the Age of the Earth— The Gap Theory

In recent years, the Day-Age Theory has fallen on hard times. Numerous expositors have outlined its shortcomings, and have shown that it is without lexical or exegetical support. It has failed utterly to secure the goals and objectives of its advocates—i.e., the injection of geological time into the Genesis account in a biblically and scientifically logical manner, with the subsequent guarantee of an ancient Earth. Therefore, even though it still has retained its popularity within limited circles, it has been rejected by many old-Earth creationists, theistic evolutionists, and progressive creationists.

Yet the Bible believer who nevertheless desires to accommodate his theology to the geologic ages, and to retain his belief in an old Earth, somehow must fit vast time spans into the creation account of Genesis 1. As I explained earlier, there are but three options. The time needed to ensure an old Earth might be placed: (a) **during** the creation week; (b) **before** the creation week; or (c) **after** the creation week. I have documented, in my review of the Day-Age Theory in the previous chapter, that the geologic ages cannot be placed into the biblical text **during** the creation week. I now would like to examine the suggestion that they may be inserted **before** the creation week.

For over 150 years, those Bible believers who were determined to insert the geologic ages into the biblical record of origins, yet who realized the inadequacy of the Day-Age Theory to accomplish that task, have suggested that it is possible to place the geologic ages **before** the creation week using what is referred to most commonly as the Gap Theory (also known by such synonyms as the Ruin-and-Reconstruction Theory, the Ruination/Re-creation Theory, the Pre-Adamic Cataclysm Theory, and the Restitution Theory).

Modern popularity of the Gap Theory generally is attributed to the writings of Thomas Chalmers, a nineteenth-century Scottish theologian. Ian Taylor, in his book, *In the Minds of Men*, provided this summary:

> An earlier attempt to reconcile geology and Scripture had been put forward by another Scotsman, Thomas Chalmers, an evangelical professor of divinity at Edinburgh University. He founded the Free Church of Scotland, and because of his outreach to the poor and destitute he later became known as the "father of modern sociology." Traceable back to the rather obscure writings of the Dutchman Episcopius (1583-1643), Chalmers formed an idea, which became very popular and is first recorded in one of his lectures of 1814: "The detailed history of Creation in the first chapter of Genesis begins at the middle of the second verse."* Chalmers went on to explain that the first statement, "In the beginning God created the Heavens and the Earth and the Earth was without form and void and darkness was on the face of the deep," referred to a pre-Adamic age, about which Scripture was essentially silent. Some great catastrophe had taken place, which

---

* See: Chalmers, Thomas (1857), "Natural Theology," in William Alanna, ed., *Select Works of Thomas Chalmers* (Edinburgh, Scotland: Thomas Constable), volume five of the twelve volume set.

left the earth "without form and void" or ruined, in which state it remained for as many years as the geologist required. Finally, approximately six thousand years ago, the Genesis account continues, "The spirit of God moved upon the face of the waters." The remaining verses were then said to be the account of how this present age was restored and all living forms, including man, created (1984, pp. 362-363).

Through the years, the Gap Theory has undergone an "evolution" of its own, and for that reason is not easy to define. There are several variations of the theory, and at times its defenders do not even agree among themselves on strict interpretations. I will define the theory as many of its advocates have, recognizing that no single definition can be all-inclusive or encompass all possible facets of the theory. A brief summation of the main tenets of the Gap Theory might be as follows.

The widely held view among Gap theorists today is that the original creation of the world by God, as recorded in Genesis 1:1, took place billions of years ago. The creation then was despoiled because of Satan's disobedience, resulting in his being cast from heaven with his followers. A cataclysm occurred at the time of Satan's rebellion, and is said by proponents of the Gap Theory to have left the Earth in darkness ("waste and void") as a divine judgment because of the sin of Satan in rebelling against God. The world as God had created it, with all its inhabitants,* was destroyed and left "waste and void," which, it is claimed, accounts for the myriad fossils present in the Earth. Then, God "re-created" (or "restored") the Earth in six literal, 24-hour days. Genesis 1, therefore, is the story of an original, perfect creation, a judgment and ruination, and a re-creation. While there are other minor details that could be included, this represents the essence of the Gap Theory.

This compromise is popular with those who wish to find a place in Genesis 1 for the geologic ages, but who, for whatever reason(s),

---

* Many holding to this theory place the fossils of dinosaurs, so-called "ape-men," and other extinct forms of life in this gap, thereby hoping to avoid having to explain them in the context of God's present creation.

reject the Day-Age Theory. The Gap Theory is intended to harmonize Genesis and geology on the grounds of allowing vast periods of time between Genesis 1:1 and Genesis 1:2, in order to account for the geologic ages. George H. Pember, one of the earliest defenders of the Gap Theory, wrote:

> Hence we see that geological attacks upon the Scriptures are altogether wide of the mark, are a mere beating of the air. There is room for any length of time between the first and second verses of the Bible. And again; since we have no inspired account of the geological formations we are at liberty to believe they were developed in the order we find them (1876, p. 28).

The *Scofield Reference Bible*,* in its footnotes on Genesis 1:11, suggested: "Relegate fossils to the primitive creation, and no conflict of science with the Genesis cosmogony remains" (1917, p. 4). Harry Rimmer, in his book, *Modern Science and the Genesis Record* (1937), helped popularize the Gap Theory. Canadian anthropologist Arthur C. Custance produced *Without Form and Void* (1970)—the text that many consider the ablest defense of the Gap Theory ever put into print. George Klingman, in *God Is* (1929), opted for the Gap Theory, as did Robert Milligan in *The Scheme of Redemption* (1972 reprint). George DeHoff advocated the Gap Theory in *Why We Believe the Bible* (1944), and J.D. Thomas, stated in his text, *Evolution and Antiquity*, that in his opinion no one "can prove that it is not true, at least in part" (1961, p. 54).

John N. Clayton has accepted major portions of the Gap Theory, but has altered it to suit his own geological/theological purposes. The end result is an extremely unusual hybrid known as the Modified Gap Theory (see: Clayton, 1976b, pp. 147-148; Jackson and Thompson, 1992, pp. 114-130; McIver, 1988b, 8[3]:1-23; Thompson, 1977, pp. 192-194; 1999a, 19:67-70).

---

* First published in 1909, by 1917 the Scofield Reference Bible had placed the Gap Theory into the footnotes accompanying Genesis 1; in more recent editions, references to the theory may be found as a footnote to Isaiah 45.

SUMMARY OF THE GAP THEORY

Those who advocate the Gap Theory base their views on several arguments, a summary of which is given here; comments and refutation will follow.

1. Gap theorists suggest that two Hebrew words in the creation account mean entirely different things. Gap theorists hold to the belief that *bara* (used in Genesis 1:1,21,27) means "to create" (i.e., *ex nihilo* creation). *Asah*, however, does not mean "to create," but instead means "to re-create" or "to make over." Therefore, we are told, the original creation was "created"; the creation of the six days was "made" (i.e., "made over").

2. Gap theorists suggest that the Hebrew verb *hayetha* (translated "was" in Genesis 1:2) should be rendered "became" or "had become"—a translation required in order to suggest a change of state from the original perfect creation to the chaotic conditions implied in verse 2.

3. Gap theorists believe that the "without form and void" of Genesis 1:2 (Hebrew *tohu wabohu*) can refer only to something once in a state of repair, but now ruined. Pember accepted these words as expressing "an outpouring of the wrath of God." Gap theorists believe the cataclysm that occurred was on the Earth, and was the direct result of Satan's rebellion against God. The cataclysm, of course, is absolutely essential to the Gap Theory. Isaiah 14:12-15 and Ezekiel 28:11-17 are used as proof-texts to bolster the theory.

4. Gap theorists believe that Isaiah 45:18 ("God created the earth not in vain"—Hebrew, *tohu*; same word as "without form" in Genesis 1:2) is a proof-text that God did **not** create the Earth *tohu*. Therefore, they suggest, Genesis 1:2 can refer only to a judgment brought upon the early Earth by God.

5. Gap theorists generally believe that there was a pre-Adamic creation of both non-human and human forms. Allegedly, Jeremiah 4:23-26 is the proof-text that requires such a position, which accounts for the fossils present in the Earth's strata.

THE GAP THEORY—A REFUTATION

The above points adequately summarize the positions of those who advocate the Gap Theory. I now would like to suggest the following reasons why the Gap Theory should be rejected as false.

1. The Gap Theory is false because of the "mental gymnastics" necessary to force its strained argumentation to agree with the actual biblical text. Even Bernard Ramm, who championed the idea of progressive creationism, found those mental gymnastics a serious argument against the theory's unorthodox nature.

> It gives one of the grandest passages in the Bible a most peculiar interpretation. From the earliest Bible interpretation this passage has been interpreted by Jews, Catholics, and Protestants as the **original creation of the universe**. In six majestic days the universe and all of life is brought into being. But according to Rimmer's view the great first chapter of Genesis, save for the first verse, is not about original creation at all, but about reconstructions. The primary origin of the universe is stated in but one verse. This is not the most telling blow against the theory, but it certainly indicates that something has been lost to make the six days of creation anti-climactic.... Or, in the words of Allis: "The first objection to this theory is that it throws the account of creation almost completely out of balance.... It seems highly improbable that an original creation which according to this theory brought into existence a world of wondrous beauty would be dismissed with a single sentence and so many verses devoted to what would be in a sense merely a restoration of it" (1954, p. 138, emp. in orig.).

2. The Gap Theory is false because it is based on a forced, artificial, and altogether incorrect distinction between God's creating (*bara*) and making (*asah*). According to the standard rendition of the Gap Theory, **these two words always must mean entirely different things**. The term *bara* always must refer to the act of "creating" (i.e., an "original" creation), while the term *asah* can refer only to the act of "making" (i.e., not an original creation, but something "re-made" or "made over"). A review of the use

of these two Hebrew words throughout the Old Testament, however, clearly indicates that quite frequently they are used interchangeably. Morris has commented:

> The Hebrew words for "create" (*bara*) and for "make" (*asah*) are very often used quite interchangeably in Scripture, at least when God is the one referred to as creating or making. Therefore, the fact that *bara* is used only three times in Genesis 1 (vv. 1,21, and 27) certainly does not imply that the other creative acts, in which "made" or some similar expression is used, were really only acts of restoration. For example, in Genesis 1:21, God "created" the fishes and birds; in 1:25, He "made" the animals and creeping things. In verse 26, God speaks of "making" man in His own image. The next verse states that God "created" man in His own image. No scientific or exegetical ground exists for distinction between the two processes, except perhaps a matter of grammatical emphasis.... Finally, the summary verse (Genesis 2:3) clearly says that **all** of God's works, both of "creating" and "making" were completed with the six days, after which God "rested" (1966, p. 32, emp. in orig.).

The insistence by Gap theorists, and by those sympathetic with them, that *bara* **always** must mean "to create something from nothing" is, quite simply, wrong. Such a view has been advocated by such writers as John Clayton* (1990c, 17[4]:7) and Hugh Ross** (1991, p. 165). Yet Old Testament scholar C.F. Keil, in his commentary, *The Pentateuch,* concluded that when *bara* appears in its basic form, as it does in Genesis 1,

> ...it always means **to create**, and is only applied to a divine creation, the production of that which had no existence before. It is never joined with an accusative of the material, **although it does not exclude a pre-existent material un-**

* The documentation for Clayton's position will be presented in chapter 12 in an examination and refutation of his Modified Gap Theory.

** Ross has stated: "The Hebrew word for 'created,' *bara*, refers **always** to divine activity. The word emphasizes the newsness of the created object. It means to bring something entirely new, something previously non-existent, into existence" (1991, p. 165, emp. added).

conditionally, but is used for the creation of man (ver. 27, ch. v. 1,2), and of everything new that God creates, whether in the kingdom of nature (Numbers xvi.30) or of that of grace (Ex. xxxiv.10; Ps. li.10, etc.) [1971, 1:47, first emp. in orig., last emp. added].

Furthermore, the Old Testament contains numerous examples which prove beyond the shadow of a doubt that *bara* and *asah* **are** used interchangeably. For example, in Psalm 148:1-5, the writer spoke of the "creation" (*bara*) of the angels. But when Nehemiah wrote of that same event (9:6), he employed the word *asah* to describe it. In Genesis 1:1, the text speaks of God "creating" (*bara*) the Earth. Yet, when Nehemiah spoke of that same event (9:6), he employed the word *asah*. When Moses wrote of the "creation" of man, he used *bara* (Genesis 1:27). But one verse before that, he spoke of the "making" (*asah*) of man. Moses also used the two words **in the same verse** (Genesis 2:4) when he said: "These are the generations of the heavens and of the earth when they were **created** [*bara*], in the day that Jehovah **made** [*asah*] earth and heaven."

Gap theorists teach that the Earth was **created** (*bara*) from nothing in Genesis 1:1. But Moses said in Genesis 2:4 that the Earth was **made** (*asah*). Various gap theorists are on record as stating that the use of *asah* can refer **only** to that which is made from something **already in existence**. Yet they do not believe that when Moses spoke of the Earth being "made," it was formed from something already in existence.

Consider also Exodus 20:11 in this context. Moses wrote: "For in six days the Lord made [*asah*] heaven and earth, the sea and all that in them is, and rested the seventh day." Gap theorists contend that this verse speaks only of God's "re-forming" from something already in existence. But notice that the verse specifically speaks of the **heaven**, the Earth, the **seas**, and **all that in them is**. Gap theorists, however, do not contend that God formed the heavens from something already in existence. The one verse that Gap theorists never have been able to answer is Nehemiah 9:6.

Thou art Jehovah, even thou alone; thou hast made [asah] heaven, the heaven of heavens, with all their host, the earth and all things that are thereon, the seas and all that is in them, and thou preservest them all; and the host of heaven worshippeth thee.

The following quotation from Fields will explain why.

...in Nehemiah 9:6 the objects of God's making (asa) include the **heavens**, the **host of heavens**, and the **earth**, and **everything contained in and on it**, and the **seas and everything they contain**, as well as the **hosts of heaven** (probably angels).

Now this is a very singular circumstance, for those who argue for the distinctive usage of asa throughout Scripture must, in order to maintain any semblance of consistency, never admit that the same creative acts can be referred to by both the verb bara and the verb asa. Thus, since Genesis 1:1 says that God **created** (bara) the **heavens** and the **earth**, and Exodus 20:11 and Nehemiah 9:6 contend that he **made** (asa) them, there must be **two distinct events** in view here. In order to be consistent and at the same time deal with the evidence, gap theorists must postulate a time when God not only "appointed" or "made to appear" the **firmament**, the **sun**, the **moon** and **stars**, and the **beasts**, but there also must have been a time when he only appointed the **heavens**, the **heaven of heavens**, the **angels** (hosts), the **earth, everything on the earth**, the **sea** and **everything in the sea**!

So that, while asa is quite happily applied to the firmament, sun, moon, stars, and the beasts, its further application to **everything else contained in the universe**, and, indeed, the universe itself (which the language in both Exodus 20:11 and Nehemiah 9:6 is intended to convey) creates a monstrosity of interpretation which should serve as a reminder to those who try to fit Hebrew words into English molds, that to straitjacket these words is to destroy the possibility of coherent interpretation completely! (1976, pp. 61-62, emp. in orig.).

Whitcomb was correct when he concluded:

These examples should suffice to show the absurdities to which we are driven by making distinctions which God never intended to make. For the sake of variety and fullness of expression (a basic and extremely helpful characteristic of Hebrew literature), different verbs are used to convey the concept of supernatural creation. It is particularly clear that whatever shade of meaning the rather flexible verb **made** (*asah*) may bear in other contexts of the Old Testament, in the context of **Genesis 1** it stands as a synonym for **created** (*bara*) [1972, p. 129, emp. and parenthetical comment in orig.].

3. The Gap Theory is false because, in the context of Genesis 1:2, there is no justification for translating the verb "was" (Hebrew, *hayetha*) as "became." Gap theorists insist upon such a translation, of course, in order to promote the idea that the Earth **became** "waste and void" after the Satanic rebellion. Yet usage of the verb *hayah* argues against the translation, "The earth **became** waste and void" (Genesis 1:2). Ramm noted:

> The effort to make **was** mean **became** is just as abortive. The Hebrews did not have a word for **became** but the verb **to be** did service for **to be** and **become**. The form of the verb **was** in Genesis 1:2 is the Qal, perfect, third person singular, feminine. A Hebrew concordance will give all the occurrences of that form of the verb. A check in the concordance with reference to the usage of this form of the verb in Genesis reveals that in almost every case the meaning of the verb is simply **was**. Granted in a case or two **was** means **became** but if in the preponderance of instances the word is translated **was**, any effort to make one instance mean **became**, especially if that instance is highly debatable, is very insecure exegesis (1954, p. 139, emp. in orig.).

4. The Gap Theory is false because the Hebrew words *tohu wabohu* do not mean only "something once in a state of repair, but now ruined." Gap theorists believe that God's "initial" creation was **perfect**, but as a result of a Satanic rebellion **became** "waste and void" (*tohu wabohu*). Whitcomb has addressed this point.

> Many Bible students, however, are puzzled with the statement in Genesis 1:2 that the Earth was without form and void. Does God create things that have no form and are void? The answer, of course, depends on what those words mean. "Without form and void" translate the Hebrew expression *tohu wa-*

bohu, which literally means "empty and formless." In other words, the Earth was not chaotic, not under a curse of judgment. It was simply empty of living things and without the features that it later possessed, such as oceans and continents, hills and valleys—features that would be essential for man's well-being. ...when God created the Earth, this was only the first state of a series of stages leading to its completion (1973b, 2:69-70).

5. The Gap Theory is false because there is no biblical evidence whatsoever to substantiate the claim that Satan's rebellion against God took place on the Earth, much less was responsible for any great "cataclysm." The idea of a so-called cataclysm that destroyed the initial Earth is not supported by an appeal to Scripture, as Morris has explained.

> The great pre-Adamic cataclysm, which is basic to the gap theory, also needs explanation.... The explanation commonly offered is that the cataclysm was caused by Satan's rebellion and fall as described in Isaiah 14:12-15 and Ezekiel 28:11-17. Lucifer—the highest of all God's angelic hierarchy, the anointed cherub who covered the very throne of God—is presumed to have rebelled against God and tried to usurp His dominion. As a result, God expelled him from heaven, and he became Satan, the great adversary. Satan's sin and fall, however, was in heaven on the "holy mountain of God," not on earth. There is, in fact, not a word in Scripture to connect Satan with the earth prior to his rebellion. On the other hand, when he sinned, he was expelled from heaven **to** the earth. The account in Ezekiel says: "Thou wast perfect in thy ways from the day that thou wast created, till iniquity was found in thee. ...therefore I will cast thee as profane out of the mountain of God; and I will destroy thee, O covering cherub, from the midst of the stones of fire. Thine heart was lifted up because of thy beauty, thou has corrupted thy wisdom by reason of thy brightness: I will cast thee to the ground [or 'earth,' the same word in Hebrew]" (Ezekiel 28:15-17).*

---

* I do not agree with Dr. Morris' comments that Ezekiel 28 and Isaiah 14 refer to Satan, and his comments are not to be construed as representative of my views (see Thompson, 1999d). I have left his statements intact, however, to show how that the alleged "proof-texts" used by Gap theorists (even when they are removed from their proper context) do not suggest a Satanic cataclysm on Earth.

> There is, therefore, no scriptural reason to connect Satan's
> fall in heaven with a cataclysm on earth... (1974a, pp. 233-
> 234, emp and bracketed material in orig.).

6. The Gap Theory is false because its most important "proof-text"
   is premised on a removal of the verse from its proper context. That
   proof-text is Isaiah 45:18, which reads:

> For thus saith the Lord that created the heavens; God him-
> self that formed the earth and made it; he hath established
> it, he created it not in vain, he formed it to be inhabited.

In their writings, gap theorists suggest the following. Since Isaiah stated that God did **not** create the Earth *tohu*, and since the
Earth of Genesis **was** *tohu*, therefore the latter could not have
been the Earth as it was created originally in Genesis 1:1. The implication is that the Earth **became** *tohu* as a result of the cataclysm precipitated by Satan's rebellion against God.

The immediate context, however, has to do with Israel, and God's
promises to His people. Isaiah reminded his listeners that just as
God had a purpose in creating the Earth, so He had a purpose
for Israel. Isaiah spoke of God's immense power and special purpose in creation, noting that God created the Earth "to be inhabited"—something accomplished when the Lord created people
in His image. In Isaiah 45, the prophet's message is that God,
through His power, likewise will accomplish His purpose for His
chosen people. Morris remarked:

> There is no conflict between Isaiah 45:18 and the statement
> of an initial formless aspect to the created earth in Genesis
> 1:2. The former can properly be understood as follows: "God
> created it not (to be forever) without form; He formed it to
> be inhabited." As described in Genesis 1, He proceeded to
> bring beauty and structure to the formless elements and then
> inhabitants to the waiting lands.

> It should be remembered that Isaiah 45:18 was written many
> hundreds of years after Genesis 1:2 and that its context
> deals with Israel, not a pre-Adamic cataclysm (1974a, p. 241,
> parenthetical item in orig.).

7. The Gap Theory is false because it cannot be reconciled with God's commentary—made at the conclusion of His six days of creative activity—that the whole creation was "very good."

> Genesis 1:31 records God's estimate of the condition of this world at the end of the sixth day of creation. We read that "God saw **every thing** that he had made, and behold, it was very good. And the evening and the morning were the sixth day." If, in accordance with the gap theory, the world had already been destroyed, millions of its creatures were buried in fossil formations, and Satan had already become as it were, the god of this world, it is a little difficult to imagine how God could have placed Adam in such a wrecked world, walking over the fossils of creatures that he would never see or exercise dominion over, walking in a world that Satan was already ruling. Could God possibly have declared that everything He had made was very good? In other words, the text of Scripture when carefully compared with this theory creates more problems than the theory actually solves (Whitcomb, 1973b, 2:68-69, emp. added).

8. The Gap Theory is false because of God's plain statement that the Earth and all things in it were made in six days. Wayne Jackson has stated: "The matter can be actually settled by one verse, Exodus 20:11a: 'for in six days Jehovah made heaven and earth, the sea, and **all that in them is**....' If **everything** was made within six days, then **nothing** was created prior to those six days!" (1974, p. 34, emp. in orig.).

9. The Gap Theory is false because it specifically implies the death of humankind on the Earth prior to Adam and Eve. Pember believed that the fossils (which he felt the Gap Theory explained) revealed death, disease, and ferocity—all tokens of sin. He suggested:

> Since, then, the fossil remains are those of creatures anterior to Adam, and yet show evident token of disease, death, and mutual destruction, they must have belonged to another world, and have a sin-stained history of their own (1876, p. 35).

229

In making such a statement, however, Pember has leveled a serious charge against the Word of God—a charge that deserves intense scrutiny.

The idea that the death of humankind occurred **prior to** Adam's sin contradicts New Testament teaching that indicates the death of humankind entered this world **as a result of** Adam's sin (1 Corinthians 15:21; Romans 8:20-22; Romans 5:12). The apostle Paul stated in 1 Corinthians 15:45 that Adam was "the first man." Yet long before Adam—if the Gap Theory is correct—there existed a pre-Adamic race of men and women with (to quote Pember) "a sin-stained history of their own." But how could Paul, by inspiration of God, have written that Adam was the **first** man if, in fact, men had lived, sinned, and died before him? The simple fact of the matter is that Paul and the Gap Theory cannot both be correct.

A word of caution is in order here, however. Allow me to explain. As certain creationists have opposed both organic evolution and its religiously based cousins, theistic evolution and progressive creation, they have pointed out (correctly) that evolution not only is by definition a purely natural process, but also one that works via natural selection and survival of the fittest in a world where (to quote the famous British poet Lord Tennyson) "nature is red in tooth and claw." Those responsible for defining and defending the General Theory of Evolution have admitted as much. Earlier in this book, I quoted Harvard University's eminent evolutionist, George Gaylord Simpson, who wrote: "Evolution is a **fully natural** process, inherent in the physical properties of the universe, by which life arose in the first place, and by which all living things, past or present, have since developed, divergently and progressively" (1960, 131:969, emp. added). I also quoted the renowned evolutionary philosopher of science, David Hull, who observed that the evolutionary process is "rife with happenstance, contingency, incredible waste, death, pain and horror" (1991, 352:486).

Creationists have noted (again, correctly) that God's creative acts were **not** those of happenstance, contingency, and incredible waste. Rather, they were acts of deliberate, purposeful, intelligent design on the part of an omnipotent Creator. But in their attempts to oppose evolution and to make the case for the biblical account of origins, some creationists (who no doubt are well intentioned) have misinterpreted, and thus misapplied, the teachings of two important New Testament passages. The first of those passages is Romans 5:12-14.

> Therefore, as through **one man sin entered into the world, and death through sin**; and so death passed unto all men, for that all sinned: for until the law sin was in the world; but sin is not imputed when there is no law. Nevertheless death reigned from Adam until Moses, even over them that had not sinned after the likeness of Adam's transgression, who is a figure of him that was to come.

The second passage is 1 Corinthians 15:20-22:

> But now hath Christ been raised from the dead, the firstfruits of them that are asleep. For since **by man came death**, by man came also the resurrection of the dead. For as in Adam all die, so also in Christ shall all be made alive.

The portions of these two verses (shown in bold type) that are emphasized by certain creationists stress the fact that **death only entered the world because of man**. The argument set forth, therefore, is as follows. Evolution suggests that there were billions of years of "happenstance, contingency, incredible waste, **death**, pain, and horror" (to use Dr. Hull's exact words). Contrariwise, the Bible states quite specifically that death did not exist until Adam and Eve sinned against God. The evolutionary scenario, therefore, is apodictically impossible—regardless of whether the evolution being advocated is that found in atheistic (organic) evolution, theistic evolution, or progressive creation. Each requires vast eons of time, during which, so we are told, nature was viciously and uncaringly culling out evolutionary dead-ends and witnessing extinctions that resulted from the deaths of untold thousands of species of plants, animals, and "hominoids."

In addressing this point, creationist Henry M. Morris wrote:

Perhaps the most serious problem is theological. If we accept the geological ages at all, in effect we are saying that God used the methods and processes which exist in the present world to finally bring into the world the goal and culmination of His creative activity—man. This means, therefore, that at least a billion years of struggle, suffering, disorder, disease, storm, convulsions of all kinds, and, above all, death troubled the world before man ever entered the world and before any sin appeared in the world. The Bible, on the other hand, teaches quite emphatically that **there was no suffering or death in the world until after sin** came in. Romans 5:12 declares, "Wherefore, as by one man sin entered into the world, and death by sin; and so death passed upon all men, for that all have sinned."

Death by sin—there was no death in the world until sin was introduced. The present groaning, struggling creation of which we read in Romans dates Biblically from the time of the great curse God put on creation because of Adam's sin. So the whole creation now is under the bondage of corruption and decay and death because of man's sin. But if the concept of the geological ages is correct, there were geological ages and over a billion years of death in the world before any sin entered the world. Therefore, God must have used the principle of decay, suffering, and disorder. This is not the God revealed in the Bible—a merciful God, a gracious God, a God of order and power, not a God of confusion, random change and chance (1973, 3:72-73, emp. added).

In his book, *Man: Ape or Image—The Christian's Dilemma*, creationist John Rendle-Short wrote:

Sin entered the world through one man, Adam. Death also entered the world through Adam. **There had been no sin or death previously**.... It may even be argued that the plants did not die before Adam. Eating the fruit or foliage of plants does not kill them.... [T]he death of a plant is of a different order from death of an animal.... [P]lants are on a par with the basic earth, of lesser worth than animals.... [P]lants are not "living" and so cannot die as an animal does. That they were eaten by animals and man before the Fall is quite consistent with the statement that there was no death....

Death and dying are always against nature, the God-given order of things. Especially would this have been so before the Fall, at a time when God declared everything to be "**very good**" (1984, pp. 139,148,149, first emp. added, last emp. in orig.).

Another well-known creationist, Ken Ham, devoted a section of his 1987 book, *The Lie: Evolution*, to "No Death Before Adam's Fall." He wrote:

> The Bible clearly teaches that death, particularly the physical and spiritual death of man, entered the world only after the first man Adam sinned.... But what about the animals? Was death a part of the created animal world? **There are a number of reasons why I believe animal death as well as human death did not occur before the Fall**.... Before sin came into the world, death wasn't even a question—God had total control of the creation and sustained it 100 percent. There was no corruption or decay. Hence, death wasn't even a possibility.... Death and bloodshed came into the world as a judgment from God for man's rebellion. But at the same time death was the very means by which man was redeemed. So bloodshed could not have existed before man's fall. There was no bloodshed before Adam sinned: everything was perfect and **death was not a part of animal existence** (1987, pp. 137-138,139, emp. added).

Thirteen years later, in his book, *Did Adam Have a Bellybutton?*, Mr. Ham repeated the same sentiments (2000, pp. 16-17, 24,88-89,91,149)

Are the conclusions of these creationist authors—that there was **absolutely no death of any kind** prior to Adam and Eve's sin —correct? And even more important, are they scriptural? The answers are "No" and "No." To say that there was no **human** death prior to the Fall of man is to make a perfectly biblical statement. The passages in Romans 5 and 1 Corinthians 15 make that crystal clear. However, using those same scriptures to suggest that not even plants or animals could die ignores the specific context of each of the passages and is a serious abuse of the texts under consideration.

233

Paul's presentation in Romans 5:12-14 and 1 Corinthians 15:20-22 had nothing whatsoever to do with the death of either plants or animals. Rather, an examination of the passages reveals that, **in the context**, he was discussing **only the death of humans** —which resulted from the tragic events that occurred in the Garden of Eden. Notice his specific phraseology, not only in Romans chapter 5, but even continuing into chapter 6. The inspired apostle spoke of: (a) "if by the trespass of the one the many died, much more did the grace of God, and the gift by the grace of the one man, Jesus Christ, abound unto **the many**" (5:15); (b) "much more shall they that receive the abundance of grace and of the gift of righteousness reign in life through the one, even Jesus Christ" (5:17); (c) "as through one trespass the judgment came unto **all men** to condemnation; even so through one act of righteousness the free gift came unto **all men**" (5:18); (d) "as through the **one man's** disobedience the many were made sinners, even so through the obedience of the one shall **the many** be made righteous" (5:19); (e) "What shall we say then? Shall **we** continue in sin, that grace may abound? God forbid" (6:1-2); (f) "Let not sin therefore reign in your **mortal body**, that ye should obey the lusts thereof" (6:12); and (g) "I speak **after the manner of men**;... ye were servants of sin,...but now being made free from sin and become servants to God" (6:19-20,22).

Notice the terms (in bold type) that Paul used in his discussion of the fact of, punishment for, and salvation from sin. He spoke of "the many," "they," "all men," mankind's "mortal body," and "after the manner of men." Who, exactly, is represented by such terms? Surely, words and phrases such as these cannot have reference to plants and animals, but must instead refer solely to human beings. Furthermore, neither plants nor animals can sin; only humans are capable of committing such a travesty by revolting against their Maker. Only humans are recipients of the "gift by the grace of...Jesus Christ" (5:15). Only of humans may it be said that "the many shall be made righteous" (5:19).

Sin and death came **on** man **by** man (notice especially Paul's comment in Romans 5:12 that "death passed unto all **men**"). Anthropologist Arthur C. Custance correctly observed: "[I]t seems clearly intended by the record in Genesis that **death was in no sense inevitable for Adam**" (1976, pp 145-146, emp. added). But, **why** was it not inevitable? The simple fact is that the suspension of man's demise was provided by his continually having access to the tree of life that stood in the midst of the Garden (Genesis 2:9; 3:22). However, as Custance went on to remark: "Adam surrendered his potential immortality..." (p. 146). Thus Paul was constrained to say: "Through **one man** sin entered into the world, and **death through sin**" (Romans 5:12). Yet it must not be overlooked that the fateful promise of imminent death that resulted from having violated God's law was made **to Adam and Eve**, not to the rest of the creation (Genesis 2:17). Custance therefore lamented: "[I]n the very day that he ate, that day the process of dying began. Thenceforth it was merely a question of time" (p. 150)—which explains why we read in Genesis 5:5 that "all the days that Adam lived were nine hundred and thirty years: **and he died**."

When, then, did death and decay begin to occur in the natural (i.e., non-human) world? In an article titled, "Was There Death Before Adam?," Trevor Major addressed this point.

> This is difficult to answer from Scripture because its special concern is for the fate of man—the only being created in the image of God (Genesis 1:26-27). Perhaps plants and animals began to die from the moment of their creation. There is every suggestion that grass, fruit trees, birds, sea creatures, cattle, insects, and other organisms functioned quite normally even in the creation week. In this period they began to grow and to reproduce, so why could they not also begin to die and decay, as is the fate of all living things? (1990, 2[7]:2).

In his book, *God's Time Records in Ancient Sediments*, Dan Wonderly agreed when he suggested:

We of course agree that both spiritual and physical death in the human race originated with the tragic event of Adam's sin. But the beginning of death in the animal and plant kingdoms is simply not mentioned in any of the Scripture passages having to do with man's sin; nor is the time of the beginning of such death given in any other place in the Bible. ...Man was given the privilege of eating the fruits of the garden, and we certainly must assume that the "beasts of the field" and the "fowls" likewise supplied themselves with food from the garden. Thus we are led to the conclusion that the supply of the biological needs of animals and of man was basically the same in the Garden of Eden before the fall of man as it is today (1977, pp 236,237).*

Some might object, however, that Genesis 1:31 records that "God saw everything He had made, and, behold it was very good." As Rendle-Short opined: "Death and dying are always against nature, the God-given order of things. Especially would this have been so before the Fall, at a time when God declared everything to be "**very good**" (1984, p. 149, emp. in orig.). The question then becomes: "How could something be 'very good' if there was death and decay in the natural world?" This seeming problem is solved quite easily, however, if we recognize that, at times, what **we** prefer to label as "good" is not necessarily what **God** considers good. [Recall God's statement via the prophet Isaiah: "For my thoughts are not your thoughts, neither are your ways my ways" (Isaiah 55:8).] As Clifford Wilson put it: "If it were not for the principle in nature of life continuing through death, **all** life would soon be extinct.... Sometimes we must reassess our ideas on the basis of newly discovered facts. Is it 'good' to kill a mosquito, a spider, a snake?.... Remember, too, the Lord said to Peter, 'Rise, Peter, kill and eat' (Acts 10:13)" [1975, p. 34, emp. in orig.]. Wonderly went on to observe:

---

* While I wholeheartedly agree with Wonderly's conclusion that plant and animal death occurred prior to the Fall, I strongly disagree with the position he takes in his book that the Earth itself is ancient, with an age measured in billions of years rather than thousands (see Thompson, 1999b).

Actually, we should not be surprised that the regular death of even complex organisms was included in the "way of life" before the fall of man. God created the whole animal kingdom, and much of the plant kingdom, with dependence upon the intake of **food** for the production of energy; and that food is always organic material produced by cells. In nearly all cases these cells which provide food for man and other organisms must die, either before being eaten or soon afterwards, as they are digested. Even most of the fungi and bacteria are dependent upon cellular organisms which have died, to provide their food for energy and growth. In fact, some kinds of fungi and bacteria are equipped with mechanisms to produce strong enzymes which digest the living cells of plants and animals which are their food. Thus if death were not a part of the original world of living organisms, then the entire basis of their lives would have had to be different from any principle known on the earth today. But, as we have seen, such a difference is not in keeping with the Genesis account of life in the Garden of Eden (1977, p. 237, emp. in orig.).

If God has established something as the "natural order of things," then: (a) by definition it qualifies as "good"; and (b) who are we to suggest otherwise? Furthermore, if we ask, "How could something be good if it involves death and decay?" this begs the question by assuming that the normal operation of the natural world, including death and decay, is not "good."

Consider also the indefensible position in which a person finds himself when he asserts that there was absolutely **no death of any kind** prior to the Fall. As Major concluded:

[T]o insist that neither death nor decay existed in the non-human world before the sin of man, is to ask for special pleading. What of bacteria, adult butterflies, and other creatures that measure their longevity in terms of hours or days? What of the luckless ant that is trodden on by an elephant, or the fly which wanders into a spider's web? These creatures lived in a world governed by natural laws instituted by God during His creation. It is unnecessary to propose that God acted during this time like a machine, constantly intervening at every level to ensure the eternal preservation of all creatures until that terrible day when sin came into the world (1990, 2[7]:2).

Each of us should remember the adage that "a text removed from its context becomes little more than a pretext." Especially is this true when Scripture is involved. Paul's statements in Romans 5 and 1 Corinthians 15 about sin having entered the human race deal with exactly that in their original context—the entrance of sin among **humans**. While God's statement to Adam that "cursed is the ground for thy sake" (Genesis 3:17) informs us that man's sin ushered in certain drastic disadvantages for the animal and plant kingdoms, the statement, in and of itself, neither says nor implies that simultaneously this was the beginning of death among nature's non-human inhabitants. Wonderly properly summarized the problem associated with taking the position that there was no death prior to Adam and Eve's sin.

> The fact of the eating of plant materials in the Garden of Eden is readily admitted by all. Since plants are living organisms, with living cells similar to those of animals, there is no question but that the terms "life" and "death" are appropriate in speaking of them. Thus when man, the beasts, and the birds ate and digested plant materials, they were bringing about the death of living organisms. This fact is intensified when we realize that seeds contain young, living embryos; so when Adam and Eve ate nuts and seeds they were killing the young embryos within those seeds.... It is not possible for us as finite human beings to say that death in the **animal** world was not in the original, good plan of God, but that death in the **plant** world was in his plan. Who are we to say that plants and animals are less "alive" than animals? Plants can carry out some activities which animals cannot. Their cells are highly complex; and many plants produce motile reproductive cells —and even some motile non-reproductive cells—which swim about by means of flagella just as actively flagellated protozoans of the animal world.

> Also, the death of small animals must have been a regular occurrence in the Garden of Eden. It is difficult to conceive of the hoofed mammals roaming the fields day after day without crushing beetles and worms with their hoofs. And how could any sheep or cow pluck grass from the earth without eating the microscopic sized insects and mites which live on

the blades and upper roots of the plants? Beyond this, how could such animals drink large quantities of water from streams and pools without ingesting many tiny aquatic arthropod animals? It should also be remembered that such tiny insects and mites are not insignificant specks, but that there is only one phylum of animals which is more complex than they, namely, the phylum which contains the vertebrates. Each such tiny insect is equipped with a complex nervous system, well-developed eyes, an elaborate respiratory system, a chemically efficient excretory system, etc....

The same wisdom of God which led Him to ordain that plant life would serve as food for certain organisms could certainly have ordained that certain animals would also serve as food. For example, when God created the kinds of whales which live on microscopic organisms (as the blue whale), He surely foresaw that as they dashed through the water scooping up planktonic organisms their diet would include many kinds of tiny crustaceans which are very complex animals. Crustaceans belong to the same phylum as insects and have a degree of organization very similar to that of insects. Even if we might say that these whales may have originally eaten seaweed, we would have to remember that a vast number of these tiny crustaceans are found in among and clinging to the branches of the seaweed (1977, pp. 236-237,238, emp. in orig.).

Wilson was correct when he stated simply but emphatically: "Only for man was death the direct result of his fall and expulsion from the Garden of Eden" (1975, p. 33).

But some will ask: "What about obviously carnivorous animals? Were they carnivorous from the beginning, or did they become carnivorous after the sin and subsequent curse of man?" There can be no doubt that all animals were created by God **initially** to be herbivorous. Early in the book of Genesis we read:

And God said, "Behold, I have given you every herb yielding seed, which is upon the face of all the earth, and every tree, in which is the fruit of a tree yielding seed; to you it shall be for food: **and to every beast of the earth**, and to every bird of the heavens, and to everything that creepeth upon the earth, wherein there is life, **I have given every green herb for food**." And it was so (1:29-30, emp. added).

Later, however, after the Fall of man, there are indicators that not only were animals killed by man—at first for clothing (Genesis 3:21) and later for sacrifice (Genesis 4:4)—but that the animals themselves had become carnivorous. When God surveyed the situation immediately prior to the Great Flood, the text indicates that "God saw the earth, and, behold, it was corrupt; for **all flesh had corrupted their way** upon the earth. And God said unto Noah, 'The end of **all flesh** is come before me; for the earth is filled with violence'" (Genesis 6:12-13, emp. added). Some conservative Bible scholars have suggested the commentary that "all flesh had corrupted their way" so that the Earth was "filled with violence" may well signify that animals already had become carnivorous by the time God sent the Flood. [Of course, after the Flood God gave humans permission to eat meat as well (Genesis 9:3), but noted that "the fear of you and the dread of you shall be upon every beast of the earth, and upon every bird of the heavens" (9:2), indicating a permanent change in man's relationship to the Earth's animals.]

The issue also has been raised about how animals that, at present, seem well equipped only for a carnivorous existence might have survived in the pre-Flood world at a time when they were forced to exist solely as vegetarians (a concept plainly taught in Genesis 1:29-30). Wonderly has responded to such an inquiry as follows:

> There is, however, one problem which seems to be particularly bothersome to us, concerning the existence of violence and death in the animal world. This is the pattern of behavior and way of life of the carnivorous mammals. The seemingly ruthless capturing of other mammals, and even of human beings by carnivores appears to be—and perhaps is—contrary to what we believe concerning God's original creation. So we are quite willing to say that the carnivorous mammals may have begun their ruthless hunting of other animals only after the fall of man.... If the specialized flesh-tearing teeth of the carnivores make us wonder if they did not possess an instinct

for ruthless hunting as soon as they were created, we should consider the possibility that in earlier times their diet was restricted to invertebrate animals (insects and sea-shore animals), and to fruits and other plant materials which their teeth could handle. After all, many carnivores even now eat large amounts of such foods. For example, cats eat grasshoppers; bears often eat fruit and honey; and raccoons eat corn, nuts, and other fruits, and even leaves and grasses (1977, 239-240, parenthetical item in orig.).

Rendle-Short wrote in agreement:

I readily agree it is difficult to see how certain creatures could ever have been solely vegetarian. Their whole anatomy and mode of life now seems adapted for catching prey. My reply must be, firstly, as biologists study the problem it becomes obvious that many so-called carnivores can easily live on a purely vegetarian diet—the domestic dog or cat for example. Teeth apparently designed to tear prey can also be used to tear tough vegetable fibre (1984, p. 147).

Furthermore, at times the "specialized" traits and characteristics that we think, at first glance, make animals better adapted to a certain activity, climate, or habitat turn out not to inure such an advantage after all. Joseph Dillow acknowledged this problem in discussing the giant, wooly mammoths whose frozen remains have been found in the Arctic regions.

The mammoth was endowed with a fur coat and a wooly overcoat 25 cm. long. This is generally taken as proof that the mammoth was well adapted to cold. However, the presence of fur or hair is not necessarily an indication of protection against cold. Consider, for example, the hairy mountain Malaysian elephant that inhabits a tropical region today. The Sumatran elephant from Burma, *R. lasiotis*, has a thick hair covering on its belly and legs, a hairy tail, and bristles at the end of its ears. In fact, thick fur means nothing, as many animals of the equatorial jungles, such as tigers, have thick fur (1981, p. 338).

Whereas one would think that a tiger's thick fur would equip it to live in an area of the world where the average temperature is low, quite the opposite is the case. Although in possession of an impressive, thick fur coat, it nevertheless lives quite comfortably in the tropical to subtropical regions of the Middle East. Other examples could be cited at length. For generations, we were taught that Arctic animals enjoyed protection from the frigid temperatures and waters of their icy environments as a result of thick, subcutaneous layers of fat that endowed them with remarkable survival skills. But, once again, what at first glance **appeared** to be the case turned out not to actually **be** the case. In a scholarly treatise on the body insulation of a variety of Arctic mammals and birds, Scholander and co-authors wrote:

> Except for a thermally insignificant localized fat pad on the rump of the reindeer and caribou, none of the mammals (except the seals) has any significant layer of subcutaneous fat or blubber. Subcutaneous fat is a heavy and poor insulator compared to fur and does not seem to play any role at all in the insulation of terrestrial arctic animals (1950, p. 226; see also Krause, 1978, p. 92).

Thus, even though certain animals possess traits (e.g., razor-sharp teeth and powerful claws) that **appear** to be best suited for carnivorous pursuits, the exact opposite may well be the case. The characteristics that we thought equipped them for one activity actually may have equipped them for something quite different.

Last, but certainly not least, what about Paul's statement in Romans 8:20-22: "For the creation was subjected to vanity, not of its own will, but by reason of him who subjected it, in hope that the creation itself also shall be delivered from the bondage of corruption into the liberty of the glory of the children of God. For we know that **the whole creation groaneth and travaileth in pain** together until now" (emp. added). Some have suggested that this particular passage from the pen of the apostle teaches that no creatures died before the Fall of Adam and Eve. But is that what the passage is saying? No, it is not.

There are two important areas of this passage that must be explored. First, we must examine the context within which the apostle placed his comments. Second, we must study to ascertain the meaning of the phrase "the whole creation." The context of the passage is this. Paul affirms that "the sufferings of this present time are not worthy to be compared with the glory which shall be revealed to us-ward" (8:18). In verses 19-23, he then continues by acknowledging that while the creation once was subjected to vanity, it now is waiting for "the revealing of the sons of God," at which time that creation "shall be delivered from the bondage of corruption into the liberty of the glory of the children of God" (8:21). The apostle concluded by reminding Christians, who possess the "first-fruits of the Spirit,...groan within ourselves, waiting for our adoption, to wit, the redemption of our body" (8:23).

While the passage certainly is brimming with eternal comfort, it also contains some admittedly difficult material, not the least of which is Paul's reference to the fact that "the whole creation" anxiously awaits deliverance from the "bondage of corruption." What does he mean by his phrase, "the whole creation"? Various writers have documented the reasons why the phrase "the whole creation" cannot apply to such things as, for example, unredeemed humanity or some kind of alleged millennial material/physical realm (see Jackson, 1990c, 26:25). But what, then, does Paul mean by his use of this intriguing phrase? In investigating this matter, Trevor Major responded as follows:

> What does Paul mean by "creation?" This word is translated from the Greek noun *ktisis*—a term meaning the act of creation, or the product of that creative act. For example, Jesus referred to the act when He used the phrase "from the beginning of the creation" (Mark 10:6; 13:19), and Paul referred to the product when he wrote that the Gentiles "served the creature rather than the Creator" (Romans 1:25). However, the product of creation does not always encompass every single part of the creation, whether human, plant, animal, or non-living matter. In Mark 16:15, Jesus instructed His disciples to "preach the gospel to the whole creation." No one would suggest that Jesus wanted the Gospel taken to human and non-human inhabitants of the world alike. Rather, "the whole creation" in Mark is equivalent to Matthew's "all the na-

tions" (28:19), and refers to all people everywhere in the world. Hence, could not "the whole creation" in Romans 8:22 apply solely to man?

Further, note the way in which the word "creation" is used in the verses preceding Romans 8:22. Verse 19 states that the creation waits "for the revealing of the sons of God," and verse 21 says that the creation "itself also shall be delivered from the bondage of corruption into the liberty of the glory of the children of God." On the one hand, the creation has suffered at the whims of men. His selfishness and greed have despoiled the Earth, and his unrepentant sin brought a destructive flood on the land and its creatures. On the other hand, it is hard to imagine how Christians would receive any comfort knowing that plants and animals would be delivered from their "bondage" into the same "liberty of glory of the children of God." Nonetheless, it seems more consistent to equate this "whole creation" with intelligent beings because, as Peter writes in his second epistle, the physical creation must itself look forward to obliteration by fervent heat and with great noise (3:10). The world of plants, animals, and inanimate matter is not included in the plan of redemption. Only in a metaphorical sense can it look forward to the deliverance of the children of God (1990, 2[7]:1).

It thus seems that Romans 8:19ff. is referring not to the inanimate creation or merely to members of the animal and/or plant kingdoms, but rather to intelligent beings who were suffering for their faith and who, as children of God, could look forward to their resurrection and glorification. Paul's discussion of "the creation" in this passage and in others of a similar import (e.g., Romans 1:20-21), offers evidence aplenty of the fact that God's concern over His handiwork never wanes. The psalmist recorded His testimony to that effect when he wrote:

Hear, O my people, and I will speak; O Israel, and I will testify unto thee: I am God, even thy God.... Every beast of the forest is mine, and the cattle upon a thousand hills. I know all the birds of the mountains; and the wild beasts of the field are mine...the world is mine, and the fulness thereof (Psalm 50:7-12).

Perhaps it was such heart-rending passages as Psalm 50 and Romans 8 that caused British theologian D. Martin Lloyd-Jones to write:

> Many people seem to think that the sole theme of the Bible is man's personal relationship with God.... This is a central theme...but it is not the only theme.... Ultimately the main message of the Bible concerns the condition of **the world** and its final destiny; you and I as individuals are part of a larger whole. That is why the Bible starts with the creation of the world, rather than that of man (1953, p. 5, emp. in orig.).

An in-depth study of God's Word, and of God's world, makes for a terribly fascinating human enterprise. As we study, however, we must make sure never to impose **our** wants and wishes upon the text, but rather to let the text speak to us instead. It is admirable that certain Bible believers are desirous of defending the biblical account of creation and opposing the concept of organic evolution and its theistic cousins. But to suggest that Romans 5 and 1 Corinthians 15 teach that **nothing** died prior to the Fall of man weakens the creationists' case and inflicts serious damage on the actual meaning of these pristine biblical passages. The biblical account of creation **does** need to be defended. And the theory of evolution **does** need to be opposed. But not via a misinterpretation and misapplication of God's Word. Two wrongs do not make a right.

God has placed the defense of His Word into the hands of men and women who have been instructed to teach it so that all who hear it might have the opportunity to obey it and be saved. Paul commented on this when he wrote: "But we have this treasure in earthen vessels, that the exceeding greatness of the power may be of God, and not from ourselves" (2 Corinthians 4:7). The thrust of the apostle's statement was that the responsibility of taking the Word of God to a lost and dying world ultimately has been given to mortal men. But the power is not in the men; rather, it is in the message! This, no doubt, accounts for the instructions Paul sent to Timothy in his second epistle when he urged the young evangelist to "give diligence to present thyself approved unto God, a workman that needeth not to be ashamed, **handling aright the word of truth**" (2 Timothy 2:15, emp. added).

Considering the fact that we, as God's "earthen vessels," have been made the instruments through which God offers to a lost and dying world reconciliation through His Son (John 3:16), the apostle's admonition is well taken. Surely it behooves us to "handle aright" so precious a commodity as the Word of God. The salvation of our own souls, and the souls of those we instruct, depends on the accuracy of the message.

In 1948, at the Winona Lake School of Theology, a graduate student, Malcolm Henkel, writing a master's thesis on "Fundamental Christianity and Evolution," polled 20 leading Hebrew scholars in the United States, asking them if there were any exegetical evidence of a gap interpretation of Genesis 1:2. They unanimously replied—No! (Henkel, 1950, p. 49). Nothing in this regard has changed since 1948.

Chapter 10

The Bible and the Age of the Earth— Biblical Genealogies

A ttempts to place the time necessary for an ancient Earth **during** the creation week (i.e., the Day-Age Theory) have proven unsuccessful. Similarly, attempts to insert the time necessary for an old Earth **before** the creation week (i.e., the Gap Theory) also have failed. Subsequently, the suggestion has been made that perhaps geologic time might be placed **after** the creation week of Genesis 1.

Those willing to offer such a suggestion, however, have been few and far between because of a major obstacle in the biblical record to such a compromise. As every student of the Sacred Scriptures is aware, the Bible contains lengthy genealogies. That these records play a vital role in biblical literature is clear from the amount of space devoted to them in God's Word. Furthermore, they provide a tremendous protection of the text via the message they tell. That message is this: **man has been on the Earth since the beginning, and that beginning was not very long ago**.

As I pointed out in chapter 7, while genealogies (and chronologies) serve various functions in the literature of Scripture, one of their main purposes is to show the historical connection of great men to the unfolding of Jehovah's redemptive plan. These lists, therefore, form a connecting link from the earliest days of humanity to the completion of God's salvation system. In order for them to have any evidential value, the lists must be substantially complete.

In the introduction to this book, I made the point that the inspired writer of Hebrews, in contending for the heavenly nature of Christ's priesthood, argued that the Savior could not have functioned as a priest while He was living upon the Earth since God had a **levitical** priesthood to accomplish that need (Hebrews 8:4). Jesus did not qualify for the levitical priesthood for "it is **evident** that our Lord hath sprung out of **Judah**" (Hebrews 7:14, emp. added). I then asked: How could it have been "evident" that Jesus Christ was from the tribe of Judah—**unless there were accurate genealogical records by which such a statement could be verified**? The writer of Hebrews based his argument on the fact that the readers of his epistle would not be able to dispute the ancestry of Christ due to the reliable nature of the Jewish documentation available— i.e., the genealogies.

Yet some Bible believers—determined to incorporate evolutionary dating schemes into God's Word—have complained that the biblical genealogies may not be used for chronological purposes because they allegedly contain huge "gaps" that render them ineffective for that purpose. Donald England has suggested, for example: "Furthermore, it is a misuse of Biblical genealogies to attempt to date the origin of man by genealogy" (1983, p. 155). John Clayton advocated the same view when he wrote: "Any attempt to ascribe a specific or even a general age to either man or the Earth from a Biblical standpoint is a grievous error" (n.d.[a], p. 3). Clayton also stated: "The time of man's beginning is not even hinted at in the Bible. There is no possible way of determining when Adam was created" (n.d.[b], p. 2).

In so commenting, most authors reference (as does Clayton) nineteenth-century author, William H. Green (1890), whose writings on the genealogies are accepted uncritically—and acclaimed unjustifiably—by those who wish to insert "gaps" (of whatever size) into the biblical genealogies. Thus, we are asked to believe that the genealogies are relatively useless in matters of chronology.

However, these same writers conspicuously avoid any examination of more recent material which has shown that certain portions of Green's work either were incomplete or inaccurate. And while references to the genealogies of Genesis 5 and 11 are commonplace, discussions of material from chapter 3 of Luke's Gospel appear to be quite rare. Two important points bear mentioning in regard to genealogical listings. First, to quote Custance:

> We are told again and again that some of these genealogies contain gaps: but what is never pointed out by those who lay the emphasis on these gaps, is that they only know of the existence of these gaps because the Bible elsewhere fills them in. How otherwise could one know of them? But if they are filled in, they are not gaps at all! Thus, in the final analysis the argument is completely without foundation (1967, p. 3).

If anyone wanted to find gaps in the genealogies, it certainly would have been Dr. Custance—who spent his entire adult life searching for a way to accommodate the Bible to an old-Earth scenario. Yet even he was forced to admit that arguments alleging that the genealogies contain sizable gaps are unfounded.

Second—and this point cannot be overemphasized—**even if there were gaps in the genealogies, there would not necessarily be gaps in the chronologies therein recorded. The issue of chronology is not the same as that of genealogy**. This is a critical point that has been overlooked by those who suggest that the genealogies are "useless" in matters of chronology. The "more recent work" mentioned above that documents the accuracy of the genealogies is from James B. Jordan, who reviewed Green's work and showed a number of his arguments to be untrustworthy. To quote Jordan:

> Gaps in genealogies, however, do not prove gaps in chronologies. The known gaps all occur in non-chronological genealogies. Moreover, even if there were gaps in the genealogies of Genesis 5 and 11, this would not affect the chronological information therein recorded, for even if Enosh were the great-grandson of Seth, it would still be the case that Seth was 105 years old when Enosh was born, according to a simple reading of the text. Thus, genealogy and chronology are distinct problems with distinct characteristics. They ought not to be confused (1979/1980, 2:12).

Unfortunately, many who attempt to defend the concept of an ancient Earth **have** confused these two issues. For example, some have suggested that abridgment of the genealogies has occurred and that these genealogies therefore cannot be chronologies, when, in fact, exactly the opposite is true—as Jordan's work has documented. Matthew, as an illustration, was at liberty to arrange his genealogy of Christ in three groups of 14 (making some omissions) because his genealogy was derived from more complete lists found in the Old Testament. In the genealogies of Genesis 5 and 11, remember also that the inclusion of a father's age at the time of his son's birth is wholly without meaning unless accurate chronology was intended. Else why would the Holy Spirit have provided such "irrelevant" information?

Unfortunately, there can be little doubt that some have painted an extremely distorted picture for their audiences and/or readers by suggesting that substantial "gaps" can be found within the biblical genealogies. Just such a distorted picture results, for example, when it is suggested that genealogy and chronology are one and the same problem, for they most certainly are not. Plus, there are other important considerations. Observe the following information in chart form. Speaking in round figures, from the present to Jesus was approximately 2,000 years—a figure obtainable via secular, historical documents. From Jesus to Abraham also was around 2,000 years —another figure that is verifiable historically.

Present to Jesus	=	2,000	years
Jesus to Abraham	=	2,000	years
Abraham to Adam	=	?	years

The only figure missing is the one that represents the date from Abraham to Adam. Since we know that Adam was the first man (1 Corinthians 15:45), and since we know that man has been on the Earth "from the beginning of the creation" (Mark 10:6; cf. Romans 1:20-21), if it were possible to obtain the figures for the length of time between Abraham to Adam, we then would have chronological information providing the relative age of the Earth (since we also know that the Earth is only five days older than man—Genesis 1; Exodus 20:11; 31:17).

The figure representing the time span between Abraham and Adam, of course, is **not** obtainable from secular history (nor should we expect it to be) since large portions of those records were destroyed in the Great Flood. But the figure **is** obtainable—via the biblical record. Permit me to explain.

First, few today would deny that from the present to Jesus has been approximately 2,000 years. [For our purposes here, it does not matter whether Christ is viewed as the Son of God since the discussion centers solely on the fact of His existence—something that secular history documents beyond doubt; see Butt, 2000, 20:1-6.] Second, in Luke 3 the learned physician provided a genealogy that encompassed 55 generations spanning the distance between Jesus and Abraham—a time frame that archaeology has shown covered roughly 2,000 years (see Kitchen and Douglas, 1982, p. 189). Third, Luke documents that between Abraham and Adam there were only twenty generations. Thus, the chart now looks like this:

Present to Jesus   =   2,000 years
Jesus to Abraham   =   2,000 years (55 generations)
Abraham to Adam   =   ?   years (20 generations)

Since Genesis 5 provides the ages of the fathers at the time of the births of the sons between Abraham and Adam (thus providing chronological data), it becomes a simple matter to determine the approximate number of years involved. In round numbers, that figure is 2,000. The chart then appears as follows.

Present to Jesus	=	2,000 years
Jesus to Abraham	=	2,000 years (55 generations)
Abraham to Adam	=	2,000 years (20 generations)*

Some have argued that there are "gaps" in the genealogies (e.g., Clayton, 1980a, 7[1]:6-7). But where, exactly, should such gaps be placed, and how would they help? Observe the following. It is impossible to place any gaps between the present and the Lord's birth because secular history accurately records that age-information. Similarly, no gaps can be inserted between the Lord's birth and Abraham because secular history also accurately records that age-information. The only place one could put any "usable" gaps (viz., usable in regard to extending the age of the Earth) would be in the 20 generations between Abraham and Adam. Yet notice that there are not actually 20 generations available for the insertion of gaps because Jude stated that "Enoch was the **seventh from Adam**" (Jude 14). An examination of the Old Testament genealogies establishes the veracity of Jude's statement since, counting from Adam, Enoch **was** the seventh. Jude's comment thus provides divinely inspired testimony regarding the accuracy of the first seven names in Luke's genealogy—thereby leaving only 13 generations into which any alleged gaps could be placed.

In a fascinating article some years ago, Wayne Jackson observed that in order to accommodate the biblical record only as far back as the appearance of man's alleged evolutionary ancestor (approximately 3.6 million years), one would have to place **291,125 years** between **each** of the remaining 13 generations (1978b, 14[18]:1). It does not take an overdose of either biblical knowledge or common sense to see that this quickly becomes ludicrous in the extreme

---

* The reader may wonder how 55 generations (Jesus to Abraham) could cover 2,000 years while 20 generations (Abraham to Adam) also cover 2,000 years. The answer, of course, lies in the ages of the patriarchs. Because they lived to such vast ages, fewer generations were required to encompass the same number of years. For a discussion of the Bible, science, and the ages of the patriarchs, see Appendix 2.

for two reasons. First, who could believe that the first seven of these generations are so **exact**—while the last thirteen are so **inexact**? Is it proper biblical exegesis to suggest that the first seven listings are correct as written, but gaps covering more than a quarter of a million years may be inserted between each of the last thirteen? Second, what good would any of this do anyone? All it would accomplish is the establishment of a 3.6 **million** year-old Earth; old-Earth creationists, progressive creationists, and theistic evolutionists need a 4.6-**billion**-year-old Earth. So, in effect, all of this insertion of "gaps" into the biblical text is much ado about nothing.

And therein lies my point. While it may be true on the one hand to say that an **exact** age of the Earth is unobtainable from the information contained within the genealogies, at the same time it is important to note that—using the best information available to us from Scripture—the genealogies hardly can be extended to anything much beyond 6,000 to 7,000 years. For someone to suggest that the genealogies do not contain legitimate chronological information, or that the genealogies somehow are so full of gaps as to render them useless, is to misrepresent the case and distort the facts.

Chapter 11

The Bible and the Age of the Earth— Additional Considerations

The topic of the Bible and the age of the Earth often engenders a great deal of controversy. It also spawns a variety of claims and counter-claims. Thus, in any discussion of what the Bible has to say regarding the age of the Earth, there are several additional considerations that should be examined.

"FROM THE BEGINNING OF THE CREATION"/ "FROM THE CREATION OF THE WORLD"

In Mark 10:6, Jesus declared concerning Adam and Eve: "**But from the beginning of the creation**, male and female made he them" (cf. Matthew 19:4). Christ thus dated the first humans from the creation week. The Greek word for "beginning" is *arché*, and is used of "**absolute**, denoting **the beginning of the world** and of its history, the beginning of creation." The Greek term for "creation" is *ktiseos* and denotes "**the sum-total of what God has created**" (Cremer, 1962, pp. 113,114,381, emp. in orig.).

Bloomfield noted that "creation" in Mark 10:6 "signifies 'the things created,' the world or universe" (1837, 1:197-198). In addressing this point, Wayne Jackson wrote:

> Unquestionably this language puts humankind at the very dawn of creation. To reject this clear truth, one must contend that: (a) Christ knew the Universe was in existence billions of years prior to man, but accommodating Himself to the ignorance of His generation, deliberately misrepresented the situation; or, (b) The Lord, living in pre-scientific times, was uninformed about the matter (despite the fact that He was there as Creator—John 1:3; Colossians 1:16). Either of these allegations is a reflection upon the Son of God and is blasphemous (1989, pp. 25-26, parenthetical comment in orig.).

Furthermore, Paul affirmed the following:

> For the invisible things of him **since the creation of the world** are clearly seen, being perceived through the things that are made, even his everlasting power and divinity; that they may be without excuse (Romans 1:20, emp. added).

The apostle declared that **from the creation of the world** the invisible things of God have been: (a) clearly seen; and (b) perceived. The phrase, "since the creation of the world," is translated from the Greek, *apo ktiseos kosmou*. As a preposition, *apo* is used "to denote the point from which something begins" (Arndt and Gingrich, 1957, p. 86). The term "world" is from the Greek, *kosmos*, and refers to "the orderly universe" (Arndt and Gingrich, p. 446). R.C. Trench observed that the *kosmos* is "the material universe…in which man lives and moves, which exists for him and of which he constitutes the moral centre" (1890, pp. 215-216). The term "perceived" is translated from the Greek, *noeo*, which is used to describe rational, **human** intelligence. The phrase "clearly seen" is an intensified form of *horao*, a word that "gives prominence to the discerning mind" (Thayer, 1962, p. 452). Both "perceived" and "clearly seen" are present tense forms, and as such denote "the continued manifestation of the being and perfections of God, by the works of creation from the beginning" (MacKnight, 1960, 1: 187).

Who observed and perceived the things that were made "from the beginning" of the creation? If no man existed on this planet for billions of years (because man is a "relative newcomer to the Earth"), who was observing—with rational, human intelligence—these phenomena? Paul undoubtedly was teaching that **man has existed since the creation of the world** and has possessed the capacity to comprehend the truth regarding the existence of the Creator; accordingly, those who refuse to glorify Him are without excuse (cf. Psalm 14:1). It is inexcusable for one who professes to believe the Bible to be God's inspired Word to ignore such verses as these—or to wrest them to make them say something they never were intended to say—to defer to evolutionary geology in an attempt to defend the concept of an ancient Earth. Yet examples of that very thing are all too prevalent.

During the question and answer session that followed my debate with Jack Wood Sears on the topic of the Bible and the age of the Earth (see chapter 7), a querist asked him how he could defend the concept of an ancient Earth in light of Christ's statements in Mark 10:6 and Matthew 19:4 which indicated that "from the beginning of the creation, male and female made he them." Astonishingly, Dr. Sears responded by suggesting that neither Mark 10:6 nor Matthew 19:4 was addressing the creation of the **world**. Rather, he insisted, both passages meant "from the time of the creation **of man and woman**." What?! Were that the case, these two passages then would have the Lord saying: "From the beginning of the creation (of man and woman), man and woman created he them." The Son of God was not in the habit of talking in such nonsensical terms. Furthermore, Mark plainly wrote about "the beginning of **the** creation," not "**their** creation." Christ's point is crystal clear, especially when connected to Paul's comment in Romans 1:20-21 that someone with rational, **human** intelligence was "perceiving" the things that had been created. Riegle was right when he suggested: "It is amazing that men will accept long, complicated, imaginative theories and reject the truth given to Moses by the Creator Himself" (1962, p. 24).

"FROM THE BLOOD OF ABEL"

In Luke 11:45-52, the account is recorded of the Lord rebuking the Jews of His day. He charged them with following in the footsteps of their ancestors. He foretold the destruction that was yet to befall them. And, He announced that upon them would come "the blood of all the prophets, which was shed **from the foundation of the world**." Then, with emphatic linguistic parallelism (which so often is characteristic of Hebrew expression), He added: "**from the blood of Abel** unto the blood of Zachariah...."

Jesus therefore placed the murder of Abel near the "foundation of the world." Granted, Abel's death occurred some years after the creation, but it was close enough to that event for Jesus to state that it was associated with "the foundation of the world." If the world actually came into existence several billion years before the first family, how could the shedding of human blood be declared by the Son of God to extend back to the "foundation of the world"?

Those who opt for an old-Earth scenario believe, of course, that man is a "recent addition" to the Earth—a "johnny-come-lately" who has been here only 3 **million** years or so out of an alleged Earth history of 4.6 **billion** years. It is apparent, however, that they are not obtaining their information from the same divine source as the prophet Isaiah, who asked the skeptics of his day: "Hath it not been told you **from the beginning**? Have ye not understood **from the foundations of the earth**?" (40:21, emp. added). Isaiah understood that man had been on the Earth "from the beginning" or, as he stressed, "from the foundations of the Earth." Sad, is it not, that so many today who claim to believe the Bible refuse to acknowledge that simple, scriptural fact?

HOW LONG WERE ADAM AND EVE IN THE GARDEN OF EDEN?

On occasion, those who defend an old Earth suggest that it is impossible to know how long Adam and Eve were in the Garden of

Eden and that untold years may have elapsed during that time period. Consider two popular arguments that frequently are offered in support of such a theory.

First, John Clayton has suggested that since a part of God's curse on Eve was that He was going to **multiply** her pain in childbirth (Genesis 3:16), she **must** have given birth to numerous children in the garden or else God's curse would have meant nothing to her. How could God "multiply" something if she never had experienced it in the first place? Furthermore, Clayton has lamented, rearing children is a process that requires considerable time, thereby allowing for the possibility that Adam and Eve were in the Garden of Eden for an extended period prior to being evicted after their sin. As Clayton has written: "Every evidence we have biblically indicates that mankind's beginning in the Garden of Eden **was not a short period** which involved one man and one woman" (1980a, 7[1]:5, emp. added).

The second argument (which is somewhat related to the first) suggests that Adam and Eve **must** have been in the garden for quite some time because after they left, it was said of Cain that "he builded a city" (Genesis 4:17). To quote Clayton, that is something "which you cannot do with you and your wife" (1980a, 7[1]:5). In other words, Cain had to have a large enough family to help him build "a city." That, suggests Clayton, would have taken a lot of time.

Mr. Clayton is completely in error when he says that "every evidence we have biblically indicates that mankind's beginning in the Garden of Eden was not a short period which involved one man and one woman." The fact is, **every evidence we have biblically proves conclusively that man and woman could not have been in the garden for very long**. Consider the following.

First, regardless of what defenders of an ancient Earth may **wish** were true, the simple fact of the matter is that the Bible sets an outer limit on the amount of time that man could have lived in the Garden of Eden. Genesis 5:5 states clearly that "**all the days** that

Adam lived were **930 years**." We know, of course, that "days" and "years" already were being counted by the time of Adam's creation because in Genesis 1:14 (day four of creation) God mentioned both in His discussion of their relationship to the heavenly bodies. Therefore, however long Adam and Eve may have been in the garden, one thing is for sure: they were not there for a time period that exceeded Adam's life span (930 years). Additionally, a significant portion of man's life was spent **outside** the Garden of Eden due to his sin against God—thereby reducing even further the portion of the 930 years that could have been spent in the garden setting.

Second, surely it is not inconsequential that **all** the children of Adam and Eve mentioned in the Bible were born **outside** the Garden of Eden. **Not one conception, or birth, is mentioned as having occurred while Adam and Eve lived in the garden** (see Genesis 4:1 for the first mention of any conception or birth—only **after** the couple's expulsion from Eden). Follow closely the importance and logic of this argument, which may be stated as follows.

One of the commands given to Adam and Eve was that they "be fruitful and multiply, and fill the Earth" (Genesis 1:28). [Interestingly, Isaiah would say many years later that God created the Earth "to be inhabited" (Isaiah 45:18).] In other words, Adam and Eve were commanded to **reproduce**.

But what is sin? Sin is: (a) **doing** what God said **not to do**; or (b) **not doing** what God said **to do**. Up until the time that Adam and Eve ate the fruit of the tree of the knowledge of good and evil (Genesis 3:6), had they sinned? No, they still were in a covenant relationship with God and everything was perfect. Since that is the case, the only conclusion that can be drawn is that Adam and Eve were doing what God had commanded them to do—reproducing. Yet, I repeat, the only conceptions and births of which we have any record occurred **outside the garden**! In other words, apparently Adam and Eve were not even in the garden long enough for Eve to conceive, much less give birth.

Third, while the Bible does not provide a **specific** time regarding how long Adam and Eve were in the Garden, it could not have been very long because Christ Himself, in referring to the curse of death upon the human family as a result of their sinful rebellion against God, specifically stated that the devil "was a murderer **from the beginning**" (John 8:44). Satan and his ignominious band of outlaws ("sons of the evil one"—Matthew 13:38) have worked their ruthless quackery on mankind from the very moment the serpent met mother Eve in the Garden of Eden. When he and his cohorts rebelled and "kept not their proper habitation," they were cast from the heavenly portals to be "kept in everlasting bonds under darkness unto the judgment of the great day" (Jude 6).

Satan fought with God—and lost. The devil's insurrection had failed miserably, and that failure had dire, eternal consequences. His obstinate attempt to usurp God's authority cost him his position among the heavenly hosts. As a result of his rebellion, he was cast "down to hell" (2 Peter 2:4). In the end, his sedition gained him nothing and cost him everything. Regardless of the battle plan he adopted to challenge the Creator of the Universe, regardless of the battlefield he chose as his theater of war, and regardless of the numbers or strength of his army, the simple fact of the matter is that—in the most important contest of his existence—he lost! The conditions of his ultimate surrender were harsh. Although his armies had been thoroughly routed, although he had been completely vanquished, and although the Victor had imposed the worst kind of permanent exile, Satan was determined not to go gently into the night. While he admittedly had lost the war, he nevertheless planned future skirmishes. Vindictive by nature (Revelation 12:12), in possession of cunning devices (2 Corinthians 2:11), and thoroughly determined to be "the deceiver of the world" (Revelation 12:9), he set his face against all that is righteous and holy—and never once looked back. His anger at having been defeated fueled his determination to strike back in revenge.

But strike back at whom? God's power was too great, and His omnipotence was too all-consuming (Job 42:2; 1 John 4:4). Another target was needed; another repository of satanic revenge would have to be found. And who better to serve as the recipient of hell's unrighteous indignation than mankind—the only creature in the Universe made "in the image and likeness of God" (Genesis 1:26-27)? As Rex A. Turner Sr. observed: "Satan cannot attack God directly, thus he employs various methods to attack man, God's master creation" (1980, p. 89). What sweet revenge—despoiling the "apple of God's eye" and the zenith of His creative genius! Thus, with the creation of man, the battle was on. Little wonder that in his first epistle the apostle Peter described Satan as an adversary that, "as a roaring lion, walketh about, seeking whom he may devour" (5:8).

Now—knowing what the Scriptures tell us about Satan's origin, attitude, and mission—is it sensible to suggest that he would take his proverbial time, and twiddle his figurative thumbs, while allowing Adam and Eve to revel in the covenant relationship they enjoyed with their Maker (Genesis 3:8 relates how God walked with them in the garden "in the cool of the day")? Would he simply "leave them alone for a long period of time" so that they could conceive, give birth to, and rear children in the luscious paradise known as the Garden of Eden? Is this how a hungry, stalking lion would view its prey —by watching admiringly from afar, allowing it hundreds or thousands of years of fulfilled joy, and affording it time to conceive, give birth to, and raise a family? Hardly—which is why Christ described Satan as a murderer "from the beginning." Satan was in no mood to wait. He was angry, he was bitter, and he was filled with a thirst for revenge. What better way to slake that thirst than introducing sin into God's perfect world?

What may be said, then, about John Clayton's suggestion that Adam and Eve must have been in the Garden for an extended period of time since God said that He was going to "multiply" Eve's pain. How could He possibly "multiply" something she never had experienced? This quibble can be answered quite easily. Does a person have to "experience" something before that something can be "multiplied"? Suppose I said, "I'm going to give you **$100**." You therefore stick out your hand to receive the $100 bill I am holding in mine. But I immediately pull back my hand and say, "No, I've changed my mind; I am going to give you **$1,000** instead!" Did you actually have to possess or "experience" the $100 bill before I could increase it to $1,000? Of course not!

The fact that God said He intended to "multiply" Eve's pain in childbirth does not mean necessarily that Eve had to have experienced **some** pain before God's decree that she would experience **more** pain. God's point was merely this: "Eve, you were going to experience some pain in childbirth, but because of your sin, now you will experience even more pain." The fact that Eve never had experienced **any** childbirth pain up to that point does not mean that she could not experience **even more** pain later as a part of her penalty for having sinned against God.

Last, what about John Clayton's idea that Adam and Eve must have been in the Garden for an extended period of time because the text indicates that when they left Cain and his wife "builded a city" (Genesis 4:17). Clayton has lamented that this is something "which you **cannot do with you and your wife**" (1980a, 7[1]:5). Of course he would be correct—**if** the city under discussion were a modern metroplex. But that is not the case here.

The Hebrew word for city is quite broad in its meaning. It may refer to anything from a sprawling village to a mere encampment. Literally, the term means "place of look-out, especially as it was fortified." In commenting on Genesis 4:17, Old Testament commentator John Willis observed: "However, a 'city' is not necessarily a large, impressive metropolis, but may be a small unimposing village of relatively few inhabitants" (1979, p. 155). Again, apply some common sense here. What would it be **more likely** for the Bible to suggest that Cain and his wife constructed (considering who they were and where they were living)—a thriving, bustling, metropolis, or a Bedouin tent city. To ask is to answer, is it not? To this very day, Bedouin tent cities are quite commonplace in that particular area of the world. And—as everyone will admit—two boy scouts can erect a tent, so it hardly strains credulity to suggest that likely Cain and his wife were able to accomplish such a task as well.

THE DOCTRINE OF APPARENT AGE

On occasion, the comment is overheard, "But the Earth **looks so old**." There are at least two responses that might be made to such a statement. First, one might ask: "Compared to what; what does a **young** Earth look like?" Who among us has anything with which to compare? Second, we should not be surprised if certain methods in science appear to support the idea of an ancient Earth. Why? The answer lies in what has been called the "doctrine of apparent age" (also known as the "doctrine of mature creation").

This concept states that when God made "heaven, and earth, the sea, and all that in them is" (Exodus 20:11), they were made perfect, complete, and ready for habitation by mankind and the multiple forms of plant and animal life. God did not create **imma-ture** forms (although He certainly could have done so, had He desired), but **mature** ones. Rather than creating an acorn, for example, He created an oak. Rather than creating an egg, He created a chicken. Rather than creating Adam and Eve as infants or young children, He created them as post-pubescent beings. We know this to be true because one of the commands God gave each living thing shortly after its creation was that it should reproduce "after its kind." This very command, in fact, was given to Adam and Eve while they still were in the Garden of Eden, prior to their sin and expulsion.

How old were Adam and Eve two seconds after their creation? **They were two seconds old**. How old were the plants and animals two seconds after their creation? **They were two seconds old**. But how old all these two-seconds-old people, plants, and animals **look** like they were? Trevor Major has commented:

> So Adam, for example, had the look and the capability of a full-grown man on the first Sabbath, even though he had lived only one day. Thus, according to the doctrine of mature creation, all living things were created in a mature state, with only the **appearance** of age (1989, 27[10]:16, emp. in orig.).

It is important to realize that the initial creation had **two** ages—a **literal** age, and an **apparent** age. It **literally** may have been just one day old, two days old, three days old, and so on. But it **appeared** to be much older.

The biblical record provides additional information concerning the accuracy of the doctrine of apparent age. In Genesis 1:14, God told Moses that the heavenly bodies (e.g., Sun, Moon, stars) were to be "for signs and for seasons, for days and for years." In order for the heavenly bodies to be useful to man for the designation of signs, seasons, days, and years, those heavenly bodies **must have been visible**. Thus, when God created them He made their light already visible from Earth. The psalmist exclaimed: "The heavens declare the glory of God, and the firmament showeth his handiwork" (19:1). There was, therefore, a specific **purpose** behind God's mature creation.

First, the Earth was prepared in a mature state so that man would find it suitable for his habitation. Christ specifically stated that man and woman had been on the Earth "since the beginning of the creation" (Matthew 19:4; Mark 10:6). Thus, it was necessary that "from the beginning" the Earth be "finished." Second, once man found himself in such a home (called "very good"—denoting complete perfection—in Genesis 1:31), it was only right to give honor and glory to the Creator Who designed and built such a magnificent edifice. This explains why Paul, in Romans 1:20ff., suggested that even God's "everlasting power and divinity" had been seen by mankind "from the creation of the world," and why those who refused to honor God would be "without excuse."

Even the miracles of the Bible reflect God's frequent use of the principle we call "apparent age." During Christ's first miracle, He transformed water into wine (John 2).* For mere mortals to produce wine (alcoholic or not) requires a lengthy process employing soil, water, grapes, sunshine, etc. Yet Jesus accomplished this task in a matter of minutes, producing what the governor of the wedding feast termed not just wine but "good wine" (John 2:10). The miracle of the feeding of the 5,000 (Matthew 14:13-21) also provides evidence regarding the principle of apparent age. The young boy present on that occasion had but a few loaves and fishes, yet Christ "multiplied" them and fed over 5,000 men alone. Major addressed this concept when he wrote:

> Thousands of loaves were distributed for which the barley had not been sown, harvested, or milled, and which had never been mixed into dough and baked in an oven. Equally amazing, thousands of dried fishes were handed out which neither had grown from an egg nor been caught in a fishermen's net. Everything was there in a prepared form, ready to eat by the recipients of this great wonder.

> The miracle of creation was also achieved in a relative instant, producing an effect which could have only a supernatural cause. In the first chapter of Genesis, God created trees and grasses, not just their seeds. He created birds which could already fly, not eggs or even chicks. He created fish which could already swim, not fish eggs. He created cattle, not calves. And He created man and woman, not boy and girl. Speaking to these animals, and to these people, God commanded: "Be fruitful and multiply" (1:22,28). Notice that the plants and animals began to multiply according to their own kind almost straightaway (1:11,24). Immature organisms could not have reproduced, and in any case, would have perished in the absence of adult forms (1989, 27[10]:16).

The moment God created matter itself, would it not have appeared "mature"—i.e., as if it already had existed? If God had decided to create Adam as a baby, how could He have produced a

---

* In the New Testament, the Greek term for wine, *oinos*, is employed to denote both alcoholic and non-alcoholic grape juice beverages, prohibiting the view that the wine spoken of in John 2 necessarily was alcoholic.

baby that did not **look** like it had gone through a nine-month ges-
tation period? If He had created an acorn, how could He have created an acorn that did not **look** like it had fallen from a mighty oak?
Did God create the Earth "mature"? Indeed He did. How could He
have done otherwise?

Frank Lewis Marsh, while serving as a professor of biology at Andrews University, was a respected scientist who frequently wrote on
matters relating to creation and evolution. In his book, *Life, Man,
and Time*, he addressed the subject of apparent age from a biblical
perspective.

> As a help in making a decision here, the Bible believer goes
> back to the first two chapters of Genesis. When Adam came
> from the hand of the Creator on Friday he had every appear-
> ance of being a mature man at least in his twenties, a man
> of marriageable age. Fruit-bearing trees appeared to be at
> least several years old. The great aquatic animals playing in
> the waters appeared to be sixty to one hundred years old.
> And the smoothed landscape with its rounded mountains and
> hills, and broad rivers, and with a vegetated layer of fertile soil
> over all land areas, from a uniformitarian viewpoint, appeared
> to be millions of years old. Nevertheless, no object in this land-
> scape was more than three solar days old. Because this land-
> scape had been specially created with an **appearance of age**,
> even the most careful application by Adam of his physical
> senses and his reasonable mind to the problem of age of the
> landscape could only lead to the wrong conclusion. It is of
> great importance to recognize here that Adam could not car-
> ry on an open-minded study of the age of the landscape and
> necessarily arrive at the truth about it. In order to please God
> and know the truth about natural things he had to place spe-
> cial revelation above natural revelation. One wonders what
> testimony would have been given by the radioactive time-
> clocks at the close of Creation Week. Would it be unreason-
> able to assume that the minerals of the earth as well as its or-
> ganic forms may have been created with an appearance of age?

> From past events we learn that **even regarding points in
> natural science, special revelation must supersede nat-
> ural revelation if the truth is to be known** on those points.
> With regard to duration since Creation Week, the Bible tells

us that only a few thousand years have elapsed. To the Bible believer this means that the various timeclocks which suggest greater ages than this are not to be depended upon regardless of how coercive or compulsive the evidence may appear to be. Because of the manner of the earth's origin, Adam could not accept the data furnished by natural processes when it came to the age of the landscape.

In like manner the Bible believer today who walks the same earth Adam walked, except for an unnatural destruction and redeposition of its surface since Creation, depends upon Bible chronology to reveal the true age of the fossil-bearing strata at the earth's surface. This record informs us that duration since life first appeared on this earth is to be counted, not in hundreds of millions but rather in a few thousands of years. In this day of jumbled talk of millions of years in this earth's history, the Bible believer faces no dilemma. His philosophy may not be popular but it is satisfyingly correct. Why? Because God in His providence has supplied in man's Guidebook the very information on this planet that he needs in this confused age (1967, pp. 59,73, first emp. in orig., last emp. added).

One of Dr. Marsh's articles on this subject, which appeared in the *Creation Research Society Quarterly*, was titled "On Creation with an Appearance of Age." Although the following quotation from that article is somewhat lengthy, I consider its inclusion in this book essential because it is, in my estimation, a one-of-a-kind, timeless masterpiece due to the simple-yet-brilliant manner in which it explains the importance of a proper understanding of the scriptural principle known as the doctrine of apparent age.

I am of the opinion that it is very essential for natural scientists frequently to meditate on Adam's situation in that early and perfect world. He learned the story of origins from the Creator. To get at the facts let us assume that some time soon after Adam's creation on Day Six (Gen. 1:27, NASB), the Creator said to him, "Adam, look about you. There is not an object in this landscape that is more than three days (evenings and mornings; 24-hour periods) old." (As far into the week as the morning of Day Three, no dry land was to be found. Gen. 1:9.)

Assume that Adam replied, "Lord you have given me this wonderful mind and these marvelous physical senses. Now suppose I study this matter open-mindedly and learn if your statement is correct."

Assume that Adam began his careful study of age by examining his own body. If he were to hypothesize that he had become mature (of marriageable age, Gen. 1:27) by normal (to us) growth processes, then he could reasonably conclude that he had lived at least twenty-five years. If his basic assumptions were correct, then by the agreement of proof from several ways of determining age, such as anatomical structure, physiological activity, and psychological maturity, he would "**know**" that he was more than three days old.

Assume that Adam continued his study and observed mature fruit trees (Gen. 1:12) which apparently were several years old. He observed great water animals (Gen. 1:21) possibly apparently sixty years old. He observed mountains (Gen. 7:19) and spreading plains with rivers (Gen. 2:10-14), erosion plains which some think require millions of years to form. If he had examined trees, I believe he would have found annual rings, and that if he had dated minerals radioactively it is possible that apparent ages of even millions of years would have been found.

After all this careful open-minded study of the Edenic world, Adam could have returned to the Creator and with great sincerity said, "Lord, I'm sorry to have to say this, but this landscape is much older than you think!"

If it had been available to him, it is very likely Adam could have had the confirmation of all our most sophisticated modern scientific apparatus in the matter of great age. Suppose this apparatus had been available to Adam, and that in making his report, he had invited the Creator to have a seat, and then had taken an hour and a half with tables, charts, and photographs, showing the agreement of inorganic radioactive time clocks, of fission-track data, of effects of solar wind in eroding moon craters, etc., etc., that our earth **had** to be at least four and one-half billion years old. Would the Creator have been impressed? Would all these data on age of the open-minded method have constituted **natural truth**?...

Why could Adam not believe what he thought he saw on the subject of age of the landscape? The answer stands clearly revealed in special revelation (the Bible). Our earth was created, along with the living forms with which it was furnished, with an **appearance of age**. Adam's open-minded method could bring the right answers for innumerable problems, **provided the phenomenon under study was not complicated by the factor of geological age**. The same situation holds for us today....

How only can we know the natural truth about the age of our earth? Adam could learn that truth only by special revelation. Today our students of earth science are studying an earth which came into being **unnaturally** with an **appearance of age**. Some sixteen centuries after that creation the surface of this earth was utterly destroyed (more here and less over there) by the unnatural activities of Noah's "Flood." Today it is fair to ask, How is it possible now to determine **in natural ways** the age of a surface which was both created and destroyed in **unnatural** ways? I submit the thesis that until man accepts the necessity of special revelation regarding our natural world, he will never know the truth out the age of our earth or the origin of life upon it. My sympathies go out to our young scientists in this skeptical day. I, as a Bible-believing creationist, associated for nine years in a total of four non-church-related universities, know from first-hand experience what these young students face. They wish not to be a laughing stock before their more mature scientific colleagues. But in the matter of age determination each Bible-believing scientist will have to choose between accepting the untruths which inevitably result from acceptance of the uniformitarian myth—and thereby enjoying the approval of his more mature skeptical colleagues, or taking the consequences of standing firmly or the truth of the simple declarations of Genesis.

How strongly the natural man wants to believe everything he thinks he sees! But regarding age, Adam could not do that, even in a perfect world, and still he, was very happy! Our own love for truth should help us follow his example (1978, 14[4]:187-188, emp. and parenthetical items in orig.).

Dr. Marsh's assessment is as accurate an assessment of this matter as I have ever seen, and I believe that we who are Bible believers are indebted to him for having reminded us of the importance of God's special revelation as presented and preserved in His Word—even (especially!) in matters like the age of the Earth that sometimes are considered scientifically sacrosanct.

However, in our discussions regarding the doctrine of apparent age, we always must be extremely careful not to abuse the concept. Some have inquired, for example, whether God might have placed fossils (or, for that matter, fossil fuels) within the Earth simply in order to make it "appear" ancient. This idea should be rejected for several reasons. First, such a suggestion implies that the formation of fossils and/or fossil fuels is an inherently slow, uniformitarian-type process—which it most certainly is not (see, for example, Major, 1996).

Second, certain geological/paleontological phenomena provide some of the best examples available in the world around us of a sudden, global, non-uniformitarian catastrophe (i.e., the Genesis Flood). When the doctrine of apparent age is invoked in an inappropriate manner, it robs mankind of powerful testimony to the workings of the Creator and weakens the similarly powerful testimony of His Word regarding what He did and how He did it.

Third, the idea that the Creator may have "planted" such things as fossils and fossil fuels in the Earth is an indictment of the nature and character of God, Who never would try to "trick" or "fool" man in such a way. Nor would He ever lie (Titus 1:2; Hebrews 6:18). If we observe things in the Earth like fossils, fossil fuels, etc., we naturally (and rightly) assume that these are the results of **real** plants and/or animals that actually lived. It will not do for us to say, "God just put them there," for such a suggestion makes God deceptive, which He is not. As Major has stated: "Tactics of confusion and deception hardly belong to a Creator Who would have humanity discern Him by His creation (Romans 1:20)" [1989, 27[10]:16].

Others have suggested that if God created things that appear older than they really are, that is deceptive on the face of it. Thus, by definition the doctrine of apparent age makes God out to be a liar and should be rejected on that count alone. However, such an

accusation overlooks the fact that **God plainly told us what He
did!** Anyone who takes the time to read Genesis 1-2 can see within those chapters God's methodology. In fact, He made certain to
tell us exactly how the Earth and its inhabitants came into existence.
Perhaps—just perhaps—if God had not told us in such numbingly
exact terms what He did, or if He had not been as specific as He
was, **then** someone might be able to accuse Him of deception or
trickery. But no one can accuse God (justifiably) of such despicable
behavior because His Word adequately explains His actions. He did
not hide the facts from us but, quite the contrary, went to great
lengths to reveal them.

Some have suggested that one of the most difficult questions relating to the doctrine of apparent age has to do with the starlight
that can be seen by those of us here on the Earth. Normally, the argument goes something like this. We understand today that light
travels at a speed slightly in excess of 186,000 miles per second.
[The time it takes light to travel one year is referred to as a light-
year.] Yet we are able to see light from stars that are multiplied millions of light-years away. How can this be if the Earth is as young as
many creationists suggest—with an age measured in thousands of
years rather than billions? A partial answer to this question, of course,
is that God created the light from heavenly bodies already en route
and visible to the Earth's inhabitants (as a part of His mature creation).
Without such light, the night sky would lack patterns necessary to
serve as signs, seasons, days, and years specified so clearly in Genesis 1:14, and mankind would have been unable to see God's "glory
and handiwork" (Psalm 19:1).

Other issues may be involved as well, a treatment of which (e.g.,
the possibility that the speed of light has diminished over time, etc.)
has been provided by various writers (see: Norman and Setterfield,
1987; Major, 1987, 7:5-7; *Ex Nihilo*, 1984, 6[4]:46; Humphreys,
1994). The reader who is interested in an examination of these matters is referred to these sources (and others that they may recommend). Such a discussion is beyond the purview of this book.

The doctrine of apparent age not only explains many of the alleged evidences for an ancient Earth, but is entirely scriptural in its foundations. It helps answer many of the questions relating to data that evolutionists, and those sympathetic to them, offer as documentation for their concept of a planet of great antiquity—which, in reality, is one of relative youth.

Chapter 12

Miscellaneous Compromises of the Genesis Record

PROGRESSIVE CREATIONISM

In this day and age, it no longer is popular for one who is an atheist to be called an atheist. The name simply is too harsh, and carries too many negative connotations. Thus, today atheists often are referred to euphemistically as humanists or free-thinkers. In some instances—though they hold to each and every tenet of atheism—they even refer to themselves as agnostic in their leanings.

Why the posturing? It is because the name carries a certain connotation; words **do** have meanings. The same is true in the creation/evolution controversy. Years ago, those who accepted the evolutionary scenario, in whole or in part, yet who professed a belief in God, were known simply as "theistic evolutionists." But today that phrase is considered by many to be too harsh, and to carry too many negative connotations. And so a new name had to be found—one that would allow essentially the same beliefs as theistic evolution (much as agnosticism allows the same essential beliefs as atheism), yet was not deemed so offensive.

Thus, the term "progressive creationism" was invented. Historically speaking, the phrase was coined by Bernard Ramm, who first used it in his influential book, *The Christian View of Science and Scripture*, published in 1954 (pp. 76-78). Five years later, two other terms arrived on the scene, each defending the essence of Ramm's viewpoint, but giving it a different label. Edward John Carnell of Fuller Theological Seminary in California spoke of "threshold evolution" (1959). James O. Buswell III, in the book, *Evolution and Christian Thought Today*, edited by Russell Mixter, dubbed it "scientific creationism" (1959).*

For a time, the three phrases—progressive creationism, threshold evolution, and scientific creationism—were recognized widely as synonyms, and were used as such in the literature of 1950s and 1960s. In his classic 1969 work, *Evolution and Christian Faith*, Bolton Davidheiser wrote:

> The position most commonly taken and taught at present by men of science who profess to be Bible-believing conservative Christians (they do not like the word **fundamental**) goes by such names as **threshold evolution**, **progressive creationism**, and **scientific creationism**. These are essentially the same thing (p. 174, emp. and parenthetical comment in orig.).

However, Buswell's terminology, "scientific creationism," eventually fell into disuse and, as of the writing of this book, no longer is employed to refer to either the idea it originally represented or the concepts of progressive creationism/threshold evolution (see footnote below). For the discussion here, therefore, I will use the term "progressive creationism."

---

* Today the terms "progressive creationism" and "threshold evolution" are used interchangeably by advocates of both theories. However, the term "scientific creationism" as suggested by Buswell no longer is used to refer to such concepts. Currently, the term is used to refer to the view held by strict creationists that the available scientific evidence supports the creationist position as the correct model of origins. For example, one of the texts quoted in this book is *Scientific Creationism* by Henry Morris. That volume is devoted to an examination of much of the scientific evidence supporting biblical creationism (see also Morris and Parker, 1987).

What is Progressive Creationism?

Ramm contended that progressive creationism—in form, not in name—was taught as early as Augustine. [For a discussion of how writers such as Ramm often employ Augustine in defense of their theories, see Bromling, 1994, 14:53.] Whether that is true or not, the popular defense and acceptance of progressive creationism actually dates from the publication of Ramm's book. When his text was published, it caused quite a stir. In fact, on the book's dust jacket the publishers expressed their view that the book "marks a historical point of no return where evangelical Christian scholars will no longer in ignorance deprecate the findings of science, but will understand them with the advantage of their Christian perspective." Since he was the originator of the phrase, it is only right that Ramm be allowed to explain its meaning.

> In progressive creationism there may be much horizontal radiation. The amount is to be determined by the geological record and biological experimentation. But there is no vertical radiation. Vertical radiation is only by fiat creation. A **root-species** may give rise to several species by horizontal radiation, through the process of unraveling of gene potentialities or recombination. Horizontal radiation could account for much which now passes as evidence for the theory of evolution. The gaps in the geological record are gaps because vertical progress takes place only by creation.
>
> **Creation and development are both indispensable categories in the understanding of geology and biology**. The fiat creationist can be embarrassed by a thousand examples of development. Progression cannot be denied geology and biology. The chasms in the order of life can only be bridged by creation. Biology cannot be rendered totally meaningful solely in terms of progression. Both Genesis and biology start with the null and void, both proceed from the simple to the complex, and both climax with man (1954, p. 191, emp. in orig.).

In his now-famous text, *Unformed and Unfilled*, Weston W. Fields observed:

It seems that most evangelical scientists today believe that while God directly created the **first** life and also the major stages of life throughout the geologic history (such as the vertebrates, the birds, the marsupials, the mammals, and man), nevertheless extensive evolution has taken place over vast expanses of geologic time within these major created groups of living things. This view is known as "progressive creationism" or "threshold evolution" and is often linked with the "day-age" view (Carnell, Mixter, Ramm, etc.) [1976, p. 167, emp. and parenthetical items in orig.].

Davidheiser provided an explanation of how the process is alleged to have worked, and why it sometimes is referred to by Carnell's term, "threshold evolution."

Whereas theistic evolutionists declare that all of evolution is true but divinely directed, progressive creationists counter that God performed creative acts along the way, and thus evolution did not produce all forms of life. That is, certain forms were created, then changed or evolved, but they could not **go the whole way**. Therefore the Lord had to create again, and so repeated His creative acts. The Lord had to lift animals over a threshold, as it were, so that they could start evolving again in more diversification (1973, 3:51-52, emp. in orig.).

Thus, progressive creationism is seen as the concept that God periodically "stepped in" to intervene in the creative process. In between divine creative acts, however, evolutionary development (covering billions of years) occurred. Hugh Ross defended this idea in his text, *Creation and Time* (1994).* Michael Pitman described it in these terms: "A creationist is not obliged to embrace Old Testament fundamentalism; indeed, many believe the creation of life may have happened in stages, each generating life-forms more complex than the one before" (1984, p. 238). John Hick, a modern-day liberal theologian, said: "I...am a creationist in the sense that I believe that the universe is God's creation, but I believe that

---

* For additional documentation on Hugh Ross' position as a progressive creationist, and a refutation of that position, see Van Bebber and Taylor (1996).

God's creative work is progressive and continuous and that biological evolution is a part of it" (1985, 5[4]:40). In other words, God
intervened not just once, but many times along the way to "help biological evolution along." This, then, is the essence of progressive
creationism.

Is Progressive Creationism Theistic Evolution?

Is progressive creationism theistic evolution? Considerable controversy has been generated over the answer to that question. Dr.
Ramm, and other proponents of progressive creationism, have
been quick to respond that it is **not** theistic evolution, and that they
are **not** theistic evolutionists. In *The Christian View of Science
and Scripture*, Ramm said of himself:

> The author of this book believes in the divine origin of the
> Bible, and therefore in its divine inspiration; and he emphati-
> cally rejects any partial theory of inspiration or liberal or neo-
> orthodox view of the Bible.... **The writer is not a theistic
> evolutionist.... We accept progressive creationism**,
> which teaches that over the millions of years of geologic his-
> tory God has been fiatly creating higher and higher forms of
> life (1954, pp. 31-32,205,256, emp. added).

Buswell, in his chapter in *Evolution and Christian Thought Today*, placed anti-evolutionists into three distinct categories. The first
grouping consisted of people whom he called "hypertraditionalists"
—those "bound to rigid interpretations of Scripture [and] who are
loath to accept any new facts which seem to contradict their interpretations, since these are seen not as interpretations but as literal
teachings of Scripture itself" (1959, p. 188). Buswell's second group
was comprised of "many Roman Catholics and Protestants" who,
he acknowledged, hold to a strict interpretation of theistic evolution. In the third category, said Buswell—between the hypertraditionalists and the theistic evolutionists—is the group that generally
is recognized as "progressive creationists." Of this particular group,
he wrote:

> There are creationists, many of whom have specialized in
> one field of science or another, or else, as theologians, have
> either taken pains to keep abreast in some measure with sci-
> entific advance, or else have sought the counsel of those who
> have, who constantly allow their interpretations to be open
> to the acceptance of newly discovered facts, so that the re-
> integration of their position has been free from the contra-
> diction of embracing one body of facts, whether from Scrip-
> ture or from nature, and excluding the other (1959, p. 188).

Ramm divided people in general into four groups.

> At the risk of oversimplification we may assert four patterns
> of thought in reference to the origin of the universe: (i) fiat
> creationism; (ii) progressive creationism; (iii) theistic evolu-
> tion; and (iv) naturalistic evolution. Much of Bible-and-science
> has been plagued with an oversimplification as if the only al-
> ternatives were fiat creation or naturalistic evolution. The hy-
> per-orthodox have as a group been very uncharitable toward
> both the progressive creationists and theistic evolutionists
> (1954, p. 76).

Ramm's separation of progressive creationism and theistic evolution into separate categories is not accidental. As Davidheiser remarked: "Those who espouse progressive creationism usually are
quite insistent that they are not theistic evolutionists" (1969, p. 175).

But how do progressive creationism and theistic evolution differ? Whatever differences exist may be summed up by the statement
that theistic evolutionists embrace the entire evolutionary dogma
(short of spontaneous generation, of course), whereas progressive
creationists allow God somewhat more activity in the process. As
Fields has argued:

> Ramm goes to great lengths to show that progressive creation-
> ism is not theistic evolution. But it seems to us that the dif-
> ference is more in **extent** than **kind**, whereas true creation-
> ism differs not only in **extent** but also in **kind** with evolution
> of whatever sort. According to the definition above, which
> we feel is accurately representative of the views of prominent
> progressive creationists, God used the process of evolution
> extensively. It appears that progressive creationists want to
> have the benefit of a great amount of evolution (which will

commend them to secular scientists), as well as benefit of
the name "creationist" (which will commend them to naive
Christians), but the name "creationist" is somewhat misleading
(1976, p. 784, emp. and parenthetical comments in orig.).

Is Progressive Creationism Acceptable?

Experience has shown that those who accept, and defend, progressive creationism often come to believe more in evolution and
less in creation as time passes. This does not seem to be the exception, but rather the rule. As Davidheiser has concluded:

> "Threshold Evolution" leads to much real evolutionary belief.
> How much evolution do these people accept? One of the men
> says of his belief in progressive creationism that he encoun-
> ters a primary difficulty—he must exercise faith to believe in
> a certain amount of creation! Others admit that their view re-
> quires considerably more evolutionary belief than they would
> have been willing to accept a few years previously. In other
> words, it leads to evolutionary beliefs and away from creation.
> It establishes another compromise which is injurious to the
> Christian faith... (1973, 3:52-53).

Is progressive creationism theistic evolution? Both call on God
to start creation. Both accept evolution (in varying amounts). Both
accept the validity of the geologic age system. Both postulate an
old Earth. Where is the difference, except that progressive creationism allows God "a little more to do"? Both systems put God (*theos*)
and evolution together. By any other standard that is **theistic evolution**. As Niessen has noted:

> It is currently fashionable for theistic evolutionists to go by the
> name "Progressive Creationists" in order to avoid the popular
> resentment in Christian circles against evolution and its non-
> theistic orientation. In practice, however, both views are es-
> sentially the same. The difference merely concerns the amount
> of God's intervention within the evolutionary process (1980,
> p. 16).

THE MODIFIED GAP THEORY

Many Christians today apparently are afflicted with the malady
of "misguided determination." Please do not misunderstand. Deter-

mination can be a wonderful thing. It might be responsible for a
new invention, the founding of a college, the building of an empire
—or ten thousand other good and wonderful things. But misguided
determination is a blight, not a blessing.

Numerous Bible believers today have seen the abject failure of
both the Day-Age and Gap theories. Yet they are as determined as
ever to find a way to force evolutionary time, as represented by the
geologic ages, into the biblical text. Their determination thus forces
them to formulate, modify, temporarily accept, and then abandon
theory after theory in search of one that they hope finally will succeed. Unfortunately, many Bible believers have not yet come to the
conclusion that the Genesis record is a literal, factual, and defensi-
ble record of God's method of creation. Rather than accept the Genesis account at face value—as Christ and His inspired writers did—
they constantly seek some way to improve upon it by appealing to
one theory after another, in the hope that ultimately they will be able
to force evolutionary time into the biblical record.

In many instances, the resulting "new" theories are little more
than a reworking of the old, discarded theories that long ago were
banished to the relic heaps of history because they could not withstand examination under the intense spotlight of God's Word. One
such theory making the rounds today is the "Modified Gap Theory."
Because of its popularity in certain quarters, I feel it bears examination here.

What is the Modified Gap Theory?

Over the past three decades, one of the most frequently used
lecturers among certain segments of the churches of Christ has
been John N. Clayton, a self-proclaimed atheist-turned-Christian
who teaches high school science in South Bend, Indiana.* Due to

---

* I coauthored, with Wayne Jackson, the book, *In the Shadow of Darwin—A Review
of the Teachings of John N. Clayton*, which examines Mr. Clayton's positions on
creation, evolution, and related topics. This review is available from the offices of Apologetics Press.

his background in historical geology, Clayton has worked at a feverish pace to produce an amalgamation between the evolutionary geologic record and the Genesis account of creation. Shortly after becoming a Christian, Clayton adopted the position of a full-fledged theistic evolutionist. Later, however, he moved away from strict theistic evolution to an "off-beat" brand of that doctrine that reflects what he has called his own "private theology" (see Francella, 1981). Consequently, he is recognized widely by those who are active in the creation/evolution controversy as the originator and primary defender of what has come to be known as the Modified Gap Theory (see: Clayton, 1976b, pp. 147-148; Thompson, 1977, pp. 188-194; McIver, 1988b, 8[3]:22; Jackson and Thompson, 1992, pp. 115-130; Thompson, 1999b, pp. 68-81).

For over thirty years, John Clayton has propagated the view that the Earth is approximately 4.5 billion years old—the standard evolutionary estimate of its age (see Clayton, 1990d, p. 130). As a result, he has struggled to find some possible way by which to accommodate the Genesis account of creation to such a concept. The Modified Gap Theory is his proposed solution. Here, in his own words, is how his Modified Gap Theory attempts to make such an accommodation possible.

> Genesis 1:1 is an undated verse. No time element is given and no details of what the Earth looked like are included. It could have taken place in no time at all, or **God may have used eons of time** to accomplish his objectives. **I suggest that all geological phenomena except the creation of warmblooded life were accomplished during this time**. There was no way God could have described amoebas, bacteria, viris [sic], or dinosaurs to the ancient Hebrew, and yet these forms of life were vital to the coal, oil and gas God knew man would need. Thus God created these things but did not describe them just as He did not describe a majority of the 110 million species of life on this planet. Changes took place in the Earth (but no gap destruction) until God began the formation of man's world with birds, whales, cattle and man in the literal days of Genesis (Clayton, 1976b, pp. 147-148, emp. added, parenthetical comment in orig.).

John Clayton has worked on this concept for most of his adult life, and along the way has polished, altered, "tweaked," and revised it in order to make it fit whatever new scientific data happen to be in vogue at the time. He has included it in his lectures, defended it in his bi-monthly journal (*Does God Exist?*), and advocated it in various other ways throughout his career. In lesson nine of his 1990 *Does God Exist? Correspondence Course*, for example, he elaborated on how the Modified Gap Theory works.

> Not only does the first verse give us the creation of celestial objects, but of a **functional earth** itself.... By the end of Genesis 1:1 there was a functional, living, working earth. If you had stood upon the earth at this point in time, you would have recognized it. Let us once again remind you that how long God chose to use to accomplish this creation is not revealed in this passage.... It is very possible that a living ecosystem operated in Genesis 1:1 to produce the earth. Bacteria may have swarmed in the oceans and giant plants may have lived in great swamps. Dinosaurs may have roamed freely accomplishing their purpose in being. The purpose of all of this would have been to prepare the earth for man. This living ecosystem would have produced the coal, oil, gas, and the like, as well as providing the basis of man's ultimate food supply! (1990a, pp. 3,4, emp. added).

Thus, in capsule form, Clayton suggests that when the Bible says God "created," what it **really** means is that God, over eons of time, "prepared" an Earth for man. Further, God did not create **everything** to exist on that "first" Earth. For example, according to the Modified Gap Theory there were no warm-blooded creatures. And, since man is warm-blooded, naturally, he was not there either. Clayton has written:

> I submit to you that Genesis 1:1 is not a summary verse. It is a record of God's action which produced an Earth ready for man's use. I further submit for your consideration that **some time may be involved in this verse and that natural processes may have been used** as well as miraculous ones to prepare the Earth for man (1982, 9[10]:5, emp. added).

Mr. Clayton has provided an explanation as to **why**, according to his theory, man was not a part of this original creation.

> The week described in Exodus refers to the week described in Genesis 1:5-31. The week in Genesis 1:5-31 describes the creation of man and a few forms with which man is familiar, but it is **not** a total description of every living thing that does [sic] or ever has existed on Earth (1976a, 3[10]:5-6, emp. in orig.).

Exodus 20:11 explicitly affirms that **everything** that was made by God was completed **within the six days** of the initial week. Clayton begs to differ with both God and His inspired writer Moses, and instead asserts that many things actually had been created (during vast epochs of time) long before the creation week ever started. Since, as I already have discussed, Clayton does not believe that Exodus 20:11 refers to **all** of the creative activity of God, but instead refers only to that which occurred in Genesis 1:5-31, he has suggested that Moses "**avoids the creation question and concentrates on his own purpose**" (1976a, 3[10]:5, emp. added). Put into chart form by Clayton himself, the Modified Gap Theory appears as you see it below.

CREATION				JUDGMENT		
		RESOURCE ECOSYSTEM				
	EARTH SUN	AMOEBA BACTERIA	CHRONOMETRY SET UP			
TIME	MOON	WATER PLANTS	GEN. 1:14-19	GEN. 1:20-28	ADAM	NOW
MATTER	STARS	DINOSAURS		CREATION WEEK		CHRIST
	GALAXIES ETC.	ETC.		BIRDS WATER MAMMALS MAMMALS MAN		
	PRECAMBRIAN	MESOZOIC	CENOZOIC ±			

Summary of John Clayton's Modified Gap Theory

A Response and Refutation

Whenever John Clayton is challenged regarding the Modified Gap Theory, his usual response is to attempt to cloud the issue by suggesting that he does not accept the **standard** Gap Theory. He has complained, for example: "You'll notice that I'm accused of advocating both the Gap Theory and the Day-Age Theory there, and of course neither one of those am I advocating.... But I would like to emphasize that I do not in any way, shape, or form embrace the Gap Theory" (1980b).

Yet, in his lecture, *Evolution's Proof of God*, he is on record as stating: "In Genesis 1:2 I'm told by the Hebrew scholars that the most accurate reading is that the earth 'became without form and void' and some have suggested that maybe **a tremendous number of years passed between the first part of Genesis 1:1 and Genesis 1:2**" (n.d.[d], emp. added). Mr. Clayton then went on to defend that very position. I wonder—what would the average person call that "tremendous number of years" between Genesis 1:1 and 1:2? A "gap" perhaps?

Those who made the "accusation" to which Clayton was responding never suggested that he accepted the **standard** Gap Theory. The issue was whether or not he accepted the **Modified** Gap Theory. [In fact, he is the one who invented the theory in the first place, in the 1976 edition of his book, *The Source*.] The standard Gap Theory suggests that in the alleged time interval between Genesis 1:1 and 1:2, the Earth was destroyed during a battle between Satan and God. Clayton is on record as stating that he does not accept that so-called "gap destruction." Mr. Clayton does not like being saddled with any label that identifies his views for what they are. He bristles at being "boxed in," to use his own words. In attempting to skirt the issues, therefore, at times he has been known to answer charges that have not even been leveled. The account of the events surrounding his Modified Gap Theory provides a good example of this very thing.

John Clayton's "private theology" (see Francella, 1981) is replete with unscriptural concepts, discrepancies, and contradictions
that bear close examination. Notice that, according to his chart (reproduced on page 285), the "creation week" does not commence
until Genesis 1:14ff. Since this section of Genesis 1 has to do with
the events of **day four and afterward**, Clayton's "week" of creative activity has only **three days**! Furthermore, Clayton's Modified Gap Theory suggests that during the eons of time prior to the
"creation week" God was **building up** a "resource ecosystem" by
the use of amoebas, bacteria, water, plants, dinosaurs, etc. (again,
refer to his chart on Genesis 1:1). Yet at other times, while attempting to defend his Modified Gap Theory, Clayton has contended that
the "most accurate reading" of Genesis 1:2 is that the Earth "**became without form and void**" (n.d.[d], emp. added). Which is it?
Was the Earth **generating** or **degenerating** during this period?
Obviously, it cannot be both.

Earlier, I quoted Clayton as suggesting that in Exodus 20:11
Moses "**avoids the creation question** and concentrates on his
own purpose" (1976a, 3[10]:5, emp. added). I would like to address
that point here, for it is a careless comment indeed. The purpose
of Moses' statement was not merely to **establish** the Sabbath law;
it also was an explanation as to the **reason** for the Sabbath. Exactly **why** were the Israelites commanded to observe the Sabbath?
Because in six days God created the Earth and its creatures and on
the seventh day rested. To state that Moses "avoids the creation
question" is wrong. The divine writer did not avoid a reference to
the **Creator**; "Jehovah" is specified. Nor did he avoid referring to
the Lord's **action**; he noted that God "made" these things.

The Modified Gap Theory flatly contradicts both Exodus 20:11
and Genesis 1. For example, Clayton has argued that the creation
of fish (cold-blooded creatures) occurred in Genesis 1:1, whereas
according to Moses they were created on the **fifth day** (Genesis 1:
20-23). The Genesis record states that creeping things (which would
include both insects and reptiles) were brought into existence on

the **sixth day** (1:21,24), but the Modified Gap Theory places them in the time period before the creation week. John Clayton simply rearranges the Genesis record to fit his own evolutionary presuppositions—without any regard whatsoever for what God had to say on the matter.

The only way that Clayton can hold to his Modified Gap Theory and his "private theology" is to convince people that **his way** of translating Genesis is the **correct way**. He has attempted to do just that for more than three decades. In order to succeed, he has found it necessary to present people with an entirely **new vocabulary**. This is the case with many false teachers. They realize they never will be able to reach the masses by using correct, biblical terminology, so they invent altogether new terms, or offer drastic reinterpretations of old ones, in an attempt to make their ideas appear plausible and acceptable (see Miller, 1987, 7[2]:2-3).

The Modified Gap Theory, with its accompanying off-beat brand of theistic evolution, rests upon the (mis)interpretation of two Hebrew words, *bara* and *asah*, used in Genesis 1-2. Here is what Mr. Clayton has said about them, and why they are so important to his "private theology."

> In the Hebrew culture and in the Hebrew language there is a difference between something being created and something being made. The idea of creation involves a miraculous act on the part of God. It is not something that man can do, nor is it something that can occur naturally.... The Hebrew word used in Genesis 1 to describe this process is the word *bara*. As one might expect, this word is not used extensively in the Bible, in fact, it is only used in verses 1, 21, and 27 in Genesis. The other concept in the Hebrew culture and in the Hebrew language that is used in reference to things coming into existence involves the process of producing something naturally. The idea is that something came into existence because of planning, wisdom, and intelligence, but not as a miraculous act of God. Many times acts of men are described in this way. The Hebrew word *asah* is the main Hebrew word translated this way in Genesis 1. It is vital to a proper understanding of Genesis that these two words not be confused because

much understanding is lost and considerable contradiction
with the scientific evidence is generated when the words are
not distinguished from each other (1991, 18[1]:6-7).

Clayton also has written:

> We have pointed out that the Hebrew word *bara* normally
> means to create something out of nothing while the word
> *asah* usually implies the re-shaping of something that was
> already in existence. ...the normal use of the word *bara* and
> the normal use of the word *asah* are distinctly different and
> this difference is important in one's interpretation of Gene-
> sis 1 (1979b, 6[5]:2-5).

The following detailed summary from John Clayton's own writings should clarify why this distinction is so important to the success
of his Modified Gap Theory.

1. God initiated the Big Bang, and the Universe developed according to evolutionary theories (Clayton, 1991, 18[1]:8). [In a "News
   and Notes" insert in the September/October 1999 issue of his
   Does God Exist? journal, Clayton wrote: "We have tried over
   and over again to point out to readers that **the big bang theory
   is not at odds with the Bible** nor with the concept of God as
   Creator" (1999, 26[5]:no page number, emp. added).]

2. The initial creation (*bara*) supposedly included such things as
   the Sun, Moon, Earth, stars, etc. (Clayton, 1991, 18[1]:8). As I
   discussed earlier, Clayton places certain living creatures in this
   period (which he refers to as "pre-history"), including such things
   as dinosaurs, bacteria, cold-blooded animals, etc., but no warm-
   blooded animals or man.

3. Sometime after the initial creation, God then began to form and
   make (*asah*) things. As Clayton has stated: "It is important to recognize that this process of creating...is described in Genesis 1:1-3.
   Verse 4ff deal with something all together different—the making, forming, and shaping of the created earth. Creation does not
   occur again until animal life is described in verses 20 and 21"
   (1991, 19[1]:8-9).

4. Beginning in the time period called Day 5, according to Clayton, God began to make new things (Clayton, 1991, 18[1]:9), which presumably would **include** marine life, birds, and man, but would **exclude** light, oceans, atmosphere, dry land, planets, stars, and beasts of the field—all of which supposedly were "created" (*bara*) in Genesis 1:1.

5. Man's spiritual part then was created (*bara*) in God's image (1:27), and his physical part was formed (*yatsar,* not *bara*) from the dust of the ground (Clayton, 1991, 18[1]:9).

6. By the end of Genesis 1, God's "creating" and "making" were finished, but "there is no indication in the Bible that the seventh day ever ended" (Clayton, 1990c, 17[4]:11).

The terribly convoluted scenario involved in what you have just read is absolutely necessary, from Clayton's viewpoint, in order to make his Modified Gap Theory work. Here, now, is what is wrong with all of this.

First, the distinction of the alleged difference between *bara* and *asah* is completely artificial, and Clayton has admitted that this is the case. In the May 1979 issue of his *Does God Exist?* journal, he wrote:

> **Because there are a few isolated exceptions** where the context seems to indicate that the word *bara* or *asah* has been used in a different way than the application we have just discussed, there are those who maintain that one cannot scripturally maintain the applications of these words as we have presented them in reference to Genesis 1. The Hebrew language, as most of us recognize, is a language which can be interpreted only in its context (1979b, 6[5]:4, emp. added).

In his *Does God Exist? Correspondence Course*, Clayton confessed: "Some may object to this superliteral interpretation of *bara* and *asah* by responding that there are exceptions to the usages I have described in the previous paragraphs. **Such a criticism is valid**" (1990b, p. 3, emp. added).

Second, the "few isolated exceptions" (as Clayton calls them) to his suggested usages of *bara* and *asah* are neither few nor isolated. Furthermore, those exceptions completely obliterate his artificial distinction in regard to *bara* and *asah* (which, in fact, often **are used interchangeably** throughout the Old Testament, and do not always have the strict interpretation that John Clayton has attempted to place on them). Notice the following.

(1) Clayton has suggested: "As one might expect, this word [*bara* —BT] is not used extensively in the Bible, in fact, it is only used in verses 1, 21, and 27 in Genesis" (1991, 18[1]:6-7). This statement is completely untrue. *Strong's Exhaustive Concordance* cites no fewer than 11 instances of *bara* in the book of Genesis. Additionally, bara and its derivatives occur 40 times in the Old Testament apart from Genesis. In over 30 instances, it means "create, shape, form, or fashion."

(2) Clayton has insisted—in keeping with the rules of his new vocabulary—that the word *bara* **always** must mean "to create something from nothing" (1990c, 17[4]:7). This, too, is incorrect, as I argued at length in Chapter 9. Henry Morris observed:

> The Hebrew words for "create" (*bara*) and for "make" (*asah*) are very often used quite interchangeably in Scripture, at least when God is the one referred to as creating or making. Therefore, the fact that *bara* is used only three times in Genesis 1 (vv. 1,21, and 27) certainly does not imply that the other creative acts, in which "made" or some similar expression is used, were really only acts of restoration. For example, in Genesis 1:21, God "created" the fishes and birds; in 1:25, He "made" the animals and creeping things. In verse 26, God speaks of "making" man in His own image. The next verse states that God "created" man in His own image. No scientific or exegetical ground exists for distinction between the two processes, except perhaps a matter of grammatical emphasis. ...Finally, the summary verse (Genesis 2:3) clearly says that **all** of God's works, both of "creating" and "making" were completed within the six days, after which God "rested" (1966, p. 32, emp. in orig.).

Clayton's insistence that *bara* **always** must mean "to create something from nothing, is, quite simply, wrong. Old Testament scholar C.F. Keil (quoted earlier in chapter 9) concluded that when *bara* appears in its basic form, as it does in Genesis 1,

> ...it always means **to create**, and is only applied to a divine creation, the production of that which had no existence before. It is never joined with an accusative of the material, **although it does not exclude a pre-existent material unconditionally**, but is used for the creation of man (ver. 27, ch. v. 1,2), and of everything new that God creates, whether in the kingdom of nature (Numbers xvi. 30) or of that of grace (Ex. xxxiv.10; Ps. li.10, etc.) [1971, 1:47, first emp. in orig., last emp. added].

Further, there is ample evidence that Clayton knows his efforts to make *bara* represent **only** that "which has been created from nothing" are incorrect. Genesis 1:27 is the passage that reveals the error of his interpretation: "So God created (*bara*) man in his own image, in the image of God created he him; male and female created he them." If Clayton's assertion is correct that *bara* can be used only to mean "to create something from nothing," then the obvious conclusion is that in Genesis 1:27 God created man and woman **from nothing**. But, of course, that conflicts with Genesis 2:7, which states that God formed man from the dust of the ground.

How has Clayton attempted to correct his obvious error? He has suggested—in keeping with his new vocabulary—that Genesis 1:27 **really** is saying that when God "created" (*bara*) man, He actually created not man's body, but **his soul** from nothing (1991, 18 [1]:9). Such a strained interpretation can be proven wrong by a simple reading of the text. Genesis 1:27 tells the reader **what** was created—"**male** and **female** created he them." Do souls come in "male" and "female" varieties? They do not. Souls are spirits, and as such are sexless, (e.g., as Jesus said angels were—Matthew 22:29-30; cf. Thompson, 2000a). Yet Clayton's Modified Gap Theory interpretation plainly implies that male and female souls exist. A well-known principle in elementary logic is that any argument with a false premise (or premises) is unsound. Thus, the Modified Gap Theory is unsound.

(3) Taking the creation passages at face value and in their proper context, it is obvious that no distinction is made between the act of creating and the act of making. For example, God's activity during this first week is described in terms other than creating or making. This includes the phrase, "Let there be," which is used to usher in each new day and the things created in that day. Also, note that God "divided" the light from the darkness, and He "set" the light-giving objects in the expanse of the sky. How would John Clayton's "new vocabulary" deal with these matters?

(4) There is compelling evidence that the words *bara* and *asah* are used **interchangeably** throughout the Old Testament. Clayton, has stated: "It is difficult to believe that there would be two words used to convey the same process" (1990c, 17[4]:7). Yet why is it difficult to imagine that two different words might be used to describe exactly the same process? Writers commonly employ different words to describe the same thing(s), thereby providing "stylistic relief"—a grammatical construct which avoids the needless repetition that occurs by using the same words over and over. For more than a hundred years, conservative scholars have made a similar point to proponents of the Documentary Hypothesis, arguing that there is no reasonable way to dissect the Old Testament on the basis of the words *Elohim* ("God") and *Yahweh* ("Jehovah").

Bible writers often employed different words to describe the same thing(s). For example, in the four Gospels, Christ is spoken of as having been killed, crucified, and slain. Where is the distinction? New Testament writers often spoke of the church, the body, and the kingdom—which are exactly the same thing (see Thompson, 1999c, pp. 60-62). Where is the difference? Why should anyone find it difficult to accept that entirely different words may be used to describe the same thing or event?

Furthermore, the Scriptures are replete with examples which prove that—beyond the shadow of a doubt—*bara* and *asah* **are** used interchangeably. For example, in Psalm 148:1-5, the writer spoke of the "creation" (*bara*) of the angels. Yet when Nehemiah addressed the creation of angels, he employed the word *asah* to describe it (9:6). In Genesis 1:1, as Clayton has admitted, the text speaks of God "creating" (*bara*) the Earth. Yet again, when Nehemiah spoke of that same event, he employed the word *asah* to do so (9:6). When Moses wrote of the "creation" of man, he used *bara* (Genesis 1:27). But one verse before that (1:26), he spoke of the "making" (*asah*) of man. Moses even employed the two words **in the same verse** (Genesis 2:4) when he said: "These are the generations of the heavens and of the earth when they were **created** [*bara*], in the day that Jehovah **made** [*asah*] earth and heaven."

John Clayton has said that the Earth was **created** (*bara*) from nothing in Genesis 1:1. Yet Moses said in Genesis 2:4 that the Earth was **made** (*asah*). Clayton is on record as stating that the use of *asah* can refer **only** to that which is made from something already in existence. Does he then believe that when Moses spoke of the Earth being "made," it was formed from something already in existence?

And what about Exodus 20:11 in this context? Moses wrote: "For in six days the Lord made [*asah*] heaven and earth, the sea and all that in them is, and rested the seventh day." Clayton has written that this speaks only of God's "forming" from something already in existence. But notice that the verse specifically speaks of the **heaven** and the **Earth** and the **sea** and **all that in them is**. Does Clayton therefore contend that God formed the heavens from something already in existence? Exodus 20:11 speaks of **everything** made by God in the six days of creation. Yet even Clayton has admitted that "creation (*bara*) does not occur again until animal life is described in verses 20 and 21." How can this be? Moses stated that God "made" (*asah*) everything in the creation week. Now Mr. Clayton suggests that there was "creation" (*bara*) going on in that week. Even John Clayton, therefore, has admitted that there are times when the two words describe the same events during the same time period!

In addition to these problems, the Modified Gap Theory has the same difficulty explaining Nehemiah 9:6 as the standard Gap Theory. Since that was discussed at length in Chapter 9, I will not repeat it here.

(5) Weston W. Fields suggested that forcing *bara* and *asah* to refer to completely separate acts eventually results in what he called a "monstrosity of interpretation"—which is exactly what John Clayton's suggested usage of these words represents. Remember that Clayton has stated plainly that at the end of Genesis 1:1 there was a **fully functional** Earth in existence (complete with various kinds of life teeming on it), and that it remained that way for eons. If that is the case—based on his *bara/asah* argument—how would he explain the following problem?

Clayton has taught that the "heavenly bodies" (Sun, Moon, stars, etc.) were a part of the *bara*-type creation of Genesis 1:1. But Exodus 20:11 specifically states that they were "made" (*asah*). Are we to believe that they were **both** "created" **and** "made"? Yes, that is exactly what Clayton has advocated.

> Applied in this literal sense to Genesis 1, one would find that the **heaven and earth** were brought into existence miraculously in Genesis 1:1. This would include the sun, moon, stars, galaxies, black holes, nebula [sic], comets, asteroids and planets.... Verses 14-19 would not describe the creation of the sun, moon and stars, but the reshaping or rearranging of them to a finished form (1989, 16[1]:6).

How were the Sun, Moon, and stars ("created," Clayton says, in Genesis 1:1) assisting the Earth in being "fully functional" when they themselves had not even been "rearranged to a finished form"? One hardly could have a fully functional Earth without the Sun and Moon. Yet by his own admission, Genesis 1:14-19 speaks of God doing **something** to those heavenly bodies. For centuries, competent Bible scholars have accepted that it is in these verses that God is described as bringing the heavenly bodies into existence. But no, says Clayton, that is not true. They were in existence from Genesis 1:1, but they had not yet been "rearranged to a finished form" —something that would not occur until billions of years later. How could these **unfinished** heavenly bodies have been of any use to a **finished** Earth? How could the Earth be "functional" unless the Sun, Moon, and other planets were "functional" as well? And if they were "functional" in Genesis 1:1, why "rearrange" them?

Clayton is on record as stating: "When we look at those places where the word 'make' is used, the context leaves absolutely no doubt about what the intention of the author is for that passage" (1979b, 6[5]:5). I could not agree more! There is **absolutely no doubt** about how the Bible writers employed these words. They used them just as any author would employ them—interchangeably.

THE NON-WORLD VIEW OF ORIGINS

Imagine, if you will, the dilemma of a person who has done all he knows to do to force the evolutionary geologic age-system into the biblical record, but who has discovered that it simply will not fit. If that person wishes to retain his belief in God, but abjectly refuses to accept the biblical account of creation at face value, what option remains open to him? For the person not wishing to become an atheist or agnostic, there is only one remaining possibility—the "Non-World View."

What is the Non-World View?

The Non-World View dates from 1972, with the publication of *A Christian View of Origins* by Donald England, distinguished professor of chemistry at Harding University. In essence, it represents a "refusal to get involved" by not taking a stand on the Genesis account of creation. England himself defined it as suggesting:

> There is no world view presented in Genesis 1. I believe the intent of Genesis 1 is far too sublime and spiritual for one to presume that it teaches anything at all about a cosmological world view. We do this profound text a great injustice by insisting that there is inherent within the text an argument for any particular world view (1972, p. 124).

In other words, this is a compromise for the person who: (a) refuses to accept the Genesis account of creation as written; but (b) cannot find a reasonable alternative. In his book, Dr. England made it clear that from a straightforward reading of the Genesis account "one gets the general impression from the Bible that the earth is young," and that "it is true that Biblical chronology leaves one with the general impression of a relatively recent origin for man" (1972, p. 109). But he also made it clear that he had no intention of accepting such positions, since they disagree with "science."

Finding himself painted into a corner, as it were, the only way out was simply to throw up his hands and, with a sigh of relief, view Genesis as containing **no world view whatsoever**. As one writer who strongly recommends the Non-World View suggested:

> By "Non-World" we mean that we don't accept any "God-limiting" position on how we interpret Genesis. We don't limit our comprehension of time, space, or process in any way Biblically; and do this unlimiting on the basis that that's what God intended....
>
> If Chapter 1 is not a detailed historical account, how do we fit the fossil record to it? The "Non-World" View says "we don't." If we are to speak where the Bible speaks and be silent where the Bible is silent we won't succumb to the pressure to make it fit. Since the Bible doesn't mention dinosaurs, bats, amoeba, bacteria, DNA, virus [sic], sea plants, algae, fungus [sic], etc., we won't attempt to match them. There are a few forms we can match, but only a few out of the millions. The Hebrew words used in Genesis do not cover whole phyla of animals but they are reasonably specific. If we take a "Non-World View," this doesn't bother us because we are only interested in God's message to man, not in satisfying man's curiosity.
>
> The "Non-World View" also finds no necessity in dealing with men's arguments on the scientific theories of creation and age. There is no necessity to argue about the "big bang," "steady state," or irtron theory of origins; nor is there any need to hassle about whether the Earth is 6, 6,000 or 6 billion years old. Genesis 1:1 says only that God did it! That is the purpose. It is **not** the purpose to state how or when (Clayton, 1977, 4[6]: 6-8, emp. in orig.).

A Response and Refutation

The careful reader soon will realize that this is indeed the compromise to end all compromises. With the Non-World View, a person may believe as much, or as little, as he wants in regard to the Genesis account of creation. If the person who holds to this view is challenged with a passage of Scripture, he may reply simply, "Oh, that passage doesn't have any particular world view in it." And the convenient thing is that it does not matter how forceful the passage may be, whether it comes from the Old Testament or the New, what biblical writer may have penned it, or even if Christ Himself spoke it. With the Non-World View, **everything** becomes subjective.

The beauty of this view, according to Clayton, is that it is not "God-limiting" (1977, 4[6]:6). Even though when one reads the creation account he gets the "general impression" that man has been here only a short while, and that the Earth is relatively young, and even though Christ Himself stated in Mark 10:6 that man and woman have been here "from the beginning of the creation," all of that becomes irrelevant. With a wave of the hand, Genesis 1 means little-to-nothing. In fact, it might as well not have been written, for it simply has "no world view" in it at all.

Yet God went to great lengths to explain what was done on day one, what was done on day two, what was done on day three, and so on. He commented to Moses that He took six days to do it. Then He set the Sabbath day as the Jews' remembrance of His creative acts on those days. If God said "in the beginning" and "in six days the Lord created," that is a **time element**. Jesus Himself said that **"from the beginning of the creation**, male and female made He them" (Mark 10:6). That is a time element. True, it does not give an exact day and hour, but it says much. It says man was on the Earth "from the beginning." That automatically rules out an ancient Earth, and those compromising theories intent on having one (e.g., the Day-Age Theory, the Gap Theory, the Multiple Gap Theory, the Modified Gap Theory, etc.). God has indicated—in a way we can understand—what He wants us to know about the time element. When He said that He created "the heavens, the earth, the seas, and all that in them is" in six days, does that sound like a "Non-World" view?

Man may not understand completely the exact "how" of God's creative activity, but that "how" is present nevertheless. When the Scriptures say, "And God said, 'Let there be light' and there was light"—that is **how**. When the Scriptures say, "And God said, 'Let the earth put forth grass,'" and later "And the earth brought forth grass"—that is **how**. The "how" is by the power of God (cf. Hebrews 1:3, wherein the writer declared that God upholds "all things **by the word of his power**").

Granted, the text of Genesis 1 is sublime and spiritual. **It also is historical**. Jesus Christ Himself said so (Matthew 19:4). So did Paul (1 Corinthians 15:45; Romans 8:22; 1 Timothy 2:13). That should settle the matter. God said **that** He did it—"by the word of his power." God said **when** He did it—"in the beginning." The honest reader eventually will come to realize just how much that **in**cludes, and just how much it **ex**cludes. The only "world view" left is the perfect one—that of Genesis 1.

The Non-World View is a neatly disguised by openly flagrant attack on Genesis 1. It not only impeaches the testimony of the New Testament writers, but even impugns the integrity of the Lord Himself. And for what purpose? What ultimate good does it accomplish? It merely compromises the truth, while leaving open the way for any and all viewpoints on creation—whether founded in Scripture or not. Furthermore, surely the question begs to be asked: **If Genesis 1 is not God's world view, then what is?**

THE MULTIPLE GAP THEORY

For those who find the Day-Age and Gap theories impossible to defend, and yet who do not wish to opt for a theory like the Non-World View that is an open door to extreme liberalism and/or mod-

ernism, the list of remaining available theories is quite short. One
concept that has become somewhat popular is called the "Multiple
Gap Theory."

What is the Multiple Gap Theory?

The Multiple Gap Theory suggests that the creation days were,
in fact, six literal, 24-hour days during which God actually performed
the special creative works attributed to Him in Genesis 1. However, these literal days tell only a small part of the whole story. Rather than representing the totality of God's work in creation, they instead represent "breaks" between the geologic ages. In other words,
after God's activity on any given literal day, that day then was followed by long ages of slow development in the style of orthodox,
historical geology. Actually, this theory is a hybridization of the Day-
Age and Gap theories. Instead of making "ages" out of the days
of Genesis 1, it merely inserts the ages **between** the days. And instead of putting a single gap between Genesis 1:1 and 1:2, it inserts multiple gaps between the days of Genesis 1.

One of the Multiple Gap Theory's strongest supporters, and certainly one of its most ardent popularizers, is, strangely enough, Donald England. The reason I say "strangely enough" is because this is
the same Donald England, mentioned above, who invented the Non-
World View of Genesis and who is on record as stating:

> Genesis 1 is far too sublime and spiritual for one to presume
> that it teaches anything at all about a cosmological world view.
> We do this profound text a great injustice by insisting that
> there is inherent in the text an argument for any particular
> world view (1972, p. 124).

Of course, as I already have pointed out, the main reason for pos-
tulating the Non-World View of Genesis 1 is so that a person may
insert into the text **any** world view that he happens to hold at any
given moment. That is exactly what has happened in the case of Dr.
England and the Multiple Gap Theory. A word of explanation is in
order.

Dr. England, as I noted earlier, is a professor at Harding University, located in Searcy, Arkansas. Harding is supported by members of the churches of Christ, who generally have been known to be quite conservative in their positions regarding the Genesis account of creation. In the past, for the most part, members of the churches of Christ have not tolerated the teachings of false doctrines associated with creation. Dr. England, of course, is well aware of that fact. The Multiple Gap Theory has the advantage of allowing him, when asked, to assert that he does, in fact, believe the days of creation to be 24-hour periods. And, if he is asked if he believes in the Gap Theory, again, he can demur, insisting that he does not.

But is this an upright approach? Or is it "playing loosely with the facts"? Interestingly, an example is available upon which one may base an answer to such questions. In March 1982, Dr. England lectured to a group of young people in Memphis, Tennessee. During that series, he told these youngsters that although he had spent a lifetime searching for "proof" that the days of Genesis 1 were 24-hour days, he never had found any such proof. He then went to great lengths to set before this audience of impressionable teenagers a number of "objections" to the days of Genesis 1 being literal days.

As a result of Dr. England's comments, and a subsequent review of them (see Thompson, 1982), the then-president of Harding University, Clifton L. Ganus, received several inquiries from the university's financial supporters about Dr. England's position on these matters. How did England respond? On October 4, 1982, he wrote Dr. Ganus a letter in which he stated:

> Dear Dr. Ganus: I enjoyed my brief visit with you on Friday afternoon. I stated in your presence that I have always believed that the creation days of Genesis One were six twenty-four hour days. Anyone who would take anything that I said in the [name of congregation omitted here—BT] lectures and try to associate me with a "day-age" theory of creation is making a mistake.... Whenever I speak on the creation theme, I am always careful to make my position clear as to my understanding of the length of days in Genesis One... (1982, p. 1).

Dr. England then offered, as proof of his position on these matters, a quotation from pages 111-113 of his 1972 volume, *A Christian View of Origins*, in which he explained that he does not recommend strict theistic evolution. But here is the interesting point in all of this. In that same book, just two pages earlier, he had written the following:

> The statements, "God created" (Genesis 1 and elsewhere) and "God spoke and it was done; He commanded and it stood fast" (Ps. 33:9) do not explicitly rule out some sort of process. Now, if the days of Genesis are taken as 24-hour days, then that certainly rules out any process extending over vast periods of time. The days could easily have been twenty-four-hour days and the earth still date to great antiquity **provided that indefinite periods of time separated the six creation days** (1972, pp. 110-111, emp. added).

Is this dealing honestly with the facts? Dr. England told the university president (who certainly had the power to dismiss him) that he **does believe** the days of Genesis 1 were 24-hours long, all the while knowing that he has defended, in print, the Multiple Gap Theory.

A Response and Refutation

At the very least, this theory requires a most "unnatural" reading of the Creation account, which apparently is continuous and meant to describe the creation of "heaven and earth, the sea, and all that in them is." The context of the creation record suggests continuity. There is absolutely no exegetical evidence to document the claim that in between each of the (literal) creation days there were millions or billions of years. In fact, such evidence is conspicuously missing. In his 1983 volume, *A Scientist Examines Faith and Evidence*, Dr. England commented on this fact when he said: "True, the silence of the Scriptures leaves open the possibility of time gaps but **it does not seem advisable to build a doctrinal theory on the basis of a silence of Scripture**" (p. 154, emp. added).

Nor does the theory harmonize with orthodox geology. If the acts of creation are left on their respective days, then there is no possible way to make the Creation account agree with the geologic-age system—gaps or no gaps. As the chart on the next page shows, the Genesis sequence and the alleged geologic sequence **do not agree**. The Multiple Gap Theory does not alter that fact.

Additionally, we must not overlook Exodus 20:11, which specifically states that "in six days the Lord made heaven and earth, the sea, and **all** that in them is, and rested on the seventh day." Either God made what He made in six days or He made what He made in six days **plus** millions or billions of years. Those respecting the Bible as the inspired Word of God have no trouble accepting the former and rejecting the latter.

THE FRAMEWORK HYPOTHESIS
[ARTISTICO-HISTORICAL THEORY]

The theory known as the "framework hypothesis" had its beginnings in 1924 when Dutch scholar Arie Noordtzij, professor at the University of Utrecht, published a work whose title may be translated into English as, *God's Word and the Testimony of the Ages*. While not as popular as it was in its heyday, I believe it at least bears mentioning here.

What is the Framework Hypothesis?

Noordtzij's "framework hypothesis" of Genesis 1-11 views these chapters as somewhat of a rhetorical framework within which are developed the spiritual themes of "creation" (the divine source and meaning of reality), man's "fall" (man's ever-recurring experience of spiritual and moral inadequacy), and reconciliation (the broad currents in history by which man seeks to understand and appropriate spiritual meaning in life). The framework hypothesis contends that the treatment of creation in Genesis was **logical, not chronological**.

DIVISION	SIGNIFICANT FOSSIL APPEARANCES	YEARS AGO (millions)	GENESIS (days)
Cenozoic			
Quaternary	*Homo erectus/H. sapiens*	2	6
Tertiary	Rabbits; Rodents; Marsupials		6
	Camels; Deer; Cattle; Horses		6
	Elephants; Pigs; Early marsupials		6
	Whales; Dolphins; Seals	65	5
Mesozoic			
Cretaceous	Flowering plants		3
	Platypus; Sloths		6
	Modern bony fishes		5
	Snakes	144	6
Jurassic	Lizards		6
	Birds		5
	First true mammals	208	6
Triassic	Turtles; Frogs; Crocodiles		5
	Tuatara; Dinosaurs		6
	Conifers	245	3
Paleozoic			
Permian	Ginkgoes; Cycads; Horsetails		3
	Marine reptiles	286	5
Carboniferous	Reptiles; Mammal-like reptiles		6
	Amphibians		5
	Ferns	360	3
Devonian	Sharks; Bony fish	408	5
Silurian	Club mosses	438	3
Ordovician	Jawless fishes	505	5
Cambrian	Worms; Shellfish; Trilobites		5
	Burgess Shale fauna; First fish?	550	5
Precambrian			
Proterozoic	Jellyfish; Ediacaran fauna		5
	Green algae	2,500	3?
Archaean	Bacteria	3,800	2?
Hadean	First single-celled organism		
	Formation of Earth and Moon		2-4
	Formation of Solar System	4,800	4

Comparison of the evolutionary geological column with the order of
creation in Genesis. Evolutionary dates and data based primarily on
Gould (1993).

Two men besides Noordtzij who have espoused the framework hypothesis are N.H. Ridderbos (in his 1957 work, *Is There a Conflict Between Genesis 1 and Natural Science?*) and Charles Hauret (in his 1955 work, *Beginnings: Genesis and Modern Science*). Ridderbos spent considerable time and effort in defense of his position. In his book, *Scientific Creationism*, Henry Morris, discussed the framework hypothesis.

> The particular "framework" in which these ideas are developed varies according to the particular expositor. Some speak of Genesis as "allegorical," others as "liturgical," others as "poetic," others as "supra-historical." All agree, however, in rejecting it as "scientific" or "historical." They concur that Genesis teaches the **fact** of "creation" and the "fall," but deny that it has anything to say concerning the **method**. They hope to retain whatever theological significance it may have while, at the same time, avoiding scientific embarrassment (1974a, p. 244, emp. in orig.).

Raymond Surburg, in addressing Hauret's reasoning, commented:

> He taught that the creation account in Genesis 1:1-2:4a was a scheme designed to aid the mind to remember the account because it was based on everyday life. The framework of Genesis 1:1-2:4a closely copies the work of man. The Hebrew people worked during the day, stopped working at night, resumed again in the morning, and this was done for six days to be followed by a seventh day, a day of rest. The Mosaic cosmogony likewise depicts the divine Creator working during the day, ceasing from His labors at night, resuming the next day, and this He does for six days. Hauret thought that the main purpose of this creation account was liturgical. It was to promulgate for the first time the law of the Sabbath rest which is given in Exodus 20:11 (1959, p. 62).

Noordtzij said the purpose of the author of Genesis could not have been "to offer a natural historically faithful account of the process of creation." He further pointed out

> that the six days of Genesis 1 are obviously intended as the sum of two triduums which consequently reveal a clearly pronounced parallelism, while the total arrangement is intended

> to place in bold relief the surpassing glory of man who at-
> tains his true destiny in the Sabbath (as quoted in Ridderbos,
> 1957, p. 11).

Although Noordtzij believed the "days" of Genesis 1 to be literal days, he also maintained that the author introduced them merely as part of a framework for the narrative of creation. They do not indicate historical sequence, but instead depict the glory of the creatures in the light of the great redemptive purpose of God.

A Response and Refutation

When Arie Noordtzij published his work, his foremost opponent was professor G.C. Aalders of the Free University of Amsterdam.[*] Aalders, while desiring to be as fair as possible to Noordtzij, declared that he was compelled to understand Noordtzij as holding that as far as the days of Genesis are concerned, there was no reality with respect to the divine creative activity (see Young, 1964, p. 47). Aalders then made two remarks that should guide every serious interpreter of Genesis 1:

> (1) In the text of Genesis itself, there is not a single allusion
> to suggest that the days are to be regarded as a form or mere
> manner of representation and hence of no significance for the
> essential knowledge of the divine creative activity. (2) In Ex-
> odus 20:11 the activity of God is presented to man as a pat-
> tern, and this fact presupposed that there was a reality in the
> activity of God which man is to follow. How could man be
> held accountable for working six days if God himself had not
> actually worked for six days? (as quoted in Young, 1964, p.
> 47).

Young then remarked: "To the best of the present writer's knowledge no one has ever answered these two considerations of Aalders" (1964, p. 47). That statement holds true even today. Surburg has noted:

---

[*] Edward J. Young, in his book, *Studies in Genesis One* (1964, pp. 44-47), provided an excellent description of Aalders' work, as well as a refutation of the framework hypothesis.

...Aalders queries: What meaning did the writer of Genesis want the readers of Genesis 1 to gain when they read this account? Would the account of Genesis 1 lead the ordinary reader to suspect that the order of created events recorded was not historical? A sound principle of Biblical interpretation must be sacrificed in order to compromise with the current theories of geologists, astronomers, and biologists.

The views of Noordtzij and Ridderbos are based on the assumption that the sequence of creative events is not to be accepted, because the historical order of Genesis 1 seems to conflict with the findings of historical geology. In view of the unique character of the opening chapter of the Bible, which does not depict the history of men but solely the activity of God, it is argued that a departure from the rules that one would normally apply to Biblical historiography is justified in treating Genesis 1 (1959, pp. 63-64).

Henry Morris also has addressed the problem of viewing Genesis 1-11 as a "literary device" rather than as actual history.

This type of Biblical exegesis is out of the question for any real believer in the Bible. It is the method of so-called "neo-orthodoxy," though it is neither new nor orthodox. It cuts out the foundation of the entire Biblical system when it expunges Genesis 1-11. The events of these chapters are recorded in simple narrative form, as though the writer or writers fully intended to record a series of straightforward historical facts; there is certainly no internal or exegetical reason for taking them in any other way....

Modern theologians who would eliminate the first eleven chapters of Genesis from the realm of true history are guilty of removing the foundations from all future history. They, in effect, reject the teachings of Peter and Paul and all other Biblical writers as naive superstition and the teachings of the infallible Christ as deceptive accommodationism. The "framework hypothesis" of Genesis, in any of its diverse forms, is nothing but neo-orthodox sophistry and inevitably leads eventually to complete apostasy. It must be unequivocally rejected and opposed by Bible-believing Christians (1974a, pp. 244, 247).

It seems fitting that I close this chapter with a quotation from G. Richard Culp in his book, *Remember Thy Creator*:

> We stand either with God and His teaching of creation, or we stand with the evolutionist in opposition to Him. The issues are sharply drawn; there can be no compromise. You are either a Christian or an evolutionist; you cannot be both. God wants prophets, not politicians; not diplomats, but soldiers in the spiritual sense (1975, p. 163).

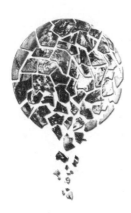

Chapter 13

What Is Wrong With Creation Compromises?

Today the constant pressure on Bible believers to compromise the Word of God is intense. Maybe it always has been that way; but it seems to be getting worse. This pressure comes from a variety of sources—some more powerful than others. What causes one person discomfort or distress may hold absolutely no sway over another.

First, there is peer pressure. As a person interacts in religious, social, occupational, or other similar settings, he may find that the views he holds are not the same as those of the people around him. [Especially is this true in the context of the creation/evolution controversy.] Everyone wants to be accepted among friends and peers. But in certain instances, "being accepted" requires compromise, or complete abandonment, of certain beliefs that may be of both an important and a long-standing nature. The pressure to conform because "everyone's doing it," or because "everyone believes it," can be acute.

Second, there is the desire to be intellectually and/or politically correct. Surely it would be safe to say that most of us desire to be "accepted" by friends, family, coworkers, etc. Few people actually **want** to be the "odd-man-out." At times, it seems that it is acceptable to be an individualist only so long as you are an individualist willing to conform to the group. Whatever is viewed currently as fashionable—whatever is in vogue—is what makes a person a valued, worthwhile member of the group. Conversely, those beliefs or actions deemed "unacceptable" according to group standards cause the group's approval to diminish or be withheld.

Third, there is the pressure of what might best be called a strictly "academic" setting. This type of pressure is altogether different than the kind that occurs as the result of a friendly discussion around the water fountain at work or in the neighborhood car pool, because this is a setting in which a person is taught two things: (a) evolution is a fact of science; and (b) all "smart" people believe it. The truth of the matter is, almost everyone wants to be considered as smart. In most modern academic settings, it is "smart" to believe in evolution. And, of course, in most of those same settings it is "not smart" to believe in either God or the Bible as His inspired Word. And it **really** is not smart to believe in creation! It is a sad-but-true fact that, as one writer stated,

> If you enter a University Campus today and declare that you are a creationist you may be ridiculed as ignorant though you may be ten times as well-informed on the subject as the ridiculer. This is nothing new. A desire for conformity to fashion has existed since the beginning of history (Camp, 1972, p. 207).

The pressure to compromise is very real, and often worsens with each passing day.

There are many reasons to compromise. But there is one good reason not to: **Truth never has been determined by popular opinion or majority vote**. Truth is determined by God and God alone (John 17:17), and that never will change (Matthew 24:35).

Jesus, in His beautiful Sermon on the Mount, explained quite clearly that "the majority" would not find their way to heaven (Matthew 7: 13-14). It is not enough to be among friends. It is not enough to go along with the crowd. It is not enough to be in the majority. Moses, in Exodus 23:2, reminded the Israelites: "Thou shalt not follow a multitude to do evil." What is important is being on the side of Truth. In the end, nothing else really matters.

Nor is compromise justified by "sincerity." It is not uncommon to hear someone say, "But he (or she) is so sincere. How could they be wrong?" Sincerity, however, is not the determining factor in deciding whether or not a person is correct. In 2 Samuel 6:6ff., the story is told of how King David had the Ark of the Covenant loaded onto a cart to be transported. As a man by the name of Ahio was driving the cart, the text says simply that "the oxen stumbled" (vs. 6). Ahio's brother, Uzzah, apparently fearing that the Ark was about to tumble from the cart and be damaged or destroyed, "put forth his hand to the ark of God, and took hold of it." But the text goes on to note that "the anger of Jehovah was kindled against him there **for his error**; and there he died" (vs. 7, emp. added). Why, exactly, did God strike Uzzah dead? God's commandments to the people of Israel were plain; they were not to touch the holy things of God (Numbers 4:15). Uzzah may have been sincere, but he disobeyed—and perished (notice that Uzzah incurred God's righteous indignation "for his error"). Saul was completely sincere in his persecution of the church (Acts 22:19-20; Galatians 1:13; 1 Corinthians 15:9). Yet God struck him blind (Acts 9:3-9). God does not want **just** sincerity; He wants obedience (John 14:15).

THE ERROR OF CREATION COMPROMISES

The thesis of this book is that compromises of the Genesis account of creation not only are unnecessary, but wrong. While they may not always spring from ill motives, in the end they all produce the same unpleasant results. Christ said that "every good tree bringeth forth good fruit; but the corrupt tree bringeth forth evil

311

fruit" (Matthew 7:17). One verse before that, He also said that "by their fruits ye shall know them." In this day and age, Bible believers desperately need to be more active "fruit inspectors." The compromises offered in place of the historical account of creation as recorded in Genesis 1, and as confirmed by writers in both the Old and New Testaments, are the "corrupt trees" of which Jesus spoke. The damage that such compromises have inflicted, and continue to inflict, is the evil fruit. Perhaps if more Christians could see those fruits, they would not be so quick to compromise.

"THE BLINDNESS OF PRECONCEIVED OPINION"

Charles Darwin once accused some of his opponents of what he called "the blindness of preconceived opinion" (1958, p. 444). One cannot help but wonder if that same accusation might be leveled against those who wish to compromise the Genesis record by incorporating into it various aspects of the General Theory of Evolution, for it is their "preconceived opinion" that evolution is true—not any statement from God's Word—which leads them to such a conclusion. The late, eminent United Nations scientist A.E. Wilder-Smith, in his book, *Man's Origin: Man's Destiny*, wrote:

> If the chance processes of evolution really are the motive force behind the upward surge of nonliving matter to complex life, and if the Bible is really telling us that life originated in this way, all we can ask ourselves is this: **Why does the author of the Bible not speak up and express himself more plainly in this matter**? Why does he not tell us more directly the truth about the role played by chance in creation? If Genesis really describes a slow process of upward development by chance over millions of years, why does its author not say so? Surely these facts could have been expressed more clearly, even in primitive language and times, if God had wished to convey to us the idea of chance operating through millions of years with natural selection as the prime motive force of creation instead of God Himself (1975, p. 37, emp. added).

This question has not been treated fairly or answered adequately by proponents of theistic evolution, progressive creation, threshold evolution, and other compromises of Genesis 1. There is no theistic statement that suggests God used any of these methods. Why is this the case? The fact is, He said just the opposite.

> ...once we admit that divine intervention has occurred at all, there is no way to determine just where and how except by divine statement. **Surely this must be obvious**.

> If we can accept any intervention at all, we can accept the ultimate intervention, which is creation. There is no suggestion here of dishonesty on the part of the theistic evolutionist but certainly there is grave inconsistency. God could have accomplished the origin of life in any way He chose, by evolution or by creation, but an admission that there is a God and that He made such an accomplishment in any way, means that we are totally dependent upon His revelation to determine which way. His revelation declares creation, not evolution (Camp, 1972, p. 206, emp. in orig.).

The "blindness of preconceived opinion" has prompted some to remove God as the Creator of His own Universe, and relegate Him to the status of "Honorary Creator." And all of this has occurred in spite of the fact that there is no biblical evidence **for** the compromising theories, and vast amounts of evidence **against** them. Robert Taylor summed up the matter like this: "This writer may be very dense of mental powers, but he cannot see where Almighty God is afforded any degree of honor by saying that he occupied a supervisory post in some remote corner of evolutionary thought and development" (1974, 116[1]:2).

TURNING THE SAVIOR INTO A LIAR

One of the first things students learn in freshman philosophy classes is that any doctrine that implies a false doctrine is itself false. This is true in every area of life. Each of the compromises discussed in this book should be rejected on that account alone. Each of these compromises not only postulates an unscriptural old-Earth scenario, but has man appearing as the end product of some sort of long, meandering "creation process." During His earthly tenure, Christ discussed human origins and commented that man and woman had been here "since the beginning of the creation" (Mark 10: 6). If the compromising theories are correct, Jesus is not. Being a member of the Godhead, He is omniscient. Therefore, He had to have known the truth of the matter. But instead of revealing it, He lied. Yet Peter spoke of Jesus as One Who "did no sin" (1 Peter 2: 22). The writer of Hebrews reiterated that point (4:15). The compromising theories, whether they intend to or not, accuse Christ of lying. Such an accusation, however, is false. And any doctrine that implies a false doctrine is itself false. The late Gus Nichols once wrote:

> **Since Jesus endorsed the Genesis record of the miraculous creation of man and woman, this record is true. If it is not, Jesus is a false Christ**. Thus, theistic evolution overthrows faith in Christ, and thereby overthrows faith in Christianity.... Yes, the theory that God created the world by means of organic evolution rejects the Bible account of creation in Genesis, and rejects Christ who endorsed these writings, and in so doing makes Christ an ignoramus and the Christian religion a false religion. It is a fact that theistic evolution is more dangerous and misleading, more deceptive, and overthrows the faith of more people, than avowed atheistic evolution and atheism (1972, p. 24, emp. added).

Taylor also commented on this point.

> For years we have been warning young people what an espousal of theistic evolution does to Jesus Christ. Jesus went on record as accepting the fact that man and woman were made at the beginning.... Evolution does not believe humanity was made but slowly evolved through long eons of time. Jesus said humanity existed from the beginning and Mark has his affirmation of man's having existed from the beginning of creation. Evolution does not believe humanity has existed from the beginning. If evolution be true, Jesus is proved to be an unreliable witness of truthfulness in Matthew 19:4 and Mark 10:6 (1974, 116[1]:6).

No Bible believer ever should accept, or ask others to accept, a doctrine that impugns the sinless nature of the Savior, and turns Him into a liar.

MAKING MAN "THE NAKED APE"

In 1967, Desmond Morris, who at the time was an eminent zoologist and curator of mammals at the London Zoological Society, authored a book that subsequently became a best-seller. He titled his volume, *The Naked Ape*, and used it to propagate the idea that man evolved from ape-like creatures millions of years ago—a view accepted by many who seek to compromise the creation account. Helmut Thielicke, a prominent European theologian, wrote: "Often our dreams, which we cannot control by our will, are an appalling reminder that we have our roots in the animal kingdom. **Men are higher animals**, related to the fish, the dogs, and the cats" (1961, pp. 64-65, emp. added). In his 1990 book, *Genesis and the Big Bang*, Gerald L. Schroeder defended a similar position.

> ...we must acknowledge that a form of animal life that was very much like human life predated Adam and Eve. This latter option is not in contradiction with the established tradition on which I am relying. Well within the scope of biblical tradition is the fact of a **directed** evolution of man, one that arises from the pristine matter of the universe (p. 149, emp. in orig.).

Seven years later, in his 1997 volume, *The Science of God*, Dr. Schroeder apparently had not changed his mind.

> The first step in a rapprochement between science and the Bible is for each camp to understand the other. Distancing the Bible from a few misplaced theological shibboleths will do wonders in furthering this mutual understanding.... The mistaken shouts of protest against the imagined heresy of gravity have faded to distant echoes. As later chapters argue, the same will happen with the more recent theological cries directed against evolution. The biblical account of animal life's development, which amounts to a mere eight verses (!), will have no problem with the final scientific understanding of how animal life evolved. ...**the universe developed**

**from its chaotic beginning, through the start of life,
and on to the appearance of humankind** (pp. 11-12,
73, emp. added, parenthetical item in orig.).

While Thielicke is a theologian and Schroeder is a scientist, they both
have two things in common: (a) they profess to believe in the God
of the Bible; and (b) they advocate the view that man sprang from
animal life via an evolutionary process. Others, while not willing to
go as far these two writers and advocate that man actually evolved
from animals, nevertheless have opted for scenarios that should give
a cautious reader pause, especially in light of Christ's statements in
Mark 10:6 and Matthew 19:4. For example, progressive creationist Hugh Ross has written:

> Man is unique among all species of life. By "spirit" the Bible
> means "aware of God and capable of forming a relationship
> with Him." Evidence of man's spiritual dimensions would in-
> clude divine worship, shown by religious relics, altars, and
> temples. From the Bible's perspective, decorating, burial of
> dead, or use of tools would not qualify as conclusive evidence
> of the spirit.... While bipedal, tool-using, large-brained homi-
> nids roamed the earth at least as long ago as one million years,
> evidence for religious relics and altars dates back only about
> 8,000 to 24,000 years. Thus, **the secular anthropological
> date for the first spirit creatures is in complete agree-
> ment with the biblical date**.... According to Genesis 1,
> the origin of the universe predates the six days of creation,
> while the origin of man occurs at the very end of the six days.
> Thus, **the creation of the universe would predate by
> far the creation of man** (1991, pp. 159,160, emp. added).

Davis A. Young has accepted a similar, if not identical, position:
"Man is created after the other animals have been formed. Man is
the crown, the culmination of creation. Paleontology has discovered
the same. **Man is a very recent inhabitant of the earth.... Again
there is no conflict between the Bible and science**" (1977, p.
132, emp. added).

But all this **does** conflict with the Bible! And no amount of posturing is going to eliminate that plain statement of fact. First, Christ
stated that man and woman have been on the Earth "since the be-

ginning of the creation." Clayton, England, Ross, Schroeder, Sears, Young, and others advocate the belief that man is a "very recent inhabitant" of the Earth. Both positions simply cannot be true. What we have to decide is this: Who are we going to believe—Jesus (the Son of God, through Whom the worlds were created; John 1:1ff.), or modern-day compromisers who are intent upon ignoring what God's Word has to say and who defer instead to current pseudoscientific theories that have been established and defended primarily by those who do not even believe in God in the first place?

Second, man is not a "higher animal," and there was no "form of animal life that was very much like human life" that "predated Adam and Eve." Such statements contradict both Old and New Testament doctrine on such issues. Andrews has said, for example:

> Adam and Eve were not beings whose bodies were prepared in some way by a process of evolution; they did not emerge from apehood, but were special creations of God. According to the creationist, man was not derived from pre-existing animal stock, but directly from the "dust of the ground," a physical being indeed, but one made also in the image of God....

> Let us now consider how theistic evolution deals with the nature and origin of man. First of all, evolution does not see human origins in terms of one unique individual, Adam, and his equally unique wife. According to evolution, it is not individuals that evolve, but populations. Whether we think of amoeba, mice, or men, it is not the individual that climbs dramatically up the ladder of evolutionary development, but the population as a whole. No accepted evolutionary theory claims that evolution occurs at the level of the individual....

> If evolution is true, therefore, we do not have a unique individual, Adam, but rather a population of emergent humankind. Adam can only be a representative man, a kind of symbol for mankind. If this view is adopted, however, it creates great difficulty in the interpretation of certain scriptures, notably Romans 5 and I Corinthians 15 (1986, pp. 86,88).

Schroeder has suggested that prior to Adam there was "a form of animal life that was very much like human life." This is not correct.

It is significant also that Gen. 2:20 records that man surveyed cattle and birds and beasts of the field but that "for the man there was not found a helper for him." Regardless of the literary form of the Genesis account, the message here is loud and clear. Man, Adam, is distinct from all the animals he surveyed, and there was no one like him. This is a completely impossible concept under the theory of evolution, where Adam would have been one of several anthropoid hominids who were approaching the status of *Homo*, through a series of mutations. There would have been many other pre-men and -women like him or at least a number of them. Certainly he would not have surveyed all of the animal kingdom and found no one who would be a helpmeet for him (Zimmerman, 1972, p. 114).

Try as they might, theistic evolutionists and progressive creationists cannot force the Genesis account into agreement with evolution. God has the inspired text too well protected.

THE PROBLEM WITH EVE

Theistic evolution and its counterparts should be rejected because they cannot explain Eve. The Bible teaches that from the beginning there were male and female (Matthew 19:4) with capability of reproduction (Genesis 1:28). Theistic evolution contends that the sexes evolved. Wilder-Smith addressed this contradiction.

But surely it is going to be very difficult to honestly interpret the biblical account of origins in a consistently evolutionary context, in spite of all the heroic efforts of sincere theistic evolutionists. Is not the account of Eve's miraculous surgical origin from Adam's side sufficient to prove that the Bible is not describing here any natural evolutionary chance process modified by natural selection through millions of years? Eve was taken during sleep direct from Adam's side, which is surely not, by any stretch of the imagination, a description of the evolutionary process....

The account of Eve's arrival on the scene, if we take the Bible seriously, surely cuts out the possibility of any "natural" evolutionary process over millions of years as the total explanation of man's origin. The biblical account is that of a plainly miraculous and nonuniformitarian origin, of woman at least. It represents a complete break with normal methods of reproduction in the whole higher animal kingdom. Evolutionary processes cannot by any stretch of the imagination be called upon to explain it (1975, pp. 41,42).

After discussing the inconsistencies between various compromises and the actual creation account in regard to the creation of woman, Davidheiser wrote:

A theistic evolutionist should honestly admit, "I do not believe the creation account," for when he attempts to interrelate the two positions, he necessarily finds evolution incompatible with Scripture (1973, 3:50).

Dr. Davidheiser was right when he urged theistic evolutionists (and, by implication, progressive creationists) to admit that they do not believe the Genesis account of creation. One cannot consistently believe both the biblical record of origins and the evolutionary position.

A "SOUL-LESS NAKED APE"?

Theistic evolution is wrong because it cannot explain where, or how, man acquired his God-given soul. Lindsell observed:

Theistic evolutionists must cross another bridge that is narrow and perilous. They cannot for one moment postulate that lower forms of animal life had souls such as we find in *Homo sapiens* today. Thus at whatever point in the evolutionary process some animal became man, God must have created and implanted in man the soul that distinguishes him from animals. To put it another way, when did the *imago dei* get into man which made man man? Something was added at some point to the evolutionary spiral. That something was not there before. It came about by direct divine intervention —God added a new component that did not spring from nature.

If this be true, why need we suppose that the body of man came through an evolutionary process when the soul did not? (1977, p. 17, emp. added).

Bales discussed the inconsistency of theistic evolution in this regard when he wrote:

> To be consistent evolutionists, theistic evolutionists must maintain that the image of God, in man, was evolved. If they call on God and a miracle to get the image of God in man, why so hesitant to call on God and a miracle for the giving of the life of the body to a physical body formed of the dust of the earth? Their non-theistic evolutionistic colleagues will not find the creation of the image of God in man any more acceptable than the creation of the body of man. What do theistic evolutionists affirm of the origin of the image of God? (1974, 116 [4]:53).

DID MAN "FALL"—OR "RISE"?

Surely one of the most serious problems with theistic evolution and similar compromises is the theological doctrine of the fall of man into sin. Once again those who are so willing to compromise the text would do better simply to admit that they do not believe the biblical record of origins.

> If evolution is true and if a man evolved from lower forms of life, whether through a mechanical process as Darwin proposed or through acts of God in accordance with theistic evolution, there was no first man who stood distinctly separate from the animal kingdom, but merely a gradual blending from animal to man. Without an Adam and Eve, it follows that there was no fall of man as recorded in Genesis. But the atonement of Christ is based upon the fall of man as a real historic event. If evolution is true, then, whether mechanistic or theistic, no historic fall of man occurred, and thus no Redeemer is needed to save us from our sins. If we are not a fallen people, unable to save ourselves, but a product of our animal ancestry, gradually improving and moving toward perfection, Christ was only a martyr, a good man ahead of His time but not the Saviour, the Redeemer (Davidheiser, 1973, 3:50-51).

Lindsell asked:

> The evolutionary approach forces us into a hermeneutic which regards the creation account as saga or myth rather than history and fact. This in turn does gross violence to even didactic

portions of the Bible in both the Old and New Testaments and creates other problems for which there are no answers. The Apostle Paul builds his theology of redemption in Romans around the first and the second Adams. Jesus for Paul is the second Adam. The first Adam was the inhabitant of the Garden of Eden, our first ancestor through whom...sin with all of its consequences came. And it was the first man's sin that made necessary the second Adam's sacrifice on the cross of Calvary. To argue that the first Adam was a mythical figure while holding that the second Adam was true man boggles the imagination and turns the Scripture on its head. Moreover, if there was no first Adam, whence did...sin come? (1977, pp. 17-18).

A MILLION CONTRADICTIONS—
NOT A MILLION YEARS

It would take a veritable encyclopedia to list the many contradictions between the various creation compromises and the Genesis account of origins. One almost is tempted to say: "There are a million of them!" While it is impossible to discuss each, I would like to offer the following list, which has been combined from a variety of sources (Culp, 1975, pp. 154-155; Thompson, 1977, pp. 109-123,215-235; Niessen, 1980, pp. 17-22; Overton, 1981, pp. 117-118; Morris, 1984, pp. 119-120; Hayward, 1985, p. 14; Jackson, 1987, pp. 127-129; Kautz, 1988, pp. 24-25).

1. The Genesis narrative states that light existed before the Sun was made (Genesis 1:3,16), while evolution contends that the Sun was Earth's first light.

2. Moses declared that the waters existed before dry land ever appeared (Genesis 1:2,6,9). Evolution alleges that Earth's first waters gradually seeped out of its interior to form the vast oceans.

3. Scripture teaches that the first biological forms of life upon the Earth were plants (Genesis 1:11), whereas evolution argues that the initial life forms were marine organisms (see Sagan, 1980, p. 30; Fortey, 1997, pp. 3-28).

4. The Bible teaches that fruit-bearing trees existed before fish were created (Genesis 1:11,20), but evolution contends that fish evolved long before fruit-bearing trees (see Sagan, 1980, p. 33).

5. Genesis states that plants came into being before the Sun was made (Genesis 1:11,14ff.), whereas evolution suggests that the Sun was burning millions of years before the first plants.

6. Moses taught that birds were made on the fifth day of the creation week, and that "creeping things" (which would include both insects and reptiles) were brought into existence on the sixth day (Genesis 1:21,24); evolution asserts that birds developed long after both insects and reptiles (see Fortey, 1997, pp. 222-237,261-288).

7. The Genesis account reveals that living creatures were created according to individual groups, and thereafter each reproduced after its own "kind" (Genesis 1:11,12,21,24,25). According to evolutionary theory, all living organisms derive from a common, primitive life-source (see Sagan, 1980, pp. 30-31).

8. The biblical record teaches that man was fashioned from the dust of the ground (Genesis 2:7; 3:19; 1 Corinthians 15:45; 2 Corinthians 5:1), but evolution suggests that humans ultimately descended from ape-like creatures (see Johanson, et al., 1994).

9. The Bible teaches that the first humans were made with distinctive sexual characteristics—male and female (Genesis 1:27; 2:7,22; Matthew 19:4); evolution suggests that sexes "evolved" approximately two billion years ago in a process that "must have been agonizingly slow" (Sagan, 1980, p. 31).

10. The Bible is plain in its teaching that mankind has existed on Earth "from the beginning of the creation" (Matthew 19:4; Mark 10:6; Romans 1:20), thus virtually "from the foundation of the world" (Isaiah 40:21; Luke 11:50-51). Conversely, evolutionists teach that man is a "Johnny-come-lately" to the planet (cf. Sagan, 1980, p. 33; Fortey, 1997, p. 16—"Imagine that the history

of the world is represented by a clockface, say, then the appearance of 'blue green' bacteria in the record happened at about two o'clock, while invertebrates appeared at about ten o'clock, and mankind, like Cinderella suddenly recalling the end of the ball, at about one minute to midnight.").

11. Genesis declares that man was appointed to exercise dominion over "every living thing that moveth upon the earth" (Genesis 1:28), but evolution argues that multiplied millions of creatures already had lived and become extinct eons before man ever set foot upon the Earth, hence before he had opportunity to have dominion over them.

12. Moses affirmed that God's work of creation was "finished" with the completion of the sixth day (Genesis 2:1-2). Evolution, on the other hand, requires that some sort of creative process has continued, hammering out new forms of living organisms across the many eons of time since life first began. [The famous evolutionist of Harvard, Kirtley F. Mather, wrote that evolution is "not only an orderly process, it is a continuing one. Nothing was finished on any seventh day; the process of creation is still going on. The golden age for man—if any—is in the future, not in the past" (1960, pp. 37-38).]

13. The Word of God teaches that man has a soul that will live forever (1 Corinthians 15:35-58; cf. Thompson, 2000a); evolution teaches that man is wholly mortal (cf. Huxley, 1960c, 3:252-253—"The earth was not created; it evolved. So did all the animals and plants that inhabit it, including our human selves, mind and soul as well as brain and body. So did religion." Cf. also Mather, 1970, pp. 37-38—"The spiritual aspects of the life of man are just as surely a product of the processes called evolution as are his brain and nervous system.").

14. Adam, according to the Bible, was to name the animals (Genesis 2:19); evolutionary geologists contend that most of the animals were extinct long before man appeared on the Earth.

15. Genesis 1:31 records that God surveyed everything He had created and called it "very good." Evolutionists claim that most of these things did not even survive to that point, and the groaning world that did survive until man's appearance was far from perfect (cf. Hull, 1991, 352:486; Russell, 1961, p. 73).

16. The Genesis account speaks of the early Earth as having been designed specifically for man's habitation; evolutionary theory postulates an early Earth endowed with a reducing atmosphere that provided no free oxygen (see Thaxton, et. al., 1984, pp. 14-41,69-98).

17. The Bible speaks of mankind as being created with a moral nature (Genesis 1:26-27, et al.; cf. Thompson, 2000b, pp. 157-181); according to evolution, mankind is by nature amoral. [Famed British evolutionist Richard Dawkins commented: "You are for nothing. You are here to propagate your selfish genes. There is no higher purpose in life" (as quoted in Bass, 1990, 124[4]:60); American evolutionist George Gaylord Simpson described "good and evil, right and wrong" as "concepts irrelevant in nature" (1967, p. 346).]

18. The Scriptures portray early civilizations as producing sophisticated musical instruments (Genesis 4:21) and refining alloys (Genesis 4:22), as well as building such structures as the ark of Noah (Genesis 6:14-16) and the Tower of Babel (Genesis 11:3-6). Evolution, contrariwise, presents early man as quite primitive and technologically immature (cf. Birdsell, 1972, pp. 192-363).

19. According to Genesis, Adam was endowed with language from the first day of his creation; evolutionary theory postulates that language evolved slowly over long periods of time as man struggled to develop means of communication (cf. Birdsell, 1972, pp. 335-336; Diamond, 1992, pp. 141-167).

20. The biblical record is clear that Adam's responsibility was to tend the Garden of Eden (Genesis 2:9,15-16); Abel, his son, was a farmer by occupation (Genesis 4:2). Evolutionary theory, however, asserts that agriculture developed late in man's history (cf. Diamond, 1992, pp. 180-191).

21. Throughout Scripture, there are events that God has orchestrated (e.g., the Flood, the long day of Joshua, et al.) that cannot be called in any sense of the word "uniformitarian" in nature. Yet one of the cardinal tenets of evolutionary dogma (and the one that is the foundation of almost all evolutionary-based dating systems) is uniformitarianism. [Geologist Charles Felix wrote: "**Uniformitarianism is the great underlying principle of modern geology!** ...Uniformitarianism endures, partly because it seems reasonable and the principle is considered basic to other fields of study, but it also persists because **this is the only way to arrive at the enormous time-frame required for placement of slow evolutionary processes.** It is probably correct to state that evolution depends on the unqualified acceptance of Uniformitarianism! (1988, pp. 29,30, emp. in orig.); cf. Eiseley, 1961, p. 115.]

22. According to Genesis, the creation took place in six literal, 24-hour days; evolution is alleged to have taken place over billions of years.

EVOLUTION AND GOD'S NATURE

Lastly, I urge rejection of compromising theories that are based, in whole or in part, on the dogma of evolution because evolution is inconsistent with God's nature. As evidence I offer the following.

(a) Evolution is inconsistent with God's omnipotence; since He has all power, He is capable of creating the Universe in an instant—or in six literal days—rather than having to stretch it out over eons of time. [For a powerful (albeit inadvertent) admission of this fact on the part of progressive creationists, see

Schroeder, 1997, p. 73—"Surely an infinite Creator did not require six days or even six pico-seconds to produce the universe we know."]

(b) Evolution is inconsistent with God's personality. If making man in His own image (Genesis 1:26-27) was the goal of His alleged evolutionary process, why would God have waited until the very tail-end of geologic time, and used such a long, drawn-out, wasteful, inefficient process before creating personalities? No personal fellowship was possible with the rocks and seas, or even with dinosaurs and gliptodons. Speaking to this very point, British agnostic Bertrand Russell noted:

> We are told that...evolution is the unfolding of an idea which has been in the mind of God throughout. It appears that during those ages...when animals were torturing each other with ferocious horns and agonizing stings, Omnipotence was quietly waiting for the ultimate emergence of man, with his still more widely diffused cruelty. Why the Creator should have preferred to reach His goal by a process, instead of going straight to it, these modern theologians do not tell us (1961, p. 73).

(c) Evolution is inconsistent with God's omniscience. The history of evolution, as interpreted from the fossil record by evolutionary geologists, is filled with extinctions, misfits, evolutionary cul-de-sacs, and other similar evidences of very poor planning. The very essence of evolution, in fact, is just the opposite of planning. Earlier in this volume, I quoted David Hull, who wrote:

> [The] evolutionary process is rife with happenstance, contingency, incredible waste, death, pain and horror. ...Whatever the God implied by evolutionary theory and the data of natural history may be like, He is not the Protestant God of waste not, want not. He is also not a loving God who cares about His productions. He is not even the awful God portrayed in the book of Job. [He] is careless, wasteful, indifferent, almost diabolical. He is certainly not the sort of god to whom anyone would be inclined to pray (1991, 352:486).

(d) Evolution is inconsistent with God's purposiveness. If God's ultimate purpose was the creation, and eventual redemption, of man (as theistic evolutionists presumably believe), why, then, would He use a process devoid of purposiveness? As Harvard's eminent evolutionist, George Gaylord Simpson, wrote: "Purpose and plan are not characteristic of organic evolution and are not a key to any of its operations" (1967, p. 293). What semblance of purpose could there have been in the hundred-million-year reign and eventual extinction of the dinosaurs, for example? (see Morris, 1974a, p. 219).

How much more would have to be wrong with creation compromises to convince people to abandon them—all of them!—once and for all?

Chapter 14

Compromise— Prelude to Apostasy

A man starting in the fish business hung out a sign with the message, "Fresh Fish For Sale Today," and invited everyone he knew to the opening. His friends eagerly congratulated him on his exciting new enterprise, but one man gently suggested that his sign might be improved. Inquired he, "Why the word 'Today'? Of course it's today; it's not yesterday, and it's not tomorrow." So the fishmonger removed the word. Another asked, "Why the 'For Sale'? Everybody knows that what you have is for sale—else why the store?" And off came the words. Another bemoaned, "Why the 'Fresh'? Your integrity guarantees every fish to be fresh." Thus, the "fresh" likewise was deleted. Finally only "Fish" remained, but one objector complained, "Why the sign? I smelled your fish two blocks away!"

This humorous story provides a simple laugh—but a powerful message. Compromise—carried too far—has disastrous results. Pity the poor fishmonger who listened ever so carefully to the impassioned urgings of those around him. Were his advisers trying to be helpful? Indeed. Were they well-intentioned? To be sure. Were they sincere? No doubt. Were they ultimately **wrong**? Yes!

The verb "compromise" generally is defined as "to adjust or settle by mutual concessions; to come to agreement by mutual concession." The concept of compromise is quite popular in our day. It is used often in social matters, business disputes, foreign relations, political affairs, and various other areas of life.

Certainly, not all compromise is bad. In the daily routine of life, on occasion it is necessary to "give a little." Admittedly, there are times when each side must move from its old position to a position closer to the other side—for the sake of peace or mutual advantage. There are times when compromise not only is necessary, but beneficial. Rather than argue over whether to paint the building green or red, perhaps a compromise settlement of blue is in order. Rather than become angry over whether to buy a compact car or a full-sized automobile, perhaps the purchase of a mid-sized car would do. None among us denies that there are times when compromise is advantageous.

Years ago, during what has come to be known as the "restoration period" in American religious history, it was common to hear the cry, "unity in matters of doctrine, liberty in matters of opinion, and charity in all things." What a wonderful attitude such a slogan exemplifies! Indeed, that attitude should be the basis for every Christian's personal walk with God. The idea behind the adage, simply put, is that sometimes there is room for compromise—and sometimes there is not.

That is especially true in religious matters. While the Lord was on the Earth, He prayed for unity among believers (John 17). He prayed for such because it not only was **desirable**, but **possible**. History bears out this fact. In Genesis 11:6, for example, we find the following summary regarding the unity of the people of that day: "And Jehovah said, 'Behold they are **one** people, and they have all one language; and this is what they begin to do: and now nothing will be withholden from them, which they purpose to do.'" An amazing commentary on a people's unity, is it not? Our Lord did not pray for something that was impossible. Rather, Christ's prayer was for something He knew very well could become a reality.

He also knew the formula for putting the ideal into practice. In His statements recorded in John 12:48 and John 14:15, He made that clear when He said: "The word that I spake, the same shall judge him in the last day," and "if ye love me, keep my commandments." Religious unity was to be based on the fact that God's Word—as the objective, inspired, inerrant, authoritative source of knowledge—is to be inviolate (John 17:17; Matthew 24:35; 2 Timothy 3:16-17; 2 Peter 1:20-21). While certain topics are open to individual discretion (as Paul eloquently discussed in Romans 14), there likewise are certain areas—where God has spoken—that are not. And when God speaks, that should settle the matter once and for all.

Apparently, however, along the way, the reality of unity somehow slipped through our fingers, and division—on matters of doctrine—overtook us. Why so? Perhaps it is because there are those among us who: (a) are ignorant of what God said on a particular matter; (b) are indifferent to what God said on a particular matter; (c) do not intend to acquiesce to what God said on a particular matter.

Regardless of the reason(s) involved, the fact is that there are many Bible believers today who have compromised, and continue to compromise, the Word of God. I suggest that such compromise is a **prelude to apostasy**. In some instances, compromisers have "crept in unaware" (Jude 4), bringing false doctrine with them. However, all too often false teachers have been invited openly to propagate their false teachings.

Again, I ask, why is this the case? Perhaps it is because some possess a spirit of compromise. Effecting a compromise of God's Word is a favorite tool of the devil. When God specifically told Adam and Eve not to eat of the fruit of the tree of the knowledge of good and evil (Genesis 3:1-3), who appeared with a compromise for Eve (Genesis 3:4)? Eve capitulated, and convinced Adam to do likewise. When Moses went to Pharaoh to tell him to let the children of Israel go, what was he offered but a compromise ("Go ye, serve the Lord; only let your flocks and your herds be stayed" Exodus 10:24). Moses re-

fused ("There shall not an hoof be left behind"—Exodus 10:26), because it was not what God had commanded. Sanballat and Geshom
wanted to stop Nehemiah's work on the walls of Jerusalem (Nehemiah 6:2). They mocked his efforts, but to no avail (Nehemiah 4:
1-2). They tried threats (vss. 7-8)—without success. Then, through
their messengers, they came to Nehemiah with a compromise. Yet
the prophet stood firm: "I am doing a great work so that I cannot
come down; why should the work cease, whilst I leave it and come
down to you?" (6:3). They persisted: "Yet they sent unto me four
times after this sort" (6:4a). Nehemiah refused to compromise: "And
I answered them after the same manner" (6:4b).

Of these (and others who could be called to our remembrance),
whose names do we cherish? Today, when Eve is mentioned, we
do not think of a woman to whom we owe a great debt of grati-
tude because of her compromising attitude. Rather, we hold her in
contempt for that vile act. Today, when Moses is discussed, Bible
believers recall a man who at first wavered under the tremendous
task given to him (Exodus 2), but who later became known for his
righteous stubbornness in the face of practically incalculable—and
seemingly overwhelming—odds. Today, when Nehemiah is mentioned, Bible believers immediately think of a man with singularity
of purpose and unbending devotion to God's Word. With a formidable task before him, and opposition pressing from every side, he
steadfastly refused to yield on a single point.

COMPROMISE—PRELUDE TO APOSTASY

Not much has changed since the days of Moses and Nehemiah.
[What was it Solomon said about there being "nothing new under
the Sun"?—Ecclesiastes 1:9] Today, efforts are being made by many
within the religious community to compromise the Word of God
and to "water down" the essence of the biblical message. Having seen
personally the horribly evil fruit that has resulted from some of the

popular, modern-day compromises of God's Word, it is my firm conviction that one of the most serious—and certainly one of the most deadly—is the unrelenting compromise of the Genesis account of creation. Many Bible believers apparently do not understand that once the first eleven chapters of Genesis are compromised, the remainder of the biblical record soon will be as well. Genesis 1-11 cannot be surgically removed from the rest of the Bible, as if it were an unsightly wart or malignant tumor. These chapters are an integral part of what God did in history, and they are woven into the very warp and woof of biblical fabric from start to finish. To allow compromise on these chapters is to invite compromise elsewhere throughout the Word of God.

Surely, by the time you have reached this particular point in this book, the conclusion that serious compromises of Genesis 1-11 have occurred, and are continuing to occur, has been rendered inescapable by the evidence. But where, exactly, are such compromises likely to lead? I would like to investigate the answer to that question in this final chapter.

In 1987, Ralph Gilmore, a professor at Freed-Hardeman University, presented a series of lectures on theistic evolution at the University's annual lectureship program. Many of his comments were recorded in a chapter he authored for the lectureship book. Among those comments were these:

> It does make a difference what we believe about the first chapters of the Bible because we do not have the prerogative to "pick and choose" which biblical passages we will accept into our theology and which we will discard (2 Tim. 3:16-17; Rev. 22:18-19) [1987, p. 142].

Indeed, it **does** make a difference what we believe concerning Genesis 1-11. It is my contention that ultimately the same spirit of compromise that causes a person to doubt the veracity and genuineness of Genesis 1-11 likewise will affect his thinking on other portions of Scripture—with disastrous results.

Compromise is a Prelude to Religious Liberalism and Modernism

Few people seem to realize how significantly the influence of Charles Darwin has impacted the modern world. In chapter 3, I mentioned a 1991 Gallup poll which suggested that almost half (49%) of the American public, to some extent or another, believed in organic evolution. Amazingly, some 40% of these professed a religious affiliation. I also discussed that in March 2000, the *New York Times* released the results of a poll commissioned by the liberal civil rights group, People for the American Way, and conducted by DYG, Inc., the highly regarded polling and public research firm in Danbury, Connecticut. The results were shocking: 68% said it was "possible to believe in evolution while also believing that God created humans and guided their development" (see Glanz, 2000, A-1). This kind of thinking has had a terrible effect on the church, as Davidheiser explained over thirty years ago.

> ...the espousal of the theory of evolution leads to compromises which in turn lead to liberalism, modernism, and a repudiation of the gospel plan of salvation through the atonement of Christ. The history of the last century has shown over and over that as the evolution theory is accepted by a society, Christian faith deteriorates. With the acceptance of evolution, the social gospel is substituted for the gospel of salvation by grace through the atonement of Christ by way of the cross (1969, pp. 38-39).

E.H. Andrews, addressed this same point when he noted that "our view of origins affects our interpretation and use of Scripture" (1986, p. 86). Eventually, of course, the **objective** standard of the Word of God becomes little more than a **subjective** treatise that may, or may not, be correct in its renderings. Where, then, does this leave the individual who has "bought into" such a compromise? Kautz warned:

> For a theistic evolutionist, particularly one who is a theologian, to generate in people distrust over the reliability of the books which constitute the Old and New Testaments is, in the

> long run, to affect adversely a person's confidence in God's
> actions and promises. The Christian is then faced with the
> problem of having to determine which chapters/verses/books
> are trustworthy and which are not—a burden no Christian
> should be made to bear (1988, p. 30).

The end result is that a person eventually slides gently into liberalism and modernism. From there, it is a slippery slope into complete
and final apostasy—a road far too many have traveled already.

Compromise is a Prelude to
the Loss of a Person's Soul

The degree to which a person's faith is affected by compromise
of the Genesis account of creation depends upon a number of factors. Ultimately, however, Culp was correct when he stated:

> At the same time, the effects of theistic evolution on a man
> are profound. His personal religious standards, his zeal for
> testifying for Christ as his Savior, and his belief in the abso-
> lutes of the Bible are all weakened. One who doubts the Gen-
> esis account will not be the same man he once was... (1975,
> p. 160).

Kautz has written in agreement:

> If **atheistic** evolution leads a person away from God totally,
> then **theistic** evolution sets a person on a path which leads
> to doubt about the credibility of the Scriptures and ultimately
> about Christianity itself (1988, p. 30, emp. in orig.).

The evidence documenting that both men are correct is overwhelming. Consider the case of E.O. Wilson of Harvard. Dr. Wilson is considered to be the "father of sociobiology" and is one of
the most brilliant lights in modern evolutionary theory. But it has
not always been so. In speaking of Wilson, Henry Morris wrote:

> The decline and fall of Darwin's faith has been echoed in the
> experiences of multitudes of others since his day. One of the
> top modern-day evolutionists, founder and chief protagonist
> of the popular system known as sociobiology, has given this
> testimony: "As were many persons in Alabama, I was a born-
> again Christian. When I was fifteen, I entered the Southern

Baptist Church with great fervor and interest in the fundamentalist religion; I left at seventeen when I got to the University of Alabama and heard about evolutionary theory"
(1984, p. 113; for documentation on Wilson quotation, see
Wilson, 1982, p. 40).

In commenting on the connection between belief in evolution and
the loss of a person's faith, philosopher Huston Smith observed that
writer Martin Lings was "probably right in saying that 'more cases
of loss of religious faith are to be traced to the theory of evolution
...than to anything else'..." (1982, p. 755).

Why is this the case? Why do so many people ultimately give
up their faith, or see it slowly but systematically destroyed, once
they have accepted the tenets of evolution or theistic evolution?

It is instructive to trace the history of this rebellion through
human history, as recorded in the Bible. In its essentials it
boils down to a conflict between those who worship and serve
the Creator and those "who changed the truth of God into a
lie and worshipped and served the creature more than the
Creator" (Romans 1:25). It is a conflict between God-cen-
tered and creature-centered religion. Any sort of religion which
denies the Creator the place of absolute primacy and sovereignty in the universe, which prescribes limits of His action or
power or which seeks to judge His deeds or His Word at the
bar of human reason, is fundamentally a system of evolution.
The universe or some aspect or component of it is held to be
the focus of ultimate Truth and the idea of God is accommodated, if at all, in some derivative place in the system. This
framework appeals to creaturely pride and thus has a strong
appeal to fallen men. **Acknowledgment of God's absolute sovereignty,...requires complete submission of
man's wisdom and will to that of God, and this hu-
miliation is stubbornly resisted by human nature** (Morris, 1966, p. 98, emp. added).

Dr. Morris has seen, as I (and so many others who deal in the cre-
ation/evolution controversy) have seen on a regular basis, literally
hundreds and hundreds of people—young and old alike—who have
lost their faith as a direct result of compromise with evolutionary
doctrine in one form or another. Compromise—just as it was in the
case of E.O. Wilson—became the prelude to apostasy.

CONCLUSION

As I was putting the finishing touches on this book, I received a telephone call from a minister. He informed me that he was calling on behalf of two parents who, quite literally, were too distraught to telephone for themselves. Their 18-year-old son had just come back to town, having completed the first few weeks of classes at the university where he went to matriculate after his high school graduation. Upon his return home for a "weekend furlough," he had boldly proclaimed to his parents: "I thought you'd want to know. I don't believe in God any more." Put yourself in the place of those two parents for a moment in time. Can you imagine the shock of hearing those awful, fateful words?

This young man had been a truly wonderful son. He had been a genuinely faithful Christian. But he now had returned home from college a self-avowed atheist. When his parents asked the obvious question—"Why?!"—he casually replied: "I no longer believe in God because I have seen the compelling evidence for organic evolution that was provided by the professor in my required biology class—evidence which proves that we have descended from ape-like creatures millions of years ago. Evolution is a **scientific fact**. Belief in God is a myth for spineless sissies and worthless weaklings who don't know any better." And so, yet another soul has been lost to compromise.

It is so very sad to see, in this pilgrimage we call life, people of obvious talent and ability who could have been such a blessing to so many, yet who have become counterproductive to the cause of biblical truth because of their compromising positions on certain issues. These people could have influenced numerous souls for Christ—in this generation and in those yet to come—had they simply retained their faith in God's Word and stood firmly upon its doctrinal statements. Instead, they have opted for compromise themselves, and have fertilized the soil of many hearts with a compromising philosophy and an arrogant disposition that subordinates clear biblical history to the baseless assertions of modern scientism.

It is my earnest desire that perhaps something I have said in this book might serve as a warning to Bible believers regarding the terrible consequences that arise from creation compromises. We simply cannot cry "peace, when there is no peace" (Ezekiel 13:10). It also is my earnest desire that perhaps something I have said in this volume might rescue from the error of their ways those not yet committed to such a path, that they might once again become useful and effective tools in the church's apologetic arsenal. What will the church of the future be like if the errors of theistic evolution, progressive creationism, and other such compromises are tolerated? Perhaps the words of the poet, Alexander Pope, can admonish us.

> Vice is a monster of such frightful mien,
>   As to be hated needs but to be seen;
>   Yet seen too oft', familiar with her face,
>   We first endure, then pity, then embrace.

Appendix 1

That "Loaded" Questionnaire

INTRODUCTION: THE HISTORY OF THIS INQUIRY*

In March 1983, I received a two-page letter, dated March 14, from Jack P. Lewis, professor, Harding Graduate School of Religion, and Chairman of the Religious Affairs Committee of the Board of Directors, Christian Student Center, University of Mississippi, Oxford, Mississippi. The letter read, in part, as follows.

> The Christian Student Center adjacent to the campus of the University of Mississippi, Oxford, Mississippi, has for a number of years presented an annual lectureship in which a speaker dealt with a question confronting university students in the course of their academic life. We feel that we have had a series of outstanding programs.

---

* This material appeared originally in *Reason & Revelation* (February 1984, 4:5-12), the monthly journal on Christian evidences published by Apologetics Press. Bert Thompson wrote the first two sections; Wayne Jackson wrote the remainder. It is reproduced here in an abridged form because of its relevance to the subjects this book discusses.

For our program of February 3,4, and 5, 1984, we would like to have a symposium on "Origins" in which various speakers would present their viewpoints. We have a few tentative agreements for participation. The following is an invitation list, not an acceptance list. We thought you would like to see the whole proposal. The Chairperson, Theme Speaker, and Moderator will be Dr. Jack Wood Sears, Harding University.

1. "The Limitations of Science," Dr. Douglas Shields, University of Mississippi

2. "An Exegesis of Genesis 1 and 2," Dr. Clyde Woods, Freed-Hardeman College

3. "Scientific Creationism," Dr. Bert Thompson, Alabama Christian School of Religion

4. "Theistic Evolution," Dr. Niel [sic] Buffalo [sic], University of Central Arkansas, Conway, Arkansas

5. "An Argument for Antiquity and Classical Geology," John Clayton, South Bend, Indiana

6. "Understanding Genesis 1-11 in the Light of Restoration Principles," Dr. Don England, Harding University

We do not intend that there be debate or cross-examination among the speakers. We would like a positive, non-debate setting.... As chairman of the Religious Affairs Committee of the Board of Directors of the Center, I have been asked to issue invitations to participants.... We believe that this will be a very enlightening and helpful symposium. We hope that you will find it possible to participate. I will look forward to your reply at your earliest convenience.

On March 21, I wrote Dr. Lewis, acknowledging his letter and politely declining his invitation to participate in the Oxford lectureship. I explained my decision in light of the following information.

First, Dr. Lewis' letter stated plainly that there would be no "debate or cross-examination among the speakers," and that the situation would consist of a "positive, **non-debate** setting." I found this format unacceptable, because several of the men on the program were well known for their false teachings on the creation account. Neal Buffaloe, for example, is the coauthor of the booklet, *Creation-*

ism and Evolution (1981), which advocates the position that Genesis 1-11 is not to be taken historically and literally, and that theistic evolution is perfectly acceptable. I had written a thorough review and refutation of the booklet in the April/May/June 1981 issue of *Sound Doctrine* published by the Alabama Christian School of Religion (see Thompson, 1981, 6[2]:11-12).

Another of the suggested speakers was John N. Clayton of South Bend, Indiana. Mr. Clayton's positions on the biblical account of creation are well known and fully documented. He is the inventor and chief proponent of the Modified Gap Theory, and has advocated numerous other compromises of the creation account as well (see Jackson and Thompson, 1992). Donald England and Jack Wood Sears of Harding University both are on record in regard to their unorthodox views of Genesis. Dr. England is the author of the so-called Non-World View, which states that Christians err when they assign **any** world view to the Genesis text. In addition, he has defended the Multiple-Gap Theory, and has criticized the view that the creative days of God were literal, 24-hour periods (see England, 1972, 1983). Dr. Sears has defended the Day-Age Theory and similar concepts, and like Buffaloe, Clayton, and England, advocates the view that the Bible allows for an ancient Earth. In fact, just eight months from the arrival of Dr. Lewis' letter, I would be debating Dr. Sears in Denton, Texas on these very points.

In my response to Dr. Lewis' letter, I explained that I could not participate conscientiously on a program—in a "non-debate" setting —with speakers known to teach this kind of error. However, I also stated that I wished to give the Religious Affairs Committee, and the Board of Directors of the Christian Student Center at Oxford, the benefit of the doubt and hope that they simply were unaware of the erroneous teachings of these men when they issued their invitations. Therefore, in order to provide documentation for both the Committee and the Board to see, I enclosed copies of articles, reviews, etc., which dealt with these issues. Furthermore, I asked Dr. Lewis for a reply concerning these matters.

On March 25, Dr. Lewis sent me a 3-sentence letter, thanking me for my prompt reply to the invitation, stating that he would refer my letter to the Board of Directors, and offering his best wishes. Since then, I have received no further correspondence from him or any member of the Committee or the Board.

THE SEARS-THOMPSON DEBATE

During the dates of November 13-18, 1983 the Annual Denton Lectureship was held at the Pearl Street Church of Christ in Denton, Texas. Each afternoon, a "Discussion Forum" occurred, during which speakers holding opposite views on a subject met in a debate setting to discuss these views.

On Monday, November 14, in public debate, I met Jack Wood Sears, then-chairman of the department of biology at Harding University in Searcy, Arkansas on the topic: "The biblical account of creation allows for a very ancient Earth." Dr. Sears affirmed the proposition; I denied it, and affirmed the proposition: "God created the Universe and all that is in it in six literal days of approximately 24 hours each; He did not employ a system requiring vast periods or long ages of time to bring the material Universe to its present state." Manuscripts of each speaker's material were prepared prior to the debate, and appear in the official lectureship book, *Studies in Hebrews* (see McClish, 1983, pp. 405-434).*

During the course of the debate, I made several important points regarding the use in the Old Testament of various Hebrew words associated with the creation and/or time elements, including such words as *yom* [day] and *bara* and *asah* [used in regard to "creating" or "making"]. Dr. Sears, though completely unable to give any instances in Old Testament usage that negated my points, nevertheless said that he disputed my conclusions. Then, during his rejoinder, he made the following statements concerning the points I had raised regarding the 24-hour days of Genesis 1:

---

* Audio and video tapes of the debate are available from the offices of Apologetics Press.

> By the way, if you'd like some more information about this, we are collecting—a colleague of mine and I—are collecting answers to a questionnaire that we've sent out to outstanding Hebrew scholars both in the church and out of the church in this country and in Europe, in this country and in foreign places, and we have yet to find one that will maintain that this has to be a twenty-four hour day. And these are conservative scholars; these are not radicals. This will be given in a lectureship the first week in February at the University of Mississippi in Oxford at the University Christian Student Center by my colleague who is at this time preparing a manuscript on this. I'll not go further because I do not want to jeopardize his manuscript or his problem there.*

It is this questionnaire and the Oxford, Mississippi lectureship to which Dr. Sears alluded in his Denton speech, that we now wish to discuss at length.

The lectureship at the University of Mississippi Christian Student Center in Oxford was held during the dates of February 3-4, 1984. The listing of speakers as given above, however, was altered somewhat. *The Magnolia Messenger*, published by Magnolia Bible College in Kosciusko, Mississippi (January 1984), listed in an advertisement for the lectureship the following speakers and assignments:

"A Scientific Proof for the Existence of God," Dr. Douglas Shields

"General Evolution and the Fossils," Dr. Jack Wood Sears

"An Exegesis of Genesis 1," Dr. Clyde Woods

"Understanding Genesis 1 & 2 in View of Restoration Principles," Dr. Donald England

The general theme and title of the sixteenth annual University Christian Student Center lectureship at Oxford was "Creation, Science, and Faith."

Dr. Sears, in his statement at Denton alluding to a "questionnaire ...sent to outstanding Hebrew scholars," made mention of the fact that he and "a colleague" were sending a questionnaire to various

---

* This quotation was transcribed directly from the debate tapes.

individuals, and preparing a manuscript regarding the compiled results of that questionnaire. The "colleague" to whom Dr. Sears referred is Donald England, also of Harding University. The "manuscript" to which Dr. Sears referred was, in fact, the presentation that
Dr. England planned to make at the Oxford lectureship.

Hugo McCord, professor emeritus of Bible and biblical languages,
Oklahoma Christian College [now Oklahoma Christian University of
Science and Arts], and a Hebrew scholar in his own right, received
one of these questionnaires, along with a cover letter on Harding
University stationery, signed by both Sears and England. Upon seeing the nature of the questionnaire, Dr. McCord answered it, but
chose in addition to "dissect" it, separating each question from the
ones before and after, and placing his comments in the appropriate places. Dr. McCord graciously sent us both a copy of the questionnaire, and his response to it. On seeing the material, we then
contacted another Hebrew scholar and professor, to see if he, too,
had received the questionnaire. He had. But, as Wayne Jackson relates in the next section, the professor refused to answer it because
of the bias built into the questions—bias that practically required a
preconditioned response. This appendix is devoted to an examination of that questionnaire.

THAT "LOADED" QUESTIONNAIRE

Jack Wood Sears is a professor of biology at Harding University. Donald England is a distinguished professor of chemistry at
the same institution. Both of these gentlemen are Christians, and
each has written books in defense of the Bible. Their writings have
not been without merit, and we salute every word of truth that has
issued from their pens. We believe, however, that in one area in
particular, both of these men have seriously compromised biblical
teaching.

Both Sears and England allow for the possible harmonization of
biblical chronology with evolutionary chronology. It must be under-

stood, of course, that from an evolutionary vantage point, "time" is crucial. Every evolutionist will painfully concede that unless he is granted vast eons of time, there is utterly no possibility that macro-evolution (i.e., change across phylogenetic boundaries) has occurred. George Wald, Nobel laureate of Harvard, expressed it like this: "Time is the hero of the plot.... Given so much time, the 'impossible' becomes possible, the possible becomes probable, and the probable becomes virtually certain. One has only to wait: time itself performs the miracles" (1979, p. 294).

But it must be stressed that "time" is not a creator. Impotence times billions of years is still impotence. A.E. Wilder-Smith thus affirmed:

> ...the postulation of huge time spans by Darwinists to allow for the "creative" activity of chance and natural selection to get to work, does not really help to solve the problem in the least. ...it is not time itself which is our problem in connection with origins, but rather the infinitely more important matter of the source of the "planning energy" behind archebiopoiesis and order in our universe. This means that the mechanism of evolution postulated by Darwinians cannot really be influenced by the allowing of huge time spans, which they regard as the *conditio sine qua non* for their ideas (1975, p. 147; see also Thompson, 1977, pp. 91-103).

Though Sears and England oppose organic evolution, it is certain that both have been influenced by it, and have yielded ground, to it, especially in the area of geochronology. England has written that: "Inasmuch as Scripture does not state how old the earth is or how long life has existed on earth, one is free to accept, if he wishes, the conclusions of science" (1983, p. 155). Sears, in his book, *Conflict and Harmony in Science and the Bible*, opposed the idea that the genealogical/chronological data of the Bible can be used to determine a relative age for the Earth or mankind (1969, pp. 17-20).

The problem is this: some who have been trained in various scientific disciplines are quite weak in their knowledge of biblical matters. Unfortunately, their scientific training has colored their view of biblical truth. Beyond that, however, it is deplorable that men some-times attempt to "manipulate" the evidence in order to buttress their cherished theories. And, if we may kindly say so, that is precisely what Sears and England have attempted to do via this questionnaire.

In late October of 1983, Sears and England submitted a ques-tionnaire to a number of Bible scholars, inquiring about certain por-tions of the Scriptures dealing with creation. Though the professors claimed that they were merely soliciting answers in "the spirit of the restoration plea" so as to "respect the silence of the Scriptures," a careful examination of the questionnaire reveals that the **real** pur-pose was to gather support for their well-known views that the Gen-esis record of origins is not necessarily opposed to the time scale postulated by evolutionists.

The form contained ten questions, along with some brief pre-liminary comments. Each of the questions contained a "YES" [ ] or "NO" [ ] space to be checked. But here is a significant factor: **the questions were carefully worded in an attempt to pur-posely produce a "NO" answer**—in other words, the question-naire was "loaded." Note the following quotation from the cover let-ter (dated October 25, 1983) written by Sears and England, and ac-companying the questionnaire.

> We recognize that a simple "yes" or "no" may not be possi-ble for some of the questions; however, we would appreci-ate such a short answer if possible. **If you feel that it is nec-essary to check "yes" for any question, we would like for you to supply additional information such as an explanatory comment or a literature reference** (emp. added).

As you survey the questions in the subsequent portion of this ap-pendix, you will see that they hardly are the epitome of objectivity. One Bible professor with whom we communicated, as Dr. Thomp-son already has mentioned, also was asked to fill out the question-naire, but declined to do so because of its obvious bias. That should tell you something. The "questionnaire" was prefaced with the fol-lowing statements.

> It is believed by many that the Bible teaches an "instanta-
> neous creation." However, we would like to know if a care-
> ful, scholarly exegesis of certain words or expressions man-
> dates such a conclusion to the exclusion of "creation by some
> sort of process" that may have involved some perceptable
> [sic] time lapse. The first four questions address this problem.

Then follows the first question.

Does the use of the Hebrew word *asah* or *bara* in Genesis one preclude or exclude some sort of process?

Several things may be observed about this question. First, it is designed to be answered "No," and thus to suggest subtly that Genesis 1 will allow for some sort of developmental "process"—as opposed to a rapid creation. Second, to my knowledge, no competent scholar has claimed that *asah* ["made" (1:16)] and *bara* ["created" (1:1)] have any intrinsic implications relative to "time." This is a straw man. Third, there are, however, **contextual** indications, both in Genesis 1 and in passages elsewhere, which suggest rapid action in contrast to a protracted, developmental process. For example, Professor Raymond Surburg has noted:

> The wording of the Genesis account seems to indicate a short
> time for the creative acts described. To illustrate, in Genesis
> 1:11 God literally commands, "Earth, sprout sprouts!" Im-
> mediately v. 12 records the prompt response to the command
> —"The earth caused the plants to go out." The Genesis ac-
> count nowhere even hints that eons or periods of time are
> involved. Instantaneous action seems to be what the writer
> stresses (1959, p. 60).

Moreover, of Paul's statement concerning the human body—"But now hath God set the members of each one of them in the body, even as it hath pleased him" (1 Corinthians 12:18)—Greek scholar W.E. Vine observed:

> The tenses of both verbs are the aorist or point tenses and
> should be translated "set" and "it pleased" (instead of the per-
> fect tenses, "hath set" and "it hath pleased") and this marks
> the formation of the human body in all its parts as a creative

act at a single point in time, and contradicts the evolutionary theory of a gradual development from infinitesimal microcosms (1951, p. 173, parenthetical comment in orig.).

But suppose the question above had been worded like this: "Does the use of the Hebrew words *asah* and *bara* in Genesis 1 suggest a developmental process?" The answer most certainly would have to be "NO," but this hardly would have been the response desired by the two professors!

Finally, it might be asked—what influences motivated the professors to frame the foregoing question, laying the groundwork for some kind of developmental process that allows for "indefinite periods of time" in Genesis 1?

Is the Hebrew word *asah* or *bara* time limiting; that is, does the use of either of these words demand instantaneous creation? By "instantaneous" is intended "no perceptable [sic] time lapse."

This question is completely irrelevant. No one has argued that a rapid creation, within six literal, consecutive days, is demonstrated merely by the use of *asah* or *bara*. But again, let us reverse the matter. "Are the Hebrew words *asah* and *bara* **time expanding**; that is, does the use of either of these words demand vast eons of time?" The answer, of course, would be a resounding, "NO!" But then, that would not have left the same impression as the question asked by the professors.

Does the Hebrew word *asah* or *bara* require an *ex nihilo* [out of nothing] conclusion?

Once more the professors are fighting figments of their own imaginations. Sound scholarship does not contend that *ex nihilo* creation is inherent in these Hebrew verbs. What we **do** contend is this: **contextual** considerations in Genesis 1, and in other biblical references, argue for an *ex nihilo* creation! Gesenius, the father of modern Hebrew lexicography, wrote:

That the first v. of Genesis teaches that the original creation of the world in its rude, chaotic state was from nothing, while in the remainder of the chapter, the elaboration and distribution of matter thus created is taught, the connection of the whole section shows sufficiently clearly (as quoted by Pearson, 1953, 11:22).

Noted scholar C.F. Keil declared that when *bara* is in the *Qal (Kal)* stem in Hebrew, as in Genesis 1:1,

...it always means **to create**, and is only applied to a divine creation, the production of that which had no existence before. It is never joined with an accusative of material, **although it does not exclude a preexistent material unconditionally**, but is used for the creation of man (ver. 27, ch. v. 1,2), and of everything new that God creates, whether in the kingdom of nature (Num. xvi.30) or that of grace (Ex. xxxiv.10; Ps. li.10, etc.). In this verse, however, the existence of any primeval material is precluded by the object created—"the heavens and the earth" (1971, 1:47).

Oswald T. Allis stated that a creation *ex nihilo* "is clearly implied" in Genesis 1:1 (1951, p. 9), and Edward J. Young wrote: "If in Genesis 1:1 Moses desired to express the thought of absolute creation there was no more suitable word in the Hebrew language at his disposal [than *bara*—WJ]" (1964, p. 7). Again, one wonders what attitude prompted the foregoing question from the two professors.

Hebrews 11:3 appears to represent *ex nihilo* creation. However, does a careful exegesis of Hebrews 11:3 require an *ex nihilo* conclusion?

Hugo McCord gave the following answer to the question:

Hebrews 11:3 states that the worlds were framed by God's word (*rhemati theou*), and that God's word did not frame them out of appearing things (*ek phainomenon*). Logically the inference remains that his word could have created the worlds out of non-appearing things. But that option is so tenuous, and imaginable reason says that Hebrews 11:3 teaches an *ex nihilo* creation. God can create (*bara*) something

> from existing materials (Isa. 65:18), but none is mentioned in Genesis 1:1 nor in Hebrews 11:3. Apparently he wanted us to understand a creation out of nothing. If that was not his intention, his word has misled millions of readers. Compare: "By the word of Jehovah were the heavens made, And all the host of them by the breath of his mouth. For he spake, and it was done; He commanded, and it stood fast" (Psa. 33:6,9).*

Of Hebrews 11:3, F.F. Bruce observed: "The visible, material universe came into being by pure creation—out of nothing. It was not fashioned from preexistent material, as most pagan cosmogonies taught" (1972, p. 125).

Once more, one cannot but wonder what prompted this question, the obvious design of which was to cast doubt on an *ex nihilo* emphasis in Hebrews 11:3. The following comment from Leon Morris may shed some light on the matter: "The suggestion that there is here [in Hebrews 11:3—WJ] a reference to the formless void of Genesis 1:2 out of which the present creation was evolved has little to support it" (1960, p. 172). Surely Sears and England were not suggesting this—were they? But the questionnaire continues.

Both of us believe that Genesis records a factual yet not exhaustive account of creation events. We believe that the days of Genesis one were twenty-four hour days, but we largely believe this from the general impression gained by reading the text. However, we wish to know if this conclusion is mandated by scripture. We would appreciate your response to these questions. Please note our emphasis on "principle of Hebrew grammar or exegesis."

Before considering the next series of questions, some comments are in order. First, the preceding paragraph is misleading. Though the professors declare their belief in twenty-four hour creation days, the subsequent questions are designed to reflect upon the credibil-

---

* Quotations from Dr. McCord's response to the professors' questionnaire are reproduced from the written copy he sent to the offices of Apologetics Press.

ity of this view. Second, one should consider the implications involved in admitting that the "general impression" of Genesis 1 argues for twenty-four hour days, while at the same time hinting that principles of grammar and exegesis may suggest otherwise. Was the inspired writer incapable of making the issue clear? The questions continue.

Are there any principles of Hebrew grammar or exegesis governing the interpretation of the Hebrew text which demand that *yom* [day] of Genesis one be understood as a twenty-four hour day to the exclusion of all other interpretations?

No conservative scholar contends that there is a grammatical rule that dictates a specific length of time inherent in *yom*. Why address arguments that have not even been made, unless one wants to prejudice the issue. Dr. McCord exploded the question when he responded:

> Nothing in the word *yom* specifies its length. However, an exegesis (including grammar, syntax, and context) of *yom* in its eleven occurrences in Genesis one shows the word has two meanings:
>
> (1) about a 12-hour period in 1:5, where it is the opposite of darkness; 1:14,16,18, where it is the opposite of night;
>
> (2) a 24-hour period in 1:5, where its length is defined as a combination of evening and morning; 1:14, where it is in the context of signs, seasons, days, and years; 1:8,13,19,23,31, where again, repeated five times, its length is defined as a combination of morning and evening. An exegetical principle mandates that normal, literal meanings must be understood unless the context indicates an abnormal significance. Nothing in Genesis one points to an abnormal meaning. To this the professors agree when they say that "the general impression gained by reading the text" is "that the days of Genesis one were twenty-four-hour days."

Yes, we are well aware of the fact that the term "day" occasionally is used in the Bible in a figurative sense. But that is not the issue.

The issue is: What does the **biblical evidence** indicate concerning the use of the term "day" in the creation week? The term "baptism" sometimes is used figuratively. In Mark 10:38 the Lord employed that word for His impending suffering. Does the fact that "baptism" may be used symbolically for suffering argue that such is a possibility in Acts 2:38? What about this question: Is there any rule of Greek grammar which would mandate that the baptism of Acts 2:38 is to be in "water"? No. But would the gentlemen from Searcy allow other options? If not, why not?

Is there a principle of Hebrew grammar or exegesis governing the interpretation of the Hebrew text which demands that *yom* be interpreted as a twenty-four hour day if it is preceded by the definite article?

I am fairly familiar with the literature on the subject, yet I cannot recall ever reading an argument for twenty-four hour creation days based upon article usage.

Is there a principle of Hebrew grammar or exegesis governing the interpretation of the Hebrew text which demands that *yom* be interpreted as a twenty-four hour day if it is accompanied by a cardinal number?

The point that creationists have made on this matter is not one of **grammar**; it is one of consistent **usage**, and that does relate to exegesis. Dr. McCord correctly replied: "The length of *yom* is not determined by the accompaniment of a number, either cardinal or ordinal. However, in over 100 citations (as, cardinals, Gen. 1:5; 7:4; ordinals, Gen. 7:11; 8:4), no exception has been found." Let the professors try this question: "Can you cite at least one example from the Pentateuch where *yom*, accompanied by a numeral, clearly indicates an indefinite period of time?" Why weren't questions of this nature included in the survey? I think the answer is obvious.

Assuming the creation days of Genesis one were twenty-four hour days, is there a principle of Hebrew grammar or

a rule of exegesis that demands the conclusion that each of the six creation days were [sic] consecutive, that is, no time could have elapsed to separate day one from day two, day two from day three, etc.?

This question solicits support for the notion advanced by Donald England in *A Christian View of Origins*: "The days of Genesis 1 could easily have been twenty-four hour days and the earth still date to antiquity, provided that indefinite periods of time separated the six creation days" (1972, p. 110). [The reader might ask where the professor got the idea that the Earth can "date to great antiquity."] Likely, Dr. McCord did not receive high marks when he responded: "The Hebrew text, if a time lapse between days occurred, could have spoken to that effect, but it does not. Any attempt to inject time lapses between days is not from exegesis but eisegesis."

A point that advocates of this "time-lapse-between-days" theory might ponder is found in Numbers 7. After the Tabernacle was set up, the head princes of the twelve tribes brought offerings for the altar's dedication. Oblations were offered on "the first day" (12), "the second day" (18), "the third day" (24), and so on through "the twelfth day (78)." Assuming that these "days" were twenty-four hour days, is there any rule of Hebrew grammar demanding the conclusion that each of these twelve days was consecutive—that is, no time could have elapsed to separate day one from day two, etc.? Of course there is no "rule" of grammar that would preclude such, but only a bizarre notion foreign to the context would ever suggest it!

Is there a principle of Hebrew grammar or a rule of exegesis which would preclude the possibility of an indefinite time lapse between verses one and two or between verses two and three of Genesis chapter one?

This question opens the door to the possibility of the Gap Theory —a concept that came into vogue about a century ago as a means of harmonizing the Bible with evolutionary time scales. I will not use space at this point in refuting this totally baseless theory. Professor W.W. Fields, in his book, *Unformed and Unfilled* (1976), has completely demolished the Gap Theory. Oswald Allis likewise rendered a death-blow to this concept in his volume, *God Spake by Moses* (1951, see his Appendix). In this connection, Allis made a very important observation: "To allow science to become the interpreter of the Bible and to force upon it meanings which it clearly does not and cannot have is to undermine its supreme authority as the Word of God" (p. 158). In short, there is neither grammatical nor exegetical substance to the Gap Theory.

Many tend to conclude, from recorded Biblical genealogies, that the earth and life on earth is [sic] relatively recent; that is, less than 10,000 years. In your judgment, was it ever the intent of Hebrew genealogies to enable one today employing scholarly exegesis of the text to calculate the age of the earth or the age of life on the earth?

The purpose of this question, of course, is to suggest that the genealogical and chronological data in the Bible are without value in determining the relative ages of the Earth and mankind. To this I would like to respond in several ways.

First, there is the matter of Scripture "intent." It is claimed that the Bible is silent on the topic of Earth and human ages (see England, 1983, p. 156), and thus it was not the "intent" of the divine writers to discuss the ages of Earth and man. Dr. McCord, with penetrating logic, replied: "It was not the intent of Paul in Romans 6:3-4 to negate sprinkling (a practice unheard of until A.D. 253), but since such a malpractice has developed, it is valid to use Romans 6:3-4 to set forth the proper action of baptism." He also observed that genealogical sources in the Bible also limit humanity's life span upon, the Earth, and so the Scriptures are **not silent** on this issue!

Consider this parallel example. In Genesis 30:32ff., we read of Jacob's bargain with Laban concerning the "ring-streaked and spotted" sheep. I don't suppose anyone would claim that it was the "intent" of Moses to discuss genetics, yet both Sears and England contend that this passage has "prescientific" genetic implications (see: Sears, 1969, p. 21; England, 1983, p. 145). Why can there not be similar biblical implications that deal with Earth/man ages?

Second, what are the actual genealogical and chronological indicators of the Bible? Consider the following facts. Luke's Gospel (3:23-28) lists the record of Christ's genealogy all the way back to Adam (the first man—1 Corinthians 15:45). There are seventy-five generations from Jesus back to the commencement of humanity. Fifty-five of these—from Christ to Abraham—consume but a mere 2,000 years (see Douglas, 1974, p. 213). How many years of human history do you suppose can be squeezed into those remaining twenty generations (even if one allows for the longevity of the patriarchs and some minor gaps in the genealogical lists)? One thing is certain—the **three to four million years** currently postulated by evolutionary anthropologists (and those sympathetic with them) **will not fit**! The Bible clearly implies a relative age limitation for humanity; there are reasonable "time" indications that can be drawn from the genealogies (see Jackson, 1976, 11:42-43).

Additionally, if Scripture is silent about the relative ages of the Earth and man, and one is free, therefore, to accept the conclusions of "science," as England alleges, then numerous Bible passages are thrown into a state of absolute confusion. Evolutionary "science" contends that the Earth is some 4.6 billion years old, while man is but a stripling of approximately 3.6 million years old (a recent evolutionary estimate). This would suggest that man is only about $1/1250^{th}$ of the age of the Earth. If we let the entire sum of Earth history, from its beginning to the present, be illustrated by a twenty-four hour day, man had his origin about **one minute and nine seconds ago**! No wonder evolutionists are fond of referring to man as a "Johnny-come-lately!"

But what does this timescale do to such Bible passages as the following: (a) Adam and Eve were made male and female "in the beginning," which, as Jack P. Lewis has correctly shown, "should be understood in the sense of 'from the beginning of creation' (cf. Romans 1:20; 2 Peter 3:4)" [1978, p. 416]. That, of course, is exactly what Mark's Gospel says (Mark 10:6). (b) Paul argued that man's unbelief is inexcusable since God's existence has been humanly perceived in His handiwork "since the creation of the world" (Romans 1:20). (c) Christ placed the first family back near the "foundation of the world" (Luke 11:45-52).

In conclusion, we must again register a strong protest at what this loaded questionnaire seeks to accomplish, as well as the implications it contains. It does not reflect benevolently upon its authors' scholastic objectivity or their regard for the plain testimony of the Holy Scriptures. Rather, it is a graphic commentary on what can happen when men attempt to strain the Word of God through ever-changing "science." As the inspired James might say, "My brethren, these things ought not so to be" (3:10).

Appendix 2

The Bible, Science, and the Ages of the Patriarchs

INTRODUCTION*

As one reads through the Bible, on occasion he is confronted with statements, situations, or events that, at first glance, seem to be either impossible or improbable—when viewed from a distinctly modern vantage point. One good example of such an occurrence might be the statements of Scripture regarding the ages of several of the Old Testament patriarchs. Genesis 5 records that prior to the Flood, people typically lived for hundreds of years, with the average age of the antediluvian patriarchs (excluding Enoch, who was taken to his reward without dying) being 912 years. As Leupold observed, "At once we are struck by the longevity of these patriarchs; all except three lived in excess of nine hundred years. It is useless to attempt to evade this fact" (1942, 1:233).

---

* This material by the author appeared originally in *Reason & Revelation* (May 1992, 12:17-20), the monthly journal on Christian evidences published by Apologetics Press. It is reprinted here in a revised, updated format.

Leupold's observation that it is "useless to attempt to evade" the clear statements of Scripture regarding the long life spans of the patriarchs is correct, of course, in the sense that no one can deny that the Bible attributes long ages to many of the ancient patriarchs. The Bible specifically states that Adam, for example, lived 930 years (Genesis 5:5), Methuselah lived 969 years (Genesis 5:27), etc. However, as Leupold himself discussed in his two-volume *Exposition of Genesis*, some have suggested that while the Bible **says** these old worthies lived to be vast ages, that is not what it **means**. In other words, while the biblical statements themselves on these matters are clear, their meaning is not.

This is the case, we are told, because it is a matter of record that men today (obviously) do not live to be centuries old. Thus, some have suggested that the biblical record is unacceptable and therefore needs to be "fixed" or "explained" to bring it more into line with modern scientific facts on these matters, and to make its message palatable to people of our day and age. What recourse is available, then, to the person who discovers that there is a disagreement between plain, historical statements of Scripture and modern scientific pronouncements?

First, one might simply acknowledge that the Bible is inspired of God (2 Timothy 3:16-17), and as such is accurate in its renderings. If such a person has studied the matter(s) at hand, and is assured that his understanding of Scripture is accurate, he will revere the Word of God as just that—the Word of God—and will accept its teachings as trustworthy, in spite of modern-day claims to the contrary. Second, of course, a person might merely dismiss the biblical record as little more than ancient folklore—worthy of about as much admiration and reverence as, say, Aesop's fables. Such an attitude rejects biblical claims of inspiration, and instead does obeisance to current scientific or philosophical pratings. Third, one might—from all outward appearances—claim to accept the Bible as speaking accurately and truthfully on whatever matters it addresses, all the while in reality compromising its teachings on a variety of subjects. Thus, while such a person pretends to respect the Bible as God's Word, he instead is sowing seeds of compromise. Generally, this is the person who waits to see what "science" has to say before making any determination on the matter. Then, if science is at odds with the Bible, the Scriptures must be "corrected" to fit the scientific data or interpretations. We never are told that science must correct its view, only the reverse—viz., the biblical record must be altered to fit currently prevailing scientific data.

DOES THE BIBLICAL RECORD OF THE PATRIARCHS' AGES NEED TO BE "FIXED"?

It is my intent here to examine and discuss the spirit of compromise exhibited by those in the third group mentioned above. There are a number of notable examples of such compromise, any one of which is illustrative of the attitudes portrayed. Two such examples will suffice.

In 1990, Ronald F. Youngblood edited a book titled, *The Genesis Debate,* in which various areas of Scripture were discussed by disputants on both sides of an issue. Chapter eight of that volume discusses the question, "Did people live to be hundreds of years old before the Flood?" In that chapter, Duane L. Christensen first advocated the view that the biblical record simply cannot be accepted as it is written. He then suggested a number of methods that could be employed to "fix" the text so as to resolve what he considered a serious discrepancy between biblical statements and current scientific knowledge (Christensen, 1990, pp. 166-183). Christensen's assessment was that these numbers are, to use his words, "excessively large," scientifically unverifiable, and therefore, quite simply, unacceptable.

In the June 1978 *Does God Exist?* journal that he edits, John Clayton addressed the patriarchs' ages in an article on "The Question of Methuselah." He suggested:

One of the most frequently asked questions that we receive
in our lecture series is "How did men live so long during early Biblical times?" The Bible indicates ages of 969, 950, etc.,
years for early men. **From a scientific standpoint we cannot verify this figure**. By studying the bones of the oldest
men we get ages of ten to thirty-five years usually, and only
rarely an age as high as fifty (1978a, 5[6]:11, emp. added).

The point made by both Christensen and Clayton is that **from a
scientific standpoint**, the patriarchs' ages as given in the Bible
cannot be verified. In the September 1978 issue of his journal,
Clayton commented:

One final difficulty that this relates to is the attempts made by
some to nail down specific historic dates to Biblical events
of great antiquity. **The ages of men in the past cannot
be answered with great accuracy** (1978b, 5[9]:9, emp.
added).

Why can the ages of men in the past not "be answered with accuracy"? Is it because the Bible is unclear on its statements regarding these men's ages? No, the biblical statements are both clear and
unambiguous. The simple fact of the matter is that neither of these
two writers is willing to accept the biblical testimony because allegedly there is **no scientific evidence**. In an April 20, 1987 letter to
a gentleman in Wyoming who had written to ask him about this
very point, Mr. Clayton wrote:

It is a fact that there is **no scientific evidence** that people
lived to be hundreds of years old. It may just be that we have-
n't found the right bones, but most bones of ancient men turn
out to be twenty or thirty years of age and none have [sic]
been found, to my knowledge, older than eighty years old.
For this reason, I have tried to point out that **there are many
possible ways in which the extreme age of Methuselah might be explained**... (p. 2, emp. added).

The absence of scientific evidence substantiating the Bible's claims
for the ages of the patriarchs is why Clayton cannot bring himself
to accept those ages. Think for just a moment how radical this position really is. What "scientific evidence" do we possess that "proves"

the virgin birth of Jesus? Since science cannot prove that such an event ever occurred, should an alternate explanation be sought? This line of reasoning could be expanded almost endlessly. Since science cannot "prove" Christ's bodily resurrection, the parting of the Red Sea, the destruction of Sodom and Gomorrah, and hundreds of other such occurrences, then must these events—which remain both scientifically unverified and unverifiable—simply be dismissed in the same way these two authors suggest that the patriarchs' ages be dismissed?

Furthermore, there is another aspect to this question that needs to be explored. Aging is a metabolic process. Various species appear to be "programmed" for death within a given age range. Fleas, for example, live for about five years. Dogs live for an average of around fifteen years. Humans, on the other hand, can live upwards of seventy, eighty, ninety, or even a hundred years. Fleas never reach such an age; their genetic package will not allow it. In an article titled "Decreased Lifespans: Have We Been Looking in the Right Place?" that he authored for the *Creation Ex Nihilo Technical Journal*, Carl Wieland commented on this matter as follows:

> Barring accidental death, one-celled organisms are potentially "immortal." A bacterial cell reproduces by dividing into two where there was one, those two then become four, and so on. Why then do multicelled organisms die? Individual human cells in tissue culture divide some fifty times and then stop—**some sort of pre-programmed genetic limit is reached**. Human tumor cells, on the other hand, can be propagated indefinitely by division—the DNA mechanisms for pre-programmed cessation of division appears to be lacking or damaged in such cancer cells.

> In multicellular organisms, once damaged and worn cells can no longer replace themselves, death is only a matter of time as the function of whole organ systems deteriorates. So even without accidents or disease there is a programmed "upper limit" on our age, which appears to be 120 years or so....

> I suggest that our ancestors simply possessed genes for greater longevity which caused this "genetic limit" to human ages to be set at a higher level in the past.

Suggestive evidence in support of this is the fact that in some other organisms (for example, fruit flies), it has been shown that changes in average life spans can be bred into or out of populations....

If this suggestion has merit as the major (if not the sole) cause of great pre-Flood ages, then the obvious question is how some of these longevity genes were lost. The human population went through a severe genetic bottleneck at the time of the Flood—only eight individuals. The phenomenon of "genetic drift" is well known to be able to account for "random," selectively neutral changes in gene frequencies which may be quite rapid. Also, loss of genes is far more likely in a small population....

It is also likely (if not more so) that genes coding for lesser longevity arose by mutational degeneration, with their frequency of possession rising as time passed. At the moment, too little is known of the exact mechanics of the way in which cells are programmed to die in order to offer more specific suggestions (1994, 8[2]:139-140, emp. added, parenthetical comments in orig.).

What if, in the past, human metabolism was much slower? What would be the end result? Gerald Schroeder, in his book, *The Science of God*, addressed such questions.

There are terrible mutations that upset the delicate aging process. Progeria speeds up the aging process almost tenfold, causing a teenager to die with the body of an old person. Within the realm of possibilities is the reverse process, slowing aging tenfold. It would be surprising but not inconceivable that manipulation of a flea's genome might allow it to live ten times longer than normal, thus reaching the age of fifty years. After all, several animals species live even longer than fifty years. The fact that no animals currently reach the long ages associated with pre-Noah biblical persons does not preclude the possibility that this potential exists within our genome.

If human metabolism was slower and life spans were longer during the pre-Noah period, fossils would not indicate this. The slower metabolisms would result in fossils that appear to have formed from younger individuals (1997, pp. 202-203, emp. added).

In a fascinating article published in *Science Digest* some years back ("How Your Bones Tell Your Age"), Frederic W. Nordsiek observed:

> Bone is hard and cannot grow from the inside out as can soft tissues like skin or muscle. Therefore, for example, each of the long bones of the arms and legs at first consists of two bones, with a growing section in between them. After growth is finished, these pairs of bones fuse together.... **Human bones continue to fuse together right up to advanced old age** (1960, 47[5]:17-18, emp. added).

Consider all of these scientific facts collectively, and you will see how they demolish arguments like those from Christensen and Clayton which suggest that "there is no scientific evidence that people lived to be hundreds of years old." Observe what happens when the scientific facts of the matter are interpreted properly.

We know—scientifically—that: (1) aging "is a metabolic process"; (2) the process is indeed controlled by a "pre-programmed genetic limit"; and (3) "human bones continue to fuse together right up to advanced old age." If people at that distant point in human history possessed slower metabolism rates (an extremely reasonable suggestion, considering the condition of the world in which they were living at the time—see Dillow, 1981), and if the human genome contained genes for greater longevity, then the patriarchs **could** have lived to vast old ages, and the slower metabolisms would result in fossils that appeared to have formed from much younger individuals. In short, scientists actually could be in possession of—could be staring at in their laboratories—bones from people who had lived to ripe old ages, and they never would know it! Thus, the allegation that "most bones of ancient men turn out to be twenty or thirty years of age and none has been found older than eighty years old" (to use Clayton's exact words) means absolutely nothing in light of the actual scientific facts concerning human aging.

And surely the question must be asked: Why do the great ages of the patriarchs need to be "explained" in the first place? Why not simply accept the biblical record as it is written? In his June 1978 article on Methuselah, John Clayton provided the answer to that question as he discussed several possible ways to "explain" the patriarchs' ages. He wrote:

> The first possibility is that God miraculously changed man's life expectancy. There is no discussion of such a miracle in the Bible, but many miracles occurred during the creation which are not recorded in Genesis I. This may well be the answer, **but since no skeptic would accept it** we'll consider some other possibilities (1978a, 5[9]:11, emp. added).

This is incredible. First we are told that because there is "no scientific evidence," the great ages of the patriarchs therefore must be "explained." Second, we are told that since "no skeptic would accept" a particular view on these matters, "other possibilities" need to be explored. What a sad commentary on how Mr. Clayton, and others like him, view God's inspired Word. It brings to mind the comment of biblical scholar Edward J. Young in his book, *Studies in Genesis One*:

> What strikes one immediately upon reading such a statement is the low estimate of the Bible which it entails. Whenever "science" and the Bible are in conflict, it is always the Bible that, in one manner or another, must give way. We are not told that "science" should correct its answers in the light of Scripture. Always it is the other way around (1964, p. 54).

The question, then, no longer becomes, "Does the Word of God affirm it?" but instead "Can science confirm it?" As Wayne Jackson observed:

> Whenever such people read the Scriptures, they do so with an eye cast back over their shoulder to see if science agrees; and whenever science asserts that which is different from what the Bible says, in desperation they are ready to append, delete, stretch, or constrict the sacred narrative to make it conform to the latest notions of the scientific community (1978a, 14:14).

SUGGESTED METHODS FOR "FIXING"
THE AGES OF THE PATRIARCHS

Exactly how do Bible critics suggest that the patriarchs' great ages be "explained"? Several methods have been offered, among which are the following.

Ages Determined by Counting Years as Months

Some have suggested that men's ages were not determined in ancient times as they are today. For example, John Clayton wrote:

> The guess that appeals to this writer is that the methods of measuring age are not the same today as they were when men lived so long.... We also know that many cultures use the moon as a measure of age (such as many American Indian tribes). If Methuselah were measured on such a system his age would be 80 years, plus the time till he became a father. This doesn't change anything as he would still be phenomenally old—especially for the day in which he lived, but it would give a modern comprehension of how such an age was calculated (1978a, 5[6]:12, parenthetical item in orig.).

Old Testament scholar John J. Davis addressed this suggestion in two of his books. In the first, *Biblical Numerology,* he observed:

> The most common method of escaping the problem connected with these large numbers is to make "year" mean a shorter period such as a month. This view, however, finds no support at all in the Biblical text for the term "year" is never used in this manner in the Old Testament. In addition to this textual weakness, there is a serious chronological problem that is raised by such a view. In Genesis 5:6 we are told that Seth begat Enos when he was 105 years old. If "years" in this text really means "months" then this verse would propose that Seth had a son when he was only about nine years old! (1968, p. 58; see also Borland, 1990, p. 171).

In his second work, *Paradise to Prison,* Dr. Davis suggested: "There seems to be no reason to regard the names and ages of the individuals in this chapter as other than fully historical." Why so? The reason is simple. It would be difficult for someone to believe a person (e.g., Seth) could beget a child when he was only nine years old, but, as Davis pointed out, "Enos, Cainan, Mahalaleel, and Enoch **would have been fathers at even younger ages**" (1975, p. 106, emp. added). Frederick Filby discussed this solution in his book, *The Flood Reconsidered*:

> This we reject completely, as not only can it be shown to be absolutely wrong, but it makes more difficulties than it solves. Enoch, we are told, had a son, Methuselah, when he was sixty-five. If we divide by twelve he had a son when he was 5.4 years old! (1970, p. 21).

John Clayton has complained that skeptics **never** would believe that men lived to the vast ages ascribed to them in the Bible. One cannot help but wonder if these same skeptics would find it any easier to believe that Enoch—to use Dr. Filby's example—produced a child when he himself was barely over five years old!

The Bible itself makes a clear distinction between the length of years and months, thereby eliminating the critics' suggestion that perhaps men's ages were counted via "moons" (i.e., months), not years. In Genesis 8:13 it is recorded: "And it came to pass in the six hundred and first **year**, in the first **month**...." Moses apparently understood the difference between a month and year. Why do the Bible's critics have so much difficulty in distinguishing between the two?

The Bible similarly presents compelling evidence to eliminate the idea that men's ages should be divided by 12 in order to arrive at an accurate figure for the number of years they actually lived. Abraham was 86 when Ishmael was born (Genesis 16:16). Divided by 12, this means that the patriarch was just over 7 years of age at the birth of his first child, and Sarah was just under 6 when she first gave birth! Further, Abraham must have died at the "good old age" of a shade over 14 (Genesis 25:7-8)! As it turns out, the critics' attempts to "fix" the Bible create a worse problem than they sought to solve.

Ages Counted from Birth of First Offspring

Another suggestion offered in response to the patriarchs' vast ages is that these ages appear larger than normal because "some primitive people measure their age not from the time of their birth, but from the time they produce offspring, or are accepted as an adult in the community in which they live" (Clayton, 1978a, 5[6]:12). In other words, the figures presented in the Bible are too large because they have not yet been "adjusted" (i.e., shortened) to allow for the **true age**—calculated from the time of the birth of the first offspring, or from the time a person was recognized as an adult.

Two things may be said regarding this idea. First, there is not a scrap of evidence that the ages of the patriarchs were counted only from the time of the birth of their firstborn. It is one thing to speculate on such, but another thing entirely to prove it. Where is the critics' evidence that the patriarchs' ages were treated in such a manner? Second, the Bible deals a death-blow to this suggestion when it specifically mentions men's ages **before they produced offspring**, eliminating the idea that their ages were not calculated prior to that event. Genesis 12:4 says: "And Abram was seventy-five years old when he departed out of Haran." Once again, the critics' attempts to "fix" the inspired text have made their last condition worse than their first.

Ages Represent not Individuals, but Dynasties

In the late 1800s, as opposition to the Bible grew and skepticism in general increased, theologians sought ways to make the Bible conform to the claims of Darwinian evolution and uniformitarian geology. While liberal theologians were working diligently to **insert vast ages** of geological time into the biblical text, somewhat ironically, they simultaneously were working to **remove the vast ages** of the patriarchs from that same text.

One novel way to do that was to offer the idea that the names in the genealogical lists (specifically those mentioned in Genesis 5 and

11) were used to refer to entire dynasties, clans, or tribes, and only rarely to actual individuals. Borland has explained what this would accomplish:

> This would mean that when the **Adam clan** had exercised dominion for 130 years, a person was born in the Adam clan who eventually either ruled or was the progenitor of the **Seth clan**. The Adam clan continued to be powerful for an additional 800 years, and then perhaps the Seth clan took over or perhaps there was a gap before the Seth clan exerted its authority for 912 years (1990, p. 174, emp. added).

There are a number of serious problems with this view. First, advocates of the "dynasty" idea cannot remain consistent, because even they are forced to admit that certain names in the lists cannot represent **only** a clan, but instead **must** represent individuals. Noah and his sons must have been real individuals, because they were on board the ark. Abraham must have been an individual, not just a dynasty, because he was the father of the Hebrew nation. If these are recognized as individuals, why should not the others be considered as such?

Second, as Leupold commented: "The attempt to let the personal names represent tribes shatters on the clear statement of how old each father was when he begot a son. A complete generation is not thus brought forth within a tribe" (1942, 1:233). Borland commented: "The notation of the age at which a father begat a particular individual (a son) eliminates the tribe concept..." (pp. 174-175). One does not speak of a "dynasty" producing a son, and then give an age for such an occurrence.

Third, in order for this strained interpretation to be acceptable, one has to read the biblical record with a large dose of imagination and a small dose of common sense. For example, when the text says that Eve bore Cain and Abel, everyone recognizes that it is speaking of individuals because one of them (Cain) slew the other (Abel). Yet, when Eve bore Seth, suddenly a distant dynasty is under discussion. Furthermore, how would an advocate of this strange theory deal with the fact that in many instances in the Old Testament, specific brothers and sisters are mentioned? Dynasties do not have brothers and sisters. Borland addressed this aspect in great detail, and gave numerous biblical examples establishing that individuals, not dynasties, are under discussion (pp. 175-176). The idea that the patriarchs' ages are so large because their names represent tribes or dynasties is completely without merit, and should be rejected.

It is not uncommon for those who refuse to accept the patriarchs' ages at face value to suggest that the numbers must have some great "theological meaning" attached to them. Time and again I have heard or seen just such a statement. But, when pressed on exactly **what** that theological meaning might be, supporters of such an idea are at a total loss to offer any explanation. Christensen was forced to admit:

> It is probably not possible to recover the key to the theological meaning of the numbers and ages in Genesis 5 and 11, at least in detail. Nonetheless it seems likely that the numbers are not to be taken as simply historical report (1990, p. 180).

In other words, while he cannot explain what the numbers **do** mean, he does know what they **do not** mean. They are **not** to be taken as literal or historical.

But why not? That is exactly how the Bible writers accepted them. Examine this remarkable statement from Moses' pen. In Genesis 47:9, Jacob, speaking to Pharaoh, said: "The days of the years of my pilgrimage are a hundred and thirty years: few and evil have been the days of my life, and **they have not attained unto the days of the years of the life of my fathers** in the days of their pilgrimage." Notice the point that Jacob was making. He was 130 years old, yet he stated that even at that great age, his days had not reached "the days of the years of the life of my fathers." If he was 130 years old, and yet he had not reached the age of some of the patriarchs who preceded him, just **how old** would "his fathers" have been?

Isn't it remarkable how well the biblical record fits together? And isn't it wonderful that it can be trusted and accepted, without the kind of "sleight of hand" tricks on which its critics have to rely in order to make their false theories attain some degree of respectability?

References

Ackerman, Paul (1986), *It's a Young World After All* (Grand Rapids, MI: Baker).

Adler, Jerry (1980), "Is Man a Subtle Accident?," *Newsweek*, November 3.

Aling, C. (1981), *Egypt and Bible History* (Grand Rapids, MI: Baker).

Allis, Oswald T. (1951), *God Spake By Moses* (Grand Rapids, MI: Baker).

Andrews, E.H. (1986), *Christ and the Cosmos* (Welwyn, England: Evangelical Press).

Archer, Gleason (1964), *A Survey of Old Testament Introduction* (Chicago, IL: Moody).

Archer, Gleason L. (1970), *Old Testament Introduction* (Chicago, IL: Moody).

Archer, Gleason L. (1979), "The Chronology of the Old Testament," *The Expositor's Bible Commentary* (Grand Rapids, MI: Eerdmans).

Archer, Gleason (1982), *Encyclopedia of Bible Difficulties* (Grand Rapids, MI: Zondervan).

Archer, Gleason L. (1994), *A Survey of Old Testament Introduction* (Chicago, IL: Moody).

Armstrong, Karen (1996), *In the Beginning: A New Interpretation of Genesis* (New York: Ballantine).

Arndt, William and F.W. Gingrich (1957), *A Greek-English Lexicon of the New Testament and Other Early Christian Literature* (Chicago, IL: University of Chicago Press).

Asimov, Isaac and Duane T. Gish (1981), "The Genesis War," *Science Digest*, 89[9]:82-87, October. [Asimov affirmed evolution and denied creation; Gish affirmed creation and denied evolution.]

Ator, Joe T. (1988), "Astronomy," *Evolution and Faith*, ed. J.D. Thomas (Abilene, TX: ACU Press).

Baikie, James (1929), *A History of Egypt* (London: A&C Black).

Bales, James D. (no date), *Forty-Two Years on the Firing Line* (Shreveport, LA: Lambert).

Bales, James D. (1971), "The Theory of Evolution: A Philosophic Problem," *The Spiritual Sword*, 2[3]:1-4, April.

Bales, James D. (1974), "Theistic Evolution and Genesis," *Gospel Advocate*, 116[4]:52-54, January 24.

Bales, J.D. and R.T. Clark (1966), *Why Scientists Accept Evolution* (Grand Rapids, MI: Baker).

Barlow, Nora, ed. (1959), *The Autobiography of Charles Darwin 1809-1882 with Original Omissions Restored* (New York: Harcourt, Brace, and World).

Barnhouse, Donald G. (1960), "Adam and Modern Science," *Eternity*, 11[5]8.

Barnes, Albert (1972 reprint), *Barnes' Notes on the Old & New Testaments—Acts* (Grand Rapids, MI: Baker).

Barzun, Jacques (1958), *Darwin, Marx, Wagner* (New York: Doubleday).

Bass, Thomas (1990), "Interview with Richard Dawkins," *Omni*, 12[4]:57-60,84-89, January.

Baxter, Batsell Barrett (1971), *I Believe Because* (Grand Rapids, MI: Baker).

Beck, Stanley (1963), "Science and Understanding," *Dialog*, pp. 316-317.

Beechick, Ruth (1997), *Genesis: Finding Our Roots* (Pollock Pines, CA: Arrow Press).

Bennetta, William J. (1987), "Scientists Decry a Slick New Packaging of Creationism," *The Science Teacher*, pp. 36-43, May.

Berra, Tim M. (1990), *Evolution and the Myth of Creationism* (Stanford, CA: Stanford University Press).

Berry, R.J. (1975), *Adam and the Ape: A Christian Approach to the Theory of Evolution* (London: Falcon).

Bethell, Tom (1985), "Agnostic Evolutionists: The Taxonomic Case Against Darwin," *Harper's*, 270[1617]:49-52,56-58,60-61, February.

Birdsell, J.B. (1972), *Human Evolution* (Chicago, IL: Rand McNally).

Bishop, George (1998), "The Religious Worldview and American Beliefs about Human Origins," *The Public Perspective*, August/September, pp. 39-48.

Blackmore, Vernon and Andrews Page (1989), *Evolution—The Great Debate* (Oxford, England: Lion).

Bloomfield, S.T. (1837), *The Greek New Testament with English Notes* (Boston, MA: Perkins and Marvin).

Blum, Harold (1968), *Time's Arrow and Evolution* (Princeton, NJ: Princeton University Press).

Bonner, John Tyler (1961), "Review of *The Implications of Evolution*," *American Scientist*, 49:240, June. [See Kerkut (1960) for the publication data of the book Dr. Bonner was reviewing.]

Borland, James A. (1990), "Did People Live to be Hundreds of Years Old Before the Flood?" *The Genesis Debate*, ed. Ronald F. Youngblood (Grand Rapids, MI: Baker). [Borland answers in the affirmative.]

Brandfon, Fredric (1988), "Archaeology and the Biblical Text," *Biblical Archaeology Review*, 14[1]:54-59, January/February.

Brantley, Garry K. (1993a), "Dating in Archaeology: Challenges to Biblical Credibility," *Reason & Revelation*, 13:82-85, November.

Brantley, Garry K. (1993b), "Pagan Mythology and the Bible," *Reason & Revelation*, 13:49-53, July.

Brantley, Garry K. (1995), *Digging for Answers* (Montgomery, AL: Apologetics Press).

Breasted, James (1912), *History of Egypt* (New York: Charles Scribner's Sons).

Bromling, Brad T. (1994), "But Augustine Said...," *Reason & Revelation*, 14:53, July.

Brown, Francis, S.R. Driver, and Charles A. Briggs (1979), *The New Brown-Driver-Briggs-Gesenius Hebrew and English Lexicon* (Peabody, MA: Hendrickson).

Browne, Harold (1981 reprint), *The Bible Commentary*, ed. F.C. Cook (Grand Rapids, MI: Baker).

Bruce, F.F. (1972), *Answers to Questions* (Grand Rapids, MI: Zondervan).

Buffaloe, Neal (1969), "God or Evolution?," *Mission*, pp. 17,20,21, April.

Buffaloe, Neal and N. Patrick Murray (1981), *Creationism and Evolution* (Little Rock, AR: The Bookmark).

Bultmann, Rudolf (1969), *Primitive Christianity* (New York: World Publishing).

Buswell, James O. (1959), "A Creationist Interpretation of Prehistoric Man," *Evolution and Christian Thought Today*, ed. Russell L. Mixter (Grand Rapids, MI: Eerdmans).

Butt, Kyle (2000), "The Historical Christ—Fact or Fiction?," *Reason & Revelation*, 20:1-6, January.

Camp, Robert (1972), "Theistic Evolution," *A Critical Look at Evolution*, ed. Robert Camp (Atlanta, GA: Religion, Science, and Communication Research and Development Corporation).

Carnell, Edward John (1959), *The Case for Orthodox Theology* (Philadelphia, PA: Westminster).

Cassel, J. Frank (1960), "Species, Concepts, and Definitions," *Journal of the American Scientific Affiliation*, 12:2.

Cassel, J. Frank (1973), "Biology," *Christ and the Modern Mind*, ed. Robert W. Smith (Downers Grove, IL: InterVarsity Press).

Christensen, Duane L. (1990), "Did People Live to be Hundreds of Years Old Before the Flood?" *The Genesis Debate*, ed. Ronald F. Youngblood (Grand Rapids, MI: Baker). [Christensen answers in the negative.]

Clark, W. LeGros (1955), *The Fossil Evidence for Human Evolution* (Chicago, IL: University of Chicago Press).

Clarke, Adam (no date), *Clarke's Commentary* (New York: Abingdon-Cokesbury).

Clayton, John N. (no date-a), "Biblical Misconceptions and the Theory of Evolution," *Does God Exist? Correspondence Course*, Lesson 4 (South Bend, IN: Privately published by author).

Clayton, John N. (no date-b), "The History of Man on Planet Earth," *Does God Exist? Correspondence Course*, Lesson 8 (South Bend, IN: Privately published by author).

Clayton, John N. (no date-c), *Questions and Answers: Number One* (South Bend, IN: Privately published by author), [taped lecture].

Clayton, John N. (no date-d), *Evolution's Proof of God* (South Bend, IN: Privately published by author), [taped lecture].

Clayton, John N. (1976a), "'Flat Earth' Bible Study Techniques," *Does God Exist?*, 3[10]:2-7, October.

Clayton, John N. (1976b), *The Source* (South Bend, IN: Privately published by author).

Clayton, John N. (1977), "The 'Non-World View' of Genesis," *Does God Exist?*, 4[6]:6-8, June.

Clayton, John N. (1978a), "The Question of Methuselah," *Does God Exist?*, 5[6]:11-13, June.

Clayton, John N. (1978b), "The History of Man's Time Problem," *Does God Exist?*, 5[9]:6-10, September.

Clayton, John N. (1979a), "Letter to the Editor," *Rocky Mountain Christian*, 7[4]:3, March.

Clayton, John N. (1979b), "The Necessity of Creation—Biblically and Scientifically," *Does God Exist?*, 6[5]:2-5, May.

Clayton, John N. (1980a), "Is the Age of the Earth Related to a 'Literal Interpretation' of Genesis?," *Does God Exist?*, 7[1]:3-8, January.

Clayton, John N. (1980b), *A Response to "Evolutionary Creationism,"* (taped lecture).

Clayton, John N. (1982), "Where Are the Dinosaurs?," *Does God Exist?*, 9[10]:2-6, October.

Clayton, John N. (1987), Personal letter to Mike Christensen of Laramie, Wyoming, pp. 1-2.

Clayton, John N. (1989), "How Much Does Modernism Rob Us of Biblical Understanding?," *Does God Exist?*, 16[1]:4-7, January/February.

Clayton, John N. (1990a), "The History of the Earth," *Does God Exist? Correspondence Course*, Lesson 9 (South Bend, IN: Privately published by author).

Clayton, John N. (1990b), "How Did God Create Man?," *Does God Exist? Correspondence Course*, Lesson 7 (South Bend, IN: Privately published by author).

Clayton, John N. (1990c), "One Week Creation—Of Man or of God?," *Does God Exist?*, 17[4]:5-12, July/August.

Clayton, John N. (1990d), *The Source* (South Bend, IN: Privately published by author).

Clayton, John N. (1991), "Creation Versus Making—A Key to Genesis 1," *Does God Exist?*, 18[1]:6-10, January/February.

Clayton, John N. (1999), "Good Quote," *Does God Exist?*, 25[6]:no page number, September/October.

Coffman, Burton (1985), *Commentary on Genesis* (Abilene, TX: ACU Press).

Coppedge, James (1975), *Evolution: Possible or Impossible?* (Grand Rapids, MI: Zondervan).

Cremer, H. (1962), *Biblico-Theological Dictionary of New Testament Greek* (London: T. &T. Clark).

Crick, Francis (1981), *Life Itself* (New York: Simon & Schuster).

Criswell, W.A. (1972), *Did Man Just Happen?* (Grand Rapids, MI: Zondervan).

Culp, G. Richard (1975), *Remember Thy Creator* (Grand Rapids, MI: Baker).

Custance, Arthur (1967), *The Genealogies of the Bible*, Doorway Paper #24 (Ottawa, Canada: Doorway Papers).

Custance, Arthur (1970), *Without Form and Void* (Brockville, Canada: Doorway Papers).

Custance, Arthur C. (1976), *The Virgin Birth and the Incarnation* [Volume V of *The Doorway Papers*] (Grand Rapids, MI: Zondervan).

Darlington, P.D. (1980), *Evolution for Naturalists* (New York: John Wiley & Sons).

Darwin, Charles (1859), *The Origin of Species* (London: J.M. Dent & Sons), sixth edition.

Darwin, Charles (1958 reprint), *The Origin of Species* (New York: New American Library), Mentor edition.

Darwin, Charles (1870), *The Descent of Man* (New York: Modern Library). This is a two-volume edition in a single binding that also includes *The Origin of Species.*

Darwin, Francis, ed. (1888), *The Life and Letters of Charles Darwin* (London: Appleton).

Darwin, Francis, ed. (1898), *The Life and Letters of Charles Darwin* (London: Appleton).

Davidheiser, Bolton (1969), *Evolution and Christian Faith* (Grand Rapids, MI: Baker).

Davidheiser, Bolton (1973), "Theistic Evolution," *And God Created*, ed. Kelly L. Segraves (San Diego, CA: Creation-Science Research Center), 3:49-53.

Davies, Paul (1988), *The Cosmic Blueprint: New Discoveries in Nature's Creative Ability to Order the Universe* (New York: Simon & Schuster).

Davis, John J. (1968), *Biblical Numerology* (Grand Rapids, MI: Baker).

Davis, John J. (1975), *Paradise to Prison—Studies in Genesis* (Grand Rapids, MI: Baker).

Davis, John J. (1985), *Evangelical Ethics* (Phillipsburg, NJ: Presbyterian and Reformed).

Dawkins, Richard (1982), "The Necessity of Darwinism," *New Scientist*, 94:130-132, April 15.

Dawkins, Richard (1986), *The Blind Watchmaker* (New York: W.W. Norton).

Dawkins, Richard (1989), "Book Review" (of Donald Johanson & Maitland Edey's *Blueprint*), *The New York Times*, section 7, April 9.

DeHoff, George (1944), *Why We Believe the Bible* (Murfreesboro, TN: DeHoff Publications).

Denton, Michael (1985), *Evolution: A Theory in Crisis* (London: Burnett Books).

Denton, Michael (1998), *Nature's Destiny: How the Laws of Biology Reveal Purpose in the Universe* (New York: Simon & Schuster).

Diamond, Jared (1992), *The Third Chimpanzee* (New York: HarperCollins).

Dillow Joseph (1981), *The Waters Above* (Chicago, IL: Moody).

Dobzhansky, Theodosius (1956), *The Biological Basis of Human Freedom* (New York: Columbia University Press).

Dobzhansky, Theodosius (1967), "Changing Man," *Science*, 55:409.

Dobzhansky, Theodosius (1975), "Darwin or 'Oriented' Evolution?," *Evolution*, 29:376.

Dods, Marcus (1948), "Genesis," *The Expositor's Bible*, ed. W.R. Nicoll (Grand Rapids, MI: Eerdmans).

Douglas, J.D., ed. (1974), *The New Bible Dictionary* (Grand Rapids, MI: Eerdmans).

Ehrlich, Paul and L.C. Birch (1967), "Evolutionary History and Population Biology," *Nature*, 214:352.

Eiseley, Loren (1961), *Darwin's Century* (Garden City, NY: Anchor Books).

Eldredge, Niles (1982), *The Monkey Business* (New York: Pocket Books).

Eldredge, Niles (2000), *The Triumph of Evolution and the Failure of Creationism* (New York: W.H. Freeman).

England, Donald (1972), *A Christian View of Origins* (Grand Rapids, MI: Baker).

England, Donald (1982), Letter to Dr. Clifton L. Ganus, President, Harding University, Searcy, Arkansas.

England, Donald (1983), *A Scientist Examines Faith and Evidence* (Delight, AR: Gospel Light).

Erickson, Millard J. (1992), *Does It Matter What I Believe?* (Grand Rapids, MI: Baker).

Eve, Raymond A. and Francis B. Harrold (1991), *The Creationist Movement in Modern America* (Boston, MA: G.K. Hall).

Evolution (n.d.), (Ontario, Canada: International Christian Crusade).

Ex Nihilo (1984), "Update," 6[4]:46, May.

Fair, Ian (1988), "Origins and the Bible," *Evolution and Faith*, ed. J.D. Thomas (Abilene, TX: ACU Press).

Felix, Charles (1988), "Geology and Paleontology," *Evolution and Faith*, ed. J.D. Thomas (Abilene, TX: ACU Press).

Ferris, Timothy (1997), *The Whole Shebang: A State of the Universe(s) Report* (New York: Simon & Schuster).

Fields, Weston W. (1976), *Unformed and Unfilled* (Grand Rapids, MI: Baker).

Filby, Frederick A. (1970), *The Flood Reconsidered* (Grand Rapids, MI: Zondervan).

Fletcher, Joseph (1979), *Humanhood: Essays in Biomedical Ethics* (Buffalo, NY: Prometheus).

Fortey, Richard (1997), *Life: A Natural History of the First Four Billion Years of Life on Earth* (New York: Knopf).

Fox, Sidney and Klaus Dose (1977), *Molecular Evolution and the Origin of Life* (New York: Marcel Dekker).

Francella, Kevin (1981), "Former Atheist Says Bible and Evolutionism Are Compatible," *The Sunday Press*, Binghamton, New York, May 17.

Futuyma, Douglas J. (1983), *Science on Trial: The Case for Evolution* (New York: Pantheon).

Futuyma, Douglas J. (1987), "World Without Design," *Natural History*, 96[3]:34,36, March.

Gabel, John B., Charles B. Wheeler, and Anthony D. York (1996), *The Bible As Literature* (New York: Oxford University Press).

Gardner, Martin (1988), *The New Age: Notes of a Fringe Watcher* (Buffalo, NY: Prometheus).

Geisler, Norman L. and J. Kerby Anderson (1987), *Origin Science* (Grand Rapids, MI: Baker).

Geisler, Norman L. and Ronald M. Brooks (1990), *When Skeptics Ask* (Wheaton, IL: Victor).

Gilman, O.M. (1971), *The Evolutionary Outlook: 1875-1900* (Clio, MI: Marston).

Gilmore, Ralph (1987), "Theistic Evolution," *Grace Abounding*, ed. Winford Claiborne (Henderson, TN: Freed-Hardeman University).

Gipson, Mike (1999), "Letter to the Editor," *The Daily Oklahoman*, November 24, p. A-8.

Gish, Duane T. and Isaac Asimov (1981), "The Genesis War," *Science Digest*, 89[9]:82-87, October. [Gish affirmed creation and denied evolution; Asimov affirmed evolution and denied creation.]

Glanz, James (2000), "Survey Finds Support is Strong for Teaching 2 Origin Theories," *The New York Times*, p. A-1, March 11.

Glass, Bentley (1971), "Science: Endless Horizons or Golden Age?," *Science*, 171:23-29.

Godfrey, Laurie, ed. (1983), *Scientists Confront Creationism* (New York: W.W. Norton).

Gould, Stephen J. (1987), "Darwinism Defined: The Difference Between Fact and Theory," *Discover*, 8[1]:64-65,68-70, January.

Gould, Stephen J., ed. (1993), *The Book of Life* (New York: W.W. Norton).

Gould, Stephen Jay (1999), "Dorothy, It's Really Oz," *Time*, 154[8]: 59, August 23.

Grassé, Pierre-Paul (1977), *The Evolution of Living Organisms* (New York: Academic Press).

Green, William H. (1890), "Primeval Chronology," *Bibliotheca Sacra*, 47:294-295.

Green, William H. (1979 reprint), *The Unity of the Book of Genesis* (Grand Rapids, MI: Baker).

Greenstein, George (1988), *The Symbiotic Universe* (New York: William Morrow).

Gribbin, John (1981), "The Universe of a Comet Born," *Science Digest*, 89[3]:14, April.

Hall, Marshall and Sandra Hall (1974), *The Truth: God or Evolution?* (Grand Rapids, MI: Baker).

Ham, Ken (1987), *The Lie: Evolution* (El Cajon, CA: Master Books).

Ham, Ken (2000), *Did Adam Have a Bellybutton?* (Green Forest, AR: Master Books).

Hanson, Robert W. (1986), *Science and Creation* (New York: Macmillan).

Harris, R.L., G.L. Archer Jr., and B.K. Waltke, eds. (1980), *Theological Wordbook of the Old Testament* (Chicago, IL: Moody).

Harrold, Francis B. and Raymond A. Eve (1987), *Cult Archaeology and Creationism* (Iowa City, IA: University of Iowa Press).

Hartshorne, M.H. (1958), *The Promise of Science and the Power of Faith* (Philadelphia, PA: Westminster).

Harvey, Van A. (1966), *The Historian and the Believer* (New York: Macmillan).

Hauret, Charles (1955), *Beginnings: Genesis and Modern Science* (Dubuque, IA: Priority Press).

Hayward, Alan (1985), *Creation and Evolution: The Facts and the Fallacies* (London: Triangle Books).

Hearn, Walter (1961), *Journal of the American Scientific Affiliation*, p. 42, June.

Hedegard, David (1964), *Ecumenism and the Bible* (London: The Banner of Truth Trust).

Hefley, James C. (1965), "Let's Be Honest About Evolution," *Eternity*, p. 21, October.

Henkel, Malcolm (1950), "Fundamental Christianity and Evolution," *Modern Science and the Christian Faith*, ed. F. Alton Everest (Wheaton, IL: Van Kampen Press).

Henry, Matthew (no date), *Matthew Henry's Commentary on the Whole Bible* (McLean, VA: MacDonald).

Hick, John (1985), "A Liberal Christian View," *Free Inquiry*, 5[4]:40.

Himmelfarb, Gertrude (1959), *Darwin and the Darwinian Revolution* (London: Chatto and Windus).

Hoehner, Harold W. (1969), "The Duration of the Egyptian Bondage" *Bibliotheca Sacra*, 126:306-316.

Hoover, Arlie J. (1992), "God and the Big Bang," *Gospel Advocate*, 134[9]:34-35, September.

Horne, Thomas H. (1970 reprint), *An Introduction to the Critical Study and Knowledge of the Holy Scriptures* (Grand Rapids, MI: Baker).

Howard, Ted and Jeremy Rifkin (1977), *Who Should Play God?* (New York: Dell).

Howe, George (1964), *Creation Research Society Annual* (Ann Arbor, MI: Creation Research Society).

Howells, W.W. (1944), *Mankind So Far* (New York: Doubleday).

Hoyle, Fred (1981a), "The Big Bang in Astronomy," *New Scientist*, 92:521-527, November 19.

Hoyle, Fred (1981b), "Hoyle on Evolution," *Nature*, 294:105,148, November 12.

Hoyle, Fred (1982), "The Universe: Past and Present Reflections," *Annual Review of Astronomy and Astrophysics*, 20:16.

Hoyle, Fred and Chandra Wickramasinghe (1981), *Evolution from Space* (New York: Simon & Schuster).

Hoyle, Fred and Chandra Wickramasinghe (1991), "Where Microbes Boldly Went," *New Scientist*, 91:412-415, August 13.

Hughes, Norman (1984a), "Monism, Belief, and Scientific Explanations," *Does God Exist?*, 11[5]:12-18, September/October.

Hughes, Norman (1984b), Personal letter to Wayne Jackson, November 23, p. 1.

Hughes, Norman (1986), "Letter to the Editor," *Journal of the American Scientific Affiliation*, 38[4]:282, December.

Hull, David (1991), "The God of the Galapagos," *Nature*, 352:486, August 8. [Dr. Hull, of the philosophy department at Northwestern University, was reviewing Philip Johnson's 1991 book, *Darwin on Trial* (Washington, D.C.: Regnery Gateway).]

The Humanist (1977), "A Statement Affirming Evolution as a Principle of Science," 37:4-5, January/February.

Humanist Manifestos I & II (1973), (Buffalo, NY: Prometheus).

Humphreys, D. Russell (1994), *Starlight and Time* (Green Forest, AR: Master Books).

Huxley, Aldous (1966), "Confessions of a Professed Atheist," *Report: Perspective on the News*, 3:19, June.

Huxley, Julian (1946), *Rationalist Annual*; cf. L.M. Davies (1947), "The Present State of Teleology," *Transactions of the Victoria Institute* (London: Victoria Institute), 79:70.

Huxley, Julian (1960a), *Time*, p. 45, August 1.

Huxley, Julian (1960b), "The Emergence of Darwinism," *The Evolution of Life* [Volume 1 of *Evolution After Darwin*], ed. Sol Tax (Chicago, IL: University of Chicago Press).

Huxley, Julian (1960c), "The Evolutionary Vision," *Issues in Evolution* [Volume 3 of *Evolution After Darwin*], ed. Sol Tax (Chicago, IL: University of Chicago Press).

Huxley, Julian (1960d), " 'At Random': A Television Preview," *Issues in Evolution*, [Volume 3 of *Evolution After Darwin*], ed. Sol Tax (Chicago, IL: University of Chicago Press).

Irenaeus, (n.d.), *Against Heresies*, 2.X.4.

Jackson, Wayne (no date), *Evolution and Science* (Stockton, CA: Courier Publications), a tract.

Jackson, Wayne (1974), *Fortify Your Faith in an Age of Doubt* (Stockton, CA: Courier Publications).

Jackson, Wayne (1976), "Biblical Geneologies and Human History," *Christian Courier*, 11:42-43, March.

Jackson, Wayne (1978a), "The Age of Methuselah," *Christian Courier*, 14:14-16, August.

Jackson, Wayne (1978b), "The Antiquity of Human History," *Words of Truth*, 14[18]:1, April 14.

Jackson, Wayne (1981), "The Chronology of the Old Testament in the Light of Archaeology," *Reason & Revelation*, 1:37-39, October.

Jackson, Wayne (1983), "Bible Contradictions—Are They Real?," *Reason & Revelation*, 3:25-28, June.

Jackson, Wayne (1984), "A Pepperdine Professor and Evolution," *Christian Courier*, 20:29-31, December.

Jackson, Wayne (1987), "Does the Genesis Account of Creation Allow for Theistic Evolution?," *Questions Men Ask about God*, ed. Eddie Whitten (Bedford, TX: Christian Supply Center), pp. 125-133.

Jackson, Wayne (1989), *Creation, Evolution, and the Age of the Earth* (Stockton, CA: Courier Publications).

Jackson, Wayne (1990a), "Destructive Criticism and the Old Testament," *Essays in Apologetics*, ed. Bert Thompson and Wayne Jackson (Montgomery, AL: Apologetics Press), 4:1-6.

Jackson, Wayne (1990b), "The Saga of Ancient Jericho," *Reason & Revelation*, 10:17-19, April.

Jackson, Wayne (1990c), "When the Creation is Delivered," *Christian Courier*, 26:25, November.

Jackson, Wayne (1993), "Is the 'Big Bang' Theory Biblical?," *Christian Courier*, 28:41-43, March.

Jackson, Wayne and Brad Bromling (no date), *Alleged Discrepancies— The Skeptics' Impotent Axe* (Montgomery, AL: Apologetics Press), a monograph.

Jackson, Wayne and Bert Thompson (1979), *Evolutionary Creationism: A Review of the Teachings of John N. Clayton* (Montgomery, AL: Apologetics Press).

Jackson, Wayne and Bert Thompson (1992), *In the Shadow of Darwin: A Review of the Teachings of John N. Clayton* (Montgomery, AL: Apologetics Press).

Jacobus, Melancthon (1864), *Notes on Genesis* (Philadelphia, PA: Presbyterian Board of Publication).

Jamieson, Robert, et al. (1945), *Jamieson, Faucett, Brown Bible Commentary* (Grand Rapids, MI: Eerdmans).

Jastrow, Robert (1977), *Until the Sun Dies* (New York: W.W. Norton).

Jauncey, James H. (1961), *Science Returns to God* (Grand Rapids, MI: Zondervan).

Johanson, Donald C., Lenora Johanson, and Blake Edgar (1994), *Ancestors* (New York: Villard).

Johnson, Phillip E. (1991), *Darwin on Trial* (Downers Grove, IL: InterVarsity Press).

Johnston, Howard Agnew (1902), *Bible Criticism and the Average Man* (New York: Revell).

Jordan, James (1979/1980), "The Biblical Chronology Question," *Creation Social Sciences and Humanities Quarterly*, 2[2]:9-15, Winter 1979; 2[3]:17-26, Spring 1980.

Kantzer, Kenneth (1982), "Guideposts for the Current Debate over Origins," *Christianity Today*, pp. 23-25, October 8.

Kautz, Darrel (1988), *The Origin of Living Things* (Milwaukee, WI: Privately published by author).

Keen, William W. (1923), *I Believe in God and in Evolution* (Philadelphia, PA: Lippincott).

Keil, C.F. (1971 reprint), *The Pentateuch* (Grand Rapids, MI: Eerdmans).

Keil, C.F. and F. Delitzsch (1974 reprint), *Commentary on the Old Testament* (Grand Rapids, MI: Eerdmans).

Keith, Arthur (1932), *The Human Body* (London: Butterworth).

Keosian, J. (1968), *The Origin of Life* (New York: Reinhold).

Kerkut, George A. (1960), *The Implications of Evolution* (London: Pergamon).

Kitchen, Kenneth A. (1966), *Ancient Orient and Old Testament* (London: Tyndale).

Kitchen, Kenneth A. and J.D. Douglas, eds. (1982), *The New Bible Dictionary* (Wheaton, IL: Tyndale), second edition.

Kitcher, Phillip (1982), *Abusing Science: The Case Against Creationism* (Cambridge, MA: MIT Press).

Klingman, George (1929), *God Is* (Cincinnati, OH: F.L. Rowe).

Klotz, John (1955), *Genes, Genesis, and Evolution* (St. Louis, MO: Concordia).

Koch, Leo (1957), "Vitalistic-Mechanistic Controversy," *Scientific Monthly*, p. 250.

Krause, Hans (1978), *The Mammoth—In Ice and Snow?* (Stuttgart, Germany: Im Selbstverlag).

Larison, Lorraine L. (1977), *The Center of Life*, excerpts as quoted in *Science Digest*, 82:46, November.

Laughlin, John (1992), "How to Date a Cooking Pot," *Biblical Archaeology Review*, 18[5]:72-74, September/October.

Leakey, Richard and Roger Lewin (1977), *Origins* (New York: E.P. Dutton).

Lenski, R.C.H. (1966a), *The Interpretation of the Epistle to the Hebrews and of the Epistle of James* (Minneapolis, MN: Augsburg).

Lenski, R.C.H. (1966b), *The Interpretation of the Epistles of Peter, St. John, and St. Jude* (Minneapolis, MN: Augsburg).

Leupold, H.C. (1942 reprint), *Exposition of Genesis* (Grand Rapids, MI: Baker).

Lever, Jan (1958), *Creation and Evolution* (Grand Rapids, MI: Grand Rapids International Publications).

Lewis, Jack P. (1978), "From the Beginning It Was Not So...," *Your Marriage Can Be Great*, ed. Thomas B. Warren (Jonesboro, AR: National Christian Press).

Lewontin, Richard (1997), "Billions and Billions of Demons," *The New York Review*, p. 31, January 9.

Lightfoot, Neil R. (1988), "The Week of Creation," *Evolution and Faith*, ed. J.D. Thomas (Abilene, TX: ACU Press).

Lindsell, Harold (1977), *Christianity Today*, pp. 17-18, June.

Lipson, H.S. (1980), "A Physicist Looks at Evolution," *Physics Bulletin*, p. 138, May.

Lloyd, James E. (1982), *Florida Entomologist*, 65:1.

Lloyd-Jones, D. Martin (1953), *From Fear to Faith* (London: InterVarsity Press).

Løvtrup, Søren (1987), *Darwinism: The Refutation of a Myth* (London: Croom and Helm).

Lygre, David (1979), *Life Manipulation* (New York: Walker).

Macbeth, Norman (1971), *Darwin Retried* (New York: Gambit).

Macbeth, Norman (1982), "Darwinism: A Time for Funerals," *Towards*, 2:22, Spring.

MacKnight, James (1960 reprint), *Apostolical Epistles* (Nashville, TN: Gospel Advocate).

Maddox, John (1994), "The Genesis Code by Numbers," *Nature*, 367: 111, January 13.

Major, Trevor J. (1987), "Questions and Answers," *Reason & Revelation*, 7:5-7, February.

Major, Trevor J. (1989), "Which Came First-The Chicken or the Egg?," *Bible-Science Newsletter*, 27[10]:16, October.

Major, Trevor (1990), "Was There Death Before Adam?," *Reasoning from Revelation*, 2[7]:1-2, July.

Major, Trevor J. (1991), "In the News—National Beliefs Polled," *Reason & Revelation*, 11:48, December.

Major, Trevor J. (1993), "Dating in Archaeology: Radiocarbon and Tree-Ring Dating," *Reason & Revelation*, 13:74-77, October.

Major, Trevor J. (1994a), "Is Creation Science?," *Reason & Revelation*, 14:17-23, March.

Major, Trevor J. (1994b), "What Do Evolutionists Think About Theistic Evolution?," *Reason & Revelation*, 14:55, July.

Major, Trevor J. (1996), *Genesis and the Origin of Coal and Oil* (Montgomery, AL: Apologetics Press).

Mammel, Lewis and Henry M. Morris (1986), *Debate on the Age of the Earth* (two audio tapes).

Marsh, Frank Lewis (1967), *Life, Man, and Time* (Escondido, CA: Outdoor Pictures).

Marsh, Frank Lewis (1978), "On Creation with an Appearance of Age," *Creation Research Society Quarterly*, 14[4]:187-188, March.

Marx, Paul (1975), *Death Without Dignity* (Collegeville, MN: Liturgical Press).

Mather, Kirtley F. (1960), *Science Ponders Religion*, ed. Harlow Shapley (New York: Appleton-Century-Croft).

Mattell, A.J. Jr., (1982), "Three Cheers for the Creationists," *Free Inquiry*, Spring.

Mauro, Philip (no date), *The Wonders of Bible Chronology* (Swengel, PA: Reiner).

McClish, Dub, ed. (1983), *Studies in Hebrews* (Denton, TX: Pearl Street Church of Christ).

McCormick, Richard (1974), "To Save or Let Die—The Dilemma of Modern Medicine," *Journal of the American Medical Association*, 229: 172-176.

McCord, Hugo (1968), "College Freshmen and Evolution," *Firm Foundation*, pp. 771,777, December 3.

McDowell, Josh (1999), *The New Evidence that Demands a Verdict* (Nashville, TN: Thomas Nelson).

McIver, Tom (1988a), *Anti-Evolution Bibliography* (Jefferson, NC: McFarland).

McIver, Tom (1988b), "Formless and Void: Gap Theory Creationism," *Creation/Evolution*, 8[3]:1-24, Fall.

McKenzie, John L. (1959), "Myth and the Old Testament," *The Catholic Biblical Quarterly*, 21:281.

McKown, Delos B. (1985), *With Faith and Fury* (Buffalo, NY: Prometheus).

McKown, Delos B. (1993), *The Myth-Maker's Magic—Behind the Illusion of "Creation Science"* (Buffalo, NY: Prometheus).

Merrill, E.H., (1978), *An Historical Survey of the Old Testament* (Phillipsburg, NJ: Presbyterian and Reformed).

Miller, David L. (1987), "Anatomy of a False Teacher," *The Restorer*, 7[2]:2-3, February.

Milligan, Robert (1972 reprint), *The Scheme of Redemption* (Nashville, TN: Gospel Advocate).

Millikan, Robert (1925), quoted in *The Nashville Banner*, August 7.

Mixter, Russell L. (1961), "Man in Creation," *Christian Life*, October, p. 25.

Montagu, Ashley, ed. (1984), *Science and Creationism* (New York: Oxford University Press).

Moody, Paul A. (1962), *Introduction to Evolution* (New York: Harper & Row).

Moody, Paul A. (1970), *Introduction to Evolution* (New York: Harper & Row), second edition.

Moore, David W. (1999), "Americans Support Teaching Creationism as Well as Evolution in Public Schools," [On-line], URL http://www.gallup.com/poll/releases/pr990830.asp (Princeton, NJ: Gallup News Service).

Moore, John N. and Harold Slusher (1974), *Biology: A Search for Order in Complexity* (Grand Rapids, MI: Zondervan).

Morris, Henry M. (1963), *The Twilight of Evolution* (Grand Rapids, MI: Baker).

Morris, Henry M. (1966), *Studies in the Bible and Science* (Grand Rapids, MI: Baker).

Morris, Henry M. (1973), "The Day-Age Theory," *And God Created*, ed. Kelly L. Segraves (San Diego, CA: Creation-Science Research Center).

Morris, Henry M. (1974a), *Scientific Creationism* (San Diego, CA: Creation-Life Publishers).

Morris, Henry M. (1974b), *The Troubled Waters of Evolution* (San Diego, CA: Creation-Life Publishers).

Morris, Henry M. (1976), *The Genesis Record* (Grand Rapids, MI: Baker).

Morris, Henry M. (1980), *King of Creation* (San Diego, CA: Creation-Life Publishers).

Morris, Henry M. (1984), *The Biblical Basis for Modern Science* (Grand Rapids, MI: Baker).

Morris, Henry M. (1989), *The Long War Against God* (Grand Rapids, MI: Baker).

Morris, Henry M. and Gary E. Parker (1987), *What Is Creation Science?* (San Diego, CA: Master Books), second edition.

Morris, John D. (1992), "Do Americans Believe in Creation?," *Acts and Facts*, p. d, February.

Morris, John D. (1994), *The Young Earth* (Green Forest, AR: Master Books).

Morris, Leon (1960), *The Epistle to the Hebrews* (Grand Rapids, MI: Eerdmans).

Muller, Hermann J. (1966), as quoted in *Arkansas Gazette*, p. 2, June 28.

Nelkin, Dorothy (1977), *Science Textbook Controversies and the Politics of Equal Time* (Cambridge, MA: MIT Press).

Newell, Norman D. (1985), *Creation and Evolution: Myth or Reality?* (New York: Praeger).

Newport, Frank (1993), "God Created Humankind, Most Believe," *Sunday Oklahoman*, A-22.

Nichols, Gus (1972), "The Scheme of Redemption," *The Bible Versus Liberalism*, ed. Thomas B. Warren (Henderson, TN: Freed-Hardeman University).

Niessen, Richard (1980), "Significant Discrepancies Between Theistic Evolution and the Bible," *UFO's, Satan, and Evolution*, ed. Sidney J. Jansma Sr. (privately published by editor).

Nordsiek, Frederic W. (1960), "How Your Bones Tell Your Age," *Science Digest*, 47[5]:17-18, May.

Norman, Trevor and Barry Setterfield (1987), *The Atomic Constants, Light, and Time* [Technical Report] (Menlo Park, CA: Stanford Research Institute International).

Numbers, Ronald L. (1992), *The Creationists: The Evolution of Scientific Creationism* (New York: Alfred A. Knopf).

O'Keefe, John (1995), as quoted in *Show Me God*, ed. Fred Heeren (Wheeling, IL: Searchlight Publications).

Oparin, A.I. (1961), *Life: Its Nature, Origin and Development* (Edinburgh: Oliver and Boyd).

Orgel, Leslie E. (1994), "The Origin of Life on Earth," *Scientific American*, 271:77-83, October.

Osborn, Henry Fairfield (1918), *The Origin and Evolution of Life* (New York: Charles Scribner's Sons).

Overton, Basil (1973), *Evolution or Creation?* (Nashville, TN: Gospel Advocate).

Overton, Basil (1981), *Evolution in the Light of Scripture, Science, and Sense* (Winona, MS: Choate).

Packer, J.I., Merrill C. Tenney, and William White Jr. (1980), *The Bible Almanac* (Nashville, TN: Nelson).

Patterson, Colin (1981), Speech given in November at American Museum of Natural History in New York City. Quotations are from audio tape transcript. See Bethell (1985) for a report on Dr. Patterson's speech.

Patterson, Colin (1982), "Cladistics," Interview on British Broadcasting Corporation, March 4; Peter Franz, interviewer; Brian Lak, producer.

Pearson, A.T. (1953), "An Exegetical Study of Genesis 1:1-3," *Bethel Seminary Quarterly*, 11:22, November.

Pember, George H. (1876), *Earth's Earliest Ages* (New York: Revell).

Penzias Arno, (1992), as quoted in *Cosmos, Bios, and Theos*, ed. Henry Margenau and Abraham Varghese (La Salle, IL: Open Court Publishers).

Pieters, Albertus (1947), *Notes on Genesis* (Grand Rapids, MI: Eerdmans).

Pilgrim, James (1976), "Day Seven," *Gospel Advocate*, 118[33]:522, August 12.

Pitman, Michael (1984), *Adam and Evolution* (London: Rider).

Poole, Michael (1990), *A Guide to Science and Belief* (Oxford, England: Lion).

Press, Frank (1984), "Preface," *Science and Creationism: A View from the National Academy of Sciences* (Washington, D.C.: National Academy of Sciences).

Provine, William (no date), "Evolution and the Foundation of Ethics," *MBL* [Marine Biological Laboratory] *Science*, 3[1]. [A shorter version of this paper appeared as a guest editorial in the September 5, 1988 issue of *The Scientist*.]

Pun, Pattle P.T. (1987), "A Theory of Progressive Creationism," *Journal of the American Scientific Affiliation*, 39:14, March.

Ramm, Bernard (1954), *The Christian View of Science and Scripture* (Grand Rapids, MI: Eerdmans).

Rehwinkle, Alfred (1974), *The Wonders of Creation* (Grand Rapids, MI: Baker).

Rendle-Short, John (1984), *Man: Ape or Image—The Christian's Dilemma* (San Diego, CA: Master Books).

Ricci, Paul (1986), *Fundamentals of Critical Thinking* (Lexington, MA: Ginn Press).

Ridderbos, N.H. (1957), *Is There a Conflict Between Genesis 1 and Natural Science?* (Grand Rapids, MI: Eerdmans).

Riegle, D.D. (1962), *Creation or Evolution?* (Grand Rapids, MI: Zondervan).

Rimmer, Harry (1937), *Modern Science and the Genesis Record* (Grand Rapids, MI: Eerdmans).

Rohl, David M. (1995), *Pharaohs and Kings: A Biblical Quest* (New York: Crown).

Ross, Hugh (1991), *The Fingerprint of God* (Orange, CA: Promise Publishing).

Ross, Hugh (1994), *Creation and Time* (Colorado Springs, CO: Navpress).

Rusch, Wilbert H. (1991), *Origins: What is at Stake?* (Kansas City, MO: Creation Research Society Books).

Ruse, Michael (1979), *The Darwinian Revolution* (Chicago, IL: University of Chicago Press).

Russell, Bertrand (1961), *Religion and Science* (London: Oxford University Press).

Russell, Bertrand (1969), *Autobiography* (New York: Simon & Schuster).

Sadler, Michael E. (1988), "Physics," *Evolution and Faith*, ed. J.D. Thomas (Abilene, TX: ACU Press).

Sagan, Carl (1980), *Cosmos* (New York: Random House).

Sagan, Carl (1997), *Billions and Billions* (New York: Random House).

Sagan, Carl and Ann Druyan (1990), "The Question of Abortion," *Parade*, April 22.

Sailhamer, John (1990), *The Expositor's Bible Commentary*, ed. Frank Gaebelein (Grand Rapids, MI: Zondervan).

Sartre, Jean Paul (1961), "Existentialism and Humanism," *French Philosophers from Descartes to Sartre*, ed. Leonard M. Marsak (New York: Meridian).

Sartre, Jean Paul (1966), "Existentialism," Reprinted in *A Casebook on Existentialism*, ed. William V. Spanos (New York: Thomas Y. Crowell Co.).

Scholander, P.F. (1953), "Body Insulation of Some Arctic and Tropical Mammals and Birds," *Biological Bulletin 99*.

Schroeder, Gerald L. (1990), *Genesis and the Big Bang* (New York: Bantam).

Schroeder, Gerald L. (1997), *The Science of God* (New York: Free Press).

Schwartz, Jeffrey H. (1999), *Sudden Origins* (New York: John Wiley & Sons).

Science and Creationism: A View from the National Academy of Sciences (1984), (Washington, D.C.: National Academy of Sciences).

Scofield, Cyrus I., ed. (1917), *Scofield Reference Bible* (New York: Oxford University Press).

Sears, Jack Wood (1969), *Conflict and Harmony in Science and the Bible* (Grand Rapids, MI: Baker).

Segraves, Kelly L. (1973), *Jesus Christ Creator* (San Diego, CA: Creation-Science Research Center).

Sheler, Jeffery L. (1999), *Is the Bible True?* (San Francisco, CA: HarperCollins).

Simpson, George Gaylord (1953), *Life of the Past* (New Haven, CT: Yale University Press).

Simpson, George Gaylord (1960), "The World into Which Darwin Led Us," *Science*, 131:966-969, April 1.

Simpson, George Gaylord (1964), *This View of Life* (New York: Harcourt and Brace).

Simpson, George Gaylord (1967), *The Meaning of Evolution* (New Haven, CT: Yale University Press), second edition.

Simpson, George Gaylord, C.S. Pittendrigh, and L.H. Tiffany (1957), *Life: An Introduction to Biology* (New York: Harcourt, Brace, and World).

Simpson, George Gaylord and W.S. Beck (1965), *Life: An Introduction to Biology* (New York: Harcourt, Brace and World), second edition.

Smith, Huston (1982), "Evolution and Evolutionism," *Christian Century*, p. 755, July 7-14.

Smith, Wilbur M. (1945), *Therefore Stand!* (Grand Rapids, MI: Baker).

Speiser, E.A. (1964), "Genesis," *The Anchor Bible Commentary* (New York: Doubleday).

Stone, Nathan (1944), *Names of God* (Chicago, IL: Moody).

Strahler, Arthur N. (1999), *Science and Earth History: The Evolution/Creation Controversy* (Buffalo, NY: Prometheus), second edition.

Sunderland, Luther (1984), *Darwin's Enigma* (San Diego, CA: Master Books).

Surburg, Raymond (1959), "In the Beginning God Created," *Darwin, Evolution, and Creation*, ed. P.A. Zimmerman (St. Louis, MO: Concordia).

Surburg, Raymond (1969), *Bible-Science Newsletter*, p. 2, April 15.

Taylor, Ian (1984), *In the Minds of Men* (Toronto: TFE Publishing).

Taylor, Kenneth (1974), *Evolution and the High School Student* (Wheaton, IL: Tyndale).

Taylor, Robert (1974), "More Problems for Theistic Evolutionists," *Gospel Advocate*, 116[1]2,6-7, January 3.

Teller, Woolsey and James D. Bales (1976), *The Existence of God—A Debate* (Shreveport, LA: Lambert).

Thayer, J.H. (1962), *Greek-English Lexicon of the New Testament* (Grand Rapids, MI: Zondervan).

Thaxton, Charles B., Walter L. Bradley, and Roger L. Olsen (1984), *The Mystery of Life's Origin* (New York: Philosophical Library).

Thiele, Edwin (1963), "Chronology, Old Testament," *Zondervan Pictorial Bible Dictionary*, ed. Merrill C. Tenney (Grand Rapids, MI: Zondervan).

Thiele, Edwin (1977), *A Chronology of the Hebrew Kings* (Grand Rapids, MI: Zondervan).

Thielicke, Helmut (1961), *How the World Began* (Philadelphia, PA: Muhlenberg Press).

Thomas, J.D. (1961), *Evolution and Antiquity* (Abilene, TX: Biblical Research Press).

Thomas, J.D. (1965), *Facts and Faith* (Abilene, TX: Biblical Research Press).

Thomas, J.D., ed. (1988), *Evolution and Faith* (Abilene, TX: ACU Press).

Thompson, Bert (1977), *Theistic Evolution* (Shreveport, LA: Lambert).

Thompson, Bert (1981), "We Told You Where Belief in Evolution Would Lead—Now See for Yourself," *Sound Doctrine*, 6[2]:11-12, April-June.

Thompson, Bert (1982), "The Day-Age Theory: Another False Compromise of the Genesis Account of Creation," *Reason & Revelation*, 2:29-32, July.

Thompson, Bert (1986), *Is Genesis Myth?* (Montgomery, AL: Apologetics Press).

Thompson, Bert (1994), "Faith and Knowledge," *Reason & Revelation*, 14:25-27,29-31, April.

Thompson, Bert (1999a), "The Bible and the Age of the Earth [Part III]," *Reason & Revelation*, 19:67-70, September.

Thompson, Bert (1999b), *The Bible and the Age of the Earth,* (Montgomery, AL: Apologetics Press).

Thompson, Bert (1999c), *My Sovereign, My Sin, My Salvation* (Montgomery, AL: Apologetics Press).

Thompson, Bert (1999d), *Satan—His Origin and Mission* (Montgomery, AL: Apologetics Press).

Thompson, Bert (1999e), *The Scientific Case for Creation* (Montgomery, AL: Apologetics Press).

Thompson, Bert (2000a), *The Origin, Nature, and Destiny of the Soul* (Montgomery, AL: Apologetics Press).

Thompson, Bert (2000b), *Rock-Solid Faith: How to Build It* (Montgomery, AL: Apologetics Press).

Thompson, Bert (2000c), *Rock-Solid Faith: How to Sustain It* (Montgomery, AL: Apologetics Press).

Thompson, Keith S. (1982), "The Meanings of Evolution," *American Scientist*, September/October.

Thompson, W.R. (1956), "Introduction," *The Origin of Species* (New York: E.P. Dutton & Sons), pp. vii-xxv.

Thurman, Clem (1986), "The Genesis 'Day' and Age of Earth," *Gospel Minutes*, 35[14]:2-3, April 4.

Tiffin, Lee (1994), *Creationism's Upside-Down Pyramid: How Science Refutes Fundamentalism* (Buffalo, NY: Prometheus).

Tipler, Frank (1994), *The Physics of Immortality* (New York: Doubleday).

Trench, R.C. (1890), *Synonyms of the New Testament* (London: Kegan, Purl, Trench, Trubner & Co.).

Turner, Rex A. Sr. (1980), *Systematic Theology* (Montgomery, AL: Alabama Christian School of Religion).

Unger, Merrill (1954), *Archaeology and the Old Testament* (Grand Rapids, MI: Zondervan).

Unger, Merrill (1966), *Unger's Bible Handbook* (Chicago, IL: Moody).

Unger, Merrill (1973), *Archaeology and the Old Testament* (Grand Rapids, MI, Zondervan).

Van Bebber, Mark and Paul S. Taylor (1996), *Creation and Time: A Report on the Progressive Creationist Book by Hugh Ross* (Gilbert, AZ: Eden Communications).

Van Till, Howard J. (1986), *The Fourth Day* (Grand Rapids, MI: Zondervan).

Van Till, Howard J., R.E. Snow, J.H. Stek, and Davis A. Young (1990), *Portraits of Creation* (Grand Rapids, MI: Eerdmans).

Vine, W.E. (1951), *First Corinthians* (Grand Rapids, MI: Zondervan).

Wald, George (1955), "The Origin of Life," *The Physics and Chemistry of Life* (New York: Simon & Schuster).

Wald, George (1979), "The Origin of Life," *Writing About Science*, ed. M.E. Bowen and J.A. Mazzeo (New York: Oxford University Press). [NOTE: This is a reprint of Dr. Wald's award-winning article, which appeared originally in *Scientific American*, 191[2]:44-53, August 1954.]

Watson, D.M.S. (1929), "Adaptation," *Nature*, 123:233, August 10.

Watson, James D. (1987), *Molecular Biology of the Gene* (New York: W.A. Benjamin).

Weiser, Arthur (1961), *The Old Testament: Its Formation and Development* (New York: Association Press).

Wells, Albert (no date), *The Christian Message in a Scientific Age* (Richmond, VA: John Knox Press).

Westminster Dictionary of the Bible (no date), (Philadelphia, PA: Westminster).

Wharton, Edward C. (no date), *Genesis Historical...Or Mythological?* (West Monroe, LA: Howard), a tract.

Whitcomb, John C. (1972), *The Early Earth* (Grand Rapids, MI: Baker).

Whitcomb, John C. (1973a), "The Days of Creation," *And God Created*, ed. Kelly L. Segraves (San Diego, CA: Creation-Science Research Center), 2:61-65.

Whitcomb, John C. (1973b), "The Gap Theory," *And God Created*, ed. Kelly L. Segraves (San Diego, CA: Creation-Science Research Center), 2:67-71.

Whitcomb, John C. (1975), "The Science of Historical Geology in the Light of the Biblical Doctrine of a Mature Creation," *Westminster Theological Journal*, Fall.

Whitcomb, John C. (1978), *The Moon: Its Creation, Form, and Significance* (Winona Lake, IN: BMH Books).

White, J.E.M. (1970), *Ancient Egypt* (New York: Dover).

Whitelaw, Thomas (no date), "Genesis," *Pulpit Commentary* (Grand Rapids, MI: Eerdmans).

Wieland, Carl (1994), "Decreased Lifespans: Have We Been Looking in the Right Place?," *Creation Ex Nihilo Technical Journal*, 8[2]: 139-140.

Wilder-Smith, A.E. (1975), *Man's Origin: Man's Destiny* (Minneapolis, MN: Bethany Fellowship).

Williams, Arthur F. (1965), *Creation Research Annual* (Ann Arbor, Michigan: Creation Research Society).

Williams, Arthur F. (1970), "The Genesis Account of Creation," *Why Not Creation?*, ed. Walter E. Lammerts (Grand Rapids, MI: Baker).

Williams, Glanville (1957), *The Sanctity of Life and the Criminal Law* (New York: Knopf).

Willis, John T. (1979), "Genesis," *The Living Word Commentary* (Austin, TX: Sweet).

Wilson, Clifford (1975), *In the Beginning God...* (Grand Rapids, MI: Baker).

Wilson, E.O. (1982), "Toward a Humanistic Biology," *The Humanist*, p. 40, September/October.

Wilson, James Maurice, et al. (1925), *Evolution in the Light of Modern Knowledge* (New York: Van Nostrand).

Wonderly, Dan (1977), *God's Time Records in Ancient Sediments* (Flint, MI: Crystal Press).

Woodmorappe, John (1999), *The Mythology of Modern Dating Methods* (El Cajon, CA: Institute for Creation Research).

Woods, Guy N. (1976a), "Man Created in God's Image," *Gospel Advocate*, 118[33]:514,518, August.

Woods, Guy N. (1976b), *Questions and Answers: Open Forum*, (Henderson, TN: Freed-Hardeman University).

Woods, Guy N. (1982), "'And be not Conformed to this World,'" *Gospel Advocate*, 124[1]:2, January 7.

Wysong, R.L. (1976), *The Creation-Evolution Controversy* (East Lansing, MI: Inquiry Press).

Young, Davis A. (1977), *Creation and the Flood* (Grand Rapids, MI: Baker).

Young, Davis A. (1982), *Christianity and the Age of the Earth* (Grand Rapids, MI: Zondervan).

Young, Davis A. (1987), "Scripture in the Hands of Geologists, Part II," *Westminster Theological Journal*, 49:303.

Young, Davis A. (1990), "Was the Earth Created a Few Thousand Years Ago?," *The Genesis Debate*, ed. Ronald F. Youngblood (Grand Rapids, MI: Baker). [Young answers in the negative.]

Young, Edward J. (1960), *An Introduction to the Old Testament* (Grand Rapids, MI: Eerdmans).

Young, Edward J. (1964), *Studies in Genesis One* (Nutley, NJ: Presbyterian and Reformed).

Young, Willard (1985), *Fallacies of Creationism* (Calgary, Canada: Detselig Enterprises, Ltd.).

Zimmerman, Paul A. (1968), "Can We Accept Theistic Evolution?," *A Symposium on Creation*, ed. Henry M. Morris (Grand Rapids, MI: Baker), 1:55-78. [Zimmerman answers in the negative.]

Zimmerman, Paul A. (1972), "The Word of God Today," *Creation, Evolution, and God's Word*, ed. P.A. Zimmerman (St. Louis, MO: Concordia).

Zirkle, Conway (1959), *Evolution, Marxian Biology, and the Social Scene* (Philadelphia, PA: University of Pennsylvania Press).

Subject Index

C

Cain, 368
  City built by, 259
Cainan, 174, 366
Calvin College, 91
Canaan, 213
Carnell, Edward John,
  Day-Age Theory and, 185
Catholic Church, 48
Childbirth, Eve's pain in, 263
Choice, freedom of, 3
Christ, Jesus, 7 - 8, 10, 14 - 15, 17
  - 19, 89, 95 - 97, 101, 104 -
  105, 119, 125, 147 - 151, 158,
  160 - 161, 176 - 178, 282, 311
  Adam and, 147 - 150
  Age of man on Earth and,
    298 - 299, 314 -
    316, 322, 356
  Authority in teaching, 15
  Creator, as, 18
  Genesis 1-11, view of, 147 -
    149
  Incarnation of, 89
  "Liar," as a, 313 - 315
  Resurrection of, 361
  Sermon on the Mount, 311
  Sinless nature of, 314
  Virgin birth of, 361
"Christian evolutionists," 118
Christianity, 13
  "Higher form of superstition,"
    as a, 125
Christianity Today, 78, 94, 178

Chronology
  Age of Earth and, 163 - 180
  Biblical, age of Earth and,
    163 - 308
City, Cain built a, 263
Clayton, John N.
  Adam's creation and, 248
  Age of Earth and, 172
  asah and, 289 - 295
  bara and, 290 - 296
  Biblical genealogies and,
    248, 252
  Big Bang and, 289
  Day-Age Theory and, 185
  Eve's curse and, 259
  Exodus 20:11, view of,
    138, 285, 294
  Garden of Eden, man's
    time in, 259
  Genesis 1:1-2 and, 283
  Historical nature of Genesis
    1-2 and, 138 - 140
  Methuselah, age of, 364
  Modified Gap Theory and,
    220, 223, 281 - 296
  Non-World View and, 297
  Patriarchs' ages and,
    359 - 360
  "Private theology" of,
    287 - 288
  Theistic evolution and, 107
Cockapoo dogs, 37
Coffman, Burton, Day-
  Age Theory and, 187
"Committees of Corre-
  spondence," 80

N

U

V

W

Y

Z

Name Index

A

Aalders, G.C., 306
Ackerman, Paul, 169
Ailing, C., 177
Allis, Oswald T., 222, 349, 354
Anderson, J. Kerby, 83
Andrews, E.H., 145, 317, 334
Archer, Gleason, 158 - 159,
        173-174, 177, 206 - 208
Armstrong, Karen, 141
Arndt, William, 256
Asimov, Isaac, 27 - 28, 52
Associated Press, 79
Astruc, Jean, 153
Ator, J.T., 111 - 113

B

Baikie, James, 177
Bales, James D., 37, 42, 51,
        117, 131, 320
Barlow, Nora, 133
Barnes, Albert, 173
Barnhouse, Donald G., 126 - 127
Barrow, John D., 64

Barzun, Jacques, 52
Bass, Thomas, 20, 324
Baxter, Batsell Barrett, 100
Beadle, George W., 102
Beck, Stanley, 101
Beck, William S., 55, 65
Beechick, Ruth, 174
Bennetta, William, 131
Berra, Tim M., 81
Berry, R.J., 137
Bethell, Tom, 60
Birch, L.C., 84
Birdsell, J.B., 324
Bishop, George, 80
Blackmore, Vernon, 81
Bloomfield, S.T., 256
Blum, Harold, 166
Bonner, John Tyler, 29
Borland, James A.,
        365 - 366, 368 - 369
Bradley, Walter, 83
Brandfon, Fredric, 179
Brantley, Garry K.,
        143, 173, 178-179
Breasted, James, 177
Bromling, Brad T., 157, 277
Brooks, Ronald M., 213

Scripture Index

SUBSCRIPTIONS

Each month *Reason & Revelation* presents articles defending the Christian faith. It aims to counterbalance the atheism, modernism, and worldly ethics with which we are confronted every day. Topics discussed include creation and evolution, archaeology, the inspiration and inerrancy of the Bible, the deity of

Christ, etc. Why not subscribe for a minister, friend, relative, or student? (Be sure to subscribe for yourself, too.) They will receive a card telling them that the gift is from you, unless you specify otherwise.

BOUND VOLUMES

At the end of each year, we produce a bound volume of *Reason & Revelation* (containing all 12 issues) that has a comb binding and an attractive, full-color, heavy-weight cover.

Once our supplies are depleted, the issues go out of print permanently. This is a good time to secure copies for posterity (for yourself, children, grandchildren, etc.).

BOUND VOLUME XX / 2000

WWW.APOLOGETICSPRESS.ORG